Collective Creation, Collaboration and Devising

Critical Perspectives on Canadian Theatre in English

volume twelve

Critical Perspectives on Canadian Theatre in English
volume twelve

Collective Creation, Collaboration and Devising

Edited by Bruce Barton

Playwrights Canada Press
Toronto • Canada

Playwrights Canada Press
215 Spadina Avenue, Suite 230, Toronto, Ontario CANADA M5T 2C7
416-703-0013 fax 416-408-3402
orders@playwrightscanada.com • www.playwrightscanada.com

Financial support provided by the taxpayers of Canada and Ontario through the Canada Council for the Arts and the Department of Canadian Heritage through the Book Publishing Industry Development Programme and the Ontario Arts Council.

 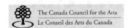

Cover image: Jin-me Yoon, between departure and arrival, 1996/1997. Partial installation view, Art Gallery of Ontario. Video projection, video montage on monitor, photographic mylar scroll, clocks with 3-D lettering, audio. Dimensions variable. Courtesy of the artist and Catriona Jeffries Gallery, Vancouver.
Production Editor/Cover Design: JLArt

Library and Archives Canada Cataloguing in Publication

Collective creation, collaboration and devising / edited by Bruce Barton.

(Critical perspectives on Canadian theatre in English ; v. 12)
Includes bibliographical references.
ISBN 978-0-88754-755-3 (bound)

1. Canadian drama (English)--20th century--History and criticism.
2. Creation (Literary, artistic, etc.). 3. Authorship--Collaboration.
I. Barton, Bruce, 1958- II. Series.

PS8163.C64 2008   C812'.5409   C2008-902839-2

First edition: May 2008
Printed and bound by Hignell Printing at Winnipeg, Canada.

For Pil and Lily…

…and for the artists on the edge
working with their hands
and heads
and hearts

Table of Contents

General Editor's Preface

Critical Perspectives on Canadian Theatre in English was launched in 2005 with the intention of making the best critical and scholarly work in the field readily available to teachers, students and scholars of Canadian drama and theatre. It set out, in individual volumes, chronologically to trace the histories of scholarship and criticism on individual playwrights, geographical regions, theatrical genres, themes and cultural communities. Over its first three years the series published nine volumes, collecting work on Aboriginal Theatre, African Canadian Theatre, playwrights Judith Thompson and George F. Walker, Feminist Theatre, Queer Theatre, Theatre in British Columbia, Environmental and Site-Specific Theatre, and Space and the Geographies of Theatre. I am very proud of this achievement, proud that these volumes have already been widely cited in subsequent scholarship, and proud that, although this is primarily a reprint series, essays newly commissioned for individual volumes have been nominated for and have won scholarly awards.

As the series continues, so do its original objectives. Each volume is edited and introduced by an expert in the field who has selected a representative sampling of the most important critical work on her or his subject since circa 1970, ordered chronologically according to the original dates of publication. Each volume also includes an introduction by the volume editor, surveying the field and its criticism, and a list of suggested further readings which recommends good work that could not otherwise be included. Where appropriate, the volume editors commission new essays on their subjects, particularly when these new essays fill in gaps in representation and attempt to correct historical injustices and imbalances, particularly those concerning marginalized communities. The volume topics have also been chosen to shed light on historically marginalized communities and work, while individual volumes have resisted the ghettoization of such work by relegating it to special topic volumes alone.

Volumes 10 through 15 carry on the work of the first nine volumes. They continue to address the work of individual playwrights, including Sharon Pollock, of geographical regions including Alberta, of genres including Collective, Collaborative and Devised Theatre, and of marginalized communities, here focusing on "Ethnic," Multicultural and Intercultural Performance. They also strike out in different directions, assembling a history of the criticism of Design in Canadian theatre, and reflecting on the multiple histories of Canada's theatre histories.

It is my hope that this series, in conjunction with the publications of Playwrights Canada Press, Talonbooks and other Canadian play publishers, will facilitate the teaching of Canadian drama and theatre in schools and universities for years to come. I hope by making available and accessible comprehensive introductions to some of the field's most provocative figures and issues, that they will contribute to the flourishing of courses on a variety of aspects of Canadian drama and theatre in classrooms across the country. And I hope that they will honour the work of some of the scholar/ pioneers of a field that is still, excitingly, young.

Ric Knowles

Acknowledgements

My thanks to my Research Assistants, Merrin Joy and Patrick Robinson, for their quick, accurate, and good-humoured efforts; to Ric Knowles, the most patient, thorough and encouraging of general editors; and to Pil Hansen... for everything. My gratitude goes out to all the authors of the previously published material for their generous contributions of such fine work. And I offer huge thanks, in particular, to the individuals whose writing appears here for the first time. Your enthusiasm, commitment and talent have made this a particularly satisfying project.

All articles are reprinted with the permission of the copyright holder.

Alan Filewod's article "Collective Creation: Process, Politics and Poetics" originally appeared in *Canadian Theatre Review* 34 (1982): 46–58; Robert Nunn's article "The Meeting of Actuality and Theatricality in *The Farm Show*" originally appeared in *Canadian Drama/L'Artdramatique canadien* 8.1 (1982): 42–54; Renate Usmiani's excerpted contribution originally appeared as part of Chapter Three, "A Success Story: Theatre Passe Muraille," in her book *Second Stage: The Alternative Theatre Movement in Canada* (Vancouver: U of British Columbia P, 1983) on pages 43–47, 54–58 and 65; Chris Brookes's contribution "Company Town – The Story of Buchans" originally appeared as Chapter Eight of *A Public Nuisance: A History of the Mummers Troupe* (St. John's: ISER, Memorial University of Newfoundland, 1988) on pages 111–27; Robert Wallace's article "Towards an Understanding of Theatrical Difference" originally appeared in *Canadian Theatre Review* 55 (1988): 5–14; Diane Bessai's excerpted contribution, "Collective Creation: Its Background and Canadian Developments," originally appeared as part of Chapter One of *The Canadian Dramatist, Volume Two: Playwrights of Collective Creation* (Toronto: Simon & Pierre, 1992; reprinted here courtesy of the Dundurn Group) on pages 13–30; Per Brask's article "Dilating the Body, Transporting the Mind: Considering Primus Theatre" originally appeared in the *Journal of Dramatic Theory and Criticism* 9.1 (1994): 207–19; Julie Salverson's article "Performing Emergency: Witnessing, Popular Theatre and The Lie of the Literal" originally appeared in *Theatre Topics* 6.2 (1996): 181–91; Ric Knowles's excerpted contribution, "The Structures of Authenticity: Collective and Collaborative Creations," originally appeared as part of Chapter Three of *The Theatre of Form and the Production of Meaning: Contemporary Canadian Dramaturgies* (Toronto: ECW, 1999) on pages 79–82 and 91–98; Erin Hurley's article "Carbone 14's Intelligent and Responsive Body" originally appeared in *Canadian Theatre Review* 109 (2002): 26–31; Paul Bettis's article "Creating the Form: Rule Plays and *Svengali's*" originally appeared in *Canadian Theatre Review* 119 (2004): 30–31 (reprinted courtesy of Linda Muir);

Shelley Scott's article "Enacting *This is for You, Anna*: Re-enacting the Collective Process" originally appeared in *Canadian Theatre Review* 121 (2005): 41–44; Bruce Barton's article "Mining 'Turbulence': Authorship Through Direction in Physically-Based Devised Theatre" originally appeared in *Directing and Authorship in Western Drama*, edited by Anna Migliarisi (New York, Ottawa, Toronto: Legas, 2006) on pages 115–33; Edward Little's article "Towards a Poetics of Popular Theatre: Directing and Authorship in Community-based Work" originally appeared in *Directing and Authorship in Western Drama*, edited by Anna Migliarisi (New York, Ottawa, Toronto: Legas, 2006) on pages 153–70; Monique Mojica's essay "Chocolate Woman Dreams the Milky Way" was originally given as an oral presentation at the Distinguished Lecture Series, University of Toronto, in January 2006 and at the Honouring Spiderwoman Conference, Native American Women Playwrights Archive, Miami University, in February 2007 – an earlier version of this article will appear in a forthcoming volume of essays on North American Native performance, edited by Steve Wilmer, to be published by Arizona UP; Kathleen Gallagher's excerpted contribution originally appeared as part of Chapter Three of *The Theatre of Urban: Youth and Schooling in Dangerous Times* (Toronto: U of Toronto P, 2007) on pages 131–37; Darren O'Donnell's article "The Social Impresario: capitalizing on the desire to be remembered for as long as it takes for wood to rot" originally appeared in *Pivot* 1 (2007): 6–13; Robert Plowman and Alex McLean's excerpted contribution "Making *Radium City*: Annotations by Alex McLean and Robert Plowman" will appear in *New Canadian Drama, Volume 9: Reluctant Texts from Exuberant Performance: Canadian Devised Theatre*, edited by Bruce Barton, Natalie Corbett, Birgit Schreyer Duarte and Keren Zaiontz (Ottawa: Borealis, 2008) in the Spring of 2008; an earlier version of Ker Wells's essay "Work With Your Hands" will appear in *Creative Expression, Creative Education*, edited by Robert Kelly (Calgary: Detselig, 2008) in the Spring of 2008; Barry Freeman's article "Cultural Meeting in Collaborative Intercultural Theatre: Collision and Convergence in the Prague-Toronto-Manitoulin Theatre Project" is published here for the first time; Modupe Olaogun's article "Cosmopolitan Time and Intercultural Collaborative Creation" is published here for the first time; Jerry Wasserman's article "The View Beyond the Stage: Collective, Collaborative and Site-Specific Performance in Vancouver" is published here for the first time; and Yvette Nolan's article "The Very Act" is published here for the first time.

Introduction: Devising the Creative Body

by Bruce Barton

I. Dramaturgy of Agency

> You cannot expect other people to create meaning for you. You cannot
> wait for someone else to define your life. You make meaning by forging
> it with your hands.   (Bogart, *And Then, You Act* 2)

Much like its title, Anne Bogart's little book *And Then, You Act: Making Art In An Unpredictable World* is filled with brief statements that encapsulate uncontainable matter(s) in a few words. The selected quotation, above, gestures towards many of the issues explored in the pages that follow in this volume in its multi-hewed (and hued) exploration. Yet what connects it most directly to much of what is written here is its call, both direct and implicit, for an understanding and approach to performance predicated on *consequential action*.

Bogart has ample, and top notch, company in this call to arms (or, precisely, to "hands") {Wells} [1]. In his meditation "On Risk and Investment," Tim Etchells of Britain's (and, subsequently, the world's) Forced Entertainment, asserts, "I ask of each performance: will I carry this event with me tomorrow? Will it haunt me? Will it change you, will it change me, will it change things? If not, it was a waste of time" (Etchells 49). Repeatedly, here and in the related literature, this image of theatre as not merely a force but, literally, a "forge" for "change"—personal *and* social change— where the *work* of the performer-creator produces not merely affect but *effect* {Brookes; Knowles; Salverson; Scott; Little; O'Donnell}, emerges as the grail to be pursued and, hypothetically, achieved within what might be deemed a "dramaturgy of agency."

Admittedly, Bogart's quoted insistence on self-determination may well appear an unlikely introductory reference for a collection of essays that focuses on collective creation, collaboration and devising. Its explicit emphasis on individual motivation and activity would seem to run counter to the agenda of a volume addressing group creativity. Yet in this, too, it is exemplary in its identification of a recurring paradox that operates on multiple levels throughout these pages. For what seems to beat emphatically at the heart of most of the collective and collaborative theatrical models explored here is an insistent, animated individuality.

Edward Albee is on record as asserting, "I dislike the term 'collaboration' ... Let us call it 'having my play done properly' rather than 'collaboration'" (20–21). This refinement of terminology offers a delightfully explicit caution against unexamined presumptions about collaboration as a, if not *the*, central tenet of theatrical activity. Yet the individuality that emerges as a persistent preoccupation within the following essays is in many ways a quite distant relative to Albee's declaration of creative authority. And it is, perhaps, the opening up of this self-consciously "alternative" understanding of theatrical collaboration that stands as this collection's most significant contribution to the study of Canadian theatrical performance.

Bringing together a fully satisfying collection of essays on such a broad and diverse combination of subject matter as collective creation, collaboration and devising is, of course, an impossibility – albeit a highly seductive one. The first obstacle—the all-too-common conflation of collective creation, on the one hand, and devising, on the other—only momentarily distracts from the insurmountable challenge of effectively representing collaboration in relation to what is ostensibly the most collaborative of all cultural activities. Perhaps, however, the saving grace resides in the full constellation of topics under consideration. Certainly, stable and distinct definitions and categorizations of these terms could only be employed as anxious and illusory distinctions – tentative, strenuous instruments for temporary and fraught analysis. Yet the insertion (and assertion) of the potentially vast expanse of "collaboration" literally *between* the magnetic poles of "collective creation" and "devising" in the volume's title provides a welcome and effective *caesura*, a practical and theoretical pause (for inquiry, for reflection, for breath) in assessing the relationship between these latter two concepts so often understood as interchangeable. Conversely, the strong common association (within the popular imagination of practitioners, audiences, critics, and no small number of scholars) between collective and devised activity equally provides a productive level of alienation to the theatrical "given" of collaboration, urging inquiry beyond or outside (or simply other than) the dominant conventions of hierarchal, vertically organized theatrical cooperation in the service of doing a playwright's play "properly."

Such self-conscious *caesurae* often emerge as resisted (even resented) yet essential moments of analytical stillness in theatrical territory so thoroughly predicated on movement. In terms of both practice and the efforts to explain practice, this tension between animation and reflection produces theoretical languages and gestures that are, simultaneously, both vigorous and precise *and* abstract and metaphorical. Even (in particular) in verbal expression, collective, devised and physically-based work is often described with a deceivingly dense brevity, resulting in conceptual collisions and conflations. In her 2007 revision of twenty-first century theatricality, *Reframing the Theatrical: Interdisciplinary Landscapes for Performance*, Allison Oddey quotes her own (much quoted) 1994 volume on theatrical devising, *Devising Theatre: A Practical and Theoretical Handbook*, as follows: "A devised theatre product is work that has emerged from and been generated by a group of people working in collaboration" (24). Even in the original context the concentration of terminology was critical; offered as a stand-alone self-quotation in the subsequent volume, the words take on an even more direct, pithy significance that seems to intentionally and irrevocably interweave collectivity, collaboration and devising practice. For Oddey, collaboration is the structure—the processual framework—that governs devising; a devised "product is work" (as opposed to *a* work) that "emerge(s) from and [is] generated by" (as opposed to *written* or *composed*) through "group" (not *individual*) authorship operating "in (as opposed to *through*) collaboration." If we push on this: collective = shared purpose and motivation, *ideology*; collaboration = self-imposed framework and structure, *context*; devising = adopted strategies and rules, *process*.

The conceptual contact improv at work (and at play) here is tangible and instructive. For Oddey, arguably, and for many others attempting to articulate collective/collaborative/devising dynamics, it is the perpetual negotiation between and navigation of these distinct yet related terms that is, in effect, *definitive*, rather than any fixed understanding of each term in isolation. Collective creation, collaboration and devising thus, potentially, become a strategic organization of concepts intentionally juxtaposed to capitalize on only apparent accessibility and familiarity – and to, in actuality, facilitate a revisiting and troubling of these impressions and the responses they evoke. In this context, "definitions" become open sites for multiplicity, for (even, enjoyably) contestation, and (following Jon McKenzie's proposal for the study of performance, in general), for *creation*. "Philosophically speaking," McKenzie suggests, "to pose the question 'What is?' presupposes a unified form while promising a single, correct answer, while the question 'Which one?' assumes a multiplicity of forces that must be actively interpreted and evaluated" (26). But asking questions is only the first stage; "[W]e must," McKenzie continues, "not only use different concepts, nor only contest and critique them; we must also *create* concepts, *initiate* models, *launch* movements of generalization." It is, then, in this spirit that the following essays have been collected between these covers and introduced in the following lines.

II. Collective Creation: *ideology*

> The group, rather than the individual, is the typical focus of the alternative society, and this is reflected in the structure of the new theatre organizations, their manner of working, and their theatre pieces … Society has become increasingly specialized and competitive. This is reflected in an established theatre based on competition and a theatrical method that focuses on individual specialists … In reaction to the fragmentation of the established society, which for many has become disorienting, the alternative society has sought wholeness. This is evident in many ways, including its focus on group living and group activities, and in its theatre, which is based on the cooperation of a creative collective. (Shrank 3–4)

Written over three and half decades ago, Theodore Shank's description of the inspiration and organization of American collaborative theatre practice feels remarkably familiar today north of the 49th parallel {Bessai; Usmiani}. Although terms such as "wholeness" are currently approached more critically, by practitioners and scholars alike, the pronounced (in all senses of that term) emphasis on "alternative" self-positioning for most present-day theatrical collective/collaborative groups in Canada remains a central preoccupation {Wasserman}.

Of course, not all Collective Creations are generated by "creative collectives" (no matter which of the numerous available definitions of this designation one settles on). But, in one sense, they might be. What I mean by this is that it is, arguably, more instructive to consider the issues of motivation and self-identification that serve as the grounds and impetus for collectively and collaboratively created theatrical works than it is to seek to fix and delimit their formal or thematic characteristics or their precise location on the continuum between "director-lead" and "fully democratic." The essays that follow in this collection present widely divergent preoccupations and processes, often more effectively experienced and analyzed through lenses of culture, orientation, gender, and/or class than through procedural or aesthetic commonalities. Yet virtually all the entries resonate with the preceding quotation in relation to its explicit and implicit *ideological* underpinnings. For the purposes of this discussion, then, I would like to consider collective creations primarily as the variable and mutable but unfailingly recognizable products of "alternative" collective ideology.

Alternative is, of course, a tricky term, an exemplar of the perpetual *différence* of "other"ness. And, as Alan Filewod asserts, alternative is a particularly elusive concept in a culture that has never truly produced nor experienced a fixed theatrical "mainstream." Arguing that the "construction of the mainstream [in Canada] was in effect an ideological fiction that rationalized larger grants to certain theatres on the basis of box office sales (or community penetration) and physical assets," Filewod contends, "[b]eyond that, the stream became a confusing delta" (204). Yet despite its "fiction[al]" status, "it is this category that underlies the whole concept of the alternative theatre, which is commonly represented as the radical challenge to a bourgeois model of theatre" (204). Of particular significance in this context, Filewod's comments address the question of the *practical* potential to distinguish between "ideological fiction" and ideological reality. Clearly, his persuasive case for the lack of an *aesthetic* model of "mainstream" theatre is not meant to preclude that mainstream's operation as an ideologically driven set of *material* conditions.

Nor does the persistently amorphous nature of the theatrical mainstream today decrease the pull (as opposed to attraction) of marginal cultural territory for many contemporary companies organized around collective and/or collaborative artistic/administrative structures. Rather, a key insight offered by Filewod's assessment emerges in the alternative (and, thus, for our purposes, collective) determination to discover one's own position on the cultural map through opposition to an ideologically, rather than aesthetically, defined "opponent." For what strategy better affords one's own aesthetic mobility? The productive ambivalence of alternative positioning—in regards to process, product, market, popular acceptance, *success*—often seems the primary constant in an otherwise constantly evolving cultural economy. Like the term itself, however, this alternative stance is very tricky to navigate.

In 1996, Winnipeg's Primus Theatre—one of the most significant theatrical collectives in Canadian history, discussed in several of the essays in this collection—

organized the "Survivors of the Ice Age" conference. The event gathered many of this country's most established and accomplished alternative theatre companies to talk, strategize, share and perform. In a conference presentation subsequently published in *Canadian Theatre Review* (CTR), Richard Paul (Ric) Knowles addressed the paradox of alternative positioning, specifically in terms of the relationship(s) to *space* thus generated:

> Many—most?—of the companies represented at "Survivors of the Ice Age" are dislocated, nomadic, or engaged in a kind of guerrilla theatre that I think is healthy, though it is also risky, and more than a little debilitating. The upsides of dislocation have to do, first, with the guerrilla practice of shifting ground, continually and purposefully refusing to settle in to entrenched positions and taken-for-granted places or starting points; and secondly, with the need, always, to ask questions about how *this* (new) cultural, social, organizational, or physical space can be made to work *this* time. (33)

However, Knowles continues, "[T]here is a down-side[:] … the problem for nomadic theatre companies is that you can't always find the spaces that you want, and when you do find them (or more often some compromise resembling them) you can't always control those spaces, and your work gets pulled around by them in unanticipated ways" (33). And certainly, this particular manifestation of what Knowles calls the "politics, not of *dislocation,* but of *displacement*" represents only the most explicit of a broad range of more subtle but equally significant repercussions of the alternative posture of "guerrilla practice," which include funding opportunities, categories and jury responses; marketing; reviewing; and audience expectations.

Knowles's immediate focus, in the passages noted above, on physical generation and performance space [2] (or lack thereof) reflects the primary significance of this factor in terms of collective identity – echoing Filewod's emphasis on "physical assets" as a primary point of distinction between ideological perceptions of "mainstream" and "alternative" theatre activity. Similarly, in her reassessment of the "Seminal Teachings" of Jerzy Grotowski on late twentieth century theatre practice, also published in the same issue of CTR, Lisa Wolford references Richard Fowler, the Canadian-born practitioner most directly responsible for the importation of Grotowski's lessons to Canada (via Fowler's extended first-hand training and collaboration with Eugenio Barba and the Odin Teatret in Denmark). Beyond a broad range of dramaturgical influences, Wolford suggests, the aspect of Fowler's practice as the director and co-founder of Primus Theatre [3] {Barton; Brask; Wells} that most profoundly reflected Grotowski's theatrical philosophy was Primus's thoroughly *collective* organization and operation. Apparently key to this conception of collectivity was the company's markedly social and "organi[c]" constitution, as opposed to a reliance upon material architecture for definition. As Fowler asserts, "The members of Primus Theatre are precisely that, *members,* the articulating limbs of a living organism; the theatre of which they are members is not a building … but the social unit which is the manifestation of their collective relationship" (qtd. in Wolford 40).

As Knowles notes, however, the benefits of organic mutability come at a significant cost, as the physical continuity—for training, rehearsal, design and administration, as well as performance—is perpetually elusive in a state of "homelessness" (33). Conversely, however, the purchase and maintenance of material space is inevitably a defining (and, almost always, problematic) process of transition for a collectively organized company, as made explicit in the evolution of Toronto's Theatre Passe Muraille (TPM). As Michael McKinnie has observed, "Passe Muraille was the first of these companies[4] to own its performance space, and, f[a]r more than any other mid-sized company in Toronto, its building can be read as an index of the ways in which theatres have been forced to incorporate the urban political economy of a late capitalist city into the heart of their work" ("Space Administration" 21). Thus, while it is easier to identify contrasts than commonalities when considering the working processes and performance products of, for instance, TPM {Filewod; Nunn; Usmiani; Bessai} and Primus, the direct and unavoidable relationship between creative strategies and material conditions in general, and between "mainstream" and "alternative" ideological positionings in particular, provides a graspable point of access into their shared "collectivity."

Not surprisingly, then, Mark Weinberg's study of collective theatre in the U.S. through to the early 1990s is titled *Challenging the Hierarchy*. Subsequent reflection on the historical collective movement has weathered the sentiment behind this confident assertion somewhat (see part IV. Devising, below), but the resulting ambivalence has merely thickened the complexity, rather than undermined the conviction, of the contemporary "alternative" ideological stance among most collaboratively organized theatre practitioners. Nowhere is this more pronounced than in relation to the most enduringly and overtly "collective" of collaborative creation processes, participatory Popular Theatre {Little; Salverson; Gallagher}. In *Popular Theatre in Political Culture: Britain and Canada in Focus*, Tim Prentki and Jan Selman describe Popular Theatre practice in terms that in fact intensify the ideological orientation of early theatrical collectives.

> Popular Theatre works to facilitate independence, to assist communities in a process of building a capacity for autonomous self-development. Participatory and democratic, its principles are at odds with those of globalization. It provides a means by which those whose indigenous culture is threatened by outside intervention can, through the agency of fiction, create a space in which to articulate that culture and to examine the social bases of communities on terms of their own devising. (200)

As the related essays in this collection attest, this confidence is not purchased at the cost of naïveté. In particular, increased multicultural exposure and its resultant anxieties have similarly increased the opportunities for unintentional intrusion, miscommunication and misunderstanding in Popular Theatre contexts {Salverson; Freeman}. Yet, John Somers contends, despite the ample difficulties—which "are mainly of an ethical and political, rather than an aesthetic, nature"—Popular Theatre practitioners remain "convinced that, notwithstanding the failures … effective drama and theatre work 'does good'" (xi).

Thus, while perhaps more selectively pronounced and self-consciously employed, Weinberg's historical list of the organizational objectives of theatrical collectives retains significant allure and regular application today:

> The principles of collective organization: nonexploitative structures, nonrestrictive norms, pluralistic leadership, equal access to information and power, equal respect and rewards, equal responsibility, and democratic decision making (i.e., the principles of *worker control*) lead to a process by which each group can create a particular working methodology that is likely to be responsive to the needs of its members and to the task and that maximizes both freedom and responsibility. (16)

True, most contemporary collaboratively structured companies enact a distinctly integrated and savvy engagement with the forces of government, business, and the media; but most also self-consciously enact Baz Kershaw's definition of performance as "an *ideological transaction* between a company of performers and the community of their audience" (78), with the intention of meeting, engaging, examining, challenging, sharing and entertaining {Wasserman}. Foremost among the attractions of "collective organization," then, would seem to be structural and procedural *mobility*—the ability to "create a particular working methodology that is likely to be responsive to the needs of its members"—coupled with a commitment to the hands-on "task" of actually, however modestly, changing the world.

III. Collaboration: *context*

> Is collaboration this: the 12 years' endless proximity to other people, physical, vocal, all day and into the night, watching people fade in and out of coherence and concentration – an intimacy that approaches that of lovers who now no longer bother to close the bathroom door whilst shitting? (Etchells 54)

The conventional (as opposed to mainstream) theatre industry threatens to show its wrinkles (or, at least, its stretch marks) most conspicuously in terms of its understanding of collaboration ("No one collaborates with me on a play" [Albee 20]). Both the hierarchal model of authority in most professional theatrical contexts in Canada and the particular mode of commercial co-operation it engenders are familiar to most practitioners and students (including researchers and instructors) of the discipline. A separate volume—indeed, several volumes—could easily be dedicated to these topics (both in terms of practices that respect traditional procedures and those that experiment within their fixed parameters) and merely scratch the surface. This collection of essays does not attempt to explore these dynamics.

Rather, as I have suggested, the collaboration that is examined in virtually every essay (on practically every page) is one in which the framework and structure of the theatrical exchanges in question are conspicuously *not* conventional nor habitual – in which the context of creation is intentionally reconfigured, consciously self-imposed and, frequently, volatile territory (with Etchell's reference to "lovers" effectively suggesting the level of the stakes involved). It is an experience of collaboration that, within these essays, claims a degree of open interpretative space for specific dynamics related to culture, class, sexuality and gender through a willed distancing from or valiant disregard for dominant and homogenizing material and disciplinary constraints. It is, ultimately, an understanding of collaboration that provides a practical bridge and a conceptual separation between the ideological presumptions of collective creation and the processual strategies of theatrical devising.

> Is collaboration this: four people in the room drunk and tired, treading again through an argument about the structure of the show, an argument which we've already had 100 times in the last week and for which all of us, by now, know all the parts and yet are always coming back in circuits to the same stalemate stand-off conclusions about how and why the show does not work and will not work? There is a word for these too familiar arguments – we call them the loop, arguments that soon are shorthand and can be indicated simply with a gesture: the circling of a hand ... Maybe collaboration is simply the process of developing new words for the strange situations in which a group can find itself. (Etchells 62)

The first essay that I intended to include in this volume is one that does not feature in these pages, having already made its appearance in the previous entry in this series dedicated to Environmental and Site-Specific Theatre practice (see Houston, *Environmental*). Originally published in CTR #126 and entitled "Please Dress Warmly and Wear Sensible Shoes," the piece is a thoroughly and *explicitly* collaborative project by the four-member company bluemouth inc. presents.[5] Each individual in the intermedia troupe took on a particular aspect of site-specific work to consider within the article; once the original sections had been completed, these were circulated among the other members, all of whom were free to write into and through the original author's contribution. Each member adopted a characteristic font, and these different typefaces were carried through to the publication of the article. The result approaches a sort of conceptual hypertext, with each shift in font (there are *many*) potentially drawing the reader to make connections across and throughout the remainder of the article, as the individual voices of the company members emerge as somehow both separate yet irresolvably intertwined.[6]

My limited experience working as dramaturge for bluemouth inc.[7] has revealed them to be, as far as I know, the most defiantly "collective" company working in Canada. Determined to generate and perform without a designated director, the troupe instead occupies a creative space of constant internal persuasion, coercion, argument, and absolute generosity, one in which they must perpetually explore, negotiate, revise and reinvent their collaborative framework. This ability and—more important—this *desire* to foreground "conflict resolution" as a centrally integrated component of the creative process reflects the company's overtly interdisciplinary composition. Anticipating divisions ranging in nature from practical and aesthetic through political and philosophical, the company members resort to an approach to agreement that offers striking contrasts to the "consensus" models described by Shank and Weinberg. In this, they perhaps reflect collaborative frameworks more familiar within exchanges in the visual and graphic arts, such as those recently proposed by Maria Lind in her discussion of "The Collaborative Turn" in north-west European visual arts culture:

> Perhaps the problem is rather that there is too much forced commonality and prescribed collaboration today in the sense of social unanimity and political consensus ... More difference and disagreement, in other words, in order to avoid the risk of "consensus of the centre," which gives scope to, for instance, right-wing extremists as the only real alternative in the political area. [Political philosopher Chantal] Mouffe's "antagonistic pluralism" can be of use here since it is not based on final resolutions but on an ongoing exchange marked by conflict. "Agonistic" relationships involve struggles with an adversary rather than with an enemy, as in antagonistic relationships. An adversary is someone with whom you share a common ground but with whom you disagree on meanings and implementation of basic principles – disagreements which simply cannot be resolved through the deliberation and rational discussion celebrated by "third-way-politicians" and defenders of the "post-political" alike. (19)

The demands of constant reassessment—not to mention attrition—prioritize individual attention, engagement, enthusiasm and consideration, thus locating bluemouth's collaborative agenda squarely within the collective objectives outlined by Weinberg. However, their collaborative *structure* requires a democracy predicated on the ability to sustain and thrive in the tension of passionate and volatile exchange (including conflict and difference), in addition to (and, at times, rather than) the equilibrium of consensus {Barton; Plowman & McLean; O'Donnell; Nolan}.

These observations highlight the important, if commonsensical, observations of Keith R. Sawyer in relation to the study of creative collaboration. In an attempt to consolidate theories of collaboration drawn from the fields of anthropology, musicology, conversation analysis, organizational behaviour, and creativity research, Sawyer argues that "[t]o properly understand group creativity, we need to think of intersubjectivity as 'a process of coordination of individual contributions to joint activity rather than as a state of agreement' (Matusov 34)." Drawing on G.H. Mead's 1930s work on "the *emergent*" [8] in group behaviour, Sawyer contends that the primary question about intersubjectivity in group creativity "is not how performers come to share identical representations, but rather, how a coherent interaction can proceed even when they do not" (9). These hypotheses lead Sawyer to propose what he terms "*collaborative emergence*" as the focal point of group creativity *in performance* – the quality which makes collaborative performance fundamentally unpredictable (and, thus, engrossing) (12).

Intriguingly, if we continue on the trail of Etchell's aforementioned "loop," we find Sawyer's equation in reverse, with performance presented as the "solution" to collaboration, rather than the other way around:

> The loop is the heart of the show, a wall you hit your heads against until you are senseless, gibbering and tired of it, tired of it, tired of it. And strangely it seems sometimes that the worst thing of all is that the loop must be tackled in public, with the group, through speech, discussion. So many times in the process I begin to envy the solitude of writers and painters – who surely have their loops but at least aren't condemned to sit up forever and talk about them. (63)

As the product of a shared motivation of collectivity (*ideology*) and a common structural framework of collaboration (*context*), the momentary, transient, unpredictable "*emergent*" of performance is understood here as the product of drudgery, repetition and persistence. Collaboration, in this instance, is thus the intake of breath—the ironically volatile and passionate semantic stillness—waiting to be animated by the strategies and rules, the devising *process*, called forth by such hard and contentious labour.

IV. DEVISING: *process*

> [C]onstraints are necessary as rules of the game for acting ... They are born of the demands of poetry. (Lecoq 76)

Two new books on theatrical devising have recently been published, providing welcome contributions on an aspect of performance creation surprisingly underexposed to both academic and practitioner examination. In a field where a few widely read and referenced studies have basically set the agenda—in some cases for over a decade—these new resources have effectively deepened and broadened the discussion. What is intriguing, however, is the degree to which, in both new studies, the same territory is explored through relatively similar optics. This is, no doubt, in part attributable to the fact that both emerge from England, the birthplace and enduring home of devising discourse; but this provides only a partial explanation.

Unsurprisingly, both of the new texts initially (and repeatedly) wrestle with issues of nomenclature. The result is regularly, though not always intentionally, a conflation of issues relating to ideological context and questions of processual strategies. In *Devising Performance: A Critical History* (2006), Deirdre Heddon and Jane Milling note that

> British and Australian companies tend to use "devising" to describe their practice, whereas in the USA the synonymous activity is referred to most often as "collaborative creation." We shall use the phrases interchange-

ably in this text, although the terminology itself offers a slight variation in emphasis. While the word "devising" does not insist on more than one participant, "collaborative creation" clearly does. (2)

Even more explicitly, in *Making a Performance: Devising Histories and Contemporary Practices* (2007), Emma Govan, Helen Nicholson and Katie Normington observe that

> Devising is widely regarded as a process of generating a performative or theatrical event, often but not always in collaboration with others. It is interesting that, in the USA, this aspect of theatre-making is often described as "collaborative creation" or, in the European tradition, as the product of "creative collectives," both terms that emphasise group interactivity in the process of making a performance. (4)

The superimposition of context and process is neither surprising nor without historical basis. Oddey's influential *Devising Theatre* effectively established this precedent by interweaving its description of ideological motivation and organizational structure with considerations of practical strategies. Whereas, for Oddey, "In the 1970s devising companies chose artistic democracy in favour of the hierarchical structures of power linked to text-based theatre ... within the last twenty years or so there has been a move from this standpoint to more hierarchical structures within many companies in response to an ever-changing economic and artistic climate" (9). Thus, by the time of Oddey's writing, "the term 'devising' ha[d] less radical implications, balancing greater emphasis on skill sharing, specialization, specific roles, increasing division of responsibilities, such as the role of the director/deviser or administrator, and more hierarchical company structures." While these parallel developments are no doubt present, an alternative interpretation of this dynamic is to identify a gradual distinction between collective and collaborative philosophies and frameworks, on the one hand, and devising techniques, on the other {Freeman}. Certainly, no absolute separation of these two aspects is possible or desirable, but an equal potential for error lies in the unquestioned folding of one factor entirely into the other.

This latter gesture seems to inform Hedding and Milling's survey of ideological connotations historically associated with devising practices (the list is instructive and worth recounting at some length):

> [I]t is possible to construct something of a "soundbite" of those qualities frequently assumed to be implicit in devising which serve to give it an almost mythical status. Devising is variously: a social expression of non-hierarchical possibilities; a model of cooperative and non-hierarchical collaboration; an ensemble; a collective; a practical expression of political and ideological commitment; a means of taking control of work and operating autonomously; a de-commodification of art; a commitment to total community; a commitment to total art; the negating of the gap between art and life; the erasure of the gap between spectator and performer; a distrust of words; the embodiment of the

> death of the author; a means to reflect contemporary social reality; a means to incite social change; an escape from theatrical conventions; a challenge for theatre makers; a challenge for spectators; an expressive, creative language; innovative; risky; inventive; spontaneous; experimental; non-literary…. (4–5)

The authors round out this inventory with the following challenge: "As processes of devising are now so firmly embedded in our training and educational institutions, can we really continue to claim for devising any 'marginal' or 'alternative' status? And why should we wish to do so?" (6). This final question is an important one – as much for its problematic conflation of closely aligned yet separate issues as for its accurate capture of much popular and scholarly perception.

Ultimately, however, both texts wisely retreat to the idea of devising as, in Heddon and Milling's terms, "best understood as a set of strategies" (2). Extending this observation in a manner reminiscent of McKenzie's portrayal of "performance," Govan et al. propose, "If devising is most accurately described in the plural—as *processes* of experimentation and sets of creative *strategies*—rather than a single methodology, it defies neat definition or categorization" (7) {Plowman & McLean}. In the next sentence, however, the seemingly inescapable hitching of process to motivation reemerges in the authors' contention that "[n]ew practices have arisen from a combination of creative conversations and dissatisfaction with how current modes of practice address contemporary climates."

In her *Devising Theatre* text, Oddey usefully identifies a series of junctures at which theatrical devising is seen to depart from (or, depending on the perspective adopted, challenge) more traditional, horizontally organized theatrical approaches. Her umbrella categorization of these junctures is "Methodology" (11), most productively understood as a set of practical principles intended to guide the creation, selection, and application of concrete process {Bettis; Mojica; Oloagun}. No doubt foremost among its characteristics is devising's refusal to accord primary or "sacred" status to the dramatic *text* (5) {Wallace; Plowman & McLean}. Indeed, text may be secondary in terms of both its "authority" within the developmental process and of the order in which the performance elements may be selected and incorporated into the final production. Theatrical devising is also seen to adopt an altered relationship to both *time* and material *resources*, shifting the priorities associated with both from preoccupations with product to a focus on the developmental process(es) involved (12–16). Devising strategies are said to involve heightened sensitivity to and engagement with the *physical spaces* [and, by extension, *places*] of development and performance (17–18) (resulting in a theoretical intersection with environmental and site-specific practices). Similarly, devising is described as inherently accommodating to the exploration of advanced and emerging *technologies* (18) (opening up a related theoretical exchange with intermedia activity). Finally, Oddey argues for a fundamental *interdisciplinarity* within devising processes (19). Each of these principles can be understood as orientations towards dramaturgical tools and their application; issues of ideological positioning (collectivity) and structural framework (collaboration) may be implicit in each, but are prerequisite to none.

What this still relevant "Methodology" directly addresses is an altered approach to and understanding of composition. Many of the essays in this collection attempt to articulate examples and formulate theories to describe the particular qualities of devised composition. The regular reliance, in theatrical devising, on improvisation, multiple authors, and found and adapted text readily prompts metaphors such as "montage" {Barton; Brask} "*con-fusion*" {Barton; Freeman} and – in what strikes me as one of the most fertile and complex of analogies, "*mola*" {Mojica}. These references effectively suggest the culturally rich and phenomenologically multiplanal nature of an approach to expression that is as deeply engaged with issues of physical gesture (tempo, rhythm, scale, direction, relation to gravity) as with spoken text (Bogart refers to composition as "writing on your feet, with others, in space and time, using the language of theater" [*Viewpoints* 12]). By extension, these methodological principles also evoke an approach to and understanding of performance—more specifically, of the *actor-creator*—just as radically altered as the relation to textual composition and communication.

Some of the hundreds of texts committed to exploring issues related to actor-creator training and performance are listed in the Works Cited pages of the following articles and in the Suggested Further Reading section of this collection. Any attempt here to briefly catalogue or summarize the diversity of perspectives on this topic would be foolhardy. Widely recognized figures such as Eugenio Barba, Augusto Boal, Anne Bogart, Peter Brook, Jerzy Grotowski, Jacques Lecoq, Philippe Gaulier, and Tadashi Suzuki, to name only some of the most conspicuous, have all been thoroughly studied; many have produced multiple volumes, most of which are available in English. All have offered ample opportunities for first-hand experience and training in their respective systems, effectively disseminating their teachings over geographical, national, cultural and generational borders. Significantly, however, very few, if any, would call (or would have called, while alive) their approach to performance creation "devising" (just as many of the practitioners included in this volume initially stumbled over this categorization of their activities). But, as noted, devising is not a *system* – it is not uniform or unified, logically organized or reliably repeatable. Rather, it consists of "*processes* of experimentation and sets of creative *strategies*." The connection to the above mentioned systems of training lies not in stable and predictable application; rather, finally, it primarily relates to an altered conception of the role of the *body* in performance {Barton; Brask; Hurley; Wells; Nolan}.

In fact, the performer's life is based on an alteration of balance. (Barba 18)

V. Collective Creation / Collaboration / Devising: *the creative body*

If any one term encapsulates Lecoq's overall goal for his students during the two years they may study with him, it is that of preparation: preparing the creative actor. Compared to the more circumscribed word

> "training," preparation seems to imply a process of getting ready, of
> open-endedness and an unwillingness to close down on possible options
> and choices. (Murray 64)

It is with the arrival, finally, at the creative body that we return, full circle, to a "dramaturgy of agency." Simon Murray's shifting of emphasis and interpretation, above, from "training" to "preparing the creative actor" in reference to the teachings of Jacques Lecoq both distinguishes the late acting teacher from many of his more conventional counterparts and firmly aligns him with a number of otherwise diverse figures associated with "preparation" for the types of theatre and performance that I have been orbiting in this introduction. Murray's semantic transition is profound. The trained body—the disciplined, contained, regimented body—is opposed to the prepared body: alert, attentive, capable, creative ... prepared, one might speculate, for ... the future? The Revolution?

Lecoq's aforementioned reliance on "constraints" is a clear point of connection across distinct cultures and complex approaches {Hurley}: "A high jumper would not jump so high if there was no obstacle to clear ... Constraints favour style; too much constraint leads to virtuosoism, to feats. Not enough constraint dilutes the intentions and the gestures in the soup of natural gestures..." (Lecoq 76). Correspondingly, Barba contends, "Extra-daily techniques ... lead to information. They literally *put* the body *into form*, rendering it artificial but *believable*. Herein lies the essential difference which separates extra-daily techniques from those which merely transform the body into the 'incredible' body of the acrobat and the virtuoso" (16, emphasis in original) {Barton; Brask; Wells}. Locating the actor's body (and, thus, the actor) at once separate from life but utterly "of life" emerges as a key objective within multiple "systems of preparation." And, as with the motivational quotations that opened this introduction, this paradox is repeatedly expressed through philosophical mysteries presented as resolvable, ultimately and thoroughly, only through phenomenological scrutiny and practical application.

However, whereas engagement with well-established and rigorous systems of preparation historically took the form of long-term master/pupil, mentor/protégé, or guru/disciple relationships, with the accompanying demands of commitment and fidelity regularly associated with such arrangements, contemporary North American performers tend to be a more eclectic cohort.[9] As Ian Watson has observed,

> The geographical underpinnings of a national identity have little to
> do with the contemporary actor. He or she can study any number of
> different techniques from a range of countries and performance genres.
> Professional identity is formed by those with whom one studies, not by
> the country in which one lives or by the ethnic group to which one
> belongs. (8)

Similarly, it is not the many distinguishing particulars of these systems that are of immediate relevance to this discussion, but rather the global ideological and/or structural frameworks that contemporary actors perceive in them, identify with, and invest in.

For the purpose of this specific argument, then, and at the risk of gross generalization, it is possible to recognize in a spectrum of related teachings [10] two general avenues to "preparation." The first involves a gesture of *emptying* – an extraction of the body (the complete body, which includes the mind) from the world and the world from the body.

> The technique of the "holy actor" is an inductive technique (i.e., a technique of elimination), whereas that of the "courtesan actor" is a deductive technique (i.e., and accumulation of skills). (Grotowski, *Towards* 35)

> The beauty of omission, in fact, is the suggestiveness of indirect action, of the life which is revealed with a maximum of intensity in a minimum of activity. (Barba 29)

> When I look around the first thing that seems to be missing is the imaginative space that art can engender. Our society, chock full of real trauma, manufactured paranoia and war, needs silence and space. (Bogart 117)

> In the darkness, the eyes lose their dominance and other senses control the activity. The body is warmed, muscles loosened, and the mind prepared, almost cleansed of distracting thoughts. (Allain 205 [discussing the training approach of Staniewski Gardzienice])

The second gesture takes the form of reengagement with the world, a bodily reconstitution through the establishment of a new, altered *balance*.

> I – I does not mean to be cut in two but to be double. The question is to be passive in action and active in seeing (reversing the habit). Passive: to be receptive. Active: to be present. (Grotowski, "Performer" 378)

> The performer, through long practice and continuous training, fixes this "inconsistency" by a process of innervation, develops new neuro-muscular reflexes which result in a renewed body culture, a "second nature," a new consistency, artificial but marked with *bios*. (Barba 26)

> Our fate as artists is to live with and accept the paradox "keep moving and slow down, simultaneously," or *festina lente*. Learn how to live in this contradiction and enjoy its inherent irritation. (Bogart and Landau 125)

> What do I teach in my School? The pleasure of the game. A child who plays forgets his sadness. Why not an actor? Where is the pleasure of a character who is about to die? It is in the actor who plays, who surprises, who turns everything upside down while being magnificently drenched in light. (Gaulier)

In isolation, these quotations can, of course, yield no specific insights or distinguishing characteristics. Yet, upon reflection, the gestures they describe—the pattern of movement in relation to society, culture, politics, ideology—emerge as familiar and evocative within the current discussion. The group sentiment identified as underpinning collective creation similarly endorses a self-conscious disengagement from dominant culture in order to effect a profound reconstitution of beliefs and values, resulting in a distinctly new and altered ideological balance. Similarly, the structural context of this transformation takes the form of a passionate and generous but also volatile preparedness: a collaborative tension predicated on the animating potential of difference and contradiction. As advocates for a "dramaturgy of agency," each of the systems of preparation touched upon here involves extensive periods of individual development, training, and material generation. [11] Yet as preparation for engagement with the hands-on forging of personal *and* collective meaning, all also reconverge in the concrete and generative strategies and rules of theatrical devising.

The creative body is the collective body is the collaborative body is the devising body.

The readiness is all.

. . .

The creative body must, of course, forever resist becoming a timeless body, a universal body. By the same token, however, it must also resist the equal but opposite erasure of quotidian invisibility. It must, instead, be both apart from the world and a part of the world, separate from life but utterly of it, simultaneously. New orientations, incorporating and bridging cognitive psychology (see Blair), neurobiology (see Hansen, "Introducing," "Dance"), material semiotics (see Knowles, *Reading*), media studies (see Barton, "Subjectivity"), and phenomenology (see Zarrilli), are bringing a prismatic lens to collective, collaborative and devising contexts, continually complicating the relationship between "the body," on the one hand, and "bodies," on the other.

As the essays in this collection illustrate, the proximate positioning of concepts can be as illuminating as that of living bodies in performance. Inserting a fresh consideration of collaboration between the easily conflated terms collective creation and devising calls for a reconsideration of all three concepts, in isolation and in conversation, in abstract idealization and in concrete historical applications. Such moments of reflection—of passionate, analytical calm in the rushing current of history—are what André Lepecki, following anthropologist Nadia Seremetakis, refers to as "still-acts."

> The still-act shows how the dust of history, in modernity, may be agitated in order to blur artificial divisions between the sensorial and the social, the somatic and the mnemonic, the linguistic and the corporeal, the mobile and the immobile. Historical dust is not simple metaphor. When taken literally, it reveals how historical forces penetrate deep into the inner layers of the body: dust sedimenting the body, operating to

rigidify the smooth rotation of joints and articulations, fixing the subject within overly prescribed pathways and steps, fixating movement within a certain politics of time and place. (15)

The theatrical connotations of "still-act"—"the moment of exit from historical dust" (Seremetakis 12)—reverberate conspicuously through this collection of articles. It is difficult to conceive of a more fitting stage for the creative body in performance, in ideology, in context, in process.

Notes

1 Author names in {braces} refer to essays of particular relevance included in this collection.

2 His article also names a) the performing body; b) organizational spaces; c) training spaces; d) discursive spaces; and e) the cultural landscape as additional sites of consequence worthy of study (31–32).

3 Fowler was Primus Theatre's director throughout the company's nine years of operation (from 1989 to 1998).

4 Specifically, Factory Theatre Lab, Tarragon and Canadian Stage Company. McKinnie's observation that Passe Muraille was particularly influenced by its move to ownership is in part related to TPM's overtly collective model of administration and creation, as compared to these other institutions. For an extensive study of the relationships of each of these and additional Canadian theatres with property purchase and maintenance, see McKinnie, *City Stages.*

5 bluemouth inc. presents is Lucy Simic, Stephen O'Connell, Sabrina Reeves and Richard Windeyer.

6 This description of "Please Dress Warmly and Wear Sensible Shoes" is taken from the introduction of a forthcoming article by the author, "Subjectivity<>Culture<>Communications<>*Intermedia*: A Meditation on the 'Impure Interactions' of Performance and the 'In-between' Space of Intimacy in a Wired World," to be published in *Theatre Research in Canada/Recherches théâtrales au Canada* in 2008.

7 I am presently working as the company's dramaturge on a project based on American dance marathons to be presented through the Harbourfront Performing Arts (Toronto) "Fresh Ground" program in 2008/09.

8 "The emergent when it appears is always found to follow from the past, but before it appears, it does not, by definition, follow from the past" (Mead 2, qtd. in Sawyer 12).

[9] I discuss Number Eleven Theatre's "postmodern" relationship with their "modernist" systems of preparation in my contribution to this volume.

[10] My selected "teachings" here are, admittedly, Eurocentric in nature, owing primarily to the facts that 1) the majority of collective and collaborative devising practitioners in Canada draw their primary influence from this region and 2) significantly more has been published in relation to European models. The regularly (and occasionally problematic) intercultural nature of many of these systems notwithstanding, therefore, the relevance of these observations for systems of preparation emerging thoroughly out of other cultures and regions will no doubt complicate these observations.

[11] "The actors work on their improvisations alone, as Barba believes that their focus should be on their particular response to the material that has been presented and not on how they might work with the other actor(s) in the space. Barba comments that when improvising with a partner you have to work in real time and the work can often be merely illustrative. When working alone, time and reactions often appear to work differently; the actor can go much further alone as he or she inhabits what Barba calls the realm of 'dreaming awake'." (Turner 32–33)

Works Cited

Albee, Edward. "Creation and Interpretation." *The Alchemy of Theatre: The Devine Science: Essays on Theatre & the Art of Collaboration.* New York: Playbill Books, 2006. 18–22.

Allain, Paul. "The Gardzienice Theatre Association of Poland." *Acting Reconsidered: A Theoretical and Practical Guide.* Ed. Phillip B. Zarrilli. London: Routledge, 1995. 200–18.

Auslander, Philip. "Just Be Yourself: Logocentrism and Difference in Performance Theory." *Acting Reconsidered: A Theoretical and Practical Guide.* Ed. Phillip B. Zarrilli. London: Routledge, 1995. 53–61.

Barba, Eugenio. *The Paper Canoe.* London: Routledge, 1995.

Barton, Bruce. "Mining 'Turbulence': Authorship Through Direction in Physically-Based Devised Theatre." In *Directing and Authorship in Western Drama.* Ed. Anna Migliarisi. New York, Ottawa, Toronto: Legas Publishing, 2006. 115–33.

———. "Subjectivity<>Culture<>Communications<>*Intermedia*: A Meditation on the 'Impure Interactions' of Performance and the 'In-between' Space of Intimacy in a Wired World." *Theatre Research in Canada/Recherches théâtrales au Canada* 28.2 (2007): forthcoming.

bluemouth inc. presents. "Please Dress Warmly and Wear Sensible Shoes." *Canadian Theatre Review* 126 (2006): 16–22.

Blair, Rhonda. "Reconsidering Stanislavsky: Feeling, Feminism, and the Actor." *Theatre Topics* 12.2 (2002): 177–90.

Bogart, Anne. *And Then, You Act: Making Art in an Unpredictable World.* New York: Routledge, 2007.

——— and Tina Landau. *The Viewpoints Book: A Practical Guide to Viewpoints and Composition.* New York: TCG, 2005.

Etchells, Tim. *Certain Fragments: Contemporary Performance and Forced Entertainment.* London and New York: Routledge, 1999.

Filewod, Alan. "Erasing Historical Difference: The Alternative Orthodoxy in Canadian Theatre." *Theatre Journal* 41.2 (1989): 201–10.

Gaulier, Philippe. "The King of My School." http://www.ecolephilippegaulier.com/archives/frames.html. Accessed 23 January 2008.

Govan, Emma, Helen Nicholson, and Katie Normington. *Making a Performance: Devising Histories and Contemporary Practices.* London: Routledge, 2007.

Grotowski, Jerzy. *Towards a Poor Theatre.* New York: Simon and Schuster, 1968.

———. "Performer." *The Grotowski Sourcebook.* Ed. Richard Schechner and Lisa Wolford. London: Routledge, 1997. 376–80.

Hansen, Pil. "Dance Dramaturgy: possible work relations and tools." *Space and Composition: Physical and Visual Dramaturgy in Theatre and Dance* (Symposium Proceedings). Ed. Miriam Frandsen and Jesper Schou-Knudsen. Copenhagen: NordScen, 2005.

———. "Introducing Mechanisms of Perception and Performativity into Dramaturgy." Seminar 4: *Foundations of Writing and Performance: The Neocognitive Turn in Performance Theory.* Annual Conference of the American Society for Theatre Research, Toronto 2005. Unpublished.

Heddon, Deirdre, and Jane Milling. *Devising Performance: A Critical History.* Houndsmill, Basingstoke: Palgrave MacMillan, 2006.

Houston, Andrew, ed. *Environmental and Site-Specific Theatre.* Toronto: Playwrights Canada, 2007.

Kershaw, Baz. "Performance, Community, Culture." *The Community Performance Reader.* Ed. Petra Kuppers and Gwen Robertson. London: Routledge, 2007. 77–96.

Knowles, Richard Paul. "Survival Spaces: Space and the Politics of Dislocation." *Canadian Theatre Review* 88 (1996): 31–37.

————. *Reading the Material Theatre.* Cambridge and New York: Cambridge UP, 2004.

Lecoq, Jacques. *Theatre of Movement and Gesture.* Ed. David Bradby. London: Routledge, 2006.

Lepecki, André. *Exhausting Dance: Performance and the Politics of Movement.* New York: Routledge, 2006.

Lind, Maria. "The Collaborative Turn." *Taking Matters into Common Hands: On Contemporary Art and Collaborative Processes.* Ed. Johanna Billing, Maria Lind, and Lars Nilsson. London: Black Dog, 2007.

Matusov, E. "Intersubjectivity Without Agreement." *Mind, Culture, and Activity* 3.1 (1996): 25–45.

Mead, G.H. *The Philosophy of the Present.* Chicago: U of Chicago P, 1932.

McKenzie, Jon. "The Liminal-Norm." *The Performance Studies Reader.* Ed. Henry Bial. Abingdon, Oxon: Routledge, 2007. 26–31.

McKinnie, Michael. *City Stages: Theatre and Urban Space in a Global City.* Toronto: U of Toronto P, 2007.

————. "Space Administration: Rereading the Material History of Theatre Passe Muraille in Toronto." *Essays on Canadian Writing* 68 (1999): 19–45.

Milling, Jane and Graham Ley. *Modern Theories of Performance.* Houndsmill, Basingstoke: Palgrave MacMillan, 2001.

Mouffe, Chantal. *The Democratic Paradox.* London: Verso, 2000.

Murray, Simon. *Jacques Lecoq.* Abingdon, Oxon: Routledge, 2004.

Oddey, Alison. *Devising Theatre: A Practical and Theoretical Handbook.* London: Routledge, 1994.

————. *Reframing the Theatrical: Interdisciplinary Landscapes for Performance.* Houndsmill, Basingstoke: Palgrave MacMillan, 2007.

Prentki, Tim and Jan Selman. *Popular Theatre in Political Culture: Britain and Canada in Focus.* Bristol: Intellect, 2000.

Santino, Jack. "Performative Commemoratives, The Personal, and The Public." *The Performance Studies Reader.* Ed. Henry Bial. Abingdon, Oxon: Routledge, 2007. 125–33.

Sawyer, R. Keith. *Group Creativity: Music, Theater, Collaboration.* Mahwah, NJ: Lawrence Erlbaum, 2003.

Seremetakis, Nadia, ed. *The Senses Still: Perception and Memory as Material Culture in Modernity.* Chicago: U of Chicago P, 1994.

Shank, Theodore. "Collective Creation." *The Drama Review* 16.2 (1972): 3–31.

Somers, John. "Introduction." *Drama As Social Intervention.* Ed. Michael Balfour and John Somers. Concord, ON: Captus U, 2006.

Turner, Jane. *Eugenio Barba.* Abingdon, Oxon: Routledge, 2004.

Watson, Ian. "Introduction." *Performer Training: Developments Across Cultures.* Ed. Ian Watson. Amsterdam: Harwood Academic, 2001. 1–10.

Wolford, Lisa. "Seminal Teachings: The Grotowski Influence: A Reassessment." *Canadian Theatre Review* 88 (1996): 38–43.

Weinberg, Mark S. *Challenging the Heirarchy: Collective Theatre in the United States.* Westport, CT: Greenwood, 1992.

Zarrilli, Phillip C. "Toward a Phenomenological Model of the Actor's Embodied Modes of Experience." *Theatre Journal* 56.4 (2004): 653–66.

Collective Creation:
Process, Politics and Poetics

by Alan Filewod

Although collective creation has been an important development in Canadian theatre over the past decade, we have not had the volume of critical writing and theoretical investigation of the form that one might find, for instance, in Latin America, where a similar movement has been analyzed systematically by directors and critics such as Boal, Buenaventura and Santiago Garcia.

It is not my purpose to give a history of collective creation in Canada, or even a thorough analysis of its significance in Canadian theatre, but I will attempt to outline several considerations which may explain why collective creation has evolved as it has in this country.

Collective creation is a form which may be analyzed in three aspects: *process*, that is, the process of theatrical development; *politics*, looking at the political and ideological relationships of the subjective experience of the creators and the objective reality of the subject matter; and *poetics*, which questions the dual nature of the play in performance as a work of art in itself, and as the culmination of a particular way of working and all that implies.

From this we can derive three primary considerations which may be applied to an understanding of the uniqueness of collective creation. They are: the relation of the collective process to the final text; the relation of the process to the subject, whether it be a community, an historic event, or a work of fiction; and the relation of the final text to the subject.

Before examining these considerations, it must be pointed out that the concept of collective creation in the modern theatre has an ideological source. This does not mean that collectively-created plays are about ideology; it means that we must be aware of the difference between a concept and a convention. Theatre is a collective art, and in one sense, all plays are created collectively, just as an automobile is created collectively: the result of a number of talents working jointly to create a single thing. The modern experiment in collective creation differs radically in that it places the *responsibility* for the play on the shoulders of the collective; instead of a governing mind providing an artistic vision which others work to express, the collectively-created play is the vision of a supra-individualist mind.

There is ample evidence to suggest that of all forms of dramatic creation, collective creation is best equipped to embody and reflect actively the objectivity of social life; consequently, there is an affinity between collective creation and documentary drama, especially in Canada. Collective creation derives its uniqueness from the synthesis of several different perspectives and experiences. This is especially true when the actors work as scenariasts and playwrights, and it suggests a fundamental difference between the imagination of the collective and the individual playwright. It is the *quality* of imagination that differs, for the skills that go into the construction of a play do not differ radically. In fact, playwrights frequently work within collectives. Rick Salutin described his function in the creation of *1837* as writer on, not of, the play. I suggest as a basic principle that collectives as a rule are no better or worse than individual playwrights when it comes to making a play. But there is a fundamental qualitative difference in the kind of imitation that underlies the play.

In Canada we look upon collective creation as an *alternative* method of play creation. Compare this to what happens in Latin America, where collective creation is often systematized as, in Buenaventura's phrase, "a way of producing meaning" (59). For Buenaventura, collective creation is a dialectical method which confronts and expresses the contradictions between what he calls "virtuality" – what one wants to say – and "alternative" – the choices one makes as to how to say it. He contrasts this to the traditional bourgeois theatre, in which the actor is suppressed, as an interpreter of someone else's *meaning*. The necessary affinity of the productive relationships in the theatre and the material world are also emphasized by the Venezuelan group T-Pos which makes the statement in its theoretical paper that its work is collective not only because of the method of work, "but because it poses the collective problems of the masses" (77). In this sense, collective creation is seen as a natural development: "[D]iscipline and hierarchal order acquire their highest expression in the collective method where the work is distributed in terms of the ability and personal experience of the individual, under the supervision of the collective" (82). This of course accords with the Marxist theory that the individual can only achieve true fulfillment and productive creativity in the collective, which frees him from the artificial constraints of social oppression.

To take this a step further, a fundamental difference between the individual and collective playwrights is that the individual synthesizes the objective world into a private vision, whereas the collective synthesizes it into a public vision. This is not to say that only the collective is capable of creating objectivist drama; that is obviously not so, and some collectives are so subjective in their artistic vision as to be virtually incomprehensible to the outsider. (I am thinking here of Italy's Communa Baires.) Once more, it is the quality of imitation that differs. Because collective creation synthesizes the artistic responses of a number of individuals, it must proceed from some kind of *shared analysis*, which differs from the private vision of the individual because it needs some kind of critical perspective to account for the differences within the collective. Again, I must stress that I am referring here to the source of the imitation process, and not the result. In this sense, art is very different from the making of a material commodity. One man may build a car in his shed, while in the next shed, a collective may build a car, and they may build similar cars, because the only real difference is the distribution of the work. But in the theatre, that distribution affects the very nature of the play.

Process: The Collective and the Final Text

When looking at the process of collective creation and its relation to the final text, we are concerned with the ways in which a concept of working is embodied in performance. Ideally, we should like to answer the question: is it possible to ascertain from the viewing of a play whether it has been created collectively? The question is deceptive, because the signals which might lead us to answer yes are not restricted to collective creation. In Robert Altman's films we can see improvisation taking place, and while film is a collective art, not even Altman's films are collective creations in the sense we are using here. Improvisation is a tool of collective creation, but it is not the substance. Yet it is by recognizing improvisation that we often recognize collective creation.

Theoretically, it should be possible to adduce whether a play has been collectively created by watching the development of the montage, by listening closely to the language, and by following the actors as they develop their characters. But theory is not always sufficient, because the collective itself is a variable, a gestalt which finds its specific talent in the range of talents it joins together. By its nature, the collective is an organism in a constant state of change, as it grows and reacts, as its membership changes, and as it redefines itself in new projects. Generally, the Canadian tradition has been the one-shot collective; very rarely has it happened that the same group of people works on more than one or two shows, although naturally, some theatres—most notably Passe Muraille—have used a basic corps on a series of projects.

The Latin American tradition takes a relatively stable and long-term collective through a series of projects which are decided by the membership, one way or another, in response to perceived needs. Out of this comes a shared analysis which is applied to, and challenged by, the subject of the play. In Canada, for reasons both financial and ideological, theatres tend to audition and hire a group of actors to work on a particular project, and usually, the analysis—that is, the political response which becomes the organizational basis of the play—is discovered through the process of research and rehearsal. The major exceptions to this are those plays in which a writer is brought into the collective as a specialist, as Rudy Wiebe was in *Far As The Eye Can See*. In such cases, the writer often provides a basic analysis, if not intentionally, then *de facto*, by the very act of shaping the actors' discoveries into a structure. Frequently, actors are cautious of writers in this situation, unless a comfortable independence of roles is developed early. When working with the Mummers Troupe as a dramaturge on a play about inner city housing in St. John's, I experienced this myself when an actor bitterly challenged a certain montage of monologues I had suggested. She felt that the juxtaposition I had suggested falsified her character, making the character say something that the actor didn't want her to say. The issue was one of honesty; the actor felt that she was being manipulated, and her character with her. And I was manipulating, as any playwright working in documentary must do. In this case, our problem was that our ideas of what was honest differed, because we did not agree about what had to be said. I mention this incident only because it is, in one form or another, probably quite common.

Especially in documentary theatre, which in Canada has been a major tendency in collective creation, the issue of honesty is never far away. When working with the lives of actual people, or with one's own deeper emotions, as the actors in *I Love You, Baby Blue* had to do, ethical questions become important. Often, they become significant within the final text. Only in collective creation do we find the ethical considerations of the process of making the play so central to the final play in performance. In the *Allen Garden Show*, directed by Cheryl Cashman, there was a scene in which an actor playing herself approached another actor in the character of an old rubby to get his "story." The scene was obviously a direct imitation of an actual event: the actor invites the drunk for a cup of soup and, as he talks, surreptitiously takes notes. The drunk notices this, and in a fit of rage accuses her of ripping him off, and storms out, leaving the actor alone on stage in poignant anguish. The subject of the play was Toronto's derelict population, but the scene was about the actor and her own gradual awareness that the subject was alien to her. These ethical conflicts are not always built so overtly into the final play, but in collective creation, every actor must at some point confront his or her real feelings and attitudes as they relate to both the subject of the play and those of the other members of the collective. What in other forms of theatre today is an ideal—the actor's confrontation with the self as a means to truth—is in collective creation a necessary part of the process.

Nissin Charin, of the ICTUS theatre of Chile, has written that with his group, the starting point of a play is always subjective, with sociological aspects built in as complements in the later development of the play. But then, he says, "the general subjective mechanisms, in unobstructed play in the process of invention, at the stage for the search for material are now substituted by the search for a viewpoint from which to approach staging the play" (51). He has a useful term for this; he calls it "the objective occurrence," a "*relation* with the internal logic which the material we have compiled acquires" (52). From that he concludes that "the actors should not work for the characters they portray, but for the play; the characters are an expression of the dramatic life and not the other way round" (53).

The objective occurrence is the point at which the process of research and investigation is transformed into an objective shape, a scenario, an analysis, a general structure. In Canada, we have had two broad developments of this idea of objective occurrence, and they can be seen in the two most successful—measured in terms of fame if nothing else—collective creations: *The Farm Show* and *Paper Wheat*.

In the spoken preface to *The Farm Show*, an actor tells the audience: "the show kind of bounces along one way or another and then it stops." Paul Thompson, in his introduction to the Coach House Press edition of the play, wrote that "There is no 'story' or 'plot' as such. The form of the play is more like a Canadian Sunday School or Christmas concert where one person does a recitation, another sings a song, a third acts out a skit, etc." But as Thompson points out, beneath this apparent formlessness there is a weave of themes and motifs.

Throughout *The Farm Show* we are reminded of the process by which the play was created. One of the most memorable scenes has actor Miles Potter learning how to bale hay from a farmer, and what makes the scene work is the ironic picture of the cocky actor getting his comeuppance. Much of the charm and truth of the play comes from a quality of self-consciousness; even in the monologues we are aware of the process of research. When an actor delivers a monologue in the play, we are seeing a mirror-image of what the actor saw, right down to the momentary interruptions as children enter and telephones ring. In that sense, *The Farm Show* is a report of what the actors saw and experienced, and it is a report made sensitive by the actors' specialized insight. We are always aware that the actors are themselves characters in the play, that they are a community looking at a community.

In *Paper Wheat* we see a different form of imitation, in which the actors portray specific characters and follow them through a schematic line of action. A similar example would be Theatre Network's *Hard Hats and Stolen Hearts*, which moves from the documentary source into what is essentially an Aristotelian fable. In *Paper Wheat* there are both tendencies, and at points the mixture creates problems. Essentially a didactic play, *Paper Wheat* portrays the human aspect of the development of the grain co-operatives in Saskatchewan, and it attempts to teach a lesson about history. The problem for the actors in this kind of play is simple: how are dynamic historical principles best illustrated, and how are dry facts to be made interesting? In the first case, the play resorts to familiar agit-prop techniques which would seem to be the results of rehearsal brainstorming:

> Four farmers wander on with small sheaves of wheat in their hands, and sorrowful expressions on their faces. They look at each other and back at their wheat, then an idea hits them. Slowly, one by one, they put their individual sheaves together. Their expressions change as all their wheat becomes one big sheaf. A sign appears on the foot of the stage: it reads: Grain Growers Grain Company 1905.... (Twenty-Fifth Street 71)

This rhetorical demonstration of a principle that underlies the drama is an undialectical illustration of a process that elsewhere the play attempts to describe as dialectical. It does nothing for the play but provide one piece of information (a date) and a transition between scenes. And because it is undialectical, it reduces the principle it attempts to illustrate, simplifying something the play has been careful to build in its human complexity.

In rehearsal, particularly in documentary theatre, much time must be spent in solving staging problems. But what often happens is that the solution becomes not a key to develop an idea, but a scene in itself. So in *Company Town* we have a magic bit where ore is turned into money. And how many other plays use the device of a barber's chair to anchor a monologue?

It often happens that when the rehearsal process is objectified in the final text, the solution to the particular rehearsal problem works against the play. In *Paper Wheat* there is a scene called "Mystery Theatre." The idea was to dramatize an episode in which grain tycoons were paying a journalist under the table to write spurious letters to the editor of his paper under an assumed name. In order to dramatize this, and send it up, the creators of the play chose a radio theatre format, and the stage direction setting the scene reads: "a not yet invented CBC radio studio in the 1910s…" (71). That invention itself is interesting, but even more to the point is the "program" selected to tell the story: *The Whistler*, a famous American radio series from the 1940s. I find it curious that this double fabrication, great fun as it is, should be necessary to dramatize a documented event in a documentary play. Essentially, it reduces the event to the level of parody, and we are not sure what is being parodied. If a showbiz format is necessary to the telling of the story, why an anachronistic American programme, rather than—for instance—a more authentic 1910 vaudeville number? The solution to a rehearsal problem in this case becomes a diverting anomaly in the play; its inauthenticity, its "lets-pretend" premise, clash[es] so strongly with the didactic purpose of the play. In plays such as *I Love You Baby Blue* and *The Farm Show*, both of which depend on our own recognition of the actors as a community within the play, this kind of anomaly presents no problem, so long as it reinforces the overall pattern of the play – hence the "Human Levitation" number in *Baby Blue*. But in *Paper Wheat*, the actors are presenting us with something more than their own subjective experiences, and while the mixture of dramatic fable and documentary collage objectifies the process of creation, anomalies such as "Mystery Theatre" and the agit-prop devices bring the process of creation into the fore in an unproductive way.

Politics: Process and Subject

If the fact of collective creation has a substantial effect on the nature of the play, this in turn would suggest that collective creation has a claim to recognition as a distinct form of theatre and drama – a conclusion which argues against those who maintain that collective creation undermines the role of the playwright.

But if collective creation involves the imagination of a community of talents, then there is of necessity a political dimension to the process as well. As it has developed in Canada, collective creation has been affected by two main political considerations: the consciousness of the collective and the analysis it develops in response to its material (which may or may not touch overtly on politics), and the external political and economic realities, which define possibilities of the work and, in a narrow sense, the quality of the work. These two considerations are related at source, for they call into question the social definition of the art.

The process of creation is obviously common to all humanity, but its social organization fulfills the historic needs of the specific society: new movements emerge in response to particular conditions. In Canada, it is a fact that theatre is primarily a bourgeois occupation. Most theatre artists come from the middle classes, and they create art which satisfies—and on occasion enrages—the tastes of the middle classes. And, of course, it is the middle classes which support most theatrical activity in the country.

Because most actors and theatre artists subscribe to middle class values, the ideological nature of collective creation differs radically from the Latin American example, where theatres are frequently radicalized in the leftist opposition. This question of class consciousness has had two effects on collective creation in Canada.

The first is the nature of the collective itself. The primary doctrine of middle class ideology in Canada is individualism, and while orthodox Marxists might argue that bourgeois individualism and collective creation cannot really be reconciled, in Canada that reconciliation is taken for granted; in fact, it is not even a subject of debate. Although there is evidence that this is changing, it would be hard to find a Canadian theatre that would agree with the Colombian director Jose Triana, who wrote that "harmony ... with the social world is precisely what guarantees that our art succeeds or even approaches the possibility of giving us a useful and clear outlook on our own moment in history" (55). What Triana means by "harmony" is a direct affinity of art and political analysis. The Venezuelan T-Pos group make the same point when they write that their theatre treats social problems scientifically: "Marxism introduces the principle of critique and self-critique, the submission of the minority to the majority" (81).

Taking an ideological analysis as an *a priori* fact, the Latin American groups can focus their working time on finding what they see as the *correct* solutions to the problems of creation. In Canada, collectives are usually formed somewhat arbitrarily, and often share little more than a vague populism; consequently, much of the research/rehearsal time is spent hammering out a basic position, sorting out the differences within the collective. This is not a problem in plays like *The Farm Show,* which works *because* of the individualist consciousness of the actors. But in plays like *Paper Wheat* or *Company Town,* plays which examine concrete social problems and events, this individualism can be problematic.

This leads to the second class consideration: the objective analysis with which the collective responds to its subject as a whole. To give what is perhaps an extreme example, in 1975 the Mummers Troupe was commissioned by the St. John's Social Planning Council to produce a play on the effects of federal home renovation grants on inner city housing. The play that evolved was an entertaining and skillful portrait of a community, and indeed, the Planning Council was pleased with it. But no mention was made of the federal grant programs, because the collective could not agree on them. Some members felt that these programs were oppressive; others saw them as beneficial; others didn't really care. The topic was avoided in the play because the actors could not find a way to solve their disagreement. The exigencies of rehearsal with a tight deadline are such that whatever works best in rehearsal as actors come in from their research tends to end up in the play; in that sense, the objective occurrence, when analysis is lacking, is a form of filtering, as the actors select and polish the overtly theatrical, at the potential expense of the more difficult and substantial.

Because of this, it often happens that the actors, conscious of themselves as outsiders, objectify their own feelings in the play. This can work to great benefit, as it did in Theatre Network's *Kicker,* which, in its portrayal of Inuvik, introduced the fictitious character of a schoolteacher from the South whose dramatic experiences objectified the actors' own culture shock. In *Company Town* we do not see an outsider as such, but the actual form of the action, with its montage of objectivity (monologues) and subjective comment (songs, puppetry, clowning) serves the same function.

In *Paper Wheat* we see an example of how this objectification can defeat its purpose. Wisely working to avoid static illustration wherever possible, the creators of the play invented a small number of characters who recur throughout the play; we follow them from their homesteading days to the establishment of the grain co-ops. Through the eyes of the common man we see great events unfold, and we see how these events are related to the working lives of the people. In that sense, Sean and William and Vasily are *typical* men; they are individualized, but we know that they are representative of many others. At the end of the first act of *Paper Wheat* the three farmers agree amongst themselves to attend a meeting called to discuss grain prices, and we are left with the knowledge that we are catching a small glimpse of a great movement. But does the fiction tell the truth? By the end of the final scene of act one, we are deeply involved with the dramatic fortunes of the specific characters, and without an analytic context to give it larger meaning, the scene effectively simplifies, rather than illustrates, the historical principle. In *Paper Wheat,* as in *Hard Hats and Stolen Hearts,* an avoidance of critical analysis results in melodrama. In a play like *The Farm Show* this condition does not arise; it is a condition particular to those documentaries which attempt to blend Aristotelian fable with reportage. It is also a condition prevalent in socialist realism, which attempts to embody a progressive concept of history in the action of specific dramatic characters.

The level of consciousness within the collective is a formative influence on the nature of the play as it develops. However we must also consider the external conditions imposed on creativity by the theatre as an institution in society. It is perhaps a commonplace that the work a theatre does, its very style and technique, is in one sense a product of economic realities. But it is also true that the economic realities can be influenced by the nature of the theatre's work.

When we look at the economic profile of theatre in Canada, we are struck by the fact that those companies which specialize in collective creation tend to be at the lower end of the funding scale. They share that plight with a number of experimental and popular theatres, popular in the sense of people's theatre. Some of the reasons for this are obvious; it could be argued for instance that these companies play to minority audiences, while the funding structures in the country developed parallel to the regional theatre network. And it is obvious that a theatre with an expensive plant, like the Citadel, requires more operating funds than a small collective like Kam Lab. But there are ideological priorities underlying these arguments.

The collective companies emerged in the late 1960s and early 1970s as "alternative theatre," and as alternatives to a mainstream establishment they were considered to be less respectable, or at least less important. It was only a few years ago that the Mummers Troupe was labelled "subversive" by a senior official of the Newfoundland public service. The god of the arts councils is the box office tally, and the regional theatre, with its subscription season, middle class audience and large-capacity house naturally brings in more revenue than the small collective touring original plays to isolated rural communities. In that sense, the small theatre is making a deliberate sacrifice, as are the artists who work with it. As a general principle, it is safe to say that the more a theatre rejects the institutional standard of theatrical production, the less money it receives from funding agencies.

In 1978, the Canada Council theatre office, in Walter Learning's words, attempted to "recognize in a positive way that collectives were different and required thorough examination." But this recognition ironically confirmed the general condition of collective companies as a principle of policy. For the year 1979–80, all collective companies, as defined by the Canada Council, were ruled ineligible for Base Operating Grants. Through correspondence, several theatres discovered that certain Council officers felt collectives were inherently unstable. When this was refuted in a storm of protest, the Council convened a meeting of collective theatres in January of 1979. The meeting constituted a *de facto* recognition that collective creation is a distinct branch in the development of Canadian theatre, but Council balked at making that recognition a financial reality. Most of the companies at that meeting received less than $25,000 (a figure the Council uses as a measuring stick) from Canada Council, and many of those companies complained that they were trapped in a "collective" ghetto, from which the only escape would be to return to a more "traditional" form of production. In 1979, Mummers Troupe artistic director Chris Brookes wrote in response to the Council's suggestion that there was "some problem in realizing the mandate the company has set for itself":

> My company's ability to deliver on its mandate is measured by its response to the society of its region … This means that our production plans may have to change as rapidly as the social issues they express. The evaluation of the social topology and the substance of the response must be decided by the artistic director of the company in the region, not by Ottawa arts bureaucrats upon consideration of "production details" on a project-by-project funding contingency.

There are two serious aesthetic implications in this contradiction between ideology and funding management. Generally, those collective companies which receive critical attention, and whose success is complemented by increased funding, are those which achieve commercial success. But what of those companies which neither receive nor want that kind of attention? What if a company like Kam Lab prefers not to take a show to Toronto every year to wow the critics? What in fact happens is what we can see now. Kam Lab is virtually unknown, as is Ottawa's Great Canadian Theatre

Company. Both theatres do fine work in their regions, and both have been ignored by the media, and granted only token recognition by the Canada Council.

The second implication is even more disturbing. In the state of collective theatre, we have a reincarnation of the familiar Bohemian-artist-in-the-garret syndrome, which works to the convenience of the funding agencies and the inconvenience of the theatres. Because these companies have survived on low budgets, usually less than $100,000 a year from all sources, it is assumed that they neither need nor deserve larger amounts. Hence they cannot tackle expensive projects, and they cannot afford to maintain and train an ensemble of artists. And because rich theatres rarely practice collective creation, an equation emerges: rich means Shakespeare, poor means collective creation. Therefore the accomplishments of collective theatre in Canada can only be measured in terms of its possibilities. When we criticize a collectively-created play because the structure is confused, the acting weak and the design unimaginative, we must remember that the play has probably been conceived, researched, written and rehearsed on an insufficient budget in the same spate of time that a richer theatre might allow for the rehearsal alone of a literary drama.

Partially in response to this condition, there is an increasing trend amongst collective theatres towards a more defined radicalization; more companies are committing themselves to specific political platforms, and they are sharing this radicalization amongst themselves. The Popular Theatre Alliance stands as an example. In the past decade, Canadian theatres reacted to the currents of cultural nationalism by building a national drama; now the nature of that nationalism is being questioned, as bourgeois nationalism is redefined in terms of its class orientation.

Poetics: Text and Subject

The economic situation of collective creation can be seen as both an historical condition and an ideological necessity. But if process and politics are essential to an understanding of the play in performance, what of the play as it exists within the body of dramatic literature? It is a tenet of dramatic theory that the play text has a double existence, as a blueprint for performance and a poetic work in its own right. No two performances of any play are the same, but *Hamlet* is always *Hamlet*, be it performed by Kean or Olivier. Is *The Farm Show* always *The Farm Show*? Or, more exactly, is our response to the play independent of our response to the performance?

In order to resolve this question, it is necessary to return again to the process of creation. I have already suggested that the process of collective creation is evident in the performance. I would like to add another way in which this happens. Anyone who has attended the performance of a documentary play at its premiere will recognize that there is an aesthetic relationship between the performers and their subject audience that cannot be repeated. Just as *The Farm Show* changed when it moved out of Ray Bird's barn, *Company Town* changed when it moved out of Buchans, *Two Miles Off* changed when it moved out of Elnora. Of course, these changes are anticipated, and the play remains the play. But something has happened. When a play is specifically created about the public and private lives of a particular community—which may be the actors themselves—then criteria by which we evaluate the play must also take into account that community.

When the Mummers Troupe was rehearsing *Company Town*, an incident occurred which may illustrate this complex fact. The actors were improvising a scene in the union hall in Buchans, watched by several retired miners. The scene was about the mining company's policy of presenting a gold watch to workers who had lasted twenty-five years. As the actors improvised, a retired miner interrupted the scene, asked permission to speak, and launched into a long speech, the speech he always wished he had delivered when he received his gold watch. In it he condemned the company for its heartlessness, and recalled the men he knew who had died of silicosis. One of the actors taped him as he spoke, and the scene, exactly as it happened in the rehearsal hall, was included in the play. As performed, the director stopped a watch-giving ceremony, told the audience what had happened when the scene was being improvised, and an actor entered to deliver the miner's speech. Aesthetically, we have here something of a conundrum: an imitation within an imitation, wrapped around an anti-illusionistic device. Several months after the show opened, the play was performed in Nova Scotia, and the man who had originally made the speech happened to be in the audience. When the actor finished the speech, the retired miner stood up and said, "Ladies and gentlemen, I am that man."

Such moments are undoubtedly familiar to anyone who has worked in this kind of collective creation, and their critical meaning can only be understood in terms of particular audiences. In that sense, collective theatre still retains its older function as a communal sharing of experience, the sense of which is closed to outsiders. Effectively, it brings into question the concept of ownership.

I don't mean here ownership in the copyright sense, although that can be a complex question itself in collective creation. Today we often hear that knowledge is a resource, and frequently a commodity; this is the basis of critiques of folklorists and anthropologists who intervene in the life of a community and give nothing in return. Who owns that speech of the retired miner? The miner? The theatre as a legal entity? The actor who performed it, thereby transforming reality into art? Conventionally, nobody owns literature once a copyright expires. But here the question may be ethical, not legal.

This is a problem not just in documentary theatre, but in all collective creation, because when subjective experiences are objectified in art and identified, the recognition of that subjectivity is essential to an understanding of the art. When the Great Canadian Theatre Company performed *Company Town* in 1979, the scene of the miner's speech was three times removed from the original event, an event inspired by a breakdown between reality and imitation. Played in a theatre far removed from Buchans before an audience substantially different than the original, the scene became a curious dramatic device. The play itself was transformed from a documentary actively involved with a community to a dramatic report on that community; originally action, it became rhetoric, and its purpose was changed. And yet, the words were the same.

Company Town and *The Farm Show* are plays in which the personal experiences of the collective are significant. What of *Paper Wheat*, where those experiences are already transformed into fiction? There is no reason why the Stratford Festival could not buy a dozen copies of *Paper Wheat* and mount the play as part of its regular season. In many respects, the production might well be similar to the original, and yet, I suggest, a significant change would take place. Once transformed into a work of dramatic literature, the play would invite criticism as such, and quite possibly, it might prove a mediocre piece of dramatic literature. This is not because we are willing to excuse faults on the basis of authenticity in the original, but because when we know a play is the specific expression of specific conditions, then the criteria by which we respond are in part shaped by that awareness. Theatre is not just literature; it is also a social event.

All art requires at some level some kind of external recognition; if we cannot recognize a work of art as art, it has no meaning to us. In this respect, collective creation is no different than any other form of art. In our hypothetical production of *Paper Wheat* at Stratford, the external significance of the play is lacking. It does not *need* to be produced at Stratford, in the sense that the original production was necessary. Perhaps we might say this of Shakespeare as well; he too was responding to particular conditions. But Shakespeare was creating a literary theatre, and collective creation is essentially non-literary. Because it is a public expression, it is rhetorical. But it is an analytic rhetoric, a public vision of reality, and it derives its power and usefulness from the fact that it is public, a community addressing a community. When that public dimension is removed, then the work is changed into something it was not meant to be.

With a decade of experience behind us, we can still say that collective creation is at an early stage of development in Canada. Beginning as a localized phenomenon, it is evolving as a particular tradition and form of theatre, and consequently, it is changing the definition of theatre in this country.

(1982)

Works Cited

Brookes, Chris. Correspondence to Walter Learning. 14 July 1979.

Buenaventura, Enrique. "Collective Creation as a Means to Popular Theatre." *Reports and Papers*. [Ed.: no page numbers available]

Charin, Nissin. "Collective Creation as a Means to Popular Theatre." *Reports and Papers*. [Ed.: no page numbers available]

Learning, Walter. Correspondence to Kam Theatre Lab. 27 September 1979.

Reports and Papers from the Colloquium on Comparisons in the Theatre of the Third World (IV World Session of the Theatre of Nations). Caracas: International Theatre Institute, Venezuela Centre, 1978.

T. Pos Group (Theatre for the Workers). "A Collective Method of Work as Experienced in the Theatre." *Reports and Papers*. [Ed.: no page numbers available]

Theatre Passe Muraille. *The Farm Show: A Collective Creation*. Toronto: Coach House, 1976.

Triana, Jose. "Collective Creation." *Reports and Papers*. [Ed.: no page numbers available]

Twenty-Fifth Street House Theatre. *Paper Wheat: A Collective Creation. Canadian Theatre Review* 17 (Winter 1978): 38–92.

The Meeting of Actuality
and Theatricality in *The Farm Show*

by Robert C. Nunn

The term "documentary," like any other, explains very little when applied to specific examples, but, if properly applied, does invite the right questions: in this instance, what precisely is the actuality which the work documents, what is the relation between the work and the actuality it reflects, what perspective toward the real-life material is embodied in the structure of the work? In short, to quote John Grierson's famous definition of documentary, what precisely is its "creative treatment of actuality"? (qtd. in Mast 367). In this essay I seek to examine Theatre Passe Muraille's *The Farm Show* as a documentary play; in so doing I hope to illuminate what I think is the source of its considerable power, and this is its imaginative exploration of the contrast between the real life which is its subject and its non-representational mode of playing that material.

Theatre Passe Muraille under the direction of Paul Thompson has been engaged in a continuous process of discovering and refining its own solutions to the aesthetic problems arising from the transformation of factual material into theatre since 1971, when it presented *Doukhobors*. It was *The Farm Show* (1972), however, which indicated the rich potential of the form, and indeed remains an exemplar. The core of Theatre Passe Muraille's work over the years has consisted of further explorations of the possibilities opened up by *The Farm Show,* in such productions as *Under The Greywacke, The West Show, Far as the Eye Can See* and *Les Maudits Anglais.* The roots of the company's work in documentary are in what Paul Thompson refers to as "the traditions of documentary that we have in this country like the work of the CBC and the NFB" (qtd. in Johns 31). [1] Its influence can be seen in the work of the 25th Street House Theatre of Saskatoon and of the Mummers' Troupe of Newfoundland, to name only the most visible offshoots.

In extending the Canadian tradition of documentary in specifically theatrical directions, *The Farm Show* radically enlarged its possibilities. The "creative treatment of actuality" specific to it and responsible for the impact it has had and still has is the way in which its relation to actuality and its intense theatricality catch fire from one another. I would go so far as to say that the possibility, always inherent in theatre, as theatre, of approaching the efficacy of ritual, is realized in *The Farm Show,* to the enrichment of the documentary form.

To enlarge briefly on this point: I am defining ritual, in terms derived from anthropology, as a performance which effects a transformation in its participants; the transformation may be of social status, as in rituals of status elevation, or of social relationships, as in weddings, or of the individual's situation in the life cycle, as in puberty rites, or of spiritual condition as in the celebration of the mass. All theatre shares the element of performance with ritual; and, as Richard Schechner points out, any theatre piece is situated on a continuum between the extreme of pure entertainment and the extreme of pure ritual efficacy. *The Farm Show,* in its original performance, was considerably more than entertainment; it did indeed effect a transformation in the relationship between the company of actors, who had created the show, and the farming community, which was the subject of the show and its first audience. Moreover, this transformation is embodied in the substance and structure of the play-script itself and can be recreated, and imaginatively experienced, in subsequent performances. All this is a large claim to make for a play with such a modest title, but I hope to substantiate it in the remarks that follow.

As a first step we must analyze how the play establishes its veracity as documentary.[2] In the introduction to the published script of the play are descriptions of the process by which it was developed. These alert us to a number of significant features:

> The idea was to take a group of actors out to a farming community [near Clinton, Ontario] and build a play of what we could see and learn ... The play was not written down; it developed out of interviews, visits, and improvisations. Most of the words used were given to us by the community along with their stories. We spent a great deal of our time trying to imitate these people both in the way they move and in the way they speak. We wanted to capture the fibre of what they were, and this seemed the best way to do it.
>
> In the early days of that summer of '72, the actors had no idea what they were doing. The dramatic techniques and the songs grew out of the actors' attempts to dramatize their discoveries in daily improvisational sessions. At first the result didn't seem like a play: no lights, no costumes, no set, a barn for a theatre, haybales for seats. Simply pure performance. (7)[3]

In the text these introductions establish the play's relation to fact: it is about real people in a real community and uses their words. And in performance the play itself repeatedly asserts its own veracity; in the first scene, the audience is told the basic facts about the six-week visit to the Clinton area; and throughout the play occur assertions like "we got to know," "we wanted to go around to some of the different farmers," "we went," "we saw," and so on.

The first scene of the play, moreover, indicates succinctly what the specific quality of that relation to actuality will be. Our attention is drawn to the stage, which is laid out as a map of the district, complete with indications of where many of the people imitated or mentioned in the play live. This stage has a dual identity: as a non-representational playing space it is capable of being transformed into barns, fields, homes, the town square of Goderich, and so on. Yet through all these transformations it maintains its relation to fact, as a map. The same point can be made of the objects on the stage. They are identified in the first scene as objects from the Clinton area: "part of a bean dryer … straw bales … an old cream can. Some crates. An actual Clinton shopping cart" (19). These objects are used as props in the play and as such undergo many transformations: for example, in the "Winter Scene" the crates covered with a white cloth become a winter landscape, the shopping cart becomes a car, a mailbox becomes a snowmobile. But through all these transformations they remain what they really are, things from Clinton.

The stage and props indicate the play's paradoxical relation to actuality: its conventions are far removed from representational realism, while the audience is continually reminded of the actuality behind the mask of performance. Thus each actor performs as a number of people of the community past and present, and as trees, animals, machines and landscapes as well, yet all the while is present to the audience as a specific person who went to Clinton and helped create the play. As we will see, this contradiction is the heart of the play's success. Given the nature of the factual material it seeks to document, an extreme theatricality was the only appropriate choice of performance style. Indeed, these indications suggest that the play does much more than simply assert: "this is real, these people are real, this really happened." For, although persuading its audience of its authentic relation to fact is the *sine qua non* of documentary, it is insufficient in itself to ensure that the work has any value beyond merely recording. Indeed, as Rick Salutin points out, "the resort to a 'documentary' style … to various kinds of assurance that this really happened … can often be attempts to avoid having to stipulate what is 'really' real i.e. essential, in the situations being depicted."

The Farm Show goes far beyond the minimal, and potentially falsifying, type of documentary Salutin is speaking of. The question, then, is: what does it do with its mass of factual material, what form does it reveal in it, what does it bring out as "most real, in the sense of most important or most essential" (Salutin)?

We can begin to deal with this question by examining what Paul Thompson states to be the essence of the play: "[W]e hope … that out of it will emerge a picture of a complex and living community … We wanted to capture the fibre of what they were" (7).

Certainly the play addresses itself to presenting a dramatic portrait of a community. The emphasis throughout is on the activities by which a community sustains itself: auctions, weddings, parades, school concerts, revival meetings, township council meetings, the community's response to an accident, and so on. The forces against which it must contend are made present as well, growing in intensity from the snowstorm near the beginning whose power to isolate is triumphantly flouted in a flurry of visiting, hockey games and square dances, to the threat identified in the "Bruce Pallett" monologue near the end (it did not appear in the original performances): the indifference of the nation to the value of farming as a way of life and as part of the national identity.

However, if that were all the play did, we would have a much less rich work of art than we do. Simply, six weeks is not enough time to "capture the fibre of what they were" except in ways that would either belie the claim the play makes to having been developed in six weeks, or settle for superficiality. In *The Clinton Special*, David Fox, a member of the company, addresses this problem.

> The problem in this improvisational form of documentary theatre is you don't get deep enough, it seems very shallow, because you haven't had very much time. We're kind of ingrained with the idea of accepting what a professional writer has to give you … What he gives you is – you believe anyway – the result of study, of insight, and so on; and as soon as we get up and try to improvise it seems we're just scratching the surface. And the only way I think that you can give a – kind of convey an in-depth thing – is through the contrast – scene following scene – the total view of the thing, I don't know – but I just worry that it's a very shallow picture of the lives of these people – because we got here for six weeks, and came in here for five hours a day and work these things out and say here's a character and there's a scene, here the danger, and these are women on the farm, and these are kids on the farm, and this is their social life, and so on – we don't really know that, and we think just from what they say at the moment … And so maybe as a result of the whole show it would be nice to think somehow that it's doing justice to them, that their lives are there.

That is, if we judge the play exclusively in terms of its success as an in-depth study of a farming community, then certainly it is superficial. However, even though Paul Thompson is responsible for the selection and arrangement of the masses of scenes his company developed, and hence can be considered the "auteur" of the play, it is worth recalling the old adage "trust the tale and not the teller." If we attend to the play itself we discover that the fibre it captures is primarily the process by which it came into being – that is, the company's six-week encounter with the farming community, the interviews, the preparation, and the first performance, in and for the community. Then the problem David Fox speaks of disappears.

We can argue in fact that the "superficiality" of the play is a proper choice, given the aesthetics of documentary.[4] That is, in developing the play, the company respected the built-in limitations of their material. People told them and showed them what they were willing to tell and show. The play presents its subjects as they were willing to present themselves to strangers. This convention is established early in the play, in the scene titled "Round the Bend," "a series of images of the people in the area at their work." The seventeen characters performed in this scene are presented as if introducing themselves to the actors, the most explicit of these short monologues being Betty Feagan's: "Oh, hi! Come on in! No, we're not busy. We saw the light on over there. We knew you were there but we didn't go over. You know, we didn't know what to expect. You must be Janet. Look who's here, Ross!" (26).

The guarded friendliness of this speech is characteristic of all the monologues in the play. The characters speak in knowledge that they are being observed by strangers. Les Jervis shows off his game sanctuary to the visitors, Jean Lobb shows them her scrapbook, the "washing woman" gives them an idea of what she did the day before they came to visit, the town council proceeds with its meeting having given the visitors permission to watch, Diane Lobb shows them the hand of God in the misadventures of the "Jesus Bus." The theatre audience finds itself for the most part cast in the role of these visiting strangers.

The play's modesty and reticence is a source of its veracity, and of its strength. It does not exceed the limits imposed by the brevity of the encounter. We notice this particularly in the absence of irony. That is, the knowledge the performer has of the character and shares with the audience is commensurate with the self-awareness of the character. The actor is "demonstrating" a character who is already perceived as "demonstrating" himself or herself to an audience. [5] The impression of genuineness which the show conveys is largely due to this congruence between the process of gathering the material from reticent people over a brief space of time and the end product. A single anomaly suggests what the show might have been like if a different aim had been pursued. The man in the washroom in I,x, is presented candid-camera-style, as if inadvertently exposing himself, so to speak, unaware that he is being observed: "She gets you out on the dance floor and pushes those tubes right through to your shoulder blades. I'm getting right back out there and see if I can take her home. She's a sure thing!" (70). For only a moment we are placed in the role of the fly on the fourth wall. If the play as a whole had been constructed on this model, something might have been gained, but at a heavy price. We might have gained access to levels of experience beyond the reach of interview and observation-with-permission in the period of six weeks. What we would have lost, however, is the visibility of the actors and farmers to each other. [6] We return, then, to the presence in the play of the actual encounter of actors and farmers.

What more does the play do with the encounter besides maintaining veracity by staying within the limits it imposed? Whatever the *Farm Show's* merits as a living portrait of a farm community it succeeds brilliantly at portraying the special experience of community that developed during the six-week encounter and reached its climax in the first performance. I am speaking of the experience of community in which diverse groups whose social roles normally keep them separate experience a unity transcending social roles in a special moment on the boundaries of normal social life. Or, to use the suggestive terminology of the anthropologist Victor W. Turner, two social groups, in a "liminal" situation, betwixt and between norm-governed social relations, encounter each other as members of "communitas." [7]

It is in capturing something of the special quality of this liminal situation that *The Farm Show* effects a fusion of documentary and ritual.

Actors' comments in *The Clinton Special* point us in the direction I wish to follow:

Paul Thompson: "The experience of going out into a community and having actors meet people who don't necessarily share the same thing – I think you know a lot of artistic worlds live too closely on each other and therefore they don't encounter these people. And the actor was forced to go out and meet people and just by the – the – rubbing together...."

Miles Potter: " ... I don't know if it will ever happen again where you do a piece of work like this that you really like and out of it develops a whole circle of friends – a whole community that you feel – in some ways – that you really belong to – not as much but almost as much as some of the people who live there."

Reading or hearing about the original performance one realizes that something very significant was happening. Before the performance, neither group had the least idea what to expect. The farmers didn't know what they would see and the actors were quite uncertain about the reaction their mimicry would get. The performance itself evidently produced an exchange of energy intense enough to leave all concerned able to talk of it only in superlatives. What happened I believe was that the liminality of the performance brought the occasion close to the pole of ritual. And within this field the experience of "communitas" was shared.

Partly this experience was due to the mere fact of the performers mirroring their audience so directly, while at the same time emphasizing their identity as performers through their openly theatrical mode of performance. Earlier I spoke of *The Farm Show's* paradoxical union of documentary veracity and extreme theatricality. Now we begin to see how vital that union is: in a play that documents above all the encounter of two communities, that encounter is present on stage in the bodies of the performers.

If we turn from a consideration of how the play was presented to what was presented, we find, again, that it is the encounter of two communities that takes shape in our imagination, for in selecting and arranging the material, Paul Thompson seems to have emphasized two kinds of activities which the company shared at a profound level with their subjects. The two activities are the art of work and the work of art.

First, let's consider working. Obviously, *The Farm Show* has a great deal of material about the work of farming. The characters are presented at work, and they talk a good deal about what they do. What is perhaps not so obvious is that the play is equally about the work of acting. We are aware of the cast not only as a group but as a group at work. We are made aware of the work that preceded the production; the presentational performance style ensures that we are conscious of the actors *at work* as we watch the play, particularly since some of the scenes are physically very taxing; and to the extent possible the non-performance aspects of putting on the show, for example, moving props, are taken care of by the cast in full view of the audience.

The presentational style also ensures that we see the actors as skilled workers doing a job well. Certain scenes are quite obviously bravura passages which demand admiration for technical virtuosity. In the town council scene, for instance, two actors play the five councillors by shifting roles as they shift from seat to seat.

Thus the play makes us conscious, by a direct appeal to the histrionic sensibility, that the objective underlying the disparate activities of performing and farming is the same: to provide something of use and value and to take pride in doing so. Thus work points to a unity transcending the separate social identities of actor and farmer.

The other objective which the two groups share is to create art and take pleasure in doing so. The creative work of the actors is immediately experienced in a number of ways. They have made the show they are performing. Their performance style calls attention to their inventiveness; there is the matter of transformation from character to character to animal to machine to landscape; there are the passages of pure invention, like the battle of the tractors in II, iv; there are the songs composed by the cast; there are the brilliant stage metaphors; for example, in II, viii, the disappearance of the family farm is movingly presented as the disappearance of one child after another out of a family portrait until, with only the parents left, it is auctioned off. Above all, there is the exuberant playfulness of the performance.

And the farming people are not only presented in a style which is exuberantly inventive, but are also presented as equally creative in their own right. Let us consider the fact that the basic gesture in the play is self-presentation, in that much of it consists of monologues delivered as if to visiting strangers. These monologues have already been subjected to processes of choice and selection and arrangement before the company set to work on them. They are the words of people who have a strong histrionic sense, who enjoy presenting themselves, and who take pleasure in shaping what they have to say. That is, much of the credit for the charm of the monologues belongs with their originators. Performance is a creative activity which both groups share; the farming people are not simply the subject-matter of the play, they are its co-creators as well.

In *The Clinton Special*, David Fox's performance of the Les Jervis monologue is intercut with an interview with Les Jervis himself on the subject of David Fox's "mimicry" of him among other things, and it becomes clear that the actor's mimicry did not add theatricality to the original as much as recognize it and call attention to it.

Dramatic performance as such is referred to frequently in the material. Characters talk about skits, parades, wedding receptions, a baseball game in which one team wears braids and grass skirts. Worth particular notice is Jean Lobb's account of the skit her sons performed at her daughter's wedding dinner:

> I don't have any pictures from the wedding dinner, but that was really something. Now at most wedding dinners you have your toasts and they have dinner and a few speeches and everybody goes home. Well, not her! She decided she wanted to have all her brothers to participate because you see only Gordon was an usher.

Now there's Don and Bruce and Murray and Hugh. Those are her brothers. Now Don is the oldest, and he represented her baby days and they pinned a diaper on him and they sang one of those songs, you know the song about the kid, the beautiful kid, what's that song – "I must have been a beautiful baby 'cause baby, look at me now" ... ha! ha! ha! They sang that. And then there was Bruce. Now Bruce is *six feet tall,* and he represented her when she was a little girl and she had braids. Well they found a hat with a brim on it and they pinned the braids onto the hat, and he wore that. And then they had another silly song. And oh, they found a red bikini bathing suit for Murray to represent her when she was a teenager. And at the last minute he couldn't get up the *courage* to put it on. Ha! ha! ha! Well they found him a *wig* or something, and then they had another little doodiddle. And then there was Hugh, with a suitcase – the days when she'd be travelling. And then they all got up with Gordon and they all sang. Well, we laughed till we died at the *stupidity* of it. It was simple you know, but it was so funny. (73–74)

This skit evidently was carried off with the high spirits that have become the signature of Theatre Passe Muraille itself; indeed, it works with conventions very like those of Theatre Passe Muraille: presentational performance, transformation, theatrical metaphors. Paul Thompson told me that before the group went to Clinton they were warned that a rural audience would have difficulty accepting their performance conventions, in particular the presentation of inanimate objects by the actors. In fact they encountered no such difficulty; Paul Thompson pointed out to me that people who can accept a man wearing a diaper—over his suit—as a presentation of his sister as a baby, have no trouble accepting a man presenting himself as a tractor. The community's highly developed sense of performance as play permitted an instant acceptance of conventions which back in Toronto would be seen as experimental.

In addition, many other activities presented or mentioned are expressions of creativity: for example:

Alma Lobb: I built this rock garden myself. This hill was just a mess when I came, and I put in the rocks and the little pond. I don't like the frogs to come around, but they do. (26)

Jean Lobb: Now for *my* wedding we went out into the garden and we picked our flowers. There was dutzia and roses and we were given the delphiniums, and there was a big white satin bow around them, and when the day was done, well so were they. But whose last much longer? It was the *colours* we wanted. (73)

Lula Merrill: Now, with Fay's wedding, they cleaned up the manure spreader with International on the side, and they painted it red and white. Well, that's the colours that Fay wanted. We had to be careful with that 'cause red's a hard colour to match. (25–26)

And there are many other examples, such as Les Jervis' beautifully landscaped game sanctuary with its birds and animals and symbolic water wheel, dark Johnson's "laughing song" (54), and the symbols and decorations in the Orange Day parade.

Thus, the play makes us aware of the continuum between art and what the farming people do in their daily lives – landscaping, organizing parades, weddings, skits, folk art displays, putting together family albums, writing poems, performing. In holding a mirror up to the community, the actors address people whom they present not only as working people like themselves but as artists like themselves.

Here again we see the striking affinity between the documentary thrust of the play and its theatricality. The presentational performance style is the appropriate vehicle for capturing the actuality of the liminal encounter between the company and the farming community. By its very nature, in this context, it permits an actualization through performance of two manifestations of *communitas* – the sharing of work and the sharing of art.

One further way in which the common humanity beneath divergent roles is enacted must be mentioned and that is the ordeal. In "The Bale Scene," Miles Potter re-enacts the hellish afternoon during which he helped Mervyn Lobb with his haying. Miles begins this scene as an actor; that is, he presents himself in terms of a defined social role; then he passes through the seemingly endless ordeal of loading haybales in a mow, and finally emerges with his identity as an actor completely submerged in his utter physical exhaustion. An anthropologist might say he has undergone a rite of passage, the significance of painful ordeal which is illuminated by Victor W. Turner: "Manifold evidence … suggests that [these trials] have the social significance of rendering [the neophytes] down into some kind of human prime *materia,* divested of specific form and reduced to a condition that, although it is still social, is without or beneath all accepted forms of status" (*The Ritual Process* 170).

In this odd approximation of a rite of passage, Miles appears to stand for the company as a whole, for the scene functions as a significant transition in the play. Before it, the actors introduce themselves as actors; Miles and Jack Merrill encounter each other in a scene which amusingly underlines the enormous distance between the roles of actor and farmer, and, in "Round the Bend," farming people introduce themselves briefly, almost entirely in terms of roles – who they are, where they live, what they do.

Immediately following the "Bale Scene" comes Les Jervis' monologue, the first intimate extended portrayal, followed shortly after by the marvellously haunting "Charlie Wilson" sketch, about which I will have more to say later.

It is as if the company, in the person of Miles Potter, have to be reduced from "actor" to "mere human being" before they can legitimately venture into the progressively more intense evocations of the shared humanity beneath the roles both groups play.

The fact that a representative figure from the farming community, the unnamed "Washing Woman," played by Janet Amos, undergoes a similar ordeal towards the end of the first act reinforces the structural significance of the "Bale Scene." Miles and the Washing Woman meet on the common ground of ritual reduction to acutely uncomfortable living tissue (the washing woman, with a squawk and a flap, turns into a chicken).[8] On that foundation can be built the celebration of the common humanity adumbrated by the shared activities of work and art.

The structure of *The Farm Show is* generated by two encounters of radically different elements: the encounter of farmers and actors, which is the content of the play, and the encounter of documentary and theatricalist conventions, which is its form. Let us examine in closer detail how this structure communicates itself. To accomplish this purpose I have chosen I, viii, titled "Charlie Wilson," for in this scene the shared work and shared creativity of which I have spoken achieves its most powerful expression.

It begins, as several of the scenes do, by recalling the real process by which it came into being as well as by reasserting its factual basis:

> Last summer we asked one of the farmers if he knew anyone in the area who was considered eccentric. Someone who was a bit strange and outside of the community. He said the only man he could think of was a man named Charlie Wilson ... Well, we went around and asked people what they remembered about Charlie. (57)

The props used in this scene are objects which belonged to the hermit: "Some of his tools, his letters and his hat" (Johns 32). These links to actuality coexist with the scene's theatricality. The small cast transforms itself into a living collage of the farming people whose recollections they gathered; one performer, David Fox, transforms himself onstage into Charlie Wilson with no more costume change than putting on the old man's hat.

The powerful effect of this encounter of theatricality and actuality is suggestively described by Paul Thompson in *The Clinton Special*:

> You have the reality and you have what we did in the play, and of course there's a difference because when you make something out of it, it changes, grows and breathes. But to be confronted with the two is just fantastic because – you feel that you can respond to both – echoing off this one and echoing off that one....

The scene is framed by two emphatic declarations to the same effect: "Well, I can tell you one thing about Charlie Wilson – he's dead" (57); "He was odd and kept apart, but he's in heaven!" (61). Yet the effect of the scene movingly contradicts these testimonials to the absence of Charlie Wilson: the dead man is made present.

If we reflect on the reanimation of Charlie Wilson that we witness in this scene, we become aware that the people of the Clinton area and the company of actors are its co-creators. The intensely moving presence of Charlie Wilson is partly the work of the people who keep him alive in their memories: memories whose power to evoke the past covers an enormous range, from the banality of "Oh, Charlie was a corker, he'd get off some good ones" (59), to the spare poetry of this recollection:

> I can tell you exactly what Charlie looked like. He had a long lean face that looked like it was hewn out of white elm. He was very pale and he had a square jaw and his chin stuck out just a little. He was always clean-shaven, but occasionally you could see his beard, and it would be white. (59)

That is, we experience recollecting as a creative act in its own right.

The work of the farm people meets that of the actors. The recollections are performed by people whose talents for mimicry were put to the severest test, the presence of their models in the original audience. David Fox's performance as Charlie Wilson is a greater creative act and took a correspondingly greater risk, in that the man who took shape in his imagination had been a familiar figure to many people in the audience over a whole lifetime.

Finally and most significantly the scene testifies to the creative work of the company in that they are responsible for the selection and arrangement of the material.

That selection and arrangement produces a total effect that is much greater than the sum of its parts. A number of people recall a hermit; he is presented in performance; these several strands are interwoven to create, paradoxically, out of Charlie Wilson's loneliness, a powerful image of community, at the levels both of social structure and *communitas*. We see his loneliness as a social role. He is by no means a non-member of the community; his outsiderhood defines his relationship to it. By the time we have heard a number of people define that relationship, in terms of regular visits to people's houses, of his role as handy-man, of his status as a self-educated man, we have as an after-image, a powerful impression of the community itself. Significantly, the scene ends with an image of a social relationship: "Wishing you the compliments of the season and again thanking you for your kindness, I remain, your friend, Charlie Wilson" (61).

Further, the scene conveys a sense of encountering Charlie Wilson in his uniqueness, his infinite value simply as a member of the human community. The carefully-assembled collage of impressions accomplishes this: detail jostles detail. *Bonanza, The Divine Comedy,* wild cabbage, tic doloreux, chewing tobacco; within the overall elegiac mood, humour confronts pathos; we have the sense of continually opening vistas, transcending yet not denying the precise description of social role also contained in the scene. Altogether we are seeing community in depth: through the image of the lonely man we see, on the surface, the community as a structure, a neat grid of roles and relationships like the network of roads on the surface of the stage; and beneath the surface, the mysterious encounter with the person in his unique individuality, which Victor W. Turner identifies as a characteristic of *communitas*. [9]

Thus the scene possesses an impressive depth and complexity, which can be attributed to the presence in the scene—as immediate experience in the theatre—of actuality and theatricality, of "communal creation," the encounter of actors and farmers as co-workers and fellow-artists. We may indeed conjecture that the energy which is ultimately responsible for the intensity of the scene has its source in the liminality of the encounter of the two communities. It is not far-fetched to guess that people's recollections of Charlie Wilson were sharpened by the mere fact that actors whom they didn't know were asking about him, or that the actors' sensitivity to the dramatic possibilities of the material was heightened by the strangeness and riskiness of their venture.

In the first performance in Ray Bird's barn, the actors from Theatre Passe Muraille brought into being a piece of theatre of great power – partly through lighting upon such a promising subject, partly through their openness and adaptability, and especially through their success at capturing what had been "most real, in the sense of most important, or most essential" about the situation.

I wish to conclude with a conjecture about the nature of that power. In periods when the theatre has played a significant part in a culture's self-definition, conditions have existed which have provided a bridge between performers and audience in such a way that their very different functions have been transcended by a sense that both groups are co-participants in a single community. In Elizabethan England, the root metaphor "*totus mundus agit histrionem*" implied that what the performers were doing on stage united them with their audiences, who were performers on the great stage of the world (see Righter). In such circumstances the possibility exists for drama to reach a deeper level of meaning than is possible when the roles of audience and performer are seen as totally distinct.

The creators of *The Farm Show* succeeded in arriving with their first audience at a vision of *communitas* through risking the meeting of actor and audience in their own bodies and through the metaphorical identification of actors and farmers in the shared activities of work and art. In so doing they accomplished the aim of so much of contemporary theatre; that is, the restoration of a measure of the efficacy of ritual to the theatrical event – specifically, in this play, the power of ritual to evoke *communitas*. [10]

To a great extent the power and efficacy of the first performance are accessible in the script, as the success of its revivals testifies. The greatest success however is indicated by Ted Johns' mention, in his introduction, of "crowds of strangers asking, 'How did you do this?'" (7). The *Farm Show* lives most significantly in its seminal influence.

(1982)

Notes

[1] Valuable discussions of Theatre Passe Muraille's work in documentary theatre can be found in Miller, Endres and Kareda. For a general discussion of the developing tradition of documentary theatre in Canada see Bessai.

[2] The strategies by which a documentary establishes its veracity are discussed by Feldman.

[3] The author of the first passage is Paul Thompson; of the second, Ted Johns, who prepared the published script. Throughout the essay I also draw on information gathered from *The Clinton Special* (1974), directed by Michael Ondaatje, a documentary film about the making of *The Farm Show*. In addition I wish to thank Paul Thompson and several members of the original and subsequent casts of *The Farm Show*—Janet Amos, Layne Coleman, Clare Coulter, David Fox and Ted Johns—for information shared in conversations over the past three years.

[4] This is an instance of what G. Roy Levin calls documentary's "inherent obligation to reality" (28). In his introduction to *Doukhobors*, Paul Thompson draws a clear distinction between the aesthetic choices suitable to a fictional play and those demanded by material gathered from the real world:

> The play ran about an hour and forty minutes. We decided to leave in Fred Davidoff's long speech at the end, even though people kept coming in and saying we should trim it. We had to leave it long. It was a hard choice to make, but we put all the information in because Fred was real and Fred was there and we felt we had to use it. We felt that if we were doing a well-made play, we would cut this speech. But *Doukhobors* isn't a well-made play.

Respect for the integrity of the source outweighs conventional aesthetic criteria. This attitude reflects an aesthetic judgment within the framework of documentary. An analogy may be drawn with the aesthetics of direct cinema, in terms of which a shot's value as an element in a structure is not determined by its formal characteristics (in fact it may be out of focus or jerky or awkwardly composed or too long) but by its authenticity. Or, in the words of Albert Maysles, "[T]here's a truth there that you can't tinker with" (qtd. in Levin 283).

[5] In this respect *The Farm Show* although Brechtian in many ways parts company with Brecht for its own good reasons. The Brechtian actor stands to one side of the character he is demonstrating in order to preserve and convey his astonishment at the character's internal contradictions. The distinction between actor and character is critical and ironic. Here, it is a gesture of respect for the integrity of the actual person being demonstrated.

[6] We see here an affinity between this play and developments in film documentary in the past two decades – the disappearance of the voice-over narration and the predominance of interview, the visibility of the whole apparatus of filmmaking in

the film itself, especially its visibility to the subjects of the film, and the awareness of the subjects that they are on film, that is, that they are performing. Examples include the films of the Maysles brothers, e.g. "Salesman" and "Gimmie Shelter," films produced for the NFB by Wolf Koenig, e.g. "Lonely Boy," Allan King's "Warrendale" and "A Married Couple." Clearly the films of Frederick Wiseman, e.g. "High School," adopt the alternate strategy of rendering the process of making the film invisible to the subjects, hence capturing their unconscious self-revelations.

[7] "See, in particular, *The Ritual Process* and *Dramas, Fields, and Metaphors.* See also Schechner, who glosses "*communitas*" in terms that are relevant to this discussion as "that levelling of all differences in an ecstasy that so often characterizes performing" ("From Ritual" 119).

[8] It is surely significant that in newspaper reviews of *The Farm Show* on tour, these two scenes are the ones most often singled out, and usually together.

[9] "Essentially, communitas is a relationship between concrete, historical, idiosyncratic individuals. These individuals are not segmentalized into roles and statuses but confront one another rather in the manner of Martin Buber's 'I and Thou'" (*The Ritual Process* 131–32).

[10] One observation of Richard Schechner's is particularly germane to this discussion:

> Within the last fifteen years the process of mounting the performance, the workshops that lead up to the performance, the means by which an audience is brought into the space and led from the space and many other previously automatic procedures, have become the subjects of theatrical manipulations. These procedures have to do with the theatre-in-itself and they are, as regards the theatre, efficacious: that is, these procedures are what makes a theatre into a theatre regardless of themes, plot or the usual "elements of drama" (207). The attention paid to the procedures of making theatre are, I think, attempts at ritualizing performance, of finding in the theatre itself authenticating acts.

Works Cited

Bessai, Diane. "Documentary Theatre in Canada: An Investigation into Questions and Backgrounds." *Canadian Drama/L'Art dramatique canadien* 6.1 (1980): 9–21.

Endres, Robin. "Many Authors Make a Play." *TV Ontario Supplement* in *The Globe and Mail* (Toronto) 14 November 1975: 1.

Feldman, Seth. "Documentary Performance." *Canadian Drama/L'Art dramatique canadien* 5.1 (1979): 11–24.

Hardy, Forsyth, ed. *Grierson on Documentary.* London: Faber, 1946.

Johns, Ted. "An Interview with Paul Thompson." *Performing Arts in Canada* 10.4 (1973): 30–32.

Kareda, Urjo. "Theatre Passe Muraille." Unpublished. 1977.

Levin, G. Roy. *Documentary Explorations.* New York: Doubleday, 1971.

Mast, Gerald, and Marshall Cohen. *Film Theory and Criticism.* New York: Oxford UP, 1971.

Miller, Mary Jane. "The Documentary Drama of Paul Thompson." *Saturday Night* (July 1974): 35–37.

Ondaatje, Michael, dir. "The Clinton Special: A Film about *The Farm Show.*" Mongrel Media, 1974.

Righter, Anne. *Shakespeare and the Idea of the Play.* London: Chatto and Windus, 1962.

Salutin, Rick. "The Culture Vulture." *This Magazine* 2.4 (1977): 23.

Schechner, Richard . "From Ritual to Theatre and Back." *Ritual, Play, and Performance.* Ed. Richard Schechner and Mady Schuman. New York: Seabury, 1976. 196–222.

Theatre Passe Muraille. *Doukhobors.* Toronto: Playwrights Co-op, 1973.

———. *The Farm Show.* Toronto: Coach House, 1976.

Turner, Victor W. *Dramas, Fields, and Metaphors.* Ithaca: Cornell UP, 1974.

———. *The Ritual Process.* Chicago: Aldine, 1969.

A Success Story:
Theatre Passe Muraille (excerpts)

by Renate Usmiani

Theatre Passe Muraille first appeared, with a bang, on the Toronto underground theatre scene in 1969. Its premiere production, *Futz,* the story of the relationship between a man and his sow, caused a public scandal and brought the morality squad down upon the young company. Truly a taboo-shattering show, *Futz* not only dealt with an unacceptable theme, but also featured such theatrical and verbal explosives as bare breasts and expressions like "shit" and "fucking pigs." One might look upon the uproar caused by *Futz* as a repetition—Canadian-style and with the usual "Canadian delay" of a little over a century—of the scandal created by *Ubu Roi* in 1896 France. In spite of this unconventional beginning, Passe Muraille eventually turned out to be the only one of all the groups participating in the Underground Theatre Festival of 1970 to survive commercially. It is now well established in a spacious permanent home on Ryerson Avenue; it has a faithful following in Toronto; and its impact has been felt nationwide over the years. Success stories such as this are not common on the alternative theatre scene: how did it all come about?

Passe Muraille owes its existence and philosophy to the energy and vision of two men, James Garrard and Paul Thompson. Garrard founded the company and gave it its initial direction; Thompson developed the now famous Passe Muraille style. It is interesting to note that both men came to the theatre from academic backgrounds. Garrard, a graduate of Queen's University and a former school principal, had become disillusioned with education and decided to study theatre in England. In the late 1960s, he attended the London Academy of Music and Dramatic Art. Returning to Canada in 1968, he quickly became a part of the growing cultural and nationalistic protest movement of the period. Part of that protest movement was Rochdale College, an experimental school set up in antithesis to traditional educational institutions. Garrard joined the Rochdale Theatre Project, which used the college population as a "laboratory" for exploring the relationships between theatre and society. In 1969, he founded an independent company, which he called "Passe Muraille." The name carried implications of his visions of a truly popular theatre: theatre "without walls," a theatre which would "pass beyond" all the conventional barriers. His first Passe Muraille manifesto, written in 1969, reflects very clearly the influence of the hippie movement of the 1960s, the ideology of the Living Theatre, and the happening as a kind of theatrical event: "The renaissance of the theatre as experience, as event, demands that contact be made, first, among the actors, who must work together as a continuing ensemble; second, between the actors and those individuals termed 'the audience'; third, because theatre is a human event, between people and people" (qtd. in Wallace 76). Like American radical theatre, Garrard included in his ideology a strong social and political concern; as a Canadian, he also felt it his duty to open up his theatre to new, unknown dramatists, since the regional theatres were obviously not taking up the challenge of creating Canadian drama. Passe Muraille, then, would be experimental, national and popular: "I'd like to make theatre as popular as bowling" (Wallace 77), Garrard said, in the true spirit of Brecht, who had envisioned theatre for the masses, preferably performed in large sports arenas.

Passe Muraille started humbly. From the basement of Rochdale College, it moved to a variety of locations in the city, playing wherever cheap space was available. Often, the lack of a permanent space led to imaginative, environmental experiments: the *Immigrant Show*, for example, was performed in a streetcar hired for the purpose, which travelled through the city as the show progressed, stopping at relevant locations to create a sense of real authenticity. By 1978, however, the company was able to acquire a permanent home, a large old warehouse which provided enough space for a main stage as well as two smaller performance areas. In fact, within ten years, the company had fulfilled most of its founder's dreams. It had produced an astounding number of shows: twenty-two collective creations (ten pure collectives, twelve in co-operation with a writer) as well as a large number of scripted works, many of them new Canadian plays. Throughout that period Passe Muraille was also actively engaged in a nationwide "seeding programme" which led to the establishment of such "paral-lel" alternative theatre groups as Codco, in St. John's; 25th Street House, in Saskatoon; and Theatre Network, in Edmonton. In Toronto itself, the theatre offered the "New Works Program" – a workshopping programme for individuals and groups, offering its own facilities, financial assistance and counselling. Passe Muraille views this activ-ity not only as assistance given to junior artists, but as a means of stimulating and renewing the company itself and safeguarding against complacency and stagnation.

Although Garrard had set the ideological pattern for Passe Muraille, it remained for his successor, Paul Thompson, to develop the specific Passe Muraille style of collective creation. This style reached full maturity with *The Farm Show* of 1974. With this production, Passe Muraille achieved its artistic identity – an achievement largely due to the vision and labour of its director.

Paul Thompson had studied English and French at the University of Western Ontario and spent some time studying French in Paris. He was one of Jean Gascon's assistant directors in Stratford; but the major influence on his artistic approach was the result of his stay in France, where he worked with Roger Planchon at the Theatre de la Cité at Villeurbanne. Planchon's work descends in a straight line from the political theatre of Piscator and Brecht and, in France, the work of Jean Vilar. His productions, like all political theatre, concentrate on the social and political behaviour of the characters, rather than on psychology; this is true also of Planchon's versions of the classics, where he stresses social class through costume and interpretation. Although a dramatist himself, Planchon always emphasizes the importance of the non-literary aspect of theatre. Describing his own work, he insists "*Notre action n'a rien de littéraire*" (qtd. in Corvin). Planchon also favours process over product in the sense that he never sees any one production as a final effort, but rather as a basis for further improvement.

Paul Thompson's approach to his work at Passe Muraille was equally dynamic ("dynamic" here meaning the antithesis to static). In fact, if one were to look for a single attribute to describe the essential quality of Theatre Passe Muraille, it would be "dynamism" – a constant flow of energy directed at finding new and better forms of expression, a total refusal to be locked into any tradition or convention, absolute openness and adaptability to new experiences. This dynamism is apparent on every level of the operations of Passe Muraille. It lies at the base of Thompson's use of collective creation, rather than the "closed" text of a finished script for most of his productions. It is equally evident in the variety of performance spaces used by the company, calculated to expose the actors to new audience reactions and relationships. As Thompson says, "We need the unexpected meeting place" (qtd. in Kareda 5). The same principle is at work in the company's encouragement of experimentation by other groups under their own roof. Passe Muraille productions usually go through a number of versions, none of them considered definitive, on the basis of the Planchon principle that "if an idea is good it only gets better by reworking" (5). It is for this reason that the published versions of the company's collective creations are usually released with a strong *caveat* to the reader: the printed text captures only one fixed moment in an ongoing, dynamic creation process. Thompson captures the essential philosophy of the group when he says: "We are defined by energy and a vital definition of what we are doing. When we run out of ideas we'll close down or die" (qtd. in *Globe*).

More specifically, Thompson's work is oriented towards two major goals: actor development and the invention of new and effective methods of collective creation. Although he does call on the services of writers quite frequently, his shows are conceived with the actors, rather than the script, in mind. This approach builds on the pattern set earlier by George Luscombe at Toronto Workshop Productions; but Thompson goes a great deal further than Luscombe in emphasizing the importance of the actor's contribution, especially in the context of collective creation:

> Part of the concept of doing collective plays is saying that the actor has more to give than often is required or demanded of him in traditional plays. I think … he should be more than a puppet. In the kind of work we're doing, we like the actor to really put some of himself in the play. We also work through the skills an actor has. If an actor could yodel, e.g., then I'd really like to put his yodel in a play. (qtd. in Wallace 77)

Actors in the traditional theatre would be quick to point out that their work indeed demands far more than being a "puppet," and that they, too, put a lot of themselves into their role; and it could reasonably be argued that it may be more difficult to "be" Phaedra, Hamlet, or Lady Macbeth than a character you have created yourself and tailored to your own strengths and limitations. There are directors working in the area of collective creation who admit that they use the technique mainly because it can be adapted to actors with little professional training and limited skills.[1] Thompson, however, firmly believes in the validity of collective creation as the most effective instrument to bring out actors' maximum potential. The success of a large number of his shows indicates that his method, if not superior to that of traditional theatre, at least represents a valid alternative, with interesting results.

Thompson's original contribution to the technique of collective creation was to put the onus for research and documentation entirely on the actors themselves. He discovered that, by forcing the actor into a first-hand relationship with his material he could achieve considerably greater immediacy and a sense of commitment, which would then be communicated to the audience. Critics have often commented on the strong sense of authenticity of Passe Muraille shows; it is a result of the actors' direct involvement with their material.

The technique was applied to two major lines of investigation: sociological and historical. The sociological shows attempt to create authentic mirror images of a specific community: *The Farm Show, The West Show, The Immigrant Show, Under the Greywacke.* To produce these, the actors and the director move into the community themselves. Through personal contact, sharing experiences and observations, the actors assemble the necessary documentation to serve as basis for the show. Improvisations follow, and gradually through the use of acting techniques, to which are added mime, song and poetry, an image of the community emerges. As Thompson has pointed out (Usmiani, "Interview with Paul Thompson"), this type of creation depends on strength and self-confidence on the part of the actors; they must be confident enough to be able to submerge their own personality and to approach the experience with openness, compassion and love. If successful, the truthfulness of the production can be striking. Sociological shows were usually first presented to the community where they originated; although members of the community could instantly identify themselves with the characters and situations on stage, nobody complained; no one's feeling[s] were ever hurt in the mirroring process – a testimony to the actors' serious desire to understand the workings of the community and to give a sympathetic picture of it. While the actors are on their own to research and develop the parts they will play in this type of show, the director acts as a necessary "outside eye," helps to shape the final product, and also arbitrates in case of disagreement among the actors.

Although the collective creation movement forms part of the general anti-naturalistic trend of the modem era, the type of sociological show developed by Passe Muraille really represents the ultimate in naturalism – an imitation of life in the most literal sense. Although Thompson maintains that his productions go beyond imitation to capture the "real spirit," the "essence" of the community portrayed (Usmiani, "Interview with Paul Thompson"), his technique amounts to the kind of photographic reproduction of reality for which modernists condemned the naturalists. The success of his shows testifies to the enduring appeal of the realistic/naturalistic mode, which has here undergone a change of style and emphasis – from authored play to collective creation, from psychological theme to sociological concern. Thompson's naturalism does not belong in the school of Ibsen; it is a post-Brechtian version of that mode, with a strong local and contemporary flavour.

The historical shows, on the other hand, do not aim at simply recreating historical events or characters; rather, they try to demonstrate the political significance of past events in relation to the present and, above all, to discover a national mythology within the material provided by Canadian history. The creation of myths which can be shared by all and provide Canadians with a sense of national identity has long been the goal of poets and novelists – largely under the influence of the teaching of Northrop Frye. Passe Muraille took up the challenge in the dramatic genre. This type of show, then, went considerably beyond the scope of the sociological shows. Beyond the need to portray individuals and communities at certain points in time, it also required the structuring of action into plotline and the interpretation of the significance of historical events. Because of the complexity of the historical shows, writers were usually called in to assist the company, but the basis for the work remained collective creation. The writers' main task was shaping the final product and helping with the structuring of scenes and plotline as the show developed. While some writers find the experience of working with a collective stimulating, others describe it as "an exercise in frustration." [2] As in the case of the actor, certain special qualities are required for a writer to work in this particular genre: self-confidence, flexibility, the capacity for self-abnegation, and above all, as Rick Salutin, who has worked successfully with Passe Muraille many times, points out, the ability to be "interested more in the general statement made by the play than in details" (Usmiani, "Interview with Rick Salutin").

$$\bullet \bullet \bullet$$

Unlike *The Farm Show,* which was universally popular, [*I Love You*] *Baby Blue* aroused a great deal of controversy. In fact, the show was closed down by the police morality squad after its twelve-week run from January to April 1975; during that period, however, it was seen by more than 26,000 people. The script was eventually published by Press Porcépic in 1977. The title of the show is based on Toronto's City-TV Friday night showings of the pornographic "Baby Blue" movies, a programme which, according to research done by Passe Muraille, captured 48 per cent of the city's television audience. *I Love You, Baby Blue,* then, was meant to be a spoof of television pornography as well as a serious analysis of the sexual mores of Torontonians. It is loosely structured into individual episodes, and, much like *The Farm Show,* builds up eventually to a climactic finale. As in most collective creations, all of the actors took on multiple roles (from four to nine each); the entire cast consisted of eight people. Because of the controversial nature of the show, Passe Muraille found itself forced to go outside the company itself to find actors, since most of the regular actors were unprepared to do nude scenes or feared negative reactions from their families if they took part in *Baby Blue.* In his introduction to the printed version of the play, Thompson defends his sociological approach against accusations of sensationalism:

> The experiences we were relating were mainstream … in the sense that
> they were currently visible activities or they were attitudes that you

could find in the households of many people. Characters were chosen not because of their exceptional nature, but because they reflected a number of people with the same attitude. (Thompson, "Introduction to Theatre Passe Muraille" 2)

The published version of the play certainly comes across as a very human and sympathetic look at the problems of sexuality, with a definite emphasis on the role of sex as a shield against the loneliness and isolation of life in a big city.

The show itself is preceded by a prologue which parodies the "Baby Blue" television programme: a young woman dressed only in a blue diaper streaks across the stage, whereupon a Narrator announces "our version of the Baby Blue movie." The parody which follows consists of several short scenes. The most outrageous of them presents a couple, Harry and Babs, who drug a young woman, Gloria, in preparation for group sex; the two women, however, change their minds, kill Harry with a kitchen knife and happily proceed to make love to each other. End of "film." The Narrator then announces the play itself, a play which will deal with "the force that brings so many people from so many situations together on the same night, to watch the same thing. We suspect that force is sex. And so, Ladies and Gentlemen, 'I Love You, Baby Blue.'"

The majority of the scenes in the play deal with some psychological implications of sex; some remain on the level of pure physiology. The opening scene presents a parody and demythification of commercial sex. It is set at "Hungry Harold's Burlesque Emporium," where an MC announces a torrid act but produces only a tired stripper who goes listlessly through her motions and then "shlumps off stage." "Toronto At Night" is probably the most moving scene of the show. It captures the loneliness of the big city through a highly poetic monologue, spoken by a woman:

> Toronto at night.
> Cold.
> Black.
> Hard, grey steel.
>
> On Saturday night there's a half a million people out there on those streets. All jacked up. All plugged in. Mainlined into that great whirring motor of the city … and these people are crying out, they're crying out, "Oh Lord, from the highrises deliver us." "Oh Lord, from the windy streets deliver us," "Oh Lord, from the moonless night and the lonely bed deliver us." And the Lord looks down on all his children and he says, "I give you neon signs! Neon signs to guide your way in all that darkness!"

The tone of despair set by this speech is further reinforced with the tavern scene that follows: it is the last call before closing, and patrons frantically make dates for the night, regardless of partner, to shut out loneliness and isolation.

Scenes between couples tend to be equally pessimistic: "Gene and Chick" shows a typical young executive on the rise who comes to Chick's apartment at regular intervals, strictly for therapeutic reasons. Even during these brief interruptions of his professional life, he is unable to stay away from the telephone. Finally, Chick, humiliated and angry, sends him away for good. "Larry and Margaret," in a lighter vein, makes fun of the new "liberated" attitudes toward sex: Margaret tells Larry there is no need for him to use the clichéd "I love you" formula just because he wants to have sexual relations with her. Harry is much relieved – but eventually finds he is unable to perform in this liberated atmosphere. The most explicit intercourse-cum-orgasm scene is handled very wittily, with the man and woman escalating to the tune of the list of stops on the Toronto subway; they simultaneously climax as they "reach" Union Station. "Human levitation" combines humour with extreme boldness: a girl in a black suit and top hat, standing in front of a black curtain, announces she will perform an act of levitation – which may or may not succeed. The object of the enterprise, it turns out, is not a human body, but a penis pushed through a hole in the curtain.

As in *The Farm Show*, the two final scenes are designed to make the audience think seriously about the implications of the play. Xaviera Hollander, the notorious madam, appears as a mother figure and sexual guru. Her method is to solve everyone's problem by way of a mass orgy. Standing behind the bed used for the purpose like some latter-day saint, she looks upon her sex worshippers with approval: "This is how it should be. This is good sex, good people. Toronto the Good" (75). Her message, however, is invalidated by the last scene, a direct counterpoint to the orgy theory, and the play ends on a serious note. Again, a stage metaphor is used: an actor centre stage holds up two chairs, trying to balance them against each other – an image of the difficulties of human relationships:

> But when you really get down to it, you're ultimately dealing with only two people. Two people in a relationship (he tries to balance the chairs). And I think you'd all agree, it's a very difficult thing to achieve … it takes a lot of give and take, push and pull … and just when you think you have it … you have to try again … (but) when you find it … it's unmistakable!

In spite of this obviously simplistic and clichéd ending, *Baby Blue* succeeds in its basic purpose. The play does convey a sense of big city life through its cross section of sexual behaviour; the parodies are highly entertaining, and in the more serious scenes, the show does achieve odd moments of poignancy.

· · ·

Although most of the sociological shows of Passe Muraille are based on pure collective creation, writers were occasionally called upon to collaborate with the production. An example in point is *Far As the Eye Can See*, which portrays the controversy surrounding the Dodds-Round Hill community in Alberta, whose residents were threatened with eviction so the land could be used for strip mining. This play was developed with the help of Rudy Wiebe, Alberta novelist and short-story writer. It is interesting to follow the genesis of the collaborative process. [3] It began with a meeting between Wiebe and Thompson, when the general concepts of place, subject, and characters were developed. Following this, their ideas were presented to a group of four actors, who went through an intensive four-week course of "jamming" sessions to explore the dramatic possibilities of the material. Wiebe was present throughout these improvisational sessions, collecting some 350 pages of notes in the process. On the basis of these notes, he wrote a first version of the play – a task which took eleven days. This first version was then presented to the actors and thoroughly reworked in three weeks of rehearsals before its eventual premiere in Edmonton's Theatre Three. Before its Toronto showing, the play underwent yet another revision. The published text is based on the final, Toronto version.

The history of *Far As the Eye Can See* clearly illustrates the large part played by the actors themselves even in the case of a production involving a writer and the need for "flexibility" on the writer's part. However, the writer's contribution is immediately apparent if we look at the finished product. Unlike the episodic structure of pure collective creation, this play follows the traditional three-act pattern, with well-developed plotline. The carefully worked-out alternation of realistic scenes and fantasy (appearances by the three "Regal Dead") also testifies to the organizing influence of a single mind. Yet, *Far As the Eye Can See* is not one of Passe Muraille's most successful ventures. The dialogue often appears stilted and the device of the Regal Dead (Crowfoot, William Aberhart, and Princess Louise Alberta) artificial and quite unnecessary. The most interesting portion of the play occurs in the second act, which portrays the confrontation of the opposed parties with careful documentation of both sides of the argument.

Passe Muraille was more successful in its collaboration with writers in the area of historical plays: *1837: The Farmers' Revolt*, with Rick Salutin; *Buffalo Jump*, with Carol Bolt; and *Them Donnellys*, with Frank MacEnaney, are all excellent examples of the potential of the genre.

1837: The Farmers' Revolt, is a good example of Passe Muraille's general approach to historical topics. While describing events of the past, it very clearly reflects the contemporary issues of nationalism as opposed to colonial dependence on the mother country; the revolt of 1837 becomes the archetypal Canadian insurrection against oppression from outside forces as well as from within the country itself. In the process, an attempt is also made to create hero figures of sufficient status to become national legends, especially in the characters of Mackenzie and Van Egmond.

Like *The Farm Show*, *1837* went through two successive, distinct versions. It was first produced under the title *1837* at Theatre Passe Muraille in Toronto in 1972; in 1974, a revised version went on tour, playing in auction barns in Southwestern Ontario, as well as at the Victoria Playhouse in Petrolia. It was published in 1976. The production process in this case began with collective creation, with the script finalized by the collaborating writer, Rick Salutin, after the actors had gone through the basic outline. This system proved more successful than the one used for *Far As the Eye Can See*.

• • •

Of course, the Passe Muraille style itself has left its mark on a considerable number of younger alternative theatre companies. But the group made a perhaps equally important contribution through its hospitality to other and different theatrical endeavours. While only some of its productions have been recorded, and will thus remain a part of the body of Canadian dramatic literature, Passe Muraille's influence on the development of that literature cannot be underestimated.

(1983)

Notes

[1] See chapter five of Usmiani's *Second Stage: The Alternative Theatre Movement in Canada.* Vancouver: UBCP, 1983, on Chris Brookes and The Mummers' Troupe.

[2] Geddes, referring to his experience with Passe Muraille and *Les Maudits Anglais* (Usmiani, "Interview with Gary Geddes").

[3] Described in Thompson, "Introduction to Rudy Wiebe."

Works Cited

Corvin, Michel. *Le nouveau theatre en l'ranee.* Paris: Playwrights Union, 1974.

Globe and Mail, The (Toronto). 6 November 1972.

Kareda, Urjo. "Theatre Passe Muraille." *1977 Stratford Festival Information Brochure.*

Salutin, Rick, and Theatre Passe Muraille. *1837: The Farmers' Revolt.* Toronto: Lorimer, 1976.

Thompson, Paul. "Introduction to Rudy Wiebe and Passe Muraille." *Far As The Eye Can See.* Edmonton: NeWest, 1977.

———. "Introduction to Theatre Passe Muraille." *I Love You, Baby Blue.* Toronto: Press Porcépic, 1977.

Wallace, Robert. "Growing Pains: Toronto Theatre in the 70's." *Canadian Literature* 85 (1980): 71–85.

Usmiani, Renate. "Interview with Gary Geddes." 11 November 1980.

———. "Interview with Paul Thompson." 20 November 1980.

———. "Interview with Rick Salutin." 18 November 1980.

Company Town –
The Story of Buchans

by Chris Brookes

> It would turn your stomach to see what American Smelting and
> Refining took out of Buchans in the years they have operated there,
> without paying to this province hardly anything in taxes and employing
> people there at miserable wages in a company town with miserable
> housing. It would really cause you to become a savage – you know,
> Marxist.
>
> John C. Crosbie, MP

The summer of 1974 was immortalized by the Newfoundland government's decision
to celebrate the glories of our twenty-five years of Confederation with Canada: Jubilee
Year. It would be a big celebration: fireworks, films, music, shows, CULTURE! The
gleeful announcements were met with a certain amount of cynicism. Confederation
is not all it's cracked up to be, baby bonuses notwithstanding, some said. Amongst
the more visible naysayers was the April Fools Society (so called because
Newfoundlanders woke up to their first day of Confederation on 1 April 1949).
The Fools ran up pink, white and green nationalist flags on public flagpoles and
circulated statements like the following:

WHY ARE WE CELEBRATING?

BECAUSE major decisions affecting Newfoundland's development are
being made in Ottawa?

BECAUSE key positions in Newfoundland have been consistently given
to outsiders rather than to Newfoundlanders of equal ability?

BECAUSE Newfoundland society is being steadily absorbed into North
American mediocrity?

BECAUSE our resources have been sold out to foreign and mainland
interests?

BECAUSE our people are forced to emigrate through a failure to
develop local opportunities?

BECAUSE our fisheries are dying?

Signed: THE APRIL FOOLS.

The provincial government, perhaps fearing that Newfoundland artists would find too little in the past quarter century to celebrate about, hired out-of-province artists to show us how to do it. It blew most of its entertainment bankroll on a flock of tired music hall comedians who were flown all the way over from Britain to be toured through the province all summer at taxpayers' expense. Nobody is quite as good as the Mother Country when it comes to celebrating the joys of colonialism.

The province also commissioned a homegrown historical pageant (a kind of official antidote to *Newfoundland Night*) which toured the island.

For Lynn [Lunde] and me it was frustrating to have to borrow the money for a sandwich while watching steak dinners being given away in front of our noses, but we figured those government grapes were sour, anyway. We had our commitment to keep us warm, right?

Our conception of celebration was somewhat different. We wanted to make a show about Buchans. Buchans didn't offer the kind of picturesque sleepiness that the government liked to show off to the tourist trade (the Department of Tourism's official promotion film was titled "Come Paint and Photograph Us"). It was a grey, scruffy mining town owned lock, stock and barrel by the American Smelting and Refining Company (ASARCO). In Buchans, for example, company cars drove around without provincial license plates. They didn't need them because the company, not the province, was the law in Buchans. The town's 2,000 residents were no-nonsense militant trade unionists who in the previous three years had been responsible for two of the province's longest and most bitter strikes. People there remembered us kindly from our free performance during their previous summer's strike, and the union local, Steelworkers 5457, encouraged our new project.

We calculated that our borrowed money would pay for a cast of six, as long as I didn't take a salary. But finding performers proved to be as difficult as finding their salaries. Lynn was due to leave for an eight-month arts administration apprenticeship with the Manitoba Theatre Centre, and most other luminaries of the local theatre scene were already contracted to the big cast, better-paying Government Pageant. After much cajoling, I convinced Donna Butt, now on her university summer holidays, to join the company for a second summer. Bembo Davies, who'd gone back to Ontario after the Christmas Mummers Play, agreed to fly down, as did a zany actor-musician I'd once worked with on a puppet project in Toronto, Allen Booth. I didn't really want to overweight our group with non-Newfoundlanders who wouldn't be able to handle the Buchans dialects, but there was no choice. Other mainlanders completed the rest of the cast: Connie Kaldor, a fine singer from Saskatchewan; Howie Cooper, who'd just completed a community documentary with Toronto's Theatre Passe Muraille; and Lee Campbell. Lee was big, down-to-earth, and fresh out of a woods camp somewhere in northern Ontario: the antithesis of a middle-class sophisticate. If anyone would be able to relate to hard-rock miners, he would. It was an exciting cast, but anyone with half an ear could notice that Donna and I were the only Newfoundlanders in the lot. Accents, however, were only the tip of the iceberg. It was as much a question of dialectics as dialect.

Newfoundlanders have keen ears for accents, and for many, the whiff of a main-land accent can cause a whole set of preconceptions to snap into place. A lot of Come-From-Aways interpret this as spurious xenophobia. Xenophobic it may be, but spurious it is not. It's the result of long-term regional economic disparity. Meet a Newfoundlander in Toronto and chances are that he'll turn out to be a labourer or industrial worker; meet a mainlander in Newfoundland and ten to one he's a boss, a manager, a professional who's running things. Here, a central Canadian accent is a symbol; in general it denotes a member of a dominant class. What is resented is not the pronunciation, but the power.

In our cast, the noticeable differences in accent echoed the obvious: as middle-class urbanites, most of the actors did not share the working-class Newfoundland background of the Buchans miners who would be the subjects of their research. But with luck, I thought pragmatically, we might be able to make our "outsiderness" work like Brecht's *verfremdungseffekt*: the "alienation effect." Placed in the right context, the cast's accents would distance Buchaneers from their reflected portraits onstage. This could encourage the audience to analyze what the play was saying about their community's history, instead of getting sucked into sentimental identification with character.

This meant challenging the actors' pride: the professional ability to *be* anyone – Othello, John Proctor, Don Head. We must be careful here. Othello and Proctor are fictional characters; Don Head is a real one, and what's more, he'd be sitting in our opening night audience. How would a Buchans miner act in a given situation? We could not be sure. We could only be sure of how a middle-class actor from outside would *imagine* acting in that situation. We must not muddy class realities.

> By not pretending to become the people of Buchans, but merely "indicating" the audience to themselves, the company committed itself to a style which reveals the idea of theatre itself while it plays. Any artifice was immediately broken. The actors made the sound effects in front of the audience. They wore no costume more elaborate than a hat or an apron. They indicated "This is a bunk now, this is a movie theatre now, now it's a house, now a mine-shaft." Even the lighting switches were fully visible, so that any manipulation of objects was stripped of mystery. This made it possible to show patterns, to be analytical without objectifying, to be informative. At the same time, because the characters were copied or made by composite from actual members of the community—the original audience—and because the bulk of the play was accurate narration, there was more reality in this verbatim accuracy than in the more slippery technique of fiction (Heindsmann).

It was a question of our attitude, as artists, towards the material. The trick was, I felt, to encourage this attitude in our research and creation process as well as in performance. So before we began, I suggested a few rules to pre-structure the experience:

1. We would rely on taped narrative. I borrowed six tape recorders and insisted that everyone use them. We would avoid inventing people's speech or lives – where invention was necessary we'd find ways to let the audience know that we were inventing on our terms, not on theirs.

2. We would create a *people's* history of Buchans. To my mind the most glaring evidence of the union-company standoff lay in the way the two parties viewed the community. To the company, Buchans was a temporary mining camp, a statistic in their annual corporate report. To the residents, it was a home with a forty-year-old history, a history which demanded an equivalent corporate responsibility.

I felt that a dramatization of oral history could emphasise the existence of Buchans as a place where people *lived*. It would document the long and tangled roots of the struggle which had recently surfaced in strike violence, and which bound the community and its union so tightly together.

3. We would be extremely careful about our image as researchers in the community.

Engineering chemistry calls this the Heisenberg Uncertainty Principle: the presence of the observer always influences the reality which is being observed.

4. We would be in a total-immersion research situation. The mine manager had given us permission to live in the bunkhouse and eat at the mess hall alongside miners and kitchen staff. He was kind enough to extend to us the "bunkhouse rate," the full-board miners' rate which would make the actors' paltry $65/week salaries a liveable allowance. We would be permitted to accompany underground work shifts. The principal of the Catholic school allowed us to use the school's gymnasium for rehearsal. It even had a piano.

We arrived in early July. The six-week creation period fell into the more-or-less typical collective creation pattern for documentaries:

Week One—Immediate Impressions

We mostly watched and listened. All of us were impressed immediately by the community's vitality, a liveliness which seemed perhaps to be a survival mechanism, developed in reaction to the company's dry balance-sheet mentality. Our habits changed: the first mineshift went on at 7:30 a.m., meaning that anyone who got to the mess hall later than 7:15 (usually Howie Cooper) got cold fried eggs.

Each morning we met at the school for a show-and-tell session: that is, we acted out the material we'd gathered, rather than just talking about it. I kept notes but made little attempt to edit any of the presented "scenes" at this point – that would come weeks later when we would have a large body of theatrical material from which to choose. In this initial phase I pushed purely for quantity. Not surprisingly, much of this early material was facile, but our sharing of first impressions helped establish a collective working pattern and a "group language" which was vital for our politically and theatrically disparate group.

We began each morning's sessions around the school piano, warming up with some of the original songs which Buchaneer Angus Lane had written as morale boosters during the 1971 and 1973 strikes. "All Because of ASARCO" was set to the well-known tune of "Surrounded by Water":

> 5457 is now out on strike;
> We seek from ASARCO what we deem is right;
> 'Til Hell freezes over, we'll continue to fight;
> We won't beg or plead from ASARCO.

> The Company makes millions on concentrate tons,
> While miners wind up with lead in their lungs;
> Mining makes old men out of our young sons,
> Producing ore for ASARCO.

> Stick to your guns boys and never relent,
> Don't go back for a few paltry cents
> To boost the wages of those New York gents
> Who get damn well paid by ASARCO.

> Our plea, our plea, is for You and for Me
> To demand what we want from this company.
> And no one here will go down on their knee
> To beg or to plead from ASARCO....

For most of the cast, this project was their first contact with labour militancy. Three days earlier, no-one had even known the words to *Solidarity Forever*.

Week Two: Up to the Elbows in Research

First impressions quickly deepened. (Example: we discovered the difficulties of doing our laundry. There *is* a laundromat in Buchans, but its use is restricted to management personnel.) Buchaneers generally viewed our group as a curiosity, and were warm and friendly. The union executive, in particular, took an active interest in our research. We began asking more intelligent questions.

We encountered Buchans' unique blend of humour. The two-man "buddy" system underground gave rise to some wonderful comic/straightman routines oriented around work. Howie and Lee spent a whole nightshift underground with miners and were able to recreate some excellent observed comedy. Bembo, meanwhile, encountered the supernatural:

Sure, there's ghosts down in the mine. That's right. I sees 'em every day. There's three or four are my personal friends. Now these ghosts, when I go down there if I don't see, well, on the average of six or seven ghosts every fortnight, well ... I'm lonesome. That's right.

Now there is this one ghost down there, well, it's just a pair o' legs. That's right. Just a pair o' legs stickin' out of the side o' the drift, from the knees down. That's right. Well, he's very good, he comes by and has a smoke, watches me work, you know.

There's a couple of others. There's a big tall one and a short one and they come by regular too, you know. You see 'em down the drift and, well, you hear the feet, eh? And eh ... the tall one whistles. And you look down the drift and you see their lights. From their hats. And ya holler out to 'em but they don't make no answer. Ya start down towards 'em and they disappears. And ya goes down to where they disappears to, and there is nothin'. Just nothin'. Just rock. That's right. And eh, the tall fella, his name's Alvin. And the short fella, he's Jack. And eh, the legs? Well, they got no name.

You believe that?

The tag line was a trick that Allan Booth had picked up from conversations with Charlie Perrier, an old trapper living up the road in Buchans Junction who had helped discover the mine forty-odd years ago. Charlie was a great storyteller with a penchant for tall tales. After earnestly relating some piece of local history he would pause to see how the listener digested the story, then ask elfishly: "You believe dat?" It was a nice snap back to reality, a reminder that his tale was open to analysis. This was exactly what we wanted our audience to remember, and so we adopted the "Perrier Technique" widely throughout the show.

Week Three: Up to the Armpits in Research

This week a remarkable thing occurred. I had become quite close to Peter Noftle, a retired driller with a photographic memory and an endless collection of recitations. Several years earlier Peter had been a recipient of the ASARCO 25-year watch. The annual watch presentation was one of those typical obsequious ceremonies by which companies commemorate long-term employee service. The spectacle of a rich multi-national company attempting to compensate victims of industrial disease with cheap jewellery was too bitter an irony for Peter, and he had refused to attend the ceremony to receive his own watch. It seemed to me that he now regretted missing that opportunity to speak publicly his mind to his employers.

One morning I switched rehearsal from the school to the Union Club where I knew Peter could usually be found, in the hope that he might be able to help us with an improvised scene. I brought my tape recorder, just in case.

I asked the actors to improvise a scene in which a miner goes to the watch presentation ceremony and raises hell. One by one the actors of our group entered the scene, refused to accept their watch, and demanded to speak. The scene was not working. The improvised speeches sounded false, unlike what a real miner would say. Peter, sitting in the back of the bar, suddenly came forward, entered the scene, accepted the watch, and politely asked the "company manager" for permission to speak. I switched on my tape recorder, and I suspect the remarkable speech which followed had already had years of rehearsals in Peter's mind.

> Friends and fellow-workers of Buchans, ladies and gentlemen. As I gaze around the audience tonight, I miss quite a few familiar faces. Men with whom I worked over the past twenty-five years. Today they are dead and gone, which brings sadness to one's heart. Those men, as you know, gave twenty-five years and more of hard, faithful and honest work to the American Smelting and Refining Company. Today they are no longer with us. WHY? Because of that dread disease that every miner fears: the disease called silicosis. What, today, did these men, or their families, receive from Buchans? From the American Smelting and Refining Company?
>
> I came here when I was thirty-three and in the prime of life. I gave the best years of my life to the American Smelting and Refining Company. After twenty-five years, I am given a watch.
>
> Now, it is not my intention, ladies and gentlemen, to criticize or to ridicule the mining company. Many will say: you made your living here, you raised your family here. I grant you that. But in over twenty-five years of hard and honest service, American Smelting and Refining Company never gave me anything I never worked for.
>
> Today, many of us are just about worn out. When we're finished, if we live until we're sixty-five and retire or if we are disabled, what do we have to look forward to? We will not be allowed to stay in a company house. We will have to leave Buchans. As you know, my pension after twenty-nine years and ten months is $63.40 a month from the company. Not very much to look forward to in the later years. But I thank God I am one of the lucky ones: I came up out of the mine and took early retirement without a trace of silicosis.
>
> However, I did lose my hearing while working underground. Now, I did not try to get any compensation for my loss of hearing. But I know of one miner who went to St. John's to the Compensation Board, and what they told him was, they said: "you can get deaf anywhere."
>
> I grant you that. There's fellows today suffered loss of hearing who have never worked underground. But why is it that so many who HAVE worked underground have suffered loss of hearing? Would they have lost their hearing if they had worked on the surface? How many that

worked on the surface have ever suffered loss of hearing? I cannot name one man.

Now, that miner got no hearing aid, no compensation from the company nor from the Compensation Board. I did not try. What I wear here on my head today cost me $740.00 out of my own pocket. And today I am offered … a watch … which I am fully prepared to say cost no more than $40.00!

Does this compensate me after more than twenty-five years of service to this company? NO! Definitely NOT! I will not, I never intend, EVER to put it on my arm and I never will.

Thank you.

We placed Peter's speech in the play exactly as he delivered it that day.

Week Four: Lost in the Woods

By this time we had accumulated masses of material and individual scenes, but had not yet edited, nor structured any long sequences. I sensed that we had a handle on the show, but some of the cast were losing faith, unsure whether any structure was possible from the material. As we began piecing together segments, frustrations surfaced. There was a showdown over working method: the question of improvisations.

The sequences must be made "more dramatic," some said, and more character invention would help. I disagreed. It was essential not to take Buchaneers' lives away from them, give them mainland accents, graceful movements, and more dramatic actions. The operative dynamic of this whole project was in the first place social. Fictionalizing Buchaneers' lives in order to spice up the entertainment value could increase the *theatrical* dynamic of our play at the expense of the social dynamic of their community. In any case the two shouldn't be mutually exclusive. The objective was to pass the ball to the audience. This didn't mean that we were restricted to being theatrically dull; it meant that we had to find new ways of being theatrically interesting. We must not take the easy way out. The play belonged to our audience. It was to be their history, their lives onstage. As actors, we needed a style which only *borrowed* characters and incidents in order to describe or represent patterns to the audience. The point was to borrow, not to co-opt.

Eventually we worked out a good compromise. We would stick faithfully to actual documentary monologue and dialogue. Our own comments on this material would be made through staging (using puppets, etc.) and by the editing process itself. When we introduced scenes entirely of our own invention, we would do so in an obviously different presentational style, using a kind of agit-prop shorthand.

For some episodes we developed a diagrammatic style of presentation for added emphasis. The intention was to place a border around important elements of the historic sequence, to frame them in bold face with repetition and rhythm.

The Les Forward Scene:

> **MINER.** Les Forward. That's the name of the fella that won the strike battle for us in '41, was Les Forward. Yup. He took on the whole thing and done a wonderful job. He got us a seven-and-a-half-cent-an-hour increase and a lot of fringe benefits that were never heard of to any other mine in Newfoundland. Well, after that, see, the company bought he over. They offered he a job, see. Foreman up to the mill. He had to leave the union. And after he was on the job a very short time they turned around and fired him. The union couldn't do a thing. That's a fact.
>
> **VOICE.** The Les Forward Story!
>
> (Shift whistle blows a short blast, like a "starting lineup.")
>
> **MINER.** Les Forward joins the union and gets his union card!
>
> **LES.** Thank you.
>
> **MINER.** Les Forward is elected president of the union!
>
> (Much clapping[.])
>
> **LES.** Thank you.
>
> **MINER.** Les Forward wins the 1941 strike almost single-handedly!
>
> (More clapping, cheers.)
>
> **LES.** Thank you.
>
> **BOSS.** Les Forward is offered a job as mill foreman.
>
> (voices: "oooooooh!")
>
> **LES.** Thank you
>
> **BOSS.** Les Forward passes over his union card! Uh … Les?
>
> **LES.** Oh … uh …. Thank you….
>
> **BOSS.** Foreman do this! (stands militarily at ease. Les obeys.)
> Foreman do this! (stands to attention. Les obeys.)
> Foreman do this! (salutes with hand to temple. Les obeys.)
> Foreman do this! (slowly waves goodbye with salute hand.)
>
> **EVERYONE.** 'Bye, Les….
>
> (The shift whistle blows for a long slow time. Les is left waving sadly.)

By now most of the actors were finding it difficult to see the woods for the trees. This stage of a collective creation period, before the show's structure is finalized, is always characterized by restlessness. It is a luxury to still have time for arguing. With impeccable timing, a theatre student from York University, Alan Filewod, showed up in Buchans to research the methodology of collective creations, and we were able to yell much of our frustration into his tape recorder instead of at each other.

Weeks Five and Six: The Home Stretch

In most collective creations this is the time when stark panic hits the participants, and most of the work gets done. Chaff is sorted out, the more important material is developed further, and over two thirds of the show-and-tell scenes are usually trashed. We rolled up our sleeves and sweated, and watched our play's structure emerge more clearly day by day. Our set, a huge 2,000-pound timber "square-set" from the mine lashed to our ubiquitous scaffold, was now erected in the school gymnasium. It brought a reassuring unity to rehearsals. We knew we must have a show – because the set was ready.

Structural gaps in the show became apparent. Earlier, Donna Butt and Connie Kaldor had problems interviewing miners' wives. As a result we had lots of scenes about men working, but very little about women's work. We wanted to show that women at home worked shifts which complemented those of their husbands in the mine. A song ("Who Says We don't Work by the Whistle?") and two good scenes eventually emerged. One of these we inserted into the middle of our underground work sequence, during a scene about the men's lunchbreak. As the miners joked over their lunchboxes, the action froze, and underneath them, at breakneck pace, Donna performed the following:

> I can't let the poor man starve to death, you know. Every Monday morning I gets up and makes him chicken sandwiches. Then every Tuesday morning I gets up and makes him cheese sandwiches. And every Wednesday I give him leftovers and if we got no leftovers I give him a big tin of meatballs. Every Thursday I gives him a bit of raw bologna, because he LOVES raw bologna and every Friday I give him fish. He has fish for lunch and fish for dinner.
>
> Now let me see ... that's three times a week I make sandwiches and I make two sets for him every time so that's 3 times 2, that's 6, and I makes 'em 52 weeks a year ... that's 312 sandwiches I makes for him every year. And most of the time I does that I uses homemade bread, except on Mondays, 'cause Mondays I got to do the wash and I don't have time to make bread. Usually I got enough to do me for the rest of the week unless of course the youngsters gets at it just when it comes outa the oven and then I got nothin', but other than that I got enough to do until Tuesday morning. I uses 4 slices on Tuesdays and I uses 4 slices on Thursdays to make sandwiches. 4 and 4 is 8. I uses 3 slices with the meatballs, that's 12, and I uses 4 slices with the biscuits, that's 16. That's 52 times ... that's 677 slices of homemade bread. Now I only uses "bought bread" on Mondays. Mondays I uses 4 slices. That's 52 fours ... that's 208 slices plus the 30 or 40 I uses when the youngsters gets at the homemade when it comes outa the oven ... that's ... 328 slices of Mammy's bread!
>
> Now cake. Every Monday morning I gets up and I makes nut-bread cake. He loves it. He eats so much I haven't got enough to put on the table for supper. Then every Tuesday I makes orange-bread cake. He can't stand that, but I makes it every Tuesday anyway. Then every Wednesday I makes date-bread cake, and what he don't like about that, well, he

brings home again. Now that's 3 lots of cake I makes, that's 3 two's ... 56 ... 257!

Cookies! You wouldn't believe the cookies I makes for that man in the run of a week! I got to give him 10 cookies on Mondays, and 12 when he don't like the cakes and 4 for when he takes the orange-bread cake ... that's 26. I give him 3 on Wednesdays and 4 on Thursdays. That's 26 and 3 and 4 that's 32 ... 52 times 32, that must be about 66,000 COOKIES I MAKES IN THE RUN OF A YEAR! AND 257 CAKES AND 1100 SLICES OF BREAD AND 312 SANDWICHES AND ... AND ... AND I'LL TELLYOUSOMETHING I'M NEVERGETTINGMARRIED AGAIN!

Work responsibilities always stratify in the home stretch. The actors focus on their roles and the director worries about piecing everything together. As Bembo put it: "Well, I hope you know where this show is heading because I'm going to get into my characters now. Goodbye." The time for discussion was past. We all pulled together to make the best show of what we had.

At the eleventh hour of a collective creation, the rehearsals draw on the lengthy immersion which by this time each member of the creative team has had in the subject. As a result, scenes take shape and polish rapidly. This is different from a scripted play, where rehearsal dwells not upon shaping the show out of the actors' experience but more upon shaping the actors' experience to fit the requirements of the show. Script actors must spend a lot of rehearsal time exploring their roles, trying to piece together a background, a past, and an environment for their characters. The advantage of collective creation is that when it comes close to actual performance, the collective actor often needs far less rehearsal than the script actor, simply because he can draw upon his weeks of immersion in the community. His conversations with residents, the time spent accompanying underground work shifts, and all the dozens of improvised scenes which didn't make it into the final show structure now make him intimately familiar with his subject matter, and provide a secure performance base.

When our show opened, the school gymnasium was packed solid for three nights and matinees. Every man, woman and child in Buchans must have seen it at least twice, and we got the community seal of approval. Management had some serious misgivings, but Local 5457 certified that the play told it like it was in Buchans. They encouraged us to show it to other areas of the province.

In 1974 touring Newfoundland was neither easy nor cheap, especially with a cast and crew of nine and a ton of mine timber for a set. The provincial government, flush with their Jubilee Year funds and a $300,000 Touring Subsidy programme, considered *Company Town* too hot to touch. (This was difficult to justify to our bank manager, who already frowned at us so hard he looked like John L. Lewis with indigestion.) But Steelworkers union locals in Baie Verte and Labrador City came through in the crunch to help out with travel costs. The eventual tour was able to link up the province's mining areas and draw attention to some common problems (particularly industrial disease). As a propaganda exercise, it acquainted spectators in St. John's and other centres with the reasons behind Buchans' recent strikes, and helped shed light on some of the problems in Newfoundland's mining industry. A Royal Commission was set up to enquire into the future of the Buchans mine (ASARCO had threatened to close the operation after the last strike because of dwindling ore deposits), and the play generated additional public interest to help prod government action.

> With each audience we have to come out and say: this is what we found. It may not be important. It may be. But here it is. And the audience goes: okay. And they get interested. It leaves a space for them to fill. It's an attitude you have to have along with the material onstage ... The question is, how much power does theatre have? About all you can do, is make people aware. And if they're concerned, it will move them. If not, it won't.

> One of the things that happened to me is, one night, one of the first shows, we played [the town of] Baie Verte, and I could FEEL everybody absorbing. And the next year they had a strike. Now, you can't know. But, like, I feel somewhat responsible for that. (Cooper and Davies)

The success of *Company Town – The Story of Buchans* knitted our own company closely together. It was our "shared language." Had the play been bad, I think we might have torn each other limb from limb. As it was, the tour together was a joy; our commitment to the show overcame many potential obstacles. When, for instance, our wheezing old tour bus wasn't able to reach the mining community of Tilt Cove because of impassable road conditions, Allen Booth walked and hitchhiked into the town alone and improvised a one-man performance of the show with the school piano.

We also brought *Company Town* to mining areas in Nova Scotia, where the national theatre critic for Southam News, Dave Billington, unexpectedly turned up and gave our company's fortunes a crucial shot in the arm:

> GLACE BAY, N.S. – When the Newfoundland group called the Mummers Troupe staged their play *Company Town* here at the miner's museum the result was as exciting as Michel Tremblay's opening night in New York City.

> The excitement was generated not just because this struggling group of theatre people were so talented and professional in their work, but because their play spoke so eloquently to the audience which was comprised of local miners and descendants of miners .... One of the most moving moments came during a sketch about the 25-year watch ... When the speech ended, the audience broke into long, heartfelt applause. But the clincher came when, at the play's end, the real miner himself, Peter Noftle, stood ... Miners are tough people, but there was a catch in Noftle's voice as he spoke and thanked the actors for telling his and others' stories so accurately and so well.

And there, in that museum with the walls hung with the picks and hammers of soft-coal miners long gone, with a real miner giving a short impromptu speech, theatre ceased to be an imitation of life and became life itself.

It was a moment rarely experienced and never to be forgotten.

Billington's review was a godsend. Previous to this, our fundraising efforts had been handicapped by a peculiar Catch-22 unknown to Toronto theatres, but familiar to many groups working in "the sticks." The catch was this: many agencies (such as the Canada Council) required evaluations of our work from recognized critics before they could consider investing in us. This was a reasonable request in areas where such recognized theatre critics tend to live and work. The problem was, Canadian critics at that time didn't travel much, and they never, ever, came to Newfoundland. The Toronto Critics Association met annually to award the Floyd Chalmers Award to the "Best Canadian Play of the Year" based exclusively on Toronto productions, in the pompous assumption that any play worth producing would be produced in Toronto. Our references from anthropologists, development educators and hometown theatre reviewers did not cut any critical mustard at all in big-time artsy circles. There simply was not, we were told, anybody in Newfoundland sufficiently qualified to assess us.

Billington's review was carried in Southam Press newspapers across the country, and helped free us from the hammer lock of regional obscurity.

Ultimately, of course, to prove that we *really* existed, it was necessary to go to Toronto itself. In the spring of 1975 Rick Salutin and Toronto's Theatre Passe Muraille won a Chalmers award, and with great fanfare gave it to us as a solidarity gesture. George and Mona Luscombe and June Faulkner of Toronto Workshop Productions offered us free use of their theatre for a two-week run, and thanks to both of these kind gestures we were able to bring *Company Town* successfully to Toronto in June of 1975.

With that, the goat was fed: the Canada Council was finally impressed.

(1988)

Works Cited

Billington, Dave. Rev. of *Company Town,* by the Mummers Troupe. Southam News. [Full information unavailable–Ed.]

Cooper, Howie and Bembo Davies. *Mayday* 1 (1975).

Heindsmann, Sandra. *Mayday* 1 (1975).

Towards an Understanding
of Theatrical Difference

by Robert Wallace

1 / In its Annual Report for 1961/62, the Canada Council stated a position on theatrical practice that has become the prototype for the creation of English-Canadian theatre: "... living theatre demands living playwrights ... the Canadian theatre demands Canadian playwrights." While the purpose of the Council's statement was laudable, its implicit direction was, and continues to be, problematic; not only does it situate the playwright at the centre of theatrical practice, but it privileges the script for the theatrical event—rather than the event itself—as primarily important. While this attitude now predominates in mainstream English-Canadian theatre, it periodically weathers serious criticism, the most sustained of which came in the late 1960s and early 70s. As Alan Filewod points out in his book, *Collective Encounters: Documentary Theatre in English Canada*, for the emerging, fiercely nationalistic generation of the 1960s, the "repudiation of 'colonial' structures of thought and methods of theatrical creation ... [resulted in] the introduction of a unique dramatic genre in the collectively created documentary play" (viii).

While Filewod restricts his discussion to the 1970s, his insights into the ways in which collective creation counters the assumptions of mainstream theatre are relevant today as a new approach to theatrical creation again emerges to attack the primacy of the playwright in theatres across Canada. Although Filewod's focus in his book is the contribution of this approach to English-Canadian theatre, his explanation of the ways in which the approach rejects imperialist culture helps to explain why it has remained more important in Quebec than in English Canada. Between 1958–1980, thousands of collective creations were produced by Québécois companies working under the umbrella organization L'Association québécoise du jeune theatre (AQJY);[1] indeed, the collective movement was so strong and so widespread in Quebec during this time that it would be impossible to pick, as Filewod does for English Canada, six plays or companies representative of its achievements. Discussing this movement in an article published in *Cahiers de théâtre Jeu* 15, Montreal theatre critic Gilbert David prefers to suggest eight of its major contributions, two of which are particularly useful to an understanding of the evolution of the differences that distinguish Québécois theatre from that of English Canada: "... *la réactivation du collectif de creation autogestionnaire face à la hiérarchisation du travail théâtral ou, plus largement, spectaculaire*;" and "... *la critique productive de la formation théâtrale institutionelle par la mise de l'avant d'un programme parallèle, orienté par des objectifs pluridisciplinaires et axé principalement sur l'animation*" (7).

While the collective movement in Québécois theatre still exists [...], its contemporary proponents are neither as predominant nor prolific as those discussed in David's article. By and large, companies devoted to collective creation have been superseded in number and significance by those like Théâtre Petit a Petit [...] which, in their collaborative approach to both the organization and creation of theatre, function as the contemporary inheritors of the collectivist spirit. Despite the change in emphasis that marks the evolution of collective creation to collaborative construction, the essential dynamic remains the same – the collaborative interaction of a group of artists, who often represent different disciplines, united around a common goal or aesthetic. While this is the primary dynamic of theatrical production everywhere, in Quebec, unlike English Canada, it still remains a major method of theatrical *creation*. In this process, the playwright, while important to the collaboration, is not its central focus, a difference in attitude between our two major theatres that has significant consequences in the work they produce. While the creation of new scripts by individual writers is as much a priority in Québécois theatre as in English Canada, the collective movement's legacy of collaboration also has affected Quebec's playwrights: most new Québécois playwrights have direct, on-going experience in the theatre as directors, actors or scenographers, a fact which influences both what and how they write. Until recently, this has been the exception rather than the rule in English-Canadian theatre.

While a thorough discussion of such differences is too large a topic for a single essay, the following notes about the possible reasons for these differences are more manageable. And inasmuch as their focus is theatrical difference, they allow me to bring together a number of ideas that have circulated in recent issues of *Canadian Theatre Review* regarding the differences between theatre and drama in general, ideas that appear to have generated constructive discussion about theatre's connection to literature. In pursuing an understanding of theatrical difference, I am reminded that the recognition of difference is essential to the formation of identity; it is in this sense that I hope these notes will be useful.

2 / The valorization of the playwright as the primary authority in theatrical practice continues to dominate English Canada's mainstream theatre. In *CTR*'s issue on new play development (Winter 1986), Urjo Kareda, artistic director of Toronto's Tarragon Theatre, summarized the attitude that prevails in establishment theatres from Vancouver to St. John's: "[T]he history of this country's theatre in the last few decades [is] its ongoing struggle toward a dramatic literature" (10–11). In the same article, Kareda explained that "[t]he challenge of succeeding Bill Glassco at the Tarragon (who had founded it in 1971) was to generate a new group of playwrights and fresh play-development programs in a theatre which had been created specifically to help create a wider dramatic literature in this country" (8).

Yet, while Urjo Kareda's idea of theatre—and his concomitant approach to new play development—is widespread in English Canada, it is not, of course, the only idea. Invariably those companies who oppose its assumptions and structures work in what has become known as "the fringe" – a region both financially and aesthetically marginal to the mainstream. It is important to note that the fringe, although it attracts little critical attention and minimal government support (at least, in comparison to that given establishment theatres), is large and active: in a report published in *CTR* 51 (Summer 1987) Jini Stolk, executive director of the Toronto Theatre Alliance, explained:

> The number of small theatre companies in Toronto has exploded in recent years, while the venues available for their use have decreased alarmingly. There is now a serious shortage of theatres suitable for the 30 or more professional companies which the Toronto Theatre Alliance defines as "small theatres" – those with annual operating budgets of less than $150,000. (31)

Another report prepared by the ITA last year noted that more than 50 productions were mounted by small Toronto theatres in 1986, playing in houses that ranged in size from 57 to 280 seats (41). In other words, Toronto's fringe theatre activity, although marginally positioned in relation to the city's dominant theatre culture, still attracts a substantial audience interested in work that challenges or departs from the status quo. This is equally the case in Winnipeg, Vancouver and Edmonton—as the increasing popularity of fringe theatre festivals in the latter two cities demonstrates— as well as in the Maritime Provinces, whose "alternative" cultural activity Richard Paul Knowles discussed in *CTR* 48.

Although the range of creative endeavour that composes the fringe makes it impossible to generalize effectively about its nature, it has a number of prevailing characteristics important to these notes. For example, while fringe artists still are concerned to create Canadian work, this concern is less important than it was to the generation that shaped and controls Canada's theatrical establishment. More importantly, for many who work in the fringe, theatre is not centred on the play-wright, nor on the creation of a body of dramatic literature. As Sky Gilbert, artistic director of Buddies in Bad Times—one of Toronto's oldest and most successful fringe companies—states: "It is important to note that theatre is not simply image (which would make it a painting or an 'installation') or idea (which would make it an essay...), but, rather, action..." (40). Gilbert doesn't even entertain the possibility that theatre exists to create a body of dramatic literature; for him, like many other fringe artists, the primary component of theatre is action, not the script, a component which is spatial and temporal in its essence. Such action is initiated not by a playwright, but by a creator – a term which attempts to encompass in English the same territory as the French words *createur* and *concepteur*. Inasmuch as the creator can be an individual or a group, this approach to theatre shares important similarities with both the structure and aesthetic of collective creation: both see theatre as a collaborative, ephemeral event, a variety of performance, not a genre of literature.

Discussing the role of the creator in an essay entitled "Towards a New Dramaturgy," Paul Leonard implicitly connects the new fringe aesthetic with that of collective creation when he says,

> This distinction between writer and creator is an important one, even if, at times, both terms ultimately refer to the same person, since it encompasses the whole range of elements that make up the presentation ... By employing the word "creator," we remind ourselves that the theatrical presentation itself, not the script, is the central focus of our attention. (48)

While Leonard's argument would have appealed to many working in English-Canadian theatre collectives in the late 60s—I'm reminded, for example, of Jim Garrard's statement in an early manifesto for Toronto's Theatre Passe Muraille that "theatre [is] experience ... a human event, between people and people" (qtd. in Wallace, "Growing Pains" 76)—today it is out of favour. Nevertheless, just as the fringe work that his insights describe is gaining in popularity, so this argument is gaining increasing importance in both performance studies and critical theory, for it challenges not only the privileged position of the playwright but, implicitly, the idea of literature as well. While the interrogation of literature and literary theory has begun to influence Canadian university English departments, it has yet to affect popular notions of literature as they are presented in the mass media. Thus, while many of us can understand, if not accept, Terry Eagleton's statement in his book *Literary Theory* that "literature, in the sense of a set of works of assured and unalterable value, distinguished by certain shared inherent properties, does not exist" (11), most North American book reviewers, and certainly the general public, cannot. This is even more the case with theatre, a much more elitist art form than, say, the novel. Still, a number of important theatre practitioners and critics are beginning to proclaim its efficacy in the North American media. In May 1987, for example, the American director and author, Robert Benedetti, made the following comments at the Directors' Colloquium at Calgary which were published in *CTR* 53:

> I don't believe in dramatic literature. I don't think that there is any such thing. I think that what we call a script is a residue of an act of creation for the living theatre, and that, at best, it transmits a kind of essential energy that can generate subsequent acts of theatrical creation. That means the writer must be writing for the living performance, not writing as a literary act. (11)

While Benedetti's comments, like Leonard's, are not received by the English-Canadian theatrical establishment (which includes, I suggest, most theatre critics writing for the mass media), their ideas are more acceptable in Quebec and Europe. Paul Lefebvre, for example, a Montreal theatre critic who has written regularly for both *Le Devoir* and *Cahiers de théâtre Jeu*, suggests in an essay entitled "Playwriting in Quebec," that "the birth of Quebec theatre resulted from its encounter with speech, after its futile attempts to be sired by literature" (68). He goes on to quote another Québécois critic, Laurent Mailhot, about the development of theatre in Quebec: "Drama entered literature the moment it left it." In this regard, it is important to recognize that critics like Leonard and Lefebvre are not asserting an anti-literary approach to the theatre; nor are the fringe and Québécois companies to which I refer engaged in creating anti-literary theatre. But while these critics and practitioners accept the importance of words in the theatrical event, they explain that the words signify speech, not literature: words are meant to be heard, not read, and they are meant to be heard within the context of the other signifying practices of the theatre. For the playwright to work effectively, it follows that he must create within the theatre—that is, with an understanding of theatrical practice based on experiential knowledge of the way theatre differs from literature—not in isolation.

For many reasons this principle is more widely understood in Québécois theatre. While the primary reason is connected to speech, it is not, as I have already alluded, simply a matter of language; it is the *practice* of French in Québécois theatre that distinguishes it from English-Canadian theatre, not French itself. For a complex variety of reasons, Québécois theatre has rejected the authority of literature to create instead a body of work in which performance is the governing impulse. While words are of extreme importance in this work, it is their spoken signification that is of primary interest, not their existence as written text. As such, this work has greater affinity with fringe theatre in English Canada than with its mainstream counterpart, which possibly results from the similarly marginal positioning that both Québécois and fringe theatre occupy in relation to Canada's dominant culture.

3 /   The ideological foundations for the use of collective creation differ
      in Quebec from those of the English-Canadian groups. (Usmiani 109)

In large part, the emphasis on speech in Québécois theatre results from a generally well-known fact: Quebec's conscious rejection of English as the dominant institution of both American cultural hegemony and Canadian federalism during the last twenty years. But it also results from another fact less generally understood outside the province: the devaluing of classical or international French that also marked the ascendancy of the Parti Québécois. In theatrical terms, this rebellion was revealed in the work of a variety of playwrights now considered responsible for creating the *nouveau théâtre québécois*—Michel Tremblay, Jean-Claude Germain, Jean Barbeau, Serge Sirois and others—whose assertion of Québécois dialects in their plays marked a radical shift from the work that preceded them. The "special" languages of Quebec were heard and acted on its stages where, previously, they had been ignored or deemed inappropriate. As a component of dramatic action, the language of Quebec had to be experienced as a public, communal event.

But it was more than the use of *joual* and other French dialects in Québécois theatre in the late 60s and early 70s that contributed to its development as a genuinely different theatre in North America. Indeed, it can be argued that theatre in Toronto and Montreal at this time shared a common attempt to break from the colonial past by affirming the priorities of indigenous work rooted in the use of local and regional dialects. No, in Quebec more than the languages of imperialist culture were being challenged – whether they be English, American or "standard" French; the methods and structures used to *shape* these languages also were under attack. Clearly, many

Quebec theatre workers recognized, if only implicitly, that the repudiation of linguistic traditions in francophone theatre also required the rejection of concomitant literary traditions—indeed, of the notion of literature itself—if theatre in Quebec was to become truly indigenous. If the theatre was to employ a genuinely new language, then the language must be liberated from forms accorded the status of convention by the prevailing tastes of received culture.

The rejection of literature as an absolute of assured and unalterable value is obviously a practical, if not necessary, strategy of survival for a society marginal to the cultural hegemony. As Terry Eagleton explains, "literature does not exist in the sense that insects do ... the value-judgements by which it is constituted are historically variable ... and have a close relation to social ideologies. They refer in the end not simply to private taste, but to the assumptions by which certain social groups exercise and maintain power over others" (16). While recognition of this idea was implicit in the work of English-Canadian collectives in the early 70s, it appears to have gone unrecognized by the dozens of other theatres across the country who championed (and still do) Canadian playwrights as the basic ingredient of a uniquely Canadian theatre, perpetuating in English Canada the hierarchical structure of theatre production that situates the playwright at the top. Because this model is predicated on literary privilege which fails to challenge the assumptions of "literature" inherited from the dominant cultures of England and the United States, it can never be truly Canadian. Something else is required.

Certainly the Quebec collectives that emerged in the 70s understood this point and made it part of their ideological position. Not satisfied with the changes achieved by Tremblay and his contemporaries, the companies who became collectively known as *les jeunes théâtres* emerged to challenge *le nouveau théâtre québécois* as a *théâtre d'auteurs*.[2] Writing in 1978, Claude Des Landes stated that,

> Liberated from its dependence on literature and its purely aesthetic pretensions, theatrical expression now relates to pragmatic given facts ... If authors like Robert Gurik, Michel Tremblay or Jean Barbeau ... had as their major preoccupation to extricate us from the ruts of passivity and the colonialism of our history, the present generation, that of collective creation, lets us foresee a utilization of the stage whose immediate results one cannot be satisfied to evaluate according to a certain scale. Our entire dramaturgy has just gone through a first cycle. (qtd. in Usmiani 109)

Both the political ideology and the imperative [of] this movement had been clear from its start. For example, in 1974 *Jeune Théâtre*, the magazine published by AQJT, quoted Andre Paradis as follows:

> Culture is no longer posited as a Manichean value ... but as the reflection of an individual and collective reality and as a means to action. It is ... the birth of a collectivist spirit as a solution to change (rather than the advent of a saviour, a leader, a star): co-operatives, citizens'

committees, committees for political action. In the sphere of theatre ...
collective creation. (qtd. in Usmiani 110)

And, as Renate Usmiani outlines in her book, *Second Stage: The Alternative Theatre
Movement in Canada,* the *jeune théâtre* "set itself up as a deliberate alternative both to
traditional theatre and to the more literary *nouveau théâtre québécois,* whose authors,
it was felt, sought success only in order to defect immediately to the well-funded
mainstream establishment." She continues by explaining that for the *jeune théâtre,*
"the traditional author-director-script triad [represented] the hold of the establishment over the 'oppressed' levels of theatrical creativity, actors and technicians who
wish to gain full equality through a democratization of the creative process" (109–11).

While this also was true of English-Canadian collectives such as Toronto's
Theatre Passe Muraille, the process of democratization did not lead to such an astute
analysis of the politics of theatrical practice, possibly because the *bête noir* of English-
Canadian theatre, the Stratford Festival, held such a stranglehold on the theatrical
imagination of the city's alternative theatres. Political analysis was deemed unnecessary in face of the Festival's power; to produce Canadian plays, whether they be
collectively created or not, was considered "political" enough. As Paul Thompson,
then artistic director of Theatre Passe Muraille, said in 1974:

> In this country, it's a political act to discover things about yourself. It's
> the same in any colonized country, which we are. But once you've
> discovered something about yourself, something like Passe Muraille
> maybe helps you to – well, I don't know where you go from there, I don't
> know what you do. Just the whole element of telling or encouraging
> other people to do things is hard for me: my most exciting function is
> working with a group of people who might discover what to do out of
> their own work, and then communicate this to another group of people.
> (qtd. in Wallace, "Paul Thompson" 62)

While Thompson clearly eschewed the idea of literature as valuable in the theatre, he
failed to go further in articulating a policy or mandate that would lead his theatre into
a radically alternative position. In this regard, his work with Passe Muraille was typical of the documentary theatre created by most of the English-Canadian collectives
that worked during this period. As Alan Filewod summarizes it,

> The Canadian documentary has tended to be anti-ideological; it does
> not try to explain the significance of the matter it documents in an intel-
> lectual scheme, but rather suggests the significance of a shared historical
> or community experience by transforming it into art ... the fact of
> that transformation is as important as the textual content of the
> performance. This preference for community affirmation over ideology
> suggests that the Canadian documentary is ultimately a moralistic
> genre. (182–83)

More importantly, Filewod also acknowledges that "in Canada ... the documentary
theatre evolved parallel to, and in some cases as part of, an emerging dramatic

literature." In Quebec, this simply wasn't the case, as an excerpt from the founding manifesto of AQIT makes clear: "That on the level of its political orientation, the AQIT support the forces which are struggling to free themselves from the economic, political, ideological oppression which the people of Quebec are subjected to…" (qtd. in Usmiani 115).

To be fair, the ideological position of the Québécois theatre collectives that founded AQJT in 1972 did not remain unified. At its annual *congres* in 1975, ten of the most radical companies left the association to pursue goals more militantly political than those of the remaining members who constituted the majority.[3] Rather than weakening the association's emphasis on collective creation, however, their departure had the opposite effect, partly because it led AQJT to open its membership to companies creating theatre for young audiences in the following year. This was a logical step inasmuch as various members of AQJT already had organized the first Festival de théâtre pour enfants in 1974 (the Festivals continued until 1986). The fact that the majority of the new members relied almost exclusively on collectivity in both the structuring of their companies and the creation of their work solidified collective creation as the primary form of indigenous theatre in Quebec until the end of the decade.[4] Just as importantly, it contributed to the shift in AQJT from theatre aiming at political intervention to that involved in research and experimentation. Writing about the *jeune théâtre* in 1980, Gilbert David was able to divide its work into three general categories which typified AQJT until its demise in 1985: theatre which pursued mainstream acceptance; theatre which aimed at social change through political intervention; and theatre which deliberately explored what could be called the "aesthetics of marginality" – the forms and processes that distinguish marginal theatre from that of the mainstream (16–18).

4 / While the demise of AQJT in 1985 prompted considerable debate about a "crisis" in Québécois theatre connected to its loss of definable goals,[5] its legacy is apparent in the high proportion of Québécois theatres that continue to work with a collaborative approach. This is particularly noticeable to an anglophone, such as myself, who enters the Québécois theatre community with the models of English-Canadian theatre as his primary referents. What is immediately obvious is that in many of the most innovative Québécois theatres (for example, Le Pool, Zoopsie, Théâtre Petit à Petit and Les Productions ma chère Pauline), artistic control resides with a group of artists, not a single artistic director; individuals in such companies initiate projects that utilize the expertise of other group members as well as outside artists who join them on a project-to-project basis. While their work often is generated collectively, it also includes the production of texts by playwrights: so, for example, the three artistic directors of Les Productions ma chère Pauline can collaborate on the creation of the text for *Tiens tes rêves*, in which they also perform the roles they created; and they also can work in a more traditional manner as the cast for Rene-Daniel Dubois' production of *Le Troisième fils de Professeur Youralov*, which their company produced this year. Other groups organized as collectives (for example, Théâtre de Carton,

Théâtre de la Manufacture, Théâtre de La Rallonge and Théâtre de Quartier), while they function similarly, place a greater emphasis on group improvisation of a script as, for example, was the case with La Rallonge's production of *Gauvreau* last February, in which texts by Claude Gauvreau, Paul Claudel and Paul-Emile Borduas were collectively chosen, organized and performed. In some of these companies—Zoopsie is an example—the artists bring not only expertise to various aspects of theatre, but knowledge of other disciplines as well: often this leads to an emphasis on interdisciplinary performance, as in Zoopsie's production of *L'Objet rêvé* at Espace Go last September, which incorporated large moveable sculptures as well as live and pre-recorded video into a production that included clown-work and a live band.

While there are companies in English Canada that function similarly to these (the two Toronto companies Theatre Columbus and VideoCabaret International provide good examples), they are fewer in number and are accorded less recognition by the media and the theatregoing public. By and large, the rise of the performer who writes and directs his or her own work is still such a new phenomenon in English Canada that companies organized to serve the priorities of such artists are mainly notable as exceptions to the general rule(s) of hierarchical production in which the various creative functions associated with theatre remain separated until the final stages of production. This also is true of the playwright who directs his or her own work. With the notable exceptions of George F. Walker and Sharon Pollock, English-Canadian playwrights who direct their own plays exist mainly in the fringe (for example, Sky Gilbert, Blake Brooker and Bañuta Rubess). In Quebec, however, the opposite is true: not only is it common for a playwright to direct his own work, but recent examples reveal the degree to which this practice has infiltrated the mainstream: consider that last October Marie Laberge directed her play *Oublier* at Théâtre Jean Duceppe, one of Montreal's biggest, most popular theatres; this spring Rene-Daniel Dubois directed his *Being at Home with Claude* at Théâtre du Rideau Vert, another well-established, mainstream house; and Claude Poissant, a member of the artistic board of Théâtre Petit à Petit, directed his play *Ce que reste du désir* at the prestigious Salle Fred-Barry last January. In many cases, Quebec playwrights also act as well as direct (this is true of the three just mentioned) – a recent, interesting case occurring in the production of *La Fern me d'intérieur* by Robert Claing, which was directed by the author in collaboration with Martine Beaulne and Marie Laberge, who also performed the two character piece.

This latter production suggests yet another manifestation of the collaborative approach to theatrical organization that differentiates Québécois theatre from that of English Canada, inasmuch as its producing company, Montreal's Le Nouveau théâtre experimental, while having an artistic director in the person of Jean-Pierre Ronfard, also utilizes a board of artists (which currently includes playwright/performers Robert Claing and Anne-Marie Provencher) whose work it regularly produces. This model is followed by a number of companies including Carbone 14 under the directorship of Gilles Maheu, and Omnibus, which is co-directed by Jean Asselin and Denise Boulanger. While both these companies have produced work by individual playwrights (Carbone 14's production of Heiner Müller's *Hamletmachine* last September being a successful example), more often they collaborate on the creation of work which, as in the case of the Omnibus show *La Dame dans l'auto avec des lunettes et un fusil* (an adaptation of a novel by Sébastien Japrisot), is a radical re-working of texts by the production team. In some cases, the director also performs in the show, as did Jean Asselin in *La Dame dans l'auto* and Gilles Maheu in Carbone 14's *L'homme rouge*. But perhaps the best known example of this model is Théâtre Repere of Quebec City, the company which collectively developed *La Trilogie des dragons,* in which Robert Lepage not only collaborated on the script but also performed in and directed the production.

The example of *La Trilogie des dragons* reveals not only the creative vitality that can result from the collaborative approach to theatrical creation but also the visionary potential of releasing theatre workers from traditional structures of production. This is not to suggest that Canadian theatre should return to the principles and processes of collective creation, or to suggest that the work which was and is produced by this approach is of higher quality than that produced in the more conventional author-director-script triad. But it is to acknowledge the essentially collaborative nature of theatrical activity and to suggest that the ephemeral qualities of the event, rather than the document of the event (such as book, videotape, or film), should dictate its methods of creation. It also is to acknowledge that theatre's unique ability to galvanize an audience into a community by providing it with a mirror of its concerns rests in its connection to that community, a connection that is shaped as much by socio-historic exigencies as by tradition. The differences between Québécois and English-Canadian theatre that have become so visible to me in the last few years are also the differences between two cultures: one that survives through the construction of its own institutions, flawed as they may be, and one that relies on the received structures of other cultures to pursue its sense of self.

(1988)

Notes

[1] Founded in 1958 as L'Association canadienne du théâtre d'amateurs (ACTA), this organization evolved into L'Association québécoise du jeune théâtre (AQJT) between 1968 and 1973. Elaine F. Nardocchio explains that the association was originally conceived as the Quebec counterpart to the Dominion Drama Festival. In 1970, the term "amateur" was replaced by "non-professional;" in 1972, when ACTA officially became AQJT, collective creations became the central focus of the association's annual festival.

[2] The term *jeune théâtre* refers not only to the members of AQJT at the time of its formation in 1972 but also to the " alternative" theatre movement in Quebec that was the genesis of the organization. After AQJT suffered a severe crisis in 1975 in

which ten of its members left (see note 1, above) the term was used to apply to all of Quebec's alternative theatre groups, whether or not they belonged to AQJT. The name also applies to the journal that was published by the AQJT until it disbanded in 1985. See Usmiani, chapter six.

3   Of these, Théâtre des Cuisines, Théâtre Euh!, La Gaboche, Les Gens d'en Bas and Le Tic Tac Boom were perhaps the most militant, the latter four theatres publishing the *Manifesto pour un théâtre au service du peuple* upon departure. See "Rousseau."

4   For an illustration of the extent to which collective creation dominated theatre for young audiences during this period, see the documentation of the annual programs of the Festival de théâtre pour enfants, 1974–1980 in Beauchamp.

5   See, for example, *Cahiers de théâtre Jeu* 36 (1985), the subject of which is "1980–1985: L'Ex-jeune théâtre dans de nouvelles voies."

Works Cited

Beauchamp, Hélène. "Publications de l'organisme: bref survol: annexe 2: repertoire des festivals de theater pour l'enfance et la jeunesse." *Cahiers de théâtre Jeu* 15.2 (1980): 171–86.

Benedetti, Robert, G. Raby, P. Hawthorne, A. McInnes, J. Biros, and B. White. "The Role of the Director in New Play Development." *Canadian Theatre Review* 52 (1987): 7–13.

Cahiers de théâtre Jeu. "1980–1985: L'Ex-jeune théâtre dans de nouvelles voies." 36.3 (1985).

David, Gilbert. "a.c.t.a./a.q.j.t.: un theatre 'intervenat' (1958–1980)." *Cahiers de theatre Jeu* 15.2 (1980): 7–18.

Eagleton, Terry. "Introduction: What is Literature?" *Literary Theory: An Introduction.* Minneapolis, U of Minnesota P, 1983.

Filewod, Alan. *Collective Encounters: Documentary Theatre in English Canada.* Toronto: U of Toronto P, 1987.

Gilbert, Sky. "Inside the Rhubarb! Festival." *Canadian Theatre Review* 49 (1986): 40–43.

Kareda, Urjo. "They Also Serve Who Only Stand and Wait For Rewrites…". *Canadian Theatre Review* 49 (1986): 6–11.

Knowles, Richard Paul, ed. *Canadian Theatre Review* 48: *Atlantic Alternatives* (1986).

Lefebvre, Paul. "Playwriting in Quebec." Trans. Barbara A. Kerslake. *Contemporary Canadian Theatre.* Ed. Anton Wagner. Toronto: Simon & Pierre, 1985. 60–68.

Paul Leonard. "Towards a New Dramaturgy." *Canadian Theatre Review* 49 (1986): 44–49.

Nardocchio, Elaine F. *Theatre and Politics in Modern Quebec.* Edmonton: U of Alberta P, 1986.

Rousseau, Pierre. "Retour sur un periode militance." *Cahiers de theatre Jeu* 15.2 (1980): 89–95.

Stolk, Jini. "The Other Housing Crisis: Facilities for Small Theatres." *Canadian Theatre Review* 51 (1987): 31.

Toronto Theatre Alliance. "Preliminary Report of Toronto Small Theatres." *Canadian Theatre Review* 51 (1987): 41.

Usmiani, Renate. *Second Stage: The Alternative Theatre Movement in Canada.* Vancouver: U of British Columbia P, 1983.

Wallace, Bob. "Paul Thompson at Theatre Passe Muraille: Bits and Pieces." *Open Letter.* 2nd Ser. 7 (1974): 49–71.

Wallace, Robert. "Growing Pains: Toronto Theatre in the 70s." *Canadian Literature* 85 (1980): 71–85.

Collective Creation:
Its Background and
Canadian Developments (excerpt)

by Diane Bessai

In the annals of English-Canadian theatre history, development during the post-Centennial period is likely the liveliest on record. Although many young theatre workers had entered the scene, most regional theatres across the country seemed unreceptive to new Canadian talent and uninterested in the development and performance of new Canadian work. Many of these new workers saw the Canadian theatre establishment during the late 1960s as either the last vestige of British imperialism or the new frontier of American colonization. Feeling like outsiders, they took advantage of alternative funding of the day—grants such as Opportunities for Youth and Local Initiative Programs—to create vibrant new theatre operations run on a shoestring. These so-called "alternative" theatres may be divided roughly into two categories: those concentrating on the development of new playwrights—for example, Tarragon Theatre and Factory Theatre Lab in Toronto—and those working in collective creation. This term refers to actor-improvised plays, created during the rehearsal period, in which theatrical rather than literary values predominate. Of the latter, Theatre Passe Muraille—under the artistic direction of Paul Thompson—was the leading innovator for what became a playmaking process among particular new theatres spread across the country.

Essentially, the collective creators were subversives—like their contemporary American and British counterparts—demystifying the gentilities of "high art" by sharing their themes and performance processes openly with the audience. For this reason, the style of play and performance can be categorized as anti-naturalistic – more often presentational than mimetic. On occasion, this style draws on the theatricality of popular entertainment and often resembles a variety show or a Christmas concert more than a conventional play. The typical structure is a collage of juxtaposed scenes rather than a strictly linear development, comprising dramatic sketch, monologue, song and expressive gesture. The actors perform multiple roles, sometimes portraying inanimate objects as well as people. Through speech and transformational body language, the actors provide the essentials of the scene without much use of props and sets. The result is a type of rough and ready theatre that can be performed almost anywhere – and was: in town halls, school gyms, churches (in either basement or nave), in auction barns and, on one unusual occasion, in a Toronto streetcar. Instead of waiting for an audience to find them, the collective companies set out to create their own audiences by addressing the local public directly on subjects of interest to the lives and traditions of those in neighbouring communities.

The first part of this study analyzes a chronological selection through the 1970s of collective creations at Theatre Passe Muraille under the direction of Paul Thompson. As the most influential Canadian practitioner of collective creation at the time, Thompson was challenged, among other things, by his observation that "the really interesting people are the ones who don't go to theatres" (qtd. in Wallace 64). Therefore, he decided to attempt a change. His innovative work with talented actors having a knack for improvisation—and sometimes with writers—resulted in a new kind of Canadian play. These plays deserved critical interest in their own right as performance pieces and were seminal in the cultivation of new audiences for indigenous theatre – in Toronto and elsewhere.

Collective creation at Theatre Passe Muraille was also influential in the development of certain writers for the theatre. There is a paradox here, given that Thompson himself never advocated the primacy of the writer in his collective enterprises and, for some years, was even indifferent to the publication of Theatre Passe Muraille's scripts. For him, theatre is an art serving the performer, not aspiring to be dramatic literature. For him, the play is in the performance, not in the packaging between covers. Yet there is a clear line of descent—the subject of the second part of this study—among certain theatrical workers who have toiled in various capacities on Theatre Passe Muraille's collective creations: Rick Salutin as a writer, John Gray as a composer and musician, and Linda Griffiths as a performer. This suggests that Canadian drama, as well as Canadian theatre, owes more to collective creation than has been acknowledged before.

1. Britain and United States

The roots of collective creation in twentieth-century theatre reach back at least as far as the radical political experiments in non-Aristotelian theatre of Erwin Piscator and Bertolt Brecht in the 1920s. At that time, they were seeking ways to express their sense of the inadequacy of conventional theatre to examine the changing cultural environment of technological mass man. [1] Brecht speaks of organizing "small collectives of specialists in various fields to 'make' the plays; among these specialists were historians and sociologists as well as playwrights, actors and other people of the theatre" (qtd. in Willett 78). Piscator as a director was notorious for his freedom with texts to suit his political intention (Innes 68) and was ingenious in his stagecraft for creating new kinds of audience recognition of the changing technological environment of the modern world.

The object, of course, was to reach a new working class rather than a bourgeois audience – an interest transmitted to Joan Littlewood in the 1930s in her attempts to establish a working-class community theatre in Manchester and later in Stratford East, London. In those first years, she directed agitprop theatre, early Brecht, and Piscator's adaptation of *The Good Soldier Schweik*. For the 1940 collective documentary *Last Edition,* about the political crises of the previous decade, she drew on the methods of the American Living Newspaper. This was a form of collective play developed in the U.S. Federal Theatre Project of the mid-1930s, founded by Hallie Flanagan. A documentary type of theatre researched and assembled by "editors," its aims were to develop a factually based theatrical shorthand to explore current issues of public concern – such as agriculture (*Triple-A Ploughed Under*), a public utility (*Power*), and housing (*One Third of a Nation*). As Arthur Arent reports, this involved improvisational techniques for "dramatizing abstraction." In *Power,* for example, the meaning of the term "holding company" was illustrated by the complicated manoeuvres of two actors and a pile of boxes (57–59).

For Littlewood, as for Brecht, ensemble playing was a strong priority. In re-forming her resident group after the war as Theatre Workshop, she introduced the company to a rigorous training in the dance techniques of Rudolph Laban, which she adapted to the needs of her actors. In her productions of classics and new plays alike, her aim was to integrate fully the resources of movement, voice, sound and light. Disciplined improvisation was a constant in her rehearsal methods, resulting in what Alan Filewod identifies as her "signature technique of portraying realistic action through mime and sound effects" (54). Her best known work is the ironically titled *Oh What a Lovely War!* (1963), a company creation built on the popular songs of the First World War (see Goomey, 125–26). This musical combines a pierrot show with Piscator's early technique of using documentary projections as backdrop to satiric versions of factual scenes.

As the basis for establishing a direct link to the community at the Victoria Theatre of Stoke-on-Trent in the 1960s, director Peter Cheeseman and his company created local documentaries that combined the Living Newspaper's concern for factuality, Joan Littlewood's emphasis on ensemble creativity, and her desire to reach a popular working-class audience. John Elsom notes that "[f]or the growing regional repertory theatre movement in the 1960s, the local documentaries provided a means of establishing a theatre's identity as part of a town or region, without losing its function as a theatre" (102).

In Britain, local creativity in the theatre was often overshadowed by the transfer systems to and from the West End. The aim of Cheeseman, and those who subse-quently took their lead from him—as in Hull, Newcastle and Leeds, for example—was to establish new local theatrical material for audiences who had seldom ventured into the theatre at all. Cheeseman's company worked "to develop a new and special style of acting, which honestly exposed the factual quality" of local history (e.g. *The Staffordshire Rebels,* 1965; *The Knotty,* 1966; *Six into One,* 1968) ("Introduction" xii). In the notable case of a local issue (*The Fight for Shelton Bar,* 1974), the company went out and learned the plant operations they were to depict on stage through combina-tions of realistic action and mime.

As with Littlewood, popular culture was often an informing principle in this kind of play, providing a way of appealing to its target audiences. The collective improvisa-tion for Alan Plater's *Close the Coalhouse Door,* produced at the Newcastle Playhouse in 1968, drew richly on English music-hall tradition. This documentary musical—about the community experience of the mining industry over the years—filled the theatre with workers both in the Newcastle Playhouse and later in the Nottingham Playhouse. At the Bradford College of Art, Albert Hunt worked collectively with his student Theatre Group to develop a theatre of alternative education. Their *John Ford's Cuban Missile Crisis* (1970), commissioned by radical Bradford University students for the Lenin Centenary celebrations, took its theatrical form as a cartoon version of the American western movie.

In 1966, Hunt had been part of the dramaturgical team assembled by Peter Brook for the Royal Shakespeare Company's collective improvisation, *US*, an English perspective on the events in Vietnam. He later said he preferred a "community core to which our communication could be directed." That had not been the case with the "undefined" audience at the Aldwych Theatre for *US*. For its Lenin Centenary assignment, his company knew it would have an audience of a specific political commitment and therefore chose a subject and popular idiom that would allow "for a cool look at what the Russian Revolution had become" (Hunt, "Introduction" 7, 9). When the play was later performed in a variety of venues—from a north-country village school to a pub to London's Open Space Theatre—Hunt was pleased most by its success with non-theatre-going audiences (*Hopes* 111). In 1974, Red Ladder (a branch of the original AgitProp Street Players formed in London in 1968) moved to Leeds "to establish a cultural presence for socialist theatre" in Yorkshire. With the same kind of audience concerns in mind as theatres in other regions, they collectively developed cabaret-club shows and plays in which they personalized issues relating to past and present working life in the area. Catherine Itsin reports that *Taking Our Time*, an examination of the textile trade in the course of the industrial revolution, reached 10,000 people in West Yorkshire (49–50).

In the United States, the specific methods, purposes and degree of collective creation were as varied as the companies working in the mode. Arthur Sainer, writing in 1975, observed that the gradual proliferation of radical ensemble troupes throughout the 1960s was a "disenchantment with commercial theatre" that "paralleled a broader disenchantment with the culture at large." In effect, he was describing the essential attitudes of the American counter-culture when he particularized that disenchantment "with America as a world power, with material well-being, with the ethic of the isolated figure labouring to merit the approval of society" (Sainer 17). Theodore Shank, in his 1972 investigation of a number of small European and American companies currently practising collective creation, spoke in broader terms of this "one process" group method of devising theatre pieces as the alternative theatre for the alternative society. He surveyed examples of collective theatre of the time as part of an international quest for wholeness "in reaction to the fragmentation of the established society" in a profession traditionally characterized by specialization, competition and internal hierarchies (3).

In general, the function of such companies was twofold: through improvisational methods, to stretch the creativity of the individual performer within the group context; and in the process, to explore radical means of engaging or encountering audiences. The latter might occur through personal consciousness-raising experiments or by establishing particular social or political objectives. For all of these, the experimental use of the performance space, indoor or outdoor, was a major factor. The creation of some form of text was a by-product of the collective process – the play emerging as a fluid rather than a fixed entity, a stimulus to group performance rather than an end in itself. The function of the writer—when included in the collective— was similar to that of the director and the performers: to contribute to the group exploration. Established texts, when used, were springboards for ensemble creativity rather than the *raison d'être* of performance as in traditional theatre. Music, movement, non-verbal sound and sometimes visual art—or the use of masks or puppets—became as important as language (Shank, "Collective" 3–4).

Three American counter-culture ensembles achieved great renown off-off-Broadway: The Living Theatre, founded by Julian Beck and his wife Judith Malina in 1951; The Open Theatre, founded by Joseph Chaikin in 1963; and The Performance Group of Richard Schechner, founded in 1967. [2] Their common features included the exploration of acting techniques that were non-verbal and physically oriented (drawing to some degree on the psycho-physical theories of Jerzy Grotowski of The Polish Laboratory Theatre); the focus on the presence of the actor rather than the fictional character he traditionally portrays; the collective "confrontation" of classical texts or the creation of radical new versions; and open, often sensational, ritualized interaction with the audience. In this last respect, we see the debt to Antonin Artaud's ideas: for a theatre of cruelty as a therapeutic externalization of latent violence and suffering; and for the return to a theatre of spectacle as well as ritualized sound and gesture. [3] Each of these groups, however, also had its own experimental emphasis.

The dedication of the Becks over the years to a political philosophy of pacifist anarchism led to The Living Theatre's increasing determination to break the barriers between life, theatre and revolution. Beginning in 1964 with *Mysteries and Smaller Pieces* (their first European show following self-exile related to problems concerning tax evasion), the Becks used collective creation along with related innovations of the period – such as onstage improvisation and aggressive interaction between performers and audience. Their production *Paradise Now* (1968), a collective creation, recklessly invited audience participation in the episode called "The Rite of Universal Intercourse" and ended with actors leading spectators out into the street. For their guerrilla-theatre work among the poor of Brazil during 1970 and 1971, they interviewed their research subjects and sometimes invited their direct participation in the collective creation. This work was done for a projected cycle of plays on the origins of violence – *The Legacy of Cain*.

At its most characteristic, The Open Theatre was committed to theatrical exploration through movement and to new body techniques of acting through improvisational exercises – rather than to political awareness and change. Nevertheless, an early phase of their work yielded Megan Terry's *Viet Rock* (1966). This full-length expression of anger against the Vietnam War was improvised from an Open Theatre workshop directed by Terry. The play was unusual at the time because of its experiments in transformational acting, by which the actors not only played multiple roles but also exchanged individual parts.

In the same year, the company produced Jean-Claude van Itallie's *America Hurrah*, a three-play theatricalization of contemporary malaise, which developed in part from The Open Theatre's acting exercises. More typically, however, Chaikin led his company in collective "meditations" on timeless human concerns. These included the Fall of Adam and Eve, based on improvisations from Genesis in *The Serpent* (1967); human response to death in *Terminal* (1969); social conditioning in *The Mutation Show* (1971); and sleep and consciousness in *Nightwalk* (1973). These works grew from the improvisational development of images, non-verbal vocal sound, and physically rendered percussion effects. Although the source of the plays was the actors' improvisations, Chaikin continued to include a participating writer. For example, van Itallie structured the final script of *The Serpent* while Susan Yankowitz provided the words for *Terminal.*

Schechner's environmental theatre, The Performance Group, combined features of the other two but with a special emphasis on creating new spatial relationships. This was done within an extended performance area that would best achieve close interaction between performers and spectators. The famous *Dionysus in 69* combined the company's variation on Euripides' *The Bacchae* with primitive and contemporary rituals as well as with "actuals" (personal interjections by actors) within a design of platforms, scaffolds and towers. The spectators chose their own places within this informal setting and were free at one point to participate in a ceremonial sexual orgy reminiscent of *Paradise Now* (described by the press as a "group grope").

There was a fourth theatre of importance in the radical developments of the period, both at home and abroad. That was Ellen Stewart's prolific Café La Mama, founded in 1961 and "dedicated to the playwright and all forms of the theatre" (185). [4] Tom O'Horgan, now known best for his Broadway productions of *Hair* and *Jesus Christ Superstar,* was a core director of this troupe. He collaborated with the actors of the La Mama Experimental Theatre Club and with Paul Foster "conjointly" to develop the latter's *Tom Paine,* which premiered at the Edinburgh Fringe Festival in 1967. The play combines text with moments set aside for actor improvisation and reflects the highly physical transformational acting styles of the time.

The influence of this company on director Max Stafford-Clark of Edinburgh's Traverse Theatre was seminal for his experiments in a kind of collective play different from those of the regional theatres. He soon established the Traverse Theatre Workshop, an experimental British fringe theatre that created plays through collaboration by a writer and a group of actors. On one occasion, the creative process included several writers. Most notable was the collective work *Hitler Dances,* done by the company in rehearsal with Howard Brenton. Later, Stafford-Clark became a founding member of Joint Stock, an alternative company whose improvisational workshops in the 1970s led to the creation of plays such as David Hare's *Fanshen* and Caryl Churchill's *Cloud Nine* (See Ansorge 47–51 and Ritchie 11–32).

In the 1960s, another type of alternative theatre prevalent in the United States was explicitly political and left-wing. "Our commitment is to change, not to art" was the unequivocal statement of purpose by the San Francisco Mime Troupe in 1971 (Lesnick 250). Since 1962, this company had been performing its *commedia dell'arte* versions of European classics—under the direction of founder Ron G. Davis—in the public parks of the Bay area. The troupe's resolve to reach a new working-class audience through popular forms of theatre was strengthened in 1969 (and continues to this day) with its reorganization into an activist and Marxist collective. Although credited to individual writers—Joan Holden being the principle one—the issue-oriented plays of this troupe reflected the collaborative study and analysis of the whole collective.

Inspired by the example of this group, Luis Valdez established the first Chicano company in 1965 – the bilingual (Spanish and English) El Teatro Campesino. Initially, the company's work supported the grape workers' strike in Delano, California. Together, Valdez and the workers devised the brief satiric sketches that they called *actos*. These sketches depicted daily issues in the lives of strikers (*huelgistas*), using the broad gestures of Mexican mime. The company often performed at union meetings, rallies and along picket lines. Later, Valdez broadened the cultural base of the plays, developing a new form he called *mito*, which explored Mayan mythological themes that are part of the Chicano inheritance (Lesnick 195).

Throughout the 1960s, there was also a strong interest in guerrilla street theatre among left wing students in the United States. Students at many university campuses formed their own "radical arts troupes" under the umbrella of the nation-wide Students for a Democratic Society. Their collectively devised plays were propaganda against the Vietnam War and related issues that they identified as class oppression. In 1968, Henry Peters described the collective genesis of a typical RAT play at Princeton. According to Peters, preparation would begin about 48 hours before the event at which the students were to perform. It took one meeting to create a 10-minute scenario from "nothing" (usually from an idea suggested by one of the actors) and a second meeting to rehearse whatever evolved. The play might be changed and enriched at another meeting or rally (91–92).

The Pageant Players, an innovative street theatre active in New York parks and other public places between 1965 and 1970, frequently performed and conducted workshops at campuses to encourage the student theatre movement. According to Michael Brown, spokesman for the Pageant Players, they worked on the principle that art and politics can enrich each other. Their approach was indebted to The Open Theatre and The Living Theatre for movement exercises as the source of images and plots, and to the San Francisco Mime Troupe for its audience-directed energies (147).

Henry Lesnick identifies two basic principles as governing the American kind of guerrilla street theatre: attempts to "bridge the gulf between players and audience" and efforts "to provide a new model for the relationship between society and social reality" (13). Gradually, the idea of an open and informal relationship to the spectator became firmly imprinted on popular theatre practice, due in large part to the wide-ranging experiments in collective creation of these years.

2. Canada

There are obvious links, both direct and indirect, between the alternative theatre movements outlined above and those that have emerged in Canada. The Canadian terms of protest against conventional theatre institutions were coloured, however, by the peculiarities of Canadian post-colonial circumstances and of geography. After 1967, with a new emphasis on indigenous Canadian culture inspired by the centennial celebrations, cultural politics became an issue in the theatre.

To the casual observer in the early 1970s, the recently established institution of professional Canadian theatre seemed to be thriving. Ever since the creation of the Canada Council in 1957, the founding of new civic theatres in major cities across the country—from Halifax to Vancouver—was an ongoing enterprise. Yet even by the late 1960s, a certain disillusionment was setting in, especially among younger and untried Canadian performers and writers. Why this should be so is not hard to determine. Little beyond the fundraising was explicitly Canadian in these theatres. The "regionals," a collective designation applied scathingly by the young, were conservative and formulaic in their annual subscription programming: one or two classics, a Shakespearean play, and some contemporary successes from Broadway or the West End. As with the Shaw and Stratford festivals, artistic directors were normally sought from elsewhere, as were major performers.

On rare occasions, a new Canadian play might find a slot on a regional second stage. Yet the idea that a regional theatre might reflect a regional culture was decidedly a minor matter. Two notable exceptions were the Manitoba Theatre Centre (MTC), under the direction of its co-founder John Hirsch, and the Globe Theatre in Regina, co-founded and directed by Ken and Sue Kramer. In 1958, the MTC grew out of a union of the long-established Winnipeg Little Theatre (WLT) with Theatre 77, a small new professional company of one season. Hirsch and Tom Hendry, co-founders of the latter, were both Winnipeggers who had served their theatrical apprenticeships with the WLT. Hirsch, the MTC's first artistic director, recalled "the excitement that can come from a theatre that grows out of a community." Although it was dependent on outside professionals in those early years, the MTC tried from the outset to work with the particular interests of its community and region in mind.

For example, the [MTC] generated new plays, founded and sent on tour its own theatre school, and maintained in its programming—in Hirsch's words—"an organic connection between the audience and what went on stage."[5] By the beginning of the 1970s, however, all this was fading under the pressures of a lack of funding and the need to fill a large new theatre. In Regina in the meantime, the Kramers—who had founded a young people's theatre in 1966 for touring schools in their region—initiated an adult season in 1971 with that "organic connection" very much in mind for their choice of new and established plays. To develop new plays of local interest, they appointed Rex Deverell in 1976 as Canada's first permanent playwright-in-residence.

However, the general direction of theatrical development initiated by the Canada Council was based on the concept of a homogeneous national theatre, not on regional identities. Geography was merely an inconvenience to be overcome. The Council's *Annual Report* in 1961–62 stated: "The essential of a *national* theatre, as we see it, is that it should reach a *national* audience – even if this audience must, for convenience, be broken down into regional audiences…" (emphasis in original). With unconscious centralist irony, the report also speculated that "in a decade or so, a fairly close working relationship might develop among them (the civic theatres outside Ontario and Québec) and with Toronto and Montreal" (qtd. in Czarnecki 35–36). In theatre parlance, the "regions" in relation to these two cities were already beginning to sound like the British "provinces" in relation to London.

One reason for the rise of alternative theatres in Canada during the 1970s was that regional theatres too often refused to be genuinely regional or, for that matter, national (in the culturally indigenous sense of the term). Cultural colonialism, long a Canadian affliction in relation to both Britain and the United States, was being duplicated within the country itself. Yet paradoxically, the parallel between these Canadian circumstances and those in Britain outside London is instructive. The need, identified by John Elsom, to establish a new theatre's local identity became a concern of Canadian alternative theatres. Yet, it was largely ignored by the Canadian regionals. In its exception to this pattern, the Globe Theatre was the one regional theatre to learn from the changing scene in the British provinces. The Kramers had observed and admired Cheeseman's work at Stoke-on-Trent. For their own collective plays about local subjects, they emulated his insistence on documentary accuracy (see Deverell 176). (As we will see later in the text, Paul Thompson rejected this principle at Theatre Passe Muraille).

In the 1960s—as already outlined—the term "alternative theatre" usually alluded to radical theatrical trends of the counter-culture, notably in the United States. In Canada, as a protest against conservative cultural dependence in the theatre, alternative theatre became associated with nationalism, Canadian content and experiment. Nevertheless, counter-culture elements hastened the formation of several alternative companies and for a time influenced their productions. At Theatre Passe Muraille, for example, the early improvisational workshops of founder Jim Garrard and his choice of contemporary American plays reflected the new ensemble techniques popular in the United States. Vancouver's Tamahnous Theatre, as Renate Usmiani notes, modelled its adaptation of *The Bacchae* in 1971 on The Performance Group's *Dionysus in 69*. In 1975, Tamahnous developed techniques of ritual and incantation for its collective creation on a native Indian theme, *The Shaman's Cure* (Usmiani 69–71). In its second season, 25th Street House Theatre of Saskatoon experimented with theatre-of-cruelty techniques in a production entitled *Sibyl*, directed by Montrealer Alexander Hausvater and based on his adaptation of a novel by Par Lagerkvist.

As already indicated, some alternative theatres in Canada were oriented very specifically to playwright's theatre and the workshopping and premiering of new plays. Yet for many others, collective creation became the solution to a lack of written Canadian material. Of course, there were other good reasons for collective creations. The presence of imported fare and personnel in Canadian theatres reinforced the aversion to the tyranny of the text – a trend initiated by the counter-culture, with its dedication to the creativity of the actor. The challenge of the informal, often improvised, performance space—with its altered relationships between performer and audience—was another important factor. This kind of counter-culture theatre seemed to offer a prescription for the alternative Canadians needed to the establishment institutions that had prevailed for a decade. Alternative theatre provided creative opportunities for new actors, directors and participating writers. It reduced the emphasis on elaborate theatre space with its elitist connotations. Most importantly, it sought direct interaction with a Canadian version of an alternative audience – Thompson's "the really interesting people ... who don't go to theatres."

That this was a regional—or often a purely local—enterprise (with all that this implies about content) was its greatest virtue. It didn't happen only in Toronto or Montreal – although, understandably, these densely populated cities were often in the forefront of change. Rather, alternative theatre became a Canada-wide phenomenon from which the country has, fortunately, never entirely recovered. Sometimes, anomalously, alternative theatres were simply protests against the absence of professional theatre in their areas. The Mummers Troupe of St. John's [and] 25th Street House Theatre are good examples of such protests. At the same time, these two theatres also represent examples of alternative artistic commitment – the one committed to political collective creation, the other to an experimental artists' co-operative in which theatre was initially one component. With the founding of the Mulgrave Road Co-Op in 1977 in the small Nova Scotia community of Mulgrave, the "alternative" designation began to lose its identifying connotations of counter-culture radicalism. In this company—as in the later developments of Edmonton's Theatre Network—the principle of community-related theatre, often through collective creation, was justified in its own right.

George Luscombe, founder of Toronto Workshop Productions (TWP) in 1959, was one important forerunner to the Canadian movement of change. For nearly 30 years, he directed the theatre in a manner that continually challenged complacency in the profession and in the audience. In the early 1950s, he had performed with Joan Littlewood's Theatre Workshop at Stratford East. He returned to Canada, greatly interested in her type of highly disciplined group theatre, with its particular social and political objectives of the working class. Thoroughly trained in the movement techniques of Littlewood and Laban, he used these to develop collaborative methods for making improvisational plays, initially as a basis for training an ensemble of actors. He also applied these methods to the interpretation of established plays—often from Europe's avant-garde repertory—and to the adaptation of prose texts. Luscombe customarily maintained strong directorial control over performance techniques and the new plays evolving from them. While the actors were encouraged to "build characterization," a dramaturge was responsible for writing the dialogue (TWP).

In contrast to Luscombe's approach, the most influential type of collective play-making in Canada during the 1970s was free-form improvisation by the actors – as initiated by Paul Thompson at Theatre Passe Muraille in *Notes from Quebec* (1970). Another contrast was the choice of subject matter. Until *Ten Lost Years* (premiered 7 February 1974), Luscombe's adaptations rarely focussed on specifically Canadian material. Thus, at an early stage of a nationalistic impulse in theatre, Toronto Workshop Productions was not considered to be an explicit model for the development of new work (Filewod 51). Yet, Luscombe led the way in introducing the idea of an alternative theatre in Toronto. His highly disciplined Littlewood methods of training and production were a revelation in the physical use of the actor and the stage. However, his main influence in Canadian theatre was through the actors who trained in his company. He certainly exercised less influence on the new generation of independent-minded collective creators. Many of the latter, such as Paul Thompson, were characterized by the accessibility of their methods to both experienced and inexperienced performers as well as to the writer.

Thompson joined Theatre Passe Muraille as a stage manager in late 1969, then served as artistic director until 1981. At his own choice, he continued with the theatre as an assistant director until he was appointed director-general at the National Theatre School in 1987. His achievement in developing collective creation at Theatre Passe Muraille is distinguished by its variety of experimentation, "putting Canadian voices and people on stage" (Wallace 57). Although based at Theatre Passe Muraille in Toronto through the 1970s, where he drew on a core of local actors who developed strong improvisational skills under his guidance, he also moved about the country. On tour, he presented successful productions (*The Farm Show*, summer 1974) and created new shows while encouraging new theatre companies to create their own collective enterprises. Touring also gave him an opportunity to find new talent for his own collective creations.

During this formative period in the growth of new Canadian theatre, Thompson was a key link in a casual network of like-minded theatre groups developing in several parts of the country: the Mummers Troupe, 25th Street Theatre, Theatre Network and The Mulgrave Road Co-Op. This personal contact was reinforced by Theatre Passe Muraille's seed show programme, by which small amounts of money were given to groups with their own ideas for collective creations. People from elsewhere working in Toronto, like Paul Kelman and *The Edmonton Show* (1975), were included. In addition, seed shows might travel – such as Clarke Rogers' *Almighty Voice*, which toured the prairies in late 1974 and early 1975.

In the fall of 1974, the national tour of *Ten Lost Years* by Toronto Workshop Productions—adapted from Barry Broadfoot's transcribed interviews of victims of the Great Depression—made a powerful impact wherever it went (see Kerr). This production helped to stimulate audience interest in populist theatre performed in a presentational style. Yet Luscombe's ensemble methods did not operate through practical outreach. On the other hand, Thompson followed up the successful tours of *The Farm Show* and *Almighty Voice* through the prairies by going to Saskatoon with a company of Passe Muraille actors in the summer of 1975. There, he not only created *The West Show* but also introduced the struggling 25th Street Theatre to collective creation by directing it in *If You're So Good, Why Are You in Saskatoon?* This production eventually led to the theatre's own creation of *Paper Wheat* in 1977. It toured nationally and became the best known collective creation from the prairies. That same year, Thompson and Theatre Passe Muraille worked with writer Rudy Wiebe to develop *Far As the Eye Can See* for its premiere at Edmonton's Theatre 3.

Another kind of outreach closer to home was the creation of Theatre Passe Muraille's own regional audience in southwestern Ontario, although it was never organized on a long-range basis. Beginning with *The Farm Show* in Clinton in 1972, the company often toured through the towns and cities of Huron and Middlesex counties and sometimes beyond with plays created for those audiences as much as for audiences in Toronto. During a tour of *1837: The Farmers' Revolt*, Thompson spotted the potential of the old Memorial Hall in Blyth, Ontario. That building became the home of the Blyth Festival, renowned for its development of new Canadian plays, some of which took shape as collective creations.

(1992)

Notes

1   See Innes 60–61.

2   Full studies of these theatres and their work may be found in Sainer; Shank, *American Alternative Theatre*; Bigsby. My account draws on these sources for the American experimental theatre except where otherwise indicated.

3   For succinct commentary on the theories of Artaud see Croyden 55–71.

4   For an informal account of Café La Mama see Stewart.

5   This account of regional theatre relies on my essay "The Regionalism of Canadian Drama."

Works Cited

Ansorge, Peter. *Disrupting the Spectacle: Five Years of Experimental and Fringe Theatre in Britain.* London: Pitman, 1975.

Arent, Arthur. "The Techniques of the Living Newspaper." *Theatre Quarterly* 1.4 (1971): 57–59.

Bessai, Diane. "The Regionalism of Canadian Drama." *Canadian Literature* 85 (1980): 7–19.

Bigsby, C.W. *A Critical Introduction to Twentieth-Century American Drama.* Vol. 3. Cambridge: Cambridge UP, 1985.

Cheeseman, Peter. "Introduction." *The Knotty.* London: Methuen, 1970. vi–xx.

Croyden, Margaret. *Lunatics, Lovers and Poets: The Contemporary Experimental Theatre.* New York: Delta, 1974.

Czarnecki, Mark. "The Regional Theatre System." *Contemporary Canadian Theatre: New World Visions.* Ed, Anton Wagner. Toronto: Simon & Pierre, 1985. 35–48.

Deverell, Rex. "Medicare! as a One-Man Collective." *Showing West: Three Prairie Docu-Dramas.* Ed. Diane Bessai and Don Kerr. Edmonton: NeWest, 1982. 175–80.

Elsom, John. *Post-War British Theatre.* London: Routledge, 1976.

Filewod, Alan. *Collective Encounters: Documentary Theatre in English Canada.* Toronto: U of Toronto P, 1987.

Goomey, Howard. *The Theatre Workshop Story.* London: Methuen, 1981.

Hirsch, John. "Healthy Disengagement." *Canadian Theatre Review* 4 (1974): 26–31.

Hunt, Albert. *Hopes for Great Happenings: Alternatives in Education and Theatre.* London: Methuen, 1976.

———. "Introduction." *John Ford's Cuban Missile Crisis.* London: Methuen, 1972.

Innes, C.D. *Erwin Piscator's Political Theatre.* Cambridge: Cambridge UP, 1972.

Itsin, Catherine. *Stages in the Revolution: Political Theatre in Britain Since 1968.* London: Methuen, 1980.

Kerr, Don. "Three Plays." *next year country* 2.5 (1975): 42–43.

Lesnick, Henry, ed. *Guerilla Street Theater.* New York: Avon, 1973.

Little, Stuart W. *Off-Broadway: The Prophetic Theatre.* New York: Coward, 1972.

Ritchie, Rob, ed. *The Joint Stock Book: The Making of a Theatre Collective.* London; Methuen, 1987.

Sainer, Arthur. *The Radical Theatre Notebook.* New York: Avon. 1975.

Shank, Theodore. *American Alternative Theatre.* London: Macmillan Modern Dramatists, 1982.

——. "Collective Creation." *The Drama Review* 16.2 (1972): 3–31.

Stewart, Ellen. "La Mama Celebrates 20 Years." *PAJ* 6.2 (1982): 7–28.

TWP. "Workshop's Technique: Building a Play." Toronto Workshop Productions release, 1967.

Usmiani, Renate. *Second Stage: The Alternative Theatre Movement in Canada.* Vancouver: U of British Columbia P, 1983.

Wallace, Bob. "Paul Thompson at Theatre Passe Muraille: Bits and Pieces." *Open Letter.* 2nd ser. 7 (1974): 49–71.

Willett, John, ed. *Brecht on Theatre.* New York: Hill and Wang, 1964.

Dilating the Body,
Transporting the Mind:
Considering Primus Theatre

by Per Brask

> What is required to shape a theatrically appropriate performance?
> First of all, it needs a presentation, an acting achievement which makes the spectator at all times feel the mastery of the actor. When a talent shows [his/her] mastery, when the solutions to stage tasks are in the hands of a true master, then it will work theatrically. (Vakhtangov 355)[1]

Alkoremmi

Audience members are led into the hall where Primus Theatre presents its show, *A Last Circus (wide and tall) a Command Performance (within the wall) of Alkoremmi*. They are led, in separate groups of five or six, by a woman dressed in a short white dress and boots. She is carrying a parasol with a lit candle poised at its top. This vision of a highwire dancer, or of the goddess Diana, lights our path with a flashlight through the darkened room and seats us, in bleachers or on the floor, in a space rectangularly surrounded by ladders connected, in twos, by wooden planks at the very top. The room seems damp and smoke rises from candles atop the ladders. A chanting woman, completely concealed in red cloth, a veil over her face, extinguishes the candles with a snuffer tied to the end of a long stick. A musty, dense smell of devotion perfumes the air. In the centre of the space a huge bolt of black cloth lies folded into the shape of a butterfly.

When every one of the approximately 70-member, capacity, audience is seated, we are called to attention, invited into this strange circus, by performers whispering into huge copper megaphones, their voices seemingly hovering right in front of our ears. An angel is called down from up high, nimbus glowing around his face. Suddenly, the large butterfly gives "birth" to a giant who, after an exhausting dance, herself gives birth to a person emerging from under her skirt, struggling to break out of his membrane.

A little person, that staple of the circus and carnival world, exerts considerable energy as he climbs a ladder, slowly, step by arduous step. He stops, stares at us, smirks and says, "You know what? Up above your heads there's a place in heaven, a sort of waiting room, where all the souls wait in line to drop like coins into the bodies of the newly born. You know what else? The last soul in line is already frightened, because when he is born, all the storytellers will be dead, and that's when the end of the world will come."

The giant serves as a kind of maypole by holding a long stick above her head, a ribbon hanging from each end, as two women dance around her chanting a Sami *joik*, evoking both the return of the spirit in the Nordic celebrations of spring and the legend of the Sami prince and his courtship in the land of the giants.

The performances are executed with a high degree of physical skill and precision. Everything here is carefully worked out; no movement, no sound is accidental. The performers carry themselves with a degree of deliberateness and artfulness more akin to what one might associate with dance rather than with the dramatic theatre. In fact, there are even, at times, hints of performance qualities one might expect to find in traditional Asian performance styles. But these are only hints; the show is thoroughly modern, avant-garde and Western in its sensibilities. A circus atmosphere is generated by the performers' acrobatic skillfulness, a rapid succession of "numbers," both solo and group, the noise and the spectacular surprises such as when the giant, on stilts, suddenly appears and when she dances, to the accompaniment of loud drum beats, around the performance space kicking her "legs" towards the audience.

The show, *Alkoremmi*, flashes of which are described above, was produced by the Primus Theatre in 1991 and it has toured since.

In his book, *Skuespillerens Vandring*, on the work of four members of the Odin theatre, the Danish scholar Erik Exe Christoffersen likens the experience of watching this kind of theatre to the passage in Italo Calvino's novel, *Invisible Cities*, where he describes the manner in which Marco Polo, unfamiliar with the Leavantine languages, communicates with Kublai Khan:

> Returning from the missions on which Kublai had sent him, the ingenious foreigner improvised pantomimes that the sovereign had to interpret: one city was depicted by the leap of a fish escaping the cormorant's beak to fall into a net; another city by a naked man running through fire unscorched; a third by a skull, its teeth green with mould, clenching a round white pearl. The Great Khan deciphered the signs, but the connection between them and the places visited remained uncertain; he never knew whether Marco wished to enact an adventure, an exploit of the city's founder, the prophecy of an astrologer, a rebus or a charade to indicate a name. But obscure or obvious as it might be, everything Marco displayed had the power of emblems, which, once seen, cannot be forgotten or confused. (20–21).

On one level, the level of narration, *Alkoremmi* tells the story of a child being born with the last available soul. After his birth all children will be born without a soul. The events of the show tell the story of this child's encounters in the last days of the world. On a more important level, however, the show is not about this story. Instead, it provides an experience which lies beyond the normal equations necessary for identification; the story is merely the instrument which keeps us in the flow of time.

These two levels are ever-present in the show, creating a tension between the despair of an impending soulless world and the rowdy, noisy, circus-like events evoked by the performers' skillful turns, a skillfulness so forceful it rouses hope. Poised in this balance between despair and hope one is reminded of Theodor Adorno's statement that,

> The only philosophy which can be reasonably practised in the face of despair is the attempt to contemplate all things as they would present themselves from the standpoint of redemption. Knowledge has no light but that shed on the world by redemption; all else is reconstruction, mere technique. Perspectives must be fashioned that displace and estrange the world, reveal it to be, with its rifts and crevices, as indigent and distorted as it will appear one day in the messianic light. (247)

Training and Dramaturgy

In 1989, Winnipeg, Canada became the home of Primus Theatre. By then Primus had already germinated for a couple of years.

It all began in 1986 when Nick Hutchinson, then the Head of the English Acting Section of the National Theatre School of Canada in Montreal, invited Richard Fowler, who had been working with Eugenio Barba's Odin Theatre in Denmark since 1980, to conduct a workshop with the school's second-year class. The kind of theatrical practice Fowler introduced these students to was based on his research with the Odin Theatre.

Since the mid-1960s Eugenio Barba, a student of Grotowski's, and his company have concentrated their work on the investigation of the art of the actor and, since 1980 with the establishment of the International School of Theatre Anthropology (ISTA), this research has focused on a transcultural study of the preconditions for the construction of actorly presence: i.e., the analysis of how a performer becomes present in front of an audience before any meaning is communicated or expressed, termed, by Barba, the pre-expressive level. This level, however, does not exist as a materially independent activity, but seems more akin to an archetype. Says Barba,

> Obviously, the pre-expressive does not exist in and of itself. Similarly, the nervous system, for example, cannot be materially separated from the entirety of a living organism, but it can be *thought* of as a separate entity. This cognitive fiction makes effective interventions possible. It is an abstraction, but is extremely useful for work on the practical level. (*Paper Canoe* 136)

Barba's interrogation of pre-expressivity has been conducted by examining training techniques and performance styles all over the world and across many cultures both through studies in the field—the Odin Theatre tours widely—as well as by bringing performers from diverse backgrounds together in seminars and labs. Since the beginning of ISTA, Richard Fowler has assisted Eugenio Barba in his work. Much of the focus of this work has concerned the manner in which a performer is able physically, bodily, to mould and shape energy and hence become present in a way that attracts the spectator's attention. Says Barba, "Energy is commonly reduced to imperious and violent behaviour models. But it is actually a personal temperature-intensity which the performer can determine, awaken, mould. But which above all needs to be explored" (Barba and Savarese 81).

Thus, when the students at Canada's foremost theatre school began working with Fowler they first had to become used to not having to express or interpret something. There was no script nor characters to be interpreted; the task rather was to generate a physical score. Some of the students in this class eventually formed the nucleus of what was to become Primus Theatre.

A show like *Alkoremmi* may be said to be the result of a particular process, a distinct way of viewing the theatrical event and, ultimately, a way of life. It is this confluence of procedures which is the topic of this essay.

In addition to its director, Richard Fowler, Primus Theatre consists of five actors: Donald Kitt, Tannis Kowalchuck, Stephen Lawson, Karin Randoja and Ker Wells. One of the central foci in the life of this group is the daily training, which is conducted both individually and as a group. Each member of the group explores her/his physical and expressive potential through a variety of exercises. Says Fowler, "The base of this physical work is the concept of action, of 'act-ing' in the literal sense of the word, rather than in the sense of representing or portraying, and the releasing, modelling and forming of energy in space."

Much of the physical training consists in the exploration of parts of the body: the head, neck, shoulders, anus, hands, chest, hips and legs; balance, breathing and the modulation of energy. These exercises are not conducted only as an investigation into how parts of the body may move. More importantly, individual actors explore how a specific part of the body may become engaged, how energy may be utilized in such a way that it assists the actor in becoming present in the theatrical sense of the term, that is, able to attract the attention of the spectator. Training, however, does not lead to the discovery of a "trick" which from then on can be successfully repeated. Says Barba, "Our training does not teach us how to be an actor—how to play a role in the Commedia dell'Arte—or how to interpret a tragic or grotesque part. It doesn't give a sense of being able to do something. Training is an encounter with the reality which one has chosen" (qtd. in Christoffersen, *In Cammino*). In the process of training the actors not only gain imaginative control over their bodies, making their bodies responsive to any impulse and making their minds responsive; they also develop sequences of action which may be used later in rehearsals for the building of a physical score for the character.

In this daily work, the voice, too, comes under scrutiny as a physical element of the actor's total body. The investigation of various resonators, whispers and singing is a frequent part of the training. Apart from the individual training the daily sessions also involve improvisational exercises with other members. In this way the group forms a strong sense of individual commitment to a particular aesthetic as well as a sense of this group as a cultural entity, a social cell, committed to working together. Said Eugenio Barba in a brief to the participants of the Encounter on Third Theatre in Belgrade, 1976, "[T]he theatre is a means to find their own way of being present— which the critics would call new expressive forms—to seek more than human relationships between men, with the purpose of creating a social cell inside which intentions, aspirations and personal needs begin to be transformed into actions" (*Beyond* 194).

Though a lot of the training for the actors is individual and independent, it is still guided by Fowler. The five actors of Primus are in many ways studying with a master. Looking for a master was what led Fowler himself to seek out Eugenio Barba's Odin Theatre in 1980.

> One of the reasons I chose to work there was that I too had been looking for a master, someone who was an expert, who could help me develop in ways I couldn't foresee. You can want to develop yourself. You can want to change your way of doing things. You can want to realize your sensed potential. But this can be very hard if you have no models, no teacher. I wanted to work with such a person, a master teacher and a director. (Fowler)

In this way a performance tradition is perpetuated along a line which goes from Grotowski to Barba to Fowler to members of Primus and so on. As the performance knowledge of this tradition moves through time, it is modified, and expanded, according to the needs of the particular artists who "inherit" it. [2]

The aim of the training is to develop an extra-daily technique, a technique which alters the actor's daily, enculturated behaviour based on functionality and conservation of energy and allows for an acculturated, fictive and chosen behaviour based on a maximum of energy. This is based on the idea that the theatrical event is not a representation of daily life, but a particular and special situation leading to an out-of-the-ordinary perceptual and emotional experience. This technique expands and dilates the actor's body, making it engaged. Says Barba, "The performer's extra-daily technique, that is, presence, derives from an alteration of balance and basic posture, from the play of opposing tensions which dilate the body's dynamics. The body is re-built for the scenic fiction" (Barba and Savarese 81). In this way a body ready for the generation of a theatrical event is constructed.

The event itself—the kind of event described in my opening, an event in which presence is everything—is the result of the creation of a performance text, that is a score of actions pertaining to an entire show. A performance text is not a written text, though writing may be part of it. A performance text is, says Richard Schechner,

"… all that happens during a performance both on stage and off, including audience participation" (22). The performance text for a work like *Alkoremmi* is not derived from an approach to a written text; the rehearsals are not focused on the interpretation of a play or on ferreting out implicit actions inscribed in one. Rather, the rehearsal process consists in the "weaving together" (Barba and Savarese 68) of sequences of action generated by the actors and put together in a montage by the director. The rehearsal process, thus, does not set out to *express* an idea or a meaning, it sets out to generate an experience which will generate meaning, though not necessarily the same one for all audience members. The performance text is therefore purposefully multivalent. In reference to Barba's work, Ian Watson has described this multivalence as a result of a dramaturgy which is open as opposed to closed. Says Watson,

> The open nature of Barba's dramaturgy, combined with the dialectic between the actors' and the director's understanding of a production's meaning[,] allows spectators a wide scope in choosing their reading of the work. These readings may vary greatly because of Barba's limited use of closed signification, and his emphasis on the synthetic level of communication. But this rejection of a closed meaning structure should not be mistaken for disregarding the audience. Barba, in fact … demands more from his audience than mere passivity. He maintains that viewing a performance is action: it is work … Barba has been accused of making theatre that is difficult to understand, but he is not interested in productions that require no effort on the part of the spectators. The audience, just like the actors, must be active during a performance, even if the action is entirely mental. (99)

The clarity sought in rehearsal is, thus, not that which will exact the communication of a distilled idea or notion. The clarity sought here concerns the precision with which a single action or sequence of actions is performed and the precision with which the actions are woven together and executed, to create a multi-layered, non-linear mosaic of meanings. Says Fowler,

> The form of preparation we do is based on the development of a psychophysical score, on which the actor's performance is built. Rather than finding a way for the actor to become a character, our technique is used by the actor, through the application of certain physical principles, to find a way to create another version of him/herself. A version which is both daily, non-daily and specifically chosen, formed, codified, through the actor's research and training. He or she then performs not the result of his or her psychological interpretation of a character, but another version of him/herself given form through a physical and vocal score. The final performance is then like a piece of music played by an orchestra, each of the musicians (actors) playing a score which when combined becomes the full performance. This full performance is not only composed of the actors' actions. There are many other elements—

the sounds they make, the songs they sing, the music they make, the way the lights are used, the scenic architecture constructed for the event, the use of props – and combinations and interactions of all these elements. The meanings, associations, and denotations perceived by the audience are arrived at by the dramaturgical relationship of these elements, of which the text is only one. Hence the text is not the primary conveyor of the performance's meaning and the actor no longer has the onus for the transmission of meaning to the spectator. The actor is no longer told to express a given meaning for the audience ... The spectator "reads" the performance on the basis of all the signs that make up the performance score. (qtd. in Brask 87)

The dramaturgy of a piece like *Alkoremmi* is "woven" (Barba and Savarese 158) [3] by running the threads of its actions in two different directions. One set of threads produce the linkage of events through the time of the piece, establishing a montage of action sequences, connecting one sequence to the next. In *Alkoremmi*, this thread is provided by the story of the child born with the last soul. The other set of threads jumps in and among the first set, producing simultaneity of many events, setting them in a synchronic montage, allowing images and events to fly like sparks from one side of the stage to the other, leaping like electrons defying fixity. The resulting opacity, in the sense that all images and figures ultimately resist transparent transcription into language, heightens the audience's experience of an experience. As Jean-François Lyotard reminds us, "By virtue of the fact that it sets up a closed circuit intercom system of the work itself, the figure surprises the eye and the ear and the mind by a perfectly improper arrangement of the parts" (30).

Like the actor dilating her/his body through extra-daily behaviour, the surprises generated by this dramaturgy provide the spectator with a sense of a dilated mind, a transporting experience, in which the experience of the non-daily becomes more important than the narrowing of specific meaning. In addition, says Barba,

> Making it possible for the spectator to decipher a story does not mean making him/her discover its "true meaning" but creating the conditions within which s/he can *ask her/himself* about its meaning. It is a question of exposing the knots of the story, those points at which extremes embrace. There are spectators for whom the theatre is essential precisely because it does not present them with solutions, but knots. (*Paper Canoe* 122–23)

Creation of the Performance Text

The sequences of action which spin the threads of the performance text are in the first instance generated by the actors' individual research and training.

Ker Wells's warrior character, Gall, appears in the show barechested, wearing a head piece made from a black horsetail, manipulating two sticks, each with a lock of hair attached to the end, and issuing loud shrieks. His presence is commanding, threatening, his dancing confident of victory. Wells's research into this character began with his interest in juggling which he had incorporated into his daily training. Says Wells of this early work,

> My objective was simple, I wanted objects that were not immediately identifiable as juggling clubs, and only useful for that purpose; I wanted objects that could "become" something else, both for me, and in the eye of an observer. In addition, I wanted something that would "hit back," that would demand my physical engagement and attention. In this respect these sticks were ideal; oak is a dense, hard, heavy wood, if I dropped a stick on my foot, or allowed it to rap my knuckles, it hurt, thus they demanded my respect. (1)

As he improvised with these sticks a character began to emerge for whom he evolved a score of physical behaviour. At the same time he would read about various extinct cultures, such as the Aztec, the Beothuk and the Yahi, and their mythologies, and look for visual stimulation in a wide variety of sources which might help build his character. During this search he came across a picture of a Japanese mythological character with long black hair. At this point he obtained the horsehair and materials necessary for constructing a head piece. The character was named Gall, after a plains Indian warrior. Through further improvisations and visual stimulation Gall's physical score became increasingly precise.

When constructing the character of the child to be born with the last soul, Wells began his work by responding to the visual stimulation found in photographs of embryonic development and out of this he created a behavioral score, beginning with the birth as the child breaks out of his enveloping membrane, through learning to walk, etc.

Each of the characters encountered in *Alkoremmi* was created by painstakingly building movement upon movement, sound upon sound. Stephen Lawson's research into angel and carnival/cabaret styles, and ways of generating the image of a nimbus, grew into characters like the Master of Ceremonies and the little person. Donald Kitt's training with stilts and his studies in shamanism evolved into the giant. Karin Randoja's investigation into the images of women in mourning in a variety of cultures produced the veiled red lady and the sensual, "wild," black lady. Tannis Kowalchuk's readings in alchemy and the hermaphrodite transformed into the woman dressed in white carrying the parasol with the lit candle atop. The process of character creation leaps in stages into existence as the actors integrate impulses and various kinds of material into their work. Says Barba, "Creative thought is actually distinguished by the fact that it proceeds by leaps, by means of an unexpected disorientation which obliges it to reorganize itself in new ways, abandoning its well-ordered shell. It is the thought-in-life, not rectilinear, not univocal (*Paper Canoe* 58).

Through the whole process the actors were guided in their search by Richard Fowler who would present them with specific challenges and tasks to be executed. All the characters were thus well under way before rehearsals began. For the twelve weeks of actual rehearsal, the company was joined by dramaturg Sean Dixon, who is a former member of the company. Dixon would throughout the process observe the actors' work, individually and as a company, and he "begins to find possible stories, connections, scenarios, texts, etc., which he develops in consultation with Richard Fowler" (Primus Theatre 2).

Using the behavioral sequences created by the actors like strips of film, Fowler slowly constructed the montage which eventually became the show *Alkoremmi*.[4] In a montage, the strips of the action which are put together and juxtaposed may not be used in a context similar to the one that generated them. In a new context they take on different meanings but their physical execution, the score, remains the same. A performance text comes into being. This "text" does not only consist of the physical scores performed in front of the audience. Since the actors control all aspects of the performance, movement behind the "set" must also be choreographed in order to maintain the proper rhythm and precision of the show, the final result generating a wealth of visual and auditory impressions for the audience. Says Fowler,

> When I go to the theatre I want a primarily kinaesthetic experience, not a primarily intellectual one. I don't go to the theatre to sit and think, activities for which I have other times and places, but to experience, to be taken out of myself, to have my presumptions about life and living surprised and changed, not confirmed and reassured. And when I go to the theatre I want to see magicians not reciters, I want to see actors using their bodies, minds, emotions, energy, in ways which astonish and transport me to other levels of reality and perception. (qtd. in Brask 88)

The Group As Culture

Since 1989, the members of Primus have trained together and rehearsed together; indeed, they have committed themselves to work together, as if forever. The commitment this group of people has to each other is thus different from what is required from the average ensemble company. Since they do not select plays to be interpreted but are dependent upon each other's contributions to a show, in the form of original artistic research leading to theatrical scores, that show can no longer be performed if someone decides to leave the company. The Odin Theatre in Denmark has existed since the mid-1960s and though there has been some change in the personnel, the nucleus of that company remains intact. Primus, too, has had some change of personnel, but the essential commitment to the integrity of the group remains unmarred. Despite the paucity of available funding and the extensive periods of creation Primus requires to produce a show, its members train daily, exploring extra-daily techniques, generating scores of action. This exacting daily mental and physical regimen, in fact, creates the group as a specific culture, a culture not only in the sense of a group of people pursuing and making manifest a set of goals, priorities. Indeed, the members of this group alter their bodies in the process of becoming Primus.

During the explorations of pre-expressive shaping of energy their bodies become sharply responsive to impulses, producing themselves as flexible theatrical instruments. The life of the group is thus both mental and physical. And since all material performed is generated by the group—whether it be based on their individual lives or on their reactions to other people, other cultures—they create a relationship with their spectators which in the first instance is not about the delivery of a message, or about communicating an idea. It is rather about sharing the results of their investigations by creating an experience, about transporting the spectator's mind to the world of the extra-daily: i.e., their shows are a way for this group to be together with their spectators.

In daily training too, the individual commitment is reaffirmed. Says Barba, "Whatever you do, do it with your whole self. It sounds like—and is—a facile and rhetorical phrase. Anybody can say it. But we have only one responsibility: To live it, to carry it out in our daily acts. And the training reminds us of this" (qtd. in Christoffersen, *In Cammino*). For the members of Primus Theatre, the enactment of their whole selves is not a mere phrase; it becomes a living theatre.

(1994)

Notes

While preparing this article I have benefited greatly from discussions with colleagues at the University of Winnipeg, Professors Bill Morgan and Neil Besner of the departments of Anthropology and English, respectively, and with Richard Fowler, Artistic Director of Primus Theatre, and Patrick Friesen, the poet.

[1] Translated by the author.

[2] Indeed, one might construct a genealogy of ideas which proceeds from Diderot's discussions of the actor's paradox, mutating through Copeau's investigations at the *Vieux Colombier*, the Stanislavski of physical action, Vakhtangov's "Fantastical Realism" (melding elements from Meyerhold, Tairov and Slanislavski), and Michael Chekov's "Psychological Gesture," and Brecht's social *Gestus*, to Grotowski's "Holy actor" and Barba's transcultural actorly presence.

[3] "To compose (to put with) also means to mount, to put together, to weave actions together...."

[4] "Restored behaviour is living behaviour treated as a film director treats a strip of film" (Schechner 35).

Works Cited

Adorno, Theodor. *Minima Moralia*. London: Verso, 1974.

Barba, Eugenio. *Beyond the Floating Islands*. New York: PAJ, 1986.

———. *The Paper Canoe: A Treatise on Theatre Anthropology*. Trans. Richard Fowler. In manuscript. To be published in 1994. [Ed.: published as *The Paper Canoe: A Guide to Theatre Anthropology*. Abingdon, Oxon: Routledge, 1995.]

——— and Nicola Savarese. *A Dictionary of Theatre Anthropology: The Secret Art of the Performer*. Trans. Richard Fowler. London: Routledge, 1991.

Brask, Per. "The Anthropology of Performance: An Interview with Richard Fowler." *Canadian Theatre Review* 71 (1992). 81–88.

Calvino, Italo. *Invisible Cities*. HBJ: London, 1979.

Christoffersen, Erik Exe. *In Cammino Attraverso il Teatro* (On the Way Though the Theatre). Video. Aarhus, Denmark: Institut for Dramaturgi, University of Aarhus. 1992.

———. *Skuespillerens Vandring*. Aarhus, Denmark: Klim, 1989. 8. (English edition: *The Actor's Way*. Trans. Richard Fowler. London: Routledge, 1993.)

Fowler, Richard. Personal letter to the author. 10 September 1991.

Lyotard, Jean-Francois. "The Dream-Work Does Not Think." *The Lyotard Reader*. Ed. Andrew Benjamin. Oxford: Blackwell, 1989. 19–55.

Primus Theatre. "Final Report on Development and Performance of 'Alkoremmi.'" Reports to Canada Council and Manitoba Arts Council. May, 1991.

Schechner, Richard. *Between Theatre and Anthropology*. Philadelphia: U of Pennsylvania P, 1985.

Vakhtangov, Yevgeny. *Meyerhold-Tairow-Wachtangow-Theateroktober*. Leipzig, 1972.

Watson, Ian. *Towards a Third Theatre: Eugenio Barba and Odin Teatret*. London: Routledge, 1993.

Wells, Ker. "Summary of source material for the character 'Gall.'" Independent Theatre Productions Grant application to *Manitoba Arts Council,* August 1990.

Performing Emergency: Witnessing, Popular Theatre and the Lie of the Literal

by Julie Salverson

Since the early 1980s, I have worked as a playwright, theatre animator, and arts educator. Much of my work is in community-based popular theatre, and involves creating theatrical events through acts of storytelling in which some or all of the performers are members of the target communities. Though popular theatre as a named genre has only emerged in Canada during the past fifteen years, it has achieved a large degree of acceptability and wide public interest. Recently I have noticed that, together with the tremendous vitality, engagement, and indisputable learning generated by popular theatre projects, there are nevertheless certain uncomfortable elements that seem to repeat themselves. These include:

> • a similarity in the political analyses generated by the projects that often present a triad of victims, villains and heroes;

> • confusion and hurt feelings expressed by a small but significant number of participants during or after projects, which indicate that telling stories is not always an empowering experience;

> • conflict among popular theatre artists/educators ourselves about the intersecting roles of art and politics, conflicts that too often result in failed communication rather than productive dialogue.

Observing these patterns has led me to question how much I understand of what is involved in the act of listening to and telling "risky stories" (see Simon and Armitage-Simon), by which I mean stories that include and embody acts of violence. In this essay I will discuss difficulties that arose on a project involving refugees in Toronto. The broader context of the article is my concern with what in Canada is an enthusiastic but perhaps not always carefully considered use of personal narratives in classrooms and community organizations. I will address the significance of form and structure to storytelling and to popular theatre's potential for advocacy, healing, or harm, and consider how the power of images may provide "containment" and an environment where difficult histories might be witnessed.

As artists and educators, we must continually ask ourselves: in what context are risky stories being told? Within what frameworks did they originate? And what is the cost to the speaker? Taking responsibility should extend beyond an ongoing inventory of who we are as individuals to an understanding that there are stakes for those with whom we work – stakes that exist, but are never more than partially knowable. Thoughtlessly soliciting autobiography may reproduce a form of cultural colonialism that is at the very least voyeuristic. This is particularly true when the voice of the artist or educator herself goes unexamined, or when the choices students or project participants make for speech are privileged over choices made for silence, neglecting the highly complex negotiations that are involved in the politics of knowing and being known.[1]

In "Beyond Psychoanalysis," Ora Avni describes a character in the Elie Wiesel story "Night." Moshe the Beadle has been taken from his home by the Nazis, survived the murder of his convoy of foreign Jews, and returns to warn the others. But those to whom he returns do not, and more importantly, cannot believe him. Accepting his story would disrupt the very foundations of what they understand to be human. This story illustrates the ancient dilemma of the messenger and the audience. According to Avni, Moshe's return to town is an attempt to reaffirm ties with the human community of his past, whose integrity was put into question by the incomprehensibility of what he had witnessed. Avni is very clear about why it is essential that this messenger speak, not privately to a friend, but publicly to the community network to which he seeks readmission: "Only by having a community integrate his dehumanizing experience into the narratives of self-representation that it shares and infer a new code of behaviour based on the information he is imparting, only by becoming part of this community's history[,] can Moshe hope to reclaim his lost humanity" (212).

The enormity of such a re-imagining of identity implies the cost to both the messenger or storyteller and the listener, something at stake "that defies storytelling, 'lifting to consciousness,' or literalized metaphors" (213). To bring this man and his story into the story line of their history compels the listeners to radically uproot who they understand themselves to be, and, with the question of how they will respond, introduces a fundamental challenge to what they intend to become.

Avni's article speaks to the ways in which personal narratives of crisis are never merely personal:

> Yes, we want to "heal." Society wants to heal; history wants to heal. But no, a simple "life goes on," "tell your story," "come to terms with your pain," or "sort out your ghosts" will not do. It will not do, because the problem lies not in the individual—survivor or not—but in his or her interaction with society, and more precisely, in his or her relationship to the narratives and values by which this community defines and represents itself. (216)

In other words, we need to take seriously what it means to speak and listen to difficult histories. In Avni's explanation of the Wiesel story, the townspeople would rather risk their lives than unpin their cognitive framework; each party must be understood as existing on opposite ends of a transaction where Moshe's need to re-enter the shared narratives of his community conflicts with their need to maintain the integrity of that community (211–15). When I consider this in light of the questions raised earlier about the difficulties of popular theatre, it becomes clear that neither speaking nor listening is easy; it is not surprising that history repeatedly shoots the messenger. An environment in which witnessing is possible takes seriously what Walter Benjamin called the "permanent emergency" in which we live (257).[2] How can educators, artists, or community workers take these issues into consideration?

Popular theatre is a public and distinctly pedagogical enterprise, with its aims historically rooted in the efforts of poor and marginalized people throughout the world to stage and realize alternatives to their current lives. When popular theatre artists and members of a community negotiate how the telling of their stories will occur, both parties are attempting to set up conditions of reception that will urge and allow the participants and the eventual audience to be affected and changed by what they hear. A climate of witnessing thus involves not only listening to someone's story, but allowing our attitudes and behaviors to be changed by it.

During the initial stages of naming assumptions and setting goals on a project, we have the opportunity to ask questions significant to establishing an orientation from which participants and audience members might take what they hear personally. I draw here upon Simon's use of the phrase "to take personally," wherein events that "explicitly function to renew a reconstructed living memory" (12) enable a transformation of the listener's understanding of her or himself not just as an individual but as a member of a community. Questions that establish such an orientation might include:

> • What are the primary narratives understood by our intended audience as their histories (collective, individual, intersecting) and in what way is our project an attempt to insert counter-narratives into those histories?

> • What do we expect from ourselves and our audiences in the way of initial resistant responses, and how can we prepare to engage them in what will perhaps be a conflicted listening?

> • How might the existence of trauma in the listeners relate to and affect the reception of traumatic narratives?

> • How can we provide an environment within which the stories told can be heard by the listeners so as to reconfigure their sense of who they are in relation to the speaker and the event – a reconfiguration that causes them to take up a stance of obligation in relation to this event as they recognize and meet it in the world?

These questions help avoid one of the dangers in the transmission of stories: the lie of the literal. A common concern among popular and community theatre workers is to be faithful to the integrity of the storyteller – not to interfere with her words, to make her the final arbiter of what gets shown or said. This idealization of "authenticity" often happens at the expense of aesthetics or theatrical form, which may be considered as distortions, or as impositions of the artist's "high" culture. Yet this overemphasis upon a single, authentic story does not allow for sufficient complexity, nuance, and multiple points of entry. Such a story may remain either outside the experience of the listener, as the exotic and impenetrable but vicariously viewed "other," or it will be collapsed and assimilated by the listener as "just like me."

I am proposing an alternative approach to popular theatre practices (particularly in respect to how such practices employ and represent personal narratives) that speaks of "story" not as a fixed, knowable, finite thing, but as an open one that changes and carries with it the possibility of reformings and retellings. "Risky stories," stories of emergency and violation, need to be constructed in such a way that the subtleties of damage, hope, and the "not nameable" can be performed.[3] I am not suggesting a theatre that privileges the aesthetic over the material, the "look" of a theatre piece or story over the urgency of its conveyed meaning. I am instead suggesting that if the overly symbolic or abstract is evasive, the overly literal is a lie. Both approaches require attention to the "form" through which the emergency is spoken. I consider form as the structure of both a) the practice of speaking/listening/translating stories in popular theatre workshops and b) the created play or event through which an audience engages those stories. Within this form, which can be usefully conceptualized as a "container," a space or "gap" must exist. It is this gap that holds the circle of knowing open and invites a current that prevents steering a straight line through the story, or arriving at a predetermined destination. What might the notion of containment and gap look like in a popular theatre project, particularly when for at least one participant the container did not hold?

In 1993 I was approached by an organization in Toronto to do a play about refugees, *Are the Birds in Canada the Same?*[4] I agreed to do the project and wanted to hire people who were both refugees and actors or artists. Eventually a theatre director, a refugee advocate, and I (the playwright/producer) began a five-week period with a group of people, one of whom I will call "Tom." Tom had worked in his country of origin as an artist but not as an actor. The group spent the first day talking. On the second day, we began to speak to each other in physical images. Although the director and I deliberately asked only general questions, Tom began to tell us, with no preamble whatsoever, about his experience of torture. What I remember most about that day was the silence in the room, the shock on everyone's face, and the complete ordinariness (something I now realize is common to retellings of torture) in the way he told the story. I now consider this what Walter Benjamin refers to as a "moment of danger" (255), one I registered but did not think through.[5] For Tom at that moment—two days into a project with strangers—there was not yet the possibility of a witness.

The group continued to work together for several weeks, after which I went away and, in a sense, wrote another story. The play I wrote took elements of what had happened to the participants and re-presented them, reshaped them, and put them into a form that they could first read, then re-enter as performers, and finally experience an audience receiving. That the audience was predominantly comprised of refugees was key, I believe, to the element of public ritual and mediation or healing in the performance. The response to each presentation was very positive, profoundly so on the part of refugees. Tom seemed extremely happy throughout the weeks we worked, but I worried about what would happen when the project was over. Unlike the others who had jobs and families, Tom was alone and had no other work. Within a matter of days after the end of our project, Tom began telling people how awful the experience had been. He refused to see any of us for weeks; when I finally met with him, he told me of the nightmares he experienced during the entire project. Tom had been settled in Canada many years, so this could not be explained away as the salting of fresh wounds.

Tom's story brought me face to face with the persistence of trauma memory. [6] I now think he told his story in a space structured to invite his pain but unable to contain it adequately, a space of relationship that did not permit the sharing of knowledge, which goes beyond mere information, knowledge the leaders of the project were not, in any case, prepared to understand. We were ready to hear stories about torture. We were not ready to hear what it would mean for Tom to remember and speak them. The container, in other words, was suggested but not fully built; the gap was a gaping hole.

The concept of container and gap that I apply to the building of an environment within which to witness stories builds upon images and ideas I borrow from alchemy, psychoanalysis, and shamanic healing practices. The word for container comes from the Greek *temenos*, meaning a sacred space and time specially prepared and set apart in order to reconnect with ancient energies. It is a term often used to describe environments built in therapy, where members of a group act as each other's witnesses, and the exchange of stories happens within a ritual space. When a ritualized act is public, as I suggest it is in popular theatre, its public nature is dependent upon the shared narratives of the communities that practice it, and the histories and beliefs that allow the recognition of common images and responses to those images. People's responses to ritual "are likely to be at several levels: physical, affective, cognitive, imaginative and metaphysical" (95). According to Jungian therapist and writer Marion Woodman,

> In every creation myth a Divine Being creates a cosmos imaged as a container and a contained. Every culture moves toward the complete adjustment of the contained to its container. Culture assumes that we dwell within a universe that is our home. The loss of this home, for whatever reason, is the origin of neuroses: the contained has lost its container. (157)

If the notion of container relates as strongly to culture and home as Woodman's description of the creation myth suggests, then aren't containers also potentially totalizing structures that readjust the "containeds" to meet social norms? [7] Certainly a "container," whether popular theatre process or story, can become a straitjacket, a set of norms imposed by a leader, rigorously followed by group members, and, tragically for some, masquerading as homes in the form of cults, rigid ideologies, or in Foucault's words, "regimes of truth." To be vigilant against this danger does not mean we must stop doing our work or telling our stories. The question mark, the gap, the possibility of being wrong – these are essential to the integrity of what remains to be seen and said about each participant, each listener, and each story. The gap ensures that there is always something more to say.

My concept of the gap as a structured space for calling up what is unmarked, or for holding in mind "the lie of the literal," gains substance from Michael Taussig's description of the lack of realism in magically effective mimetic images. Taussig gives the example of dolls and drawings used in healing that display little likeness to the people they are meant to heal or bewitch (51), suggesting to me that a too perfect likeness might be like a too literal representation, or a too tight container. In other words, what might appear to an outsider as a bad copy is really a structure that contains both connection and space. Such a space offers room for the listener to enter, and for the unmarked, or Other, or dissenter, to remain. The gap is for me the pivotal element of the container. If it is too large it will destroy the structure, and there will be no connection between listeners and storytellers. Perhaps there will even be no connection between the storytellers and their own stories. If the gap is too small or nonexistent, there is no room for the Other, no space across which the familiar and the strange can gaze upon each other. Within such a balancing act of negotiations, it is not surprising to feel off balance.

Very particular suggestions of containment were structured into *Are the Birds in Canada the Same?* that, I now realize, created for Tom a place with the possibility of testifying and being witnessed. These elements include the multidimensional and corporeal aspect of the theatre work, the heightened ritualistic power of the performance space, and the presence of significant listening others. The backlash experience afterwards happened in part because we—and I mean here the leadership team—did not realize that we had created such a container, were not aware of the extent of the bargain being made, and so did not adequately stay in touch or "in-tension" with the participant through the experience. We could not hold the impact of this collision of personal narratives together with our desire to listen. The result for Tom, as he revealed to me later, was a sense of having been used and discarded. The cause was not our reluctance, but our actual inability to "stand to hear" him (Herman 138), to hold ground and accompany him through a process we had initiated but did not ourselves fully understand or recognize.

The final critical element in the story of Tom concerns the way he "acted" in the play about refugees. Tom, who was not an actor, spoke lines he had created and told stories he had lived. My mistake as a playwright was not writing for Tom a character sufficiently new and different from "Tom" – one that would allow him to step into a character who was not himself. By acting his own story, the theatre project prevented him from taking the step psychoanalyst Dori Laub describes as the re-externalization of the event. Laub says this reconstructing of history can take place "only when one can articulate and transmit the story, literally transfer it to another outside oneself and then take it back again, inside" (Felman and Laub 69). Taussig describes how Navajo sand paintings are said to help people not through their looking at the pictures, "but by their placing their body in the design itself" (57). Our project gave Tom no design to step into.

In a similar vein, Sue Jennings explains her choice to use theatre in her therapeutic practice because its main process "is that of dramatic or aesthetic distance, which paradoxically allows us to experience reality at a deeper level" (22). The language of theatre can produce the quality of "double seeing" that permits the state Augusto Boal calls metaxis: "the state of belonging completely and simultaneously to two different, autonomous worlds: the image of reality and the reality of the image ... In order for metaxis to come about, the image must become autonomous. When this is the case, *the image of the real is real as image*" (43–44, italics in original). When an image is created to work with, it forms a kind of container, allowing the theatre space itself to hold contradictory material without insisting upon its resolution. If successful, such an image permits the "self-othering" to which Laub refers, allowing the speaker to see trauma as "outside herself."

I have referred to the moment when Tom first told the story of his torture as, in Benjamin's sense, "a moment of danger." Perhaps that moment was an opportunity none of us were able to take up. How could we together have grappled with and entered the images that were "flashing up"? What is at stake is a notion of the power of the image to provide a containment of its own.

Theatre is a powerful and popular vehicle through which people can speak their stories, have fun, and learn to work with others. However, if the importance of moving personal stories to "form" is not understood, or the leader insufficiently experienced in creating the forms of such a theatre, then participants can be subject to what Luce Irigaray calls "the danger of unmediated relations becoming a source of pathology" (77). In such cases, as in the story of Tom as I am relating it, there is no external image for the participants to step into, and they are caught recycling a story they may wish they had never remembered. Ideally, popular theatre can act as an object of symbolic exchange; histories and memories can be translated, heard, and, if not made sense of, at least taken into a narrative shared within some kind of community.

Acts of witnessing may be possible through a theatre that sets out to pose questions and not to provide answers, and/or one that employs fantasy, epic theatre, ritualistic celebrations, parable, and the many forms that, in Artaud's words, "rescue theatre from its human, psychological prostration" (qtd. in Jennings 110). Such a theatre may provide a larger-than-life drama that is also a container, one that, Sue Jennings contends, "keeps the person's identity intact, but also give[s] a form for them to interact with" (110). Through such aesthetic forms, the story and the act of the trauma are marked in such a way as to be visible and yet, at the same time, not utterly pinned down. The form then speaks of trauma, but remains open to possibilities of resistance, to different ways both trauma and agency are and can be known. Risky stories in popular theatre must be able to be told in public spaces and understood as events situated within history, remembering that the artists who solicit and shape such stories need to listen not only for damage, but also for hope and resistance. We should attend to Laura S. Brown's caution against defining trauma in terms that "create a social discourse on 'normal life' that then imputes psychopathology to the everyday" (103). Such a project challenges me as popular theatre artist to consider my own relationship to trauma and the stories with which I engage. In order to be able to hear resistance, possibility, and examples of hope in action, I have to be able, at the very least, to imagine them myself.

The forms of popular theatre I like to "imagine" carry the dangerous task of facing both teller and listener with the terrible literality of the emergency that demands to be named and known, while including the unanswerability of truth, through whose elusive nature the guilty too often remain free. This theatre demands the recognition of inevitable separateness and absence, while holding central what can be named and judged. Such a theatre proceeds hopefully, with hope understood not as a dream but a choice, attempting "to tell the truth, without being absolutely sure" (Boal 39).

(1996)

Notes

1 Elisabeth Ellsworth has written about the role of silence, speech, and the interplay of identities as they operate in the classroom in her critique of critical pedagogy. See Ellsworth.

2 When I speak of witnessing I am referring to an act through which an incident of violence is understood as significant and is responded to by someone other than the direct victim of that violence, an act ultimately perceivable by the survivor as actual changed conditions in the world around him or her; e.g., the conditions that encourage people to drink and drive become conditions that discourage such behaviour. My work with the concept of witnessing is informed by my collaboration on a research project at the Ontario Institute for Studies in Education with Claudia Eppert, Christine Louise Hiller, Sharon Rosenberg, Florence Sicoli and Roger I. Simon.

3 There is an evident paradox here: gesturing towards what cannot be pinned down, holding open space within structures of naming for what Peggy Phelan calls the unmarked space, an immateriality or the "hole in the signifier" which is lost in the "full fling forward into representation" (10).

4 *Are the Birds in Canada the Same?* is a play about the experience of three refugees to Canada, one from Central America, one from the former Yugoslavia, and one from Sri Lanka. The development of the play involved some refugees from other locations, and it was produced by Flying Blind Theatre Events, with executive producer The Jesuit Centre for Social Faith and Justice in Toronto. The play was developed through a process of improvisation and discussion, directed by Aida Jordao, and

written by Julie Salverson from stories by Jorge Barahona, Mima Vulovic, Aida Jordao, Colin MacAdam and others. It was performed in May, 1994 for refugees and refugee advocates. A video adaptation of the play was produced in 1995.

[5] Writing his *Theses on the Philosophy of History* in the 1930s, trying to understand the rise of fascism, Benjamin wrote the following: "To articulate the past historically does not mean to recognize it 'the way it really was' (Ranke). It means to seize hold of a memory as it flashes up at a moment of danger. Historical materialism wishes to retain that image of the past which unexpectedly appears to man singled out by history at a moment of danger. The danger affects both the context of the tradition and its receivers. The same threat hangs over both: that of becoming a tool of the ruling classes. In every era the attempt must be made anew to wrest tradition away from a conformism that is about to overpower it" (255).

[6] Cathy Caruth has edited a valuable series of essays that explore trauma and memory. She says, "[F]or those who undergo trauma, it is not only the moment of the event, but of the passing out of it that is traumatic; ... survival itself, in other words, can be a crisis" (9).

[7] If so, this would mark what Adorno calls the end of the dissenter and a world in which "[t]he Other must go under for the people to become one" (qtd. in Cornell 48–49).

Works Cited

Alcoff, L. and L. Gray. "Survivor Discourse: Transgression or Recuperation?" *Signs* 18:2 (1993): 260–91.

Avni, Ora. "Beyond Psychoanalysis: Elie Wiesel's Night in Historical Perspective." *Auschwitz and After: Race, Culture, and "The Jewish Question" in France.* Ed. L. D. Kritzman. New York: Routledge, 1995. 203–18.

Benjamin, Walter. *Illuminations.* Trans. Harry Zohn. Ed. Hannah Arendt. New York: Shocken, 1969.

Boal, Augusto. *The Rainbow of Desire: The Boal Method of Theatre and Therapy.* Trans. A. Jackson. New York: Routledge, 1995.

Brown, Laura S. "Not Outside the Range: One Feminist Perspective on Psychic Trauma." *Trauma: Explorations in Memory.* Ed. Cathy Caruth. Baltimore: Johns Hopkins UP, 1995. 100–12.

Caruth, Cathy, ed. *Trauma: Explorations in Memory.* Baltimore: Johns Hopkins UP, 1995.

Cornell, Drucilla. *The Philosophy of the Limit.* New York: Routledge, 1992.

Ellsworth, Elizabeth. "Why Doesn't This Feel Empowering? Working Through the Repressive Myths of Critical Pedagogy." *Harvard Educational Review* 59.3 (1989): 297–324.

Felman, Shoshona, and Dori Laub. *Testimony: Crises of Witnessing in Literature, Psychoanalysis and History.* New York: Routledge, 1992.

Herman, Judith. *Trauma and Recovery: The Aftermath of Violence – From Domestic Abuse to Political Terror.* New York: Basic Books, 1992.

Irigaray, Luce. *The Irigaray Reader.* Cambridge, MA: Basil Blackwell, 1991.

Jennings, Sue, et. al. *The Handbook of Dramatherapy.* New York: Routledge, 1994.

Lather, Patricia. "Troubling Praxis." *Mourning Marxism? Feminism, Poststructuralism and Educational Praxis Symposium.* American Educational Studies Association Convention, Cleveland. November 1995.

Peck, J. "Talk About Racism: Framing a Popular Discourse of Race on Oprah Winfrey." *Cultural Critique* (Spring 1994): 89–126.

Phelan, Peggy. *Unmarked: The Politics of Performance.* New York: Routledge, 1993.

Simon, R. I. "Forms of Insurgency in the Production of Popular Memories: The Columbus Quincentenary and the Pedagogy of Counter-Commemoration." *Cultural Studies* 7.1 (1993): 73–88.

Simon, R. I. and W. Armitage-Simon. "Teaching Risky Stories: Remembering Mass Destruction Through Children's Literature." *English Quarterly* 28.1 (1995): 27–31.

Taussig, Michael. *Mimesis and Alterity: A Particular History of the Senses.* New York: Routledge, 1993.

———. *The Nervous System.* New York: Routledge, 1992.

Wiesel, Elie. *The Refugee Sanctuary: A Resource Guide for Understanding and Participating in the Central American Refugee's Struggle.* Ed. G. MacEoin. New York: Harper & Row, 1985.

Woodman, M. *Addiction to Perfection: The Still Unravished Bride.* Toronto: Inner City Books, 1982.

The Structures of Authenticity: Collective and Collaborative Creations (excerpts)

by Ric Knowles

To turn from naturalistic dramaturgical structures based on cause-and-effect development through time, on the "author-ity" of fictional narrative and of the symbolic structure shaped by the imagination of a single author, to the "authenticity" of collective and collaborative creation is in part to turn from what Alan Sinfield calls the universal/individual polarity to the historical/social one, where meaning can be contested,[1] and from the realm of general, metaphysical truth to that of particular historical facts, events, experiences, or interests. It is to turn from the heroically sweating artist, the "one" who kills into perfectly formed art [...], to the multiplica-tion of the "one" into many, the surrender of individual creative control, and the welcoming of collective sweat and other bodily and structural excesses, fissures, fluids and imperfections.[2] Finally, it is to turn from Aristotelian and archetypally tragic or comic "action," oedipally structured with a beginning, middle and end, explicitly derivative of a stable (preformed) subject, to "doing," which takes place as unstruc-tured event (as phenomenon), is constitutive of individual or collective subjectivity in progress, and is the mode less of the tragic or comic than of the epic or annal.[3]

Not surprisingly, much collective creation is epi(sodi)c in structure. Theatre Passe Muraille director Paul Thompson, in famously describing the form of that company's *The Farm Show* as "more like a Canadian Sunday School or Christmas Concert where one person does a recitation, another sings a song, a third acts out a skit, etc." (Theatre Passe Muraille, *Farm Show* 7), or when he says in the opening monologue that "the show kind of bounces along one way or another and then it *stops*" (19), could be talking about the structures of many or most collective creations, which are often described by reviews as "free-form" or "revue-style" entertainments.[4] As such, this type of theatre tends to concern itself with events rather than actions and to employ an acting style concerned with "what" rather than "why," behaviour rather than motive.

Having surrendered claims to the authority of (author-ized) symbolic narrative structure and (author-itative) authorial voice, however, what claims can these plays make on their audiences' attention? As Alan Filewod notes, "some form of authenti-cation" is required *(Collective Encounters* 10). But how is the contract between the stage and the auditorium cemented? I want to look in this chapter at four principles of authentication at work in collective and collaborative creation in Canada since the early 1970s, together with their related or emergent authenticating structures.

The first and most familiar structure, that of the documentary collective creation as represented by the work of Theatre Passe Muraille, relies on claims to fact (versus Truth), to the employment of an authenticating document or documents, and often to the "real," lived experiences of actors, the phenomenological "thingness" of things, and the stability of place over time. The truth claims of the second type of collaborative work that I will look at rely on shared experience, shared commitment, or shared process, and they are represented here by the synchronic and diachronic communities of women forged in a group of feminist collectives and women-centred plays produced by Nova Scotia's Mulgrave Road Co-op Theatre. Related to this achievement of authenticity through the mutual validation of shared experience and community is the third authenticating device that I will consider, the political one provided by shared *interest*, or social purpose, represented here by the feminist collectives that produced *Aphra* and *This Is for You, Anna*. Finally, and returning in a sense to documentary strategies of authentication but ones not usually discussed in the context of collective creation, is the appeal to both the "reality" of (physical) presence and the shared experience of biology to which much performance art turns for its truth claims. This work will be represented here by *Mary Medusa*, a performance piece created in Winnipeg in 1992–93 by Shawna Dempsey and Lorri Millan. [5]

These authenticating devices—appeals to "fact" (or document); to shared experience, process, or community; to shared political interest or commitment; and to the physical presence of the actor—are not, of course, discrete, nor are they newly observed: Robert Nunn has effectively demonstrated Theatre Passe Muraille's creation of *communitas* in *The Farm Show* (see "Meeting"); the women of Mulgrave Road Co-op Theatre rely on the authentication of place as much as do the creators of Theatre Passe Muraille's "sociological" collectives; *Aphra* and *This Is for You, Anna* employ documentary material to great effect; and almost all collective creations to a greater or lesser extent emerge from shared political commitment of some sort. And there are other modes of authentication and validation employed in these and many other Canadian collectively or collaboratively created plays, discussed with considerable sophistication by scholars such as Diane Bessai ("Documentary Theatre," *Playwrights*'), Alan Filewod ("Collective Creation," *Collective Encounters*), and Robert Nunn ("Performing Fact"). Nevertheless, I want to isolate in this chapter some of these authenticating structures and analyze their political impacts and implications within their particular cultural contexts and in some degree of isolation from one another.

Before doing so, however, I should point to the political and structural implications that these works *share* by virtue of their rejection of the inherited Aristotelian, modernist, and above all oedipal models discussed in part I [of Knowles' *The Theatre of Form and the Production of Meaning*] and to their assumption—and this is the source of their *political* commitment—of what Filewod refers to as collective *responsibility* for the work ("Collective Creation" 47). And in this regard I will begin by quoting at length from Michel Foucault's preface to *Anti-Oedipus: Capitalism and Schizophrenia*, not as a purported source for the creators of the work that we'll be examining, but as a kind of structural and political touchstone against which the accomplishments of that work can be tested or measured. Foucault proposes what he calls "a certain number of essential principles" that he derives from Gilles Deleuze and Felix Guattari, read as "a manual or guide" to "This art of living counter to all forms of fascism…" (xiii):

> • Free political action from all unitary and totalizing paranoia.
> • Develop action, thought and desires by proliferation, juxtaposition and disjunction, and not by subdivision and pyramidal hierarchization.
> • Withdraw allegiance from the old categories of the Negative (law, limit, castration, lack, lacuna), which Western thought has so long held sacred as a form of power and an access to reality. Prefer what is positive and multiple, difference over uniformity, flows over unities, mobile arrangements over systems. Believe that what is productive is not sedentary but nomadic.
> • Do not think that one has to be sad in order to be militant, even though the thing one is fighting is abominable. It is the connection of desire to reality (and not its retreat into the forms of representation) that possesses revolutionary force.
> • Do not use thought to ground a political practice in Truth; nor political action to discredit, as mere speculation, a line of thought. Use political practice as an intensifier of thought, and analysis as a multiplier of the forms and domains for the intervention of political action.
> • Do not demand of politics that it restore the "rights" of the individual, as philosophy has defined them. The individual is the product of power. What is needed is to "de-individualize" by means of multiplication and displacement, diverse combinations. The group must not be the organic bond uniting hierarchized individuals, but a constant generator of de-individualization.
> • Do not become enamored of power. (xiii–xiv)

Mark Seem summarizes these principles in his introduction to the same book and adds another "goal" closely related to the dramaturgical structures at which I will be looking:

> Once we forget about our egos a non-neurotic form of politics becomes possible, where singularity and collectivity are no longer at odds with each other, and where collective expressions of desire are possible. Such a politics does not seek to regiment individuals according to a totalitarian system of norms, but to de-normalize and de-individualize through a multiplicity of new, collective arrangements against power. Its goal is the transformation of human relationships in a struggle against power. (xxi)

It is not accidental, I think, that unlike the dramaturgical strategies analyzed in part I [of *The Theatre of Form*...], in which reversal (or, resistantly, perversion) is structurally central, *transformation* is the structural commonality between all the works and methods that I will be discussing in this chapter – including, as Filewod notes, acting methods (*Collective Encounters* 39) and, as Nunn notes, the use of props, places, or bodies ("Meeting" 50, 43). And, as Helene Keyssar argues ("Drama," *Feminist Theatre*), transformative dramatic structures function to enable rather than resist fundamental social transformation.[6]

[...]

AnOther Story

In an essay first published in 1978, Teresa de Lauretis called for "a *feminist theory of textual production*" that was neither a "*theory of women's writing* nor just a theory of textuality" (92) but a theory of "women as subjects – not commodities but social beings producing and reproducing cultural products, transmitting and transforming cultural values" (93).[7] It is neither my purpose nor my place to propose such a theory, but it may be useful here to examine some of the ways in which women as subjects and social beings—theatre workers, community members and audiences—have engaged in the production, transmission and transformation of cultural values in the limited context of a small rural theatre company—the Mulgrave Road Co-op Theatre in Guysborough, Nova Scotia—inspired in part by the work of Theatre Passe Muraille. In doing so, I want to suggest that these women, both individually and as a group, have constructed what de Lauretis calls "a new practice and vision of the relation between subject and modes of textual production" (92). That is, they have developed one model through which Maritime women, as theatre workers and as audiences, can take possession of their cultural (re)production, including the construction of gender.

Mulgrave Road is not a women's company (it was founded as a collective in 1977 by three men—Michael Fahey, Robbie O'Neill and Wendell Smith—and one woman, Gay Hauser); rather, it is a touring company dedicated to the production of new work by Nova Scotians about the Maritimes, primarily northeastern Nova Scotia.[8] Nevertheless, although its organizational structure has varied over the years, the co-op was, until its move to a more traditional board structure in 1994, dedicated to operating collectively and consensually, and, as Cindy Cowan (one of its best-known playwrights) has suggested, this procedure made the company congenial to many women theatre workers in a way that regional theatres with more traditional administrative structures were not (105).[9]

Women's dramaturgy began at Mulgrave Road in 1977 with a monologue and song created and performed by Hauser in the company's first production, a collective creation called *The Mulgrave Road Show*. The actor used the now familiar image of the quilt in a song woven into the narrative form of a woman's monologue about loneliness and isolation. Hauser sat alone on stage with an old quilt in her lap, and as she told her story she punctuated it with verses of a song about a quilt "of a thousand pieces," of "... moments sewn in heartache/Cuttings joined in joy and pain" (Mulgrave Road Co-op Theatre 14). The song, the speech, and the image of quilting created, according to Cowan, "a powerful moment of recognition for any woman watching in the audience" (106).

This moment worked first to deconstruct the conventional and condescending distinction between arts (including theatre) and crafts (including quilting), a division that privileges the former term and relegates to secondary status much of the cultural production of women, and second to represent for Mulgrave Road the communal creativity of women in rural Nova Scotia, as the quilting metaphor has done for other communities of rural women (notably in Donna Smyth's 1982 novel *Quilt* [10]). With this monologue, in fact, Hauser initiated a pattern of cultural production that helped to shape a broad range of women's plays from Mulgrave Road in subsequent years. [11] Included in that pattern was an informal but interdependent kind of networking in which women who took part in one collective creation, scripted play, workshop, or other project [12] eventually produced or initiated the production of their own plays, often involving women from the earlier shows, workshops, or working groups. Cowan suggests, moreover, that

> what gives strength to the women in the Mulgrave Road Co-op is the attempt they have made to build upon each other's work from year to year. Picking up where the last woman left off, they have incorporated the last "message" or experience and attempted to go one step further in developing plays for women. (105)

In any case, all of the women who eventually emerged from the co-op as playwrights, including Mary Vingoe, Cindy Cowan, Carol Sinclair, Jenny Munday, and Mary Colin Chisholm, had been involved with other women in the co-op in collective creations and/or scripted plays, and this pattern has often been reflected in diachronic series of intertexts between the shows, as well as in structural reflections and parallels in what seems to be an evolving women's dramaturgy at Mulgrave Road.

Because of the unique material conditions shaping the production of theatre in Guysborough County, moreover, there is a kind of parallel synchronic process involved in any one production. There's not much else to do in Guysborough when a show is in rehearsal – the population of the town is just over 500, there is only one real restaurant (closed much of the time during the off-season – i.e., the theatre season), and the determinedly masculinist Legion Hall houses the town's only bar. The result is that the rehearsal hall itself—which, together with the usual collection of musical instruments assembled for a show, contains a small kitchen, tape decks, and other comforts—usually becomes a focal unit and social centre apart from scheduled rehearsal hours. Conversations, not surprisingly, tend to revolve around the current project. Individual shows, then, evolve through an intensely focused process of creation and rehearsal in which a group of theatre professionals engages in concentrated interactions with one another and with the community through an extended period of creative isolation and immersion. And, as Jan Kudelka said about her production of

Another Story, "the positive thing about collective drama is that when it works in a community, you end up getting a bonding sense with that community" (qtd. in Deakin). Theatre workers in Guysborough either are part of the community in and about which they write—Gay Hauser and Cindy Cowan lived and raised their families there, and Jenny Munday remained in the town for a time after her stint as artistic director ended and later returned to work there—or are more often billeted with local residents throughout the workshop and rehearsal processes, often with the same people over several shows. This arrangement has resulted in a number of close and long-standing friendships between women of the co-op and residents of the town, friendships that become a part of the production and reproduction of theatre, and of cultural values, at Mulgrave Road and in Guysborough County. In its most immediate form, this type of contact and bonding results in characters in plays, such as Chisholm's portrait of a prominent Guysborough citizen, Co-op Theatre Society member, and friend in her play *Safe Haven,* a character performed by the playwright herself in the revival at the Blyth Festival, Ontario, in 1993. More significantly, however, as Hauser suggests, the ways in which women's plays are produced at the co-op reproduce the social interactions of the women who are the plays' subjects and audiences. Portraying these women theatrically, she claims, reinforces "bonding" *within* the company: "Rural women aren't aggressive," she continues. "What gives them strength is their friendships, their open dependence on each other, and their community. The result is if they need to mobilize to help each other they can do so quickly" (qtd. in Cowan 106-07). [13]

I have suggested that "women's plays" at Mulgrave Road incorporate an interconnected and associative range of intertexts between the plays themselves. This pattern was set by the 1980 collective creation *One on the Way,* the co-op's first "women's play," which developed from the original quilting monologue in *The Mulgrave Road Show* and from a workshop held by Hauser at Guysborough Municipal High School. Created by director Svetlana Zylin and actors Mary Vingoe, Nicola Lipman, and Hauser herself (five months pregnant at the time), the play used an evocative associative structure to deal with social issues of direct concern to rural women in 1980; it contained echoes of and references to material from the earlier collective creations, *The Mulgrave Road Show* (1977), *Let's Play Fish* (1978) and *The Coady Co-op Show* (1979); and it anticipated characters and situations later developed by, for example, Cowan in *Spooks* (1984) and Kudelka and the company (including Cowan and Vingoe) in *Another Story* (1982), a collective creation about the daytime "soaps" and the women who watch them. These shows in turn inspired and were reflected in others, in an expanding intertextual (and intertextural) pattern that, among other things, insists on the *recognition* of women's work and the refusal to let it be lost (Cowan 108).

The intertextuality of these productions derives directly from their *mode* of production, it is typical of women's work at Mulgrave Road, and it forms a central part of the plays' deep structures. It also combines with the productions' immediate and recognizable references to and reflections of their specific social and cultural contexts in Guysborough County to open the shows outward to the audience as community.

It attempts, that is, to create an interactive dramaturgy in which the subject is at once writer, performer and audience, and in which participation in the theatrical event functions as a constitutive act of the participant *as* subject. Achieving their sense of authenticity from a structural grounding in shared experience rather than from authenticating documents or objects, these plays seem more fully than most of Theatre Passe Muraille's sociological collectives to root themselves in the community that they share with their audiences – and more fully to function *as* collectives, even on those occasions when one woman officially fulfilled what Foucault calls the "author function" *(Foucault Reader* 101–20).

I have been concerned to this point primarily with the social production and reproduction of cultural values in women's plays at Mulgrave Road, but what is in question, of course, is not simply the *transmission* of cultural values in the Maritimes based on community, landscape and history but also their *transformation*, including the (re)construction of gender. These plays are socially *produced,* of course, performed *in* the world, but they are also socially *productive,* "performed *upon* the world," as Louis Montrose has put it in reference to Renaissance theatre, "by gendered individual and collective human agents" (23).Versions of society, history and gender are instantiated, but they are also contested and, potentially, transformed.

As I indicated above, transformation has been seen by feminist theatre critic Helene Keyssar not only as a theme but also as a frequently employed structural principle in women's dramaturgy. In this formulation, transformation replaces what we saw in chapter I [of *The Theatre of Form*] to be the essentialist, universalist and "affirmative" (in Marcuse's sense) Aristotelian principles of reversal and recognition (of a preexisting normative subject) with an activist structural encoding of the possibility of social change. It is possible to see a development in women's dramaturgy at Mulgrave Road of transformative modes of theatrical representation that not only reject traditionally self-contained patriarchal structures of linear narrative—reversal, recognition and closure—but also reproduce structurally and represent dramatically their own modes of production. Play after women's play at Mulgrave Road [14] experiments "interstructurally" with and around forms in which community, and the circulation of community values, serve as both subject matter and organizing principle. These plays are different from one another, and they employ different strategies for cultural intervention, but they also seem *structurally* to "quote" one another in much the same way as they contain networks of situational and linguistic intertexts.

I'd like to spend the remainder of my discussion of women's dramaturgy at Mulgrave Road looking briefly at some of the ways in which a few representative plays function. Each of these plays eschews mystification or mythologizing in favour of directly and explicitly addressing concrete historical or social situations; [15] each replaces a focus on a single central character with a structure in which the community itself functions as hero; each employs, in its own way, interwoven strands of story and lyrical expression rather than traditional linear narrative; and each explicitly or implicitly explores issues surrounding women's cultural production – or the production of women's culture.

Mary Vingoe's *Holy Ghosters, 1776* focuses on three strong women at the precise historical moment of the Jonathan Eddy rebellion and the battle that kept New Brunswick and Nova Scotia from becoming the fourteenth American colony. *Holy Ghosters, 1776* is typical of women's plays at the co-op in that it is structured around an ensemble of actors playing a community of characters rather than around the story of its best-known (male) historical figure, Richard John Uniacke (in its first production, the play was criticized for this focus by reviewers; see Senchuk). As Cindy Cowan remarks," I suppose when you put a famous man on stage and then upstage him with three women you are inviting trouble" (108); in fact, though, the overlapping narrative structure, built around four stories at various stages of development over the course of the action, functions to create, for the audience as well as the characters, a diachronic sense of community over time that reflects the play's own intertextual and interstructural relationship to its dramatic predecessors at Mulgrave Road. [16] In spite of the almost overwhelming sense of displacement that is the experience of all the play's *characters,* Vingoe uses history, community and landscape to create for the audience a somehow reassuring sense of *constant* change, finding in the shared experience of displacement an ironic but unsentimental sense *of continuity* over time. The play ends, moreover, with a powerful theatrical image of the promise of renewed community among the women as its two central female characters share a baked potato dug from earth scorched by the victorious British troops, leaving a sense of dislocation and destruction that is also, ironically, a nourishing "site" of potential change and a recognition of fragmentation and isolation as experiences that are or can be shared. [17]

Jenny Munday's *Battle Fatigue,* even more clearly than *Holy Ghosters, 1776,* sets out to recover women's history and is based on extensive personal research on the experiences of women in World War II. Like Vingoe, Munday structures the play around an ensemble of actors doubling roles and acting out different but parallel stories, and both playwrights portray the coming together of women of different backgrounds and sensibilities to frame the possibility—not always realized—of new or different *kinds* of community. Both plays, then, echo the experiences of the groups of women from different backgrounds in the communities—theatrical and other— through which they were produced. *Battle Fatigue,* moreover, makes its potential for intervention in the contemporary culture of its audiences explicit by framing its historical action within a series of present-tense scenes in which a feminist daughter stands in for the audience as she and we learn from her mother about the older woman's wartime past.

Both *Holy Ghosters, 1776* and *Battle Fatigue* also move toward a characteristic of the "new textual form" called for by de Lauretis, in which "rational historical inquiry is continually intersected by the lyrical and the personal" (92). Not only do both plays intercut the documented "facts" with explorations of their subjective impacts, [18] but they also introduce lyrical passages, personal "arias" that problematize the historical and document what de Lauretis calls the "resonance of the (documented) historical event in the subjects" (92). *Holy Ghosters, 1776,* for example, features a choric character, an ageless and homeless Acadian woman. Old Aboideaux, who wanders among the marshes and whose Lear-like odes to wind and weather provide historical and poetic resonances even as the character embodies the direct and personal impacts of abstract historical events such as the expulsion of the Acadians prior to the play's action. *Battle Fatigue* less clearly and less frequently employs the lyric mode (though scene-change songs are used effectively), but the play is full of subjective expression in personal narratives about the historical past that function as personal histories or what might usefully be called "documentaries of subjectivity."

Carol Sinclair's musical play *Idyll Gossip* moves still further away from the formal realm of historical documentary and further toward both lyrical expression—through song—and the explicit exploration of rural Maritime women as producers and transformers of culture. This play also employs an ensemble of actors to portray a community as its central character; more clearly than in any of the other plays under discussion, though, it both partakes of and is about women's circulation of cultural values through the arts and women's reclaiming of agency in the construction of gender in the Maritimes. A metatheatrical musical created by Maritime women about Maritime women creating music, *Idyll Gossip* was inspired by stories of women such as Rita MacNeil—or the women of Mulgrave Road—who struggle against the overwhelming and functionally hegemonic resistance within the conservative patriarchal culture of the rural Maritimes to women's participation in the performing arts. The plays external action is concerned with a group of rural women who gradually overcome first their own (hegemonically internalized) and then their society's reluctance to take their musical aspirations and abilities seriously; however, the sensual life and energy of the play derive from the songs that the women perform throughout, songs that assume and demonstrate the subjectivity of women as cultural workers and audience members. Ranging from satirical or parodic to deeply expressive in tone, these songs cumulatively create a powerful sense of women's subjectivity; in fact, there is a sense in which, as in the plays of Margaret Hollingsworth discussed in part I [of *The Theatre of Form*], the subjective—traditionally regarded as inappropriate to the supposed "objectivity" "natural" to the dramatic mode—takes over from and transforms the play's external narrative, which by traditional wisdom is the *essence* of drama but which in this play is often improbable, farcical, or absurd.

These plays, then, like all of the women's plays so far produced at Mulgrave Road Co-op Theatre, function both as *products* of the cultural conditions (theatrical and otherwise) through which they have emerged and as *agents* of transformation within those cultures. But it is important not to romanticize the involvement of Mulgrave Road in the community. Although the engagements that I have described are central and essential, the degree to which the co-op is capable of effecting meaningful cultural intervention derives in part from its existence at a point of intersection *between* cultures, including its bringing to Guysborough theatre workers of different backgrounds and interests. Mulgrave Road's efficacy rests in its being at once part of, mimetic of, and external to the community in and through which it works. As such, it functions as a potentially transformative "fissure" in an often rigidly closed culture by introducing elements new to it and by providing focal points for women and others who are *members* of the community but are constructed by it as "Other" or ex-centric. The co-op itself has functioned, in part, as a continually shifting and liminal community that is both transformed by and transformative of the culture and society of Guysborough County but within parameters that, though fluid, are defined at any time by the degree to which the company's shows are products of the culture that they represent. It may not be incidental to note, for example, that Mulgrave Road has so far been able to intervene only in very limited and almost imperceptible ways in the gendered construction of class, race, ethnicity, or sexual orientation in Guysborough County, except perhaps insofar as its work has helped to make possible future interventions in these areas as the products of a shifting cultural ground.[19]

(1999)

Notes

[1] Sinfield argues that

> The twin manoeuvres of bourgeois ideology construct two dichotomies: universal versus historical and individual versus social. In each case the first term is privileged and so meaning is sucked into the universal/ individual polarity, draining it away from the historical and social – which is where meaning is made by people together in determinate conditions and where it might be contested. ("Give" 141)

[2] Bert States, talking of surplus of presence (beyond signification) in the theatre, notes that, for example, "with running water something indisputably real leaks out of the illusion" (31). See also Gail Kern Paster on "Leaky Vessels."

[3] Alice Rayner usefully makes distinctions between acting and doing and, drawing on Hayden White, between the epic and the annal that are useful to the analysis of collective creations in Canada:

> Doing does not have the kind of linear temporality of Aristotelian action because it is not shaped by the extension between intentions and ends, with delay in the middle. For both performer and audience the temporality is the same. In doing there is no dilatory space or delay. At most, the intention and the gesture are simultaneous and therefore shapeless. Doing is emphatically in the present and has no duration through time. Though it may take time, it does not make time, insofar as it has no residue. It thus requires no pre-, con-, or re-figuring of time: doing is the figuring itself ... Doing can thus be aligned with epic time rather than

tragic, for it concerns events more than intentional actions, and epic is the form for relating deeds. The annal is perhaps the closest historical record of doing in the way that it exhibits a peculiar kind of emptiness in pure facticity, as though there were no context for facts. As Hayden White describes the annal:

> It possesses none of the attributes that we normally think of as a story: no central subject, no well-marked beginning, middle and end, no peripeteia, and no identifiable narrative voice ... [T]here is no suggestion of any necessary connection between one event and another.... (23–24)

(Rayner is quoting from White's article "The Value of Narrativity in the Representation of Reality." *Critical Inquiry* 7 [1980]: 11–12.) Rayner's analysis of "doing" in the pages that follow this passage has particular resonances with the acting method developed by Theatre Passe Muraille, in which motivation is subordinated to a kind of mimicry and emotion, thought and meaning occur as a *result* of "doing" rather than as a motivation for "action."

4   Renate Usmiani contests this description of the structure of *The Farm Show*, finding "a definite design in its inner structure": "The episodes of the second act deal with the more serious issues of farm life and, therefore, have a greater dramatic impact on the audience. There is a definite heightening of tension and emotion as the play progresses, a heightening which leads up to a climactic final scene" (52). Thompson's description is somewhat disingenuous—some shaping of the material clearly goes on in all collectives—but Usmiani seems unduly constrained to find "in" a play that she admires a structure that in her description sounds Aristotelian. Having "uncovered the shape," moreover, Usmiani then finds that "the subtle emotional manipulation of the public through the inner structure of the play is one of the reasons for its success" (52). The most detailed structural analysis of *The Farm Show*, which works from the premise that it is "episodic and anecdotal," is in Bessai, *Playwrights* 67–78.

5   Beyond the scope of this chapter, but also well worth looking at in its terms, are the complex truth claims of what Philip Auslander (following Baudrillard) calls "mediatized" performance (see "Live Performance"), perhaps best represented in Canada by the early work of Michael Hollingsworth and the Hummer Sisters at Videocabaret.

6   Alan Filewod employs a different but extremely useful model for the analysis of the "process, politics and poetics" of collective creation in Canada in his 1982 article "Collective Creation."

7   The essay, "Gramsci Notwithstanding: Or, The Left Hand of History," was first published in *Heresies: A Feminist Publication on Art and Politics* 4 (1978), under the title "The Left Hand of History."

8 My position in relation to the material discussed in this section is significantly different than it is in other sections and chapters in ways that may affect its unusual focus on the material conditions for the production of the plays in question. The section is both a product of and an intervention external to the workings of Mulgrave Road and the larger communities of Guysborough and the Maritimes. As a man from urban Ontario, I have an outsider's tendency to romanticize my own discursively constructed pastoral understandings of both "the Maritime sense of community" and "the community of women" and thereby potentially to gloss over practical problems and less than ideal (or even adequate) material circumstances surrounding and shaping the production of theatre in an impoverished and isolated area. As a playwright, director, and longtime member of Mulgrave Road, moreover, who has lived and worked in the Maritimes, and as an academic who has written about the theatre company, I have a stake in celebrating and perpetuating the work of the co-op. I hope, nevertheless, that there is a limited liminal role for a discussion such as this one in reproducing (with an inevitable and perhaps salutary shift) the work of co-op women in the frame of another discourse, in supporting (and publicizing) the production and reproduction of cultural work by the women of Mulgrave Road, and in transmitting and transforming cultural values in the Maritimes.

9 For a history of the early years of the company, see Knowles, "Mulgrave Road Co-op"; for a discussion of one representative version of the company's administrative structure, see Knowles, "Voices" 108–09.

10 Smyth's description of quilting provides a remarkable parallel to the process of play production at Mulgrave Road that I am outlining: "It was their quilt now, a thing they were doing together … As the design became clear, so did all the stories … They'd told each other these stories, all the time working and stitching. Watching how it fit together, becoming something other than the pieces they held in their hands" (49). The breakdown between male "art" and female "craft" has been actively pursued, of course, by visual artists such as Joyce Weiland, whose famous *Reason over Passion* quilt provides a particularly apt example.

11 "Women's plays" at Mulgrave Road prior to 1994, when the company's administrative structure changed, include, with dates of first productions; *One on the Way* (collective, 1980, unpublished); *Another Story* (collective, 1982, unpublished); *Holy Ghosters, 1776* (by Mary Vingoe, 1983, unpublished); *Spooks: The Mystery of Caledonia Mills* (by Cindy Cowan, 1984, unpublished); *A Child Is Crying on the Stairs* (collective with writer Nanette Cormier and based on her book of the same title [Windsor, ON: Black Moss, 1983], 1985, unpublished); *A Woman from the Sea* (by Cindy Cowan, 1986, published in *Canadian Theatre Review* 48 [1986]: 62–110; and in Filewod, ed., *CTR Anthology*); *Beinn Bhreagh* (by Cindy Cowan, 1986, unpublished); *Idyll Gossip* (by Carol Sinclair, 1987, Playwrights Union copyscript, 1987); *Battle Fatigue* (by Jenny Munday, 1989, published in *Canadian Theatre Review* 62 [1990]: 50–74); and *Safe Haven* (by Mary Colin Chisholm, 1992, published in *Theatrum* 38 [1994]: S1–S15). This list is somewhat arbitrary in that

other collective creations were predominantly the work of women, were directed by women, and/or cast women in central roles. I have, however, selected productions of plays that were identified by their creators as plays by, for, or about women.

[12] Mulgrave Road has initiated or hosted many community-based projects within its theatre building, around which theatrical activities revolve. These projects include hosting meetings of GLOW (Guysborough Learning Opportunities for Women); initiating and hosting the meetings of a weekly creative writing workshop open to anyone in the community; producing the interventionist play/workshop on child abuse, *Feeling Yes, Feeling No,* in local schools; undertaking school tours of Christmas shows; and putting on Roadies, a theatre camp for children offered each summer. Interestingly, writing about the co-op, including my own here and elsewhere, has tended to focus on the so-called major productions and to marginalize these other, equally important, projects, many of which have to do with areas traditionally seen as "women's issues."

[13] Many of the women in the community who have forged friendships with theatre workers have been of sufficient economic means to afford homes with extra rooms to billet actors. This situation has often (but not always) meant that the theatre's connections have been with women in positions of leadership in the community – doctors, schoolteachers, and so on. There have been fewer direct associations with working-class women and fewer still with the relatively large Black community at the edge of town. For a less sanguine account of the material conditions for the production of theatre in Guysborough than the one here, told from the perspective of an artistic director of the company, see Munday.

[14] A group of plays including the collective collaboration with Nanette Cormier, *A Child Is Crying on the Stairs,* and Cindy Cowan's three plays, *Spooks, A Woman from the Sea* and *Beinn Bhreagh,* are partial exceptions to the patterns that I am examining here and require separate treatment. Cowan's plays, moreover, especially *A Woman from the Sea,* seem both to take and to invite a radical or cultural feminist approach that I don't think is appropriate for or available to me as a male critic, unlike the materialist feminist theory on which I am drawing (but that I hope I am not appropriating). For a radical feminist reading of A *Woman from the Sea,* see Hodkinson 133–58.

[15] See de Lauretis 92. Interestingly, again, Cowan's *Spooks* and *A Woman from the Sea* seem to be the only exceptions to the general rule that plays by women at Mulgrave Road have avoided mysticism and mythologizing. In the former play, Cowan attempts to deconstruct media manipulations of the story of a young girl accused of setting fires in her parents' home in 1921; in the latter play, she tries to construct a radical feminist and socially conscious myth of origins and other things.

[16] Cowan notes that *Another Story* was instrumental in leading Vingoe "to initiate her own production, *Holy Ghosters*" (108).

[17] For a more detailed discussion of *Holy Ghosters,* see Knowles, "Sense."

[18] The primary source of *Holy Ghosters* is Thomas Raddall's novel *His Majesty's Yankees*, but Raddall is famous for his original and detailed historical research, and Vingoe also drew extensively on primary sources, notably John Robinson and Thomas Rispin's *Journey through Nova Scotia* (1774).

[19] The co-op has addressed some of these issues in productions such as *Victory! The Saga of William Hall, V.C.* (1981), which told the story of the first Nova Scotian, and the first Black man, to win the Victoria Cross, in the battle of Lucknow; Chisholm's *Safe Haven* (1992), which treated the intrusion of AIDS into the community; and *Another Story* (1982), in which class is at least implicitly at the heart of the play. These interventions have been important and, if vestigial, are in no way insignificant. Rarely, however, has the co-op faced racism, classism, or homophobia in the community itself head on.

Works Cited

Auslander, Philip. "Live Performance in a Mediatized Culture." *Essays in Theatre / Études théâtrales* 11.1 (1992): 33–40.

Bessai, Diane. *The Canadian Dramatist, Vol. 2: Playwrights of Collective Creation.* Toronto: Simon & Pierre, 1992.

———. "Documentary Theatre in Canada: An Investigation into Questions and Backgrounds." *Canadian Drama/L'Art dramatique canadien* 6.1 (1980): 9–21.

Cowan, Cindy. "Messages in the Wilderness." *Canadian Theatre Review* 43 (1985): 100–10.

de Lauretis, Teresa. *Technologies of Gender: Essays on Theory, Film, and Fiction.* Bloomington: Indiana UP, 1987.

Deleuze, Gilles, and Felix Guattari. *Anti-Oedipus: Capitalism and Schizophrenia.* Trans. Helen R. Lane, Robert Hurley and Mark Seem. Minneapolis: U of Minnesota P, 1983.

Filewod, Alan. "Collective Creation: Process, Politics and Poetics." *Canadian Theatre Review* 34 (Spring 1982): 46–58.

———. *Collective Encounters: Documentary Theatre in English Canada.* Toronto: U of Toronto P, 1987.

———, ed. *The CTR Anthology: Fifteen Plays from* Canadian Theatre Review. Toronto: U of Toronto P, 1993.

Foucault, Michel. *The Foucault Reader.* Ed. Paul Rabinow. New York: Pantheon, 1984.

———. "Preface." Deleuze and Guattari. xi–xiv.

Hodkinson,Yvonne. *Female Parts: The Art and Politics of Female Playwrights.* Montreal: Black Rose, 1991.

Keyssar, Helene. "Drama and the Dialogic Imagination: *The Heidi Chronicles* and *Fefu and Her Friends.*" *Modern Drama* 34.1 (1991): 88–106.

———. *Feminist Theatre: An Introduction to Plays of Contemporary British and American Women.* New York: Grove, 1985.

Knowles, Richard Paul. "The Mulgrave Road Co-op: Theatre and the Community in Guysborough County, N.S." *Canadian Drama/L'Art dramatique canadien* 12.1 (1986): 18–32.

———. "'A Sense of History Here': Mary Vingoe's *Holy Ghosters, 1776.*" *The Red Jeep and Other Landscapes: A Collection in Honour of Douglas Lochhead.* Ed. Peter Thomas. Fredericton: Goose Lane, 1987. 20–27.

———. "Voices (off): Deconstructing the Modern English-Canadian Dramatic Canon." *Canadian Canons: Essay in Literary Value.* Ed. Robert Lecker. Toronto: U of Toronto P, 1991. 91–111.

Montrose, Louis A. "Professing the Renaissance: The Poetics and Politics of Culture." *The New Historicism.* Ed. H. Aram Veeser. London: Routledge, 1989. 15–36.

The Mulgrave Road Co-op. "The Mulgrave Road Show." Unpublished ts., 1977.

Munday, Jenny. "The View from Inside the Electrolux." *Canadian Theatre Review* 71 (1992): 88–91.

Nunn, Robert C. "The Meeting of Actuality and Theatricality in *The Farm Show.*" *Canadian Drama/L'Art dramatique canadien* 8.1 (1982). 42–54.

———. "Performing Fact: Canadian Documentary Theatre." *Canadian Literature* 103 (1984): 51–62.

Paster, Gail Kern. "Leaky Vessels: The Incontinent Women of City Comedy." *Renaissance Drama* n.s. 18 (1987): 43–66.

Rayner, Alice. *To Act, to Do, to Perform: Drama and the Phenomenology of Action.* Ann Arbor: U of Michigan P, 1994.

Senchuck, Barbara. Rev. of *Holy Ghosters*, by Mary Vingoe, Mulgrave Road Co-op touring production. *Chronicle-Herald / Mail Star* (Halifax) 3 November 1983. E3.

Seem, Mark. "Introduction." Deleuze and Guattari. xv–xxiv.

Sinfield, Alan. *Faultlines: Cultural Materialism and the Politics of Dissident Reading.* Berkeley: U of California P, 1992.

Smyth, Donna. *Quilt.* Toronto: Women's Educational, 1982.

States, Bert. *Great Reckonings in Little Rooms: On the Phenomenology of Theater.* Berkeley: U of California P, 1985.

Theatre Passe Muraille. *The Farm Show*. Toronto: Coach House, 1976.

Usmiani, Renate. *Second Stage: The Alternative Theatre Movement in Canada.* Vancouver: U of British Columbia P, 1983.

Wallace, Robert. "Holding the Focus: Paul Thompson at Theatre Passe Muraille: Ten Years Later." *Canadian Drama/L'Art dramatique canadien* 8.1 (1982): 55–65.

Carbone 14's
Intelligent and Responsive Body

by Erin Hurley

Available definitions of *le théâtre de l'image*, or "image theatre," often contradict each other. For some *le théâtre de l'image* is a distinctive theatrical aesthetic emphasizing visual spectacle and minimizing spoken language (Lévesque "Carbone 14"). For others, it is a technique akin to sculpture (Pavlovic, "Gilles Maheu"; Hood). Still others emphasize its desired effects (Vigeant). Despite the differences in emphasis, most of the criticism privileges the role of the body in the technique and production of images. The body is understood as the primary sign among stage-signs whose goal is to create a strong sensory impression. For example, Bonnie Marranca describes the actor's function in the U.S.-based "theatre of images" as "media through which the playwright expresses his [*sic*] ideas; they serve as icons and images" (Marranca xi).

In this paper, I would like to concentrate on the role of the body and the meanings it creates in the work of one image/dance-theatre troupe: Montreal's Carbone 14. Carbone 14 might well be considered an unstable isotope in the Quebec theatre scene. Incorporating the neutrons of dance and music (and, to a lesser extent, mime, architecture and electronic media), Carbone 14 practices a new form of québécois theatre – a hybrid performance form some call "image-theatre," others "dance-theatre." Since 1980, Carbone 14 has innovatively performed some of the plays of Heiner Müller and Peter Weiss including *Hamletmachine, Rivage à l'abondon,* and *Marat/Sade.* However, the bulk of its creative output, and that for which it is best known both nationally and internationally, are its own non-text-based creations. Since 1984, these are: *Le Rail* (1984), *Le Dortoir* (1988), *La Forêt* (1994), *Les Âmes mortes* (1996), *L'Hiver – Winterland* (1998) and *Silences et cris* (2001). Gilles Maheu, the troupe's *concepteur* and *metteur en scène,* constructs image-based spectacles around particular themes through the shifting combinations of movement, light, environmental design and music.

Maheu's dramaturgy—his *écriture scénique*—is a body and image-based creative process. Carbone 14 builds their spectacles around a set of images, drawn from specific yet generous themes chosen by Maheu.[1] The company then improvises based on their own responses to the chosen images. Maheu says of their creative process, "The actors improvise from images, born of these [pre-selected] themes; they are confronted with discrete objects, and afterward, we keep what is most meaningful" (qtd. in Lévesque, "*Le rail*"). Carbone 14's creative process is similar to the *théâtre repère* technique developed by Jacques Lessard of the Conservatoire d'art dramatique de Québec and most famously employed by his protégé, Robert Lepage.[2] The similarities of his creative process to that of the *repère* cycle notwithstanding, Maheu distinguishes his approach saying, "Contrary to traditional *écriture (scénique)*, the show unfolds little by little, without text and without a firm plan" (qtd. in St. Hilaire). The primary means of its unfolding is the collective dancing body.

Given its predominance in Carbone 14's theatrical work and in their creative process, it is important to consider what kind of body Carbone 14 creates; this warrants analysis of Maheu's choreographic style. For it is via "style" that the body and the dance become carriers of cultural identity. Dance styles grow out of "the most fundamental assumptions about the subject and the body" (Foster, *Reading Dancing* 88). For example, modern dance styles conceive of the body as conduit for the expression of internal forces. That assumption plays itself out in movement vocabularies which stress the dynamic struggle between internal compulsion and external resistance: "The modern dancer's body registers the play of opposing forces, falling and recovering, contracting and releasing" (Dempster 28). Every dance style requires and, in its technique, creates a "specialized and specific body, one that represents a given choreographer's or tradition's aesthetic vision of dance" (Foster, "Dancing Bodies" 241). As such, each style has certain "techniques of the body." In dance, those techniques are communicated and practiced during a dancer's training and rehearsal processes. The purpose of training in a particular style—be it Graham or Duncan, Laurin or Maheu—is to ensure the full incorporation of the style's movement vocabulary, syntax and lexicons of meaning in the neuromusculature of the performer. Style also gives a dance its particular identity, distinguishing it from others. It exhibits a certain quality of movement, establishes relationship of bodies and body parts to each other in movement patterns, and directs the relationship of the performer to the audience.

In the most general terms, Carbone 14's choreographic style is firmly rooted in the "postmodern dance" tradition in which movements' meanings are generated from the context of the dance itself. The bodily signs, apprehended over the course of the show, gather symbolic force over time and in relation to themselves, not to an external interpretive grid. The movement systems deployed across Carbone 14's dancers do not cohere into plot, character, or narrative.

Rather, the organizational principle of Carbone 14 dances is what Patrice Pavis calls "gestural narrativity." It is "organized syntactically rather than semantically – for example, by systems of thematic or meaningful oppositions" (Pavis 58). In Carbone 14 shows, short scenes, images and tableaux—often separated by blackouts—elaborate the pre-selected themes in various ways. For instance, *La Forêt* concerns itself with the passage of time, its vagaries, and humanity's responses to it. Its scenes are organized nonsequentially around the stages of a lifespan: childhood is represented by a rebellious boy in his tree-house, youth and maturity by a group of young men and women, and old age by a decrepit elderly man. Often, these representatives mix, appearing in the same sequences – foreshadowing future actions, reenacting past ones. Even on the level of staging, dance critic Brigitte Purkhardt writes, *La Forêt* is organized like a "game of mirrors": "Sometimes the action is repeated. What is performed stage right seems to be the perfect reply to what is transpiring stage left. Or, it is upstage and downstage which are projected in each other" (164). What unites the scenes despite the blackouts that separate them and their non-sequential order is not plot-line but their mutual, if varied, reflections on the production's theme. This theme-and-variations approach to organizing movement, called "parataxis," dominates Carbone 14's work; it forms the super-structure of Carbone 14 shows, dictating the order of scenes. Within that super-structure and on the level of movement phrases appear other syntactic choices.

Carbone 14's postmodern style employs multiple dance languages on the level of syntax to reflect on production themes. Maheu demonstrates little interest in the lifts, turns, or *pas de deux* characteristic of ballet and modern dance, preferring instead to plumb the expressive possibilities of movement drawn from other cultural repertoires and from pedestrian activities. His choreography quotes such diverse styles of dance as Native American, modern, Indian and New Wave, creating a pastiche of unreconciled movement vocabularies. Moreover, some of the movement vocabularies are not even recognizably "dance." Maheu's choreography often blurs the boundaries between dance movement and everyday movement; stage movements are lifted from everyday activities, which are then elaborated and transformed.[3]

For instance, the movement vocabularies of *L'Hiver-Winterland* contrast an agrarian past with an urban present. The Native American dance vocabulary which opens the piece demonstrates a light quality: dancers turn bouncing on the balls of their feet; arms outstretched and palms turned up, their focus is skyward. Two scenes later, after an explicit reference to the 1995 referendum on sovereignty, four dancers mimic contemporary club-dancing: the quality of the movement is closed, frenetic, thrashing; it is recursive in its leaps and crashes, and staccato in its rhythm. Following a similar pattern, the next sequence of scenes opens with three self-mortifying *curés*, illuminated by top-spots, who turn their gently swinging, encircling arms against their torsos. Two scenes later, after another reference to the referendum, stylized self-mortification transmutes into percussive jabs directed away from the body as two *danseurs* and one *danseuse* perform break-dancing moves which subsequently segue into boxing moves, again embodying a contemporary urban aesthetic or style.

In *Le Dortoir* the movement vocabulary is drawn largely from children's games and play activity. In the first half of the piece, the quality of the choreography is light, innocent, fluid. For example, two girls play a relaxed game of catch, tossing the ball, underhand, in easy arcs to each other. Their central torsos lift and open in the toss, contract and stoop in the catch. In the second half of the piece, these playlike movements are distorted into those of violent conflict. The girls extend and contract their midsections in response to torture, their tossing hands tied to the top of an up-ended bed. The boys from the dormitory appear behind them, slightly elevated; their bodies open and close in response to self-flagellation. (This movement sequence is "mimetic" in its syntax, repeating a pivotal movement in time and across a number of different bodies.)

By venturing into international dance traditions and quotidian movement, Maheu expands the movement repertoire of his choreography, locating it culturally and socially. This move also confounds to some extent the modernist understanding of the body as expressive of internal states or inner forces. Maheu's postmodern body is available to a number of discourses, not only that of its inner life. It presents a range of movements, from the intimate terrain of childhood play to the social terrain of plural cultural influences.

Carbone 14 style also bears the earmarks of a more culturally and historically specific style than "postmodern dance" called the "Montréal style" or "*le nouveau bouger montréalais.*" Developed by dancers and choreographers during the 1980s, the *nouveau bouger* is inventive in its choreography and imagery, high-risk in its physicality, personal in its themes, and theatrical in its structure and use of scenery, text and props (Tembeck 231). This kind of cross-genre performance blossomed during the 1980s.[4] Commenting on this crossover trend, André-G. Bourassa writes, "If dance and mime steal the text from the theatre and attribute more than ever an actantial function to the object ... the theatre steals from dance and mime the exclusivity of body language for 'phrases,' even entire scenes" (Bourassa 76). As a trained mime interested in expanding that form's idiom, Maheu gravitated toward this kind of cross-genre performance, focusing on poses, tableaux and group work. Although his work is exemplary in many ways of the *nouveau bouger*'s theatrical expression and formal concerns, it nonetheless retains a distinctive style of its own.

Susan Leigh Foster suggests that "[s]tyle results from three related sets of choreographic conventions: the quality with which the movement is performed, the characteristic use of parts of the body, and the dancer's orientation in the performance space" (*Reading Dancing* 77). Using these three rubrics of analysis, the Carbone 14 style might be described as follows:

> 1) *Quality with which the movement is performed*: Maheu's choreography is generally organized in abbreviated, even abrupt, phrases. These accumulate force not via their extension in time, but rather through their extension in space. The movements are grounded, their flow more horizontal than vertical. The quality of the phrases themselves varies widely, alternating between elegiac and "punk." His choreography demonstrates little interest in the middle-ground of expression; pacing is rarely moderate, quality of movement infrequently "usual." Movement is generally either arranged in sustained poses or slow motion phrases on the one hand, or frenetic expenditures of energy on the other. Whether composed or excessive, movements are virtuosic; they display the precision and technical mastery of the dancers.
>
> 2) *Characteristic use of parts of the body*: Movement is generated from all different parts of body – there is no one centre from which movement flows. In the more contemplative or lyric sequences, full body extension is common; however, there is little emphasis on "line" in the balletic sense of the term. The quality of the extension is more athletic or

gymnastic than balletic, demonstrating physical strength, not the body's conformation to geometric patterns. One of Maheu's choreographic signatures is the complex movement by many body parts at once – its quality is ornate, almost baroque. These movements do not generally require full extension of the limbs; the focus is more on a kind of rippling, moving bits and pieces of limbs. It emphasizes articulate extremities, the ornamentation of already intricate movement.

3) *Dancer's orientation in the performance space:* As Diane Pavlovic has noted, "With the exception of *L'Homme rouge* [1983], Maheu has created group spectacles" (Pavlovic, "l'espace vital" 17). Given the emphasis on group choreography, Carbone 14 shows employ the full performance space in its breadth and depth. In the group scenes (of wandering sleepwalkers, pillow-fighting boarders, resting tundra-dwellers), movement tends to be expansive and performers fan out to fill most pockets of the stage environment. Group movement patterns tend to be laterally organized; dancers move across the stage (from stage left to stage right, or vice-versa) in profile. Performers dancing by themselves or in pairs are usually more confined in their movement patterns; restricted to precise areas, they are held in place by overhead spotlights. These are display sequences; the dancers face the audience directly. Occasionally, dancers will perform display sequences with their backs to the audience. This presentation generally demonstrates a complex articulation of the back musculature.

From this analysis of Carbone 14's style, the following conclusions regarding the kind of body produced by/for it can be drawn. The Carbone 14 body is open to the play of many influences, a responsive instrument that can embody a wide range of emotions, situations, classes and moments. It is able to express extremes (of emotion, of rhythm, of quality of movement, of cultural inflection). Physically, the Carbone 14 body-type exhibits muscular legs and visible, all-over body strength. It is often displayed – topless, naked, in form-fitting clothing. Maximizing *"l'effet vidéoclip"* of which the *nouveau bouger* has been accused (Tembeck 216), the Carbone 14 body exerts itself completely, utilizing an excessive amount of energy for short amounts of time.

The Carbone 14 body is a responsive body, articulating a pastiche of choreographic traditions. Yet, it is also an intelligent body whose intelligence can be tapped both in the creative process (in improvisations) and in the performance event (in its execution abilities). It generates its own lexicons of meaning (movement vocabularies) and establishes axes of signification (parataxis, mimesis, pathos) that can be read within individual productions and across the troupe's *oeuvre*.

That Carbone 14 privileges the body in performance is a fact worthy of investigation for it reveals certain assumptions about the body, its communicative abilities, and its relationship to culture. Carbone 14's choice to use the dancing body as the primary signifier of meaning in performance assumes that the body is an adequately communicative vessel that does not require further elaboration or interpretation by spoken or written text. This assumption underscores the role of the body as a culturally inscribed "document." Maheu stresses the body's participation in cultural processes, its inscription by outside factors, its location at the nexus of historical change. Carbone 14 relies on its dancing bodies not to bypass specific cultural discourses to discover a "universal" bodily language, but rather to revivify and represent them as cast in all of their corporeal realities.

(2002)

Notes

I would like to express my gratitude to Isabelle Jalbert and Carbone 14 for access to their video archive in the preparation of this article. Descriptions of specific sequences are drawn from my notes taken at live performances and from videotaped performances. All translations from the French are mine.

[1] Some of Carbone 14's generative themes have included "soul," "duality," and "urges." Themes are usually inspired by Maheu's own eclectic reading list. (For example, *Le Rail* was inspired by his reading of D. M. Thomas's *L'hôtel blanc* and Jack Henry Abbott's *In the Belly of the Beast.*)

[2] Lessard adapted Anna Halprin's RSVP cycle for dancers to the theatre in 1980, innovating the creative process called the *repère* cycles. (*Repère* means landmark or reference point.) The cycle includes the following stages: *resources, partition, évaluation, représentation.* "*Resources*" (resources) comprise all elements of creation, i.e., objects, light, costume, emotion, music, character, scene. "*Partition*" (scoring) is the exploration and organization of the resources, often conducted through improvisation. In the *évaluation* (evaluation) stage, resources and their scoring are evaluated according to the creative goals and objectives. The *repère* cycle's final stage, *représentation,* is the public performance of the created work (Beauchamp).

[3] This is also a feature of German dance-theatre choreographer Pina Bausch's work with Tanztheater (see Kozel).

[4] Some of its most innovative and familiar proponents in the dance world are Édouard Locke's La La La Human Steps and Ginette Laurin's Ô Vertigo danse.

Works Cited

Beauchamp, Hélène. "The Repère Cycles: From basic to continuous education." *Canadian Theatre Review* 78 (1994): 26–29.

Bourassa, André G. "Scène québécoise : permutations de formes et de fragments en danse, mime et théâtre." *Études littéraires* 18.3 (1985): 73–85.

Dempster, Elizabeth. "Women Writing the Body: Let's Watch a Little How She Dances." *Bodies of the Text: Dance as Theory, Literature as Dance.* Ed. Ellen W. Goellner and Jacqueline Shea Murphy. New Brunswick, NJ: Rutgers UP, 1995. 21–38.

Foster, Susan Leigh. "Dancing Bodies." *Meaning in Motion: New Cultural Studies of Dance.* Ed. Jane C. Desmond. Durham: Duke UP, 1997. 235–58.

———. *Reading Dancing: Bodies and Subjects in Contemporary American Dance.* Berkeley: U of California P, 1986.

Hood, Sarah B. "Theatre of Images: New Dramaturgies." *Contemporary Issues in Canadian Drama.* Ed. Per Brask. Winnipeg: Blizzard, 1995. 50–67.

Kozel, Susan. "'The Story is Told as a History of the Body': Strategies of Mimesis in the Work of Irigaray and Bausch." *Meaning in Motion: New Cultural Studies of Dance.* Ed. Jane C. Desmond. Durham: Duke UP, 1997. 101–10.

Lévesque, Robert. "Carbone 14 se surpasse." *Le Devoir* 9 May 1984: 8.

———. "*Le rail,* un théâtre de l'intuition et de l'urgence." *Le Devoir* 27 October 1984.

Marranca, Bonnie. "Introduction." *The Theatre of Images.* Ed. Bonnie Marranca. New York: Drama Book Specialists, 1977. ix–xv.

Pavis, Patrice. "The Discourses of (the) Mime." *Languages of the Stage: Essays in the Semiology of the Theatre.* New York: PAJ, 1982. 51–65.

Pavlovic, Diane. "Gilles Maheu : Corps à Corps." Trans. Roger E. Gannon and Rosalind Gill. *Canadian Theatre Review* 52 (1987): 22–29.

———. "Gilles Maheu : l'espace vital." *Cahiers de theatre Jeu* 63 (1992): 16–30.

Purkhart, Brigitte. "La Forêt." *Cahiers de theatre Jeu* 70 (1994): 162–64.

St-Hilaire, Jean. "La vie des ombres: Gilles Maheu et *Les Âmes mortes.*" *Le Soleil* 23 November 1996.

Tembeck, Iro. *Danser à Montréal: Germination d'une histoire choréographique.* Québec: Presses de l'U du Québec, 1992.

Vigeant, Louise. "du réalisme à l'expressionisme." *Cahiers de theatre Jeu* 58 (1991): 7–16.

Creating the Form:
Rule Plays and *Svengali's*

by Paul Bettis

Rule Plays were developed, by myself, as a way of creating original theatrical entertainments. And—over rather more than thirty years—they have become, I suppose, a personal method of playmaking. They are not the only thing I do; but they are a favourite professional pursuit.

The key point about Rule Plays is that their action is governed by choices made by the actors in performance, within a structure of variously organized and set limitations – or rules. In effect, a game is played with the dramatic material. And, in some ways, Rule Plays are comparable to cards or a sport: the rules of the game are a constant, but the play is expected to vary. The show, so to speak, is always the same (the rules), but it is always different (the play). And, as in a game, the play always tells a number of stories.

Of course, as in any piece of theatre, the whole process is committed to the creation of a fictional experience that makes sense. And the basic requirements for an evening of drama (such as exposition, development, crisis, climax, resolution, closure and so on) are built into the rules, to ensure the coherence of the event. But with Rule Plays, these aims are achieved by a nightly manipulation of the prepared routines and given variables, rather than by any set pattern of repetition. There is always a climax, for instance, but it is always—within limits—different: it is open to variation. And the means whereby a climax is achieved in one Rule Play are quite different from those whereby it is achieved in another. Different projects, different dramatic concepts, call for different legislative structures, different patterns of rules. Each work in the form aims to be distinct and original. And each aims to be expressive of quite different ideas.

The first stage of work on a Rule Play is, therefore, conceptual. And, in imagining a show, I set myself some formal requirements. These are intended to govern the character and development of the project and to focus its inventions.

Generally, Rule Plays are based on

- a theatrical subject – or topic
- a theatrical idea – or dynamic topic
- a theatrical form – or pattern of action
- a theatrical text – or selection of writings
- other source material – pictorial, musical, choreographic

For example, *The Freud Project* (Toronto 1996) was conceptually based on the following: the subject of incest; the idea of a family portrait; the form of psychiatric sessions; the texts of Freud; and source material drawn from Odilon Redon, Brahms and Viennese waltzes.

The construction of a rule system for any Rule Play project is based on procedures drawn from practice and experience. The following list, though partial, describes some of the basics:

> • the selection of a core of texts, quotations, images, ideas, poems, songs, pieces of music and so on
> • the division of this selection into useful dramatic categories (e.g., settings, introductions, statements, narratives, species of thoughts, etc.)
> • the invention of performance idioms and styles for the delivery of the various selections and categories
> • the invention of rationales and procedures for making choices and initiating routines
> • the determining of particular rules for modes of entry and exit and for modes of address and response
> • the determining of rules for engagement, contact and conflict –and for acceptance and refusal of the same
> • the legislation of crucial initiatives (e.g., who acts or speaks first/next/ last in any given unit)
> • the devising of methods to deal with the problems of play (i.e. errors, infractions, collisions, interruptions, contusions, overlaps and all forms of enforcement and violence)

And so on. Each mechanism inevitably leads to further elaboration and refinement.

A single example: once a category of, say, "scene-setting speeches" has been established, a set of rules is developed to determine which speech is delivered, who delivers it, when it is delivered, in what style it is delivered, to whom it is delivered, for what purpose it is delivered and what is to happen as a consequence of its delivery. Thus, the speech is made to function, not only as a scene, but also as both a signal and a structural component of the developing piece. Necessarily, the execution and management of this speech/scene/signal/component have an immediate and significant influence on the progress and character of any given evening's performance. The routine (of scene setting, in this instance) becomes one of the many units of agreed group enactment out of which the overall shape and meaning of the night's entertainment is collectively fashioned.

The Rule Play I am working on at the moment—it is somewhere between development and full production, I suppose—is a piece called *Svengali's*. It has a sort of subtitle – *Featuring "Trilby's Foot."* And it comes with a descriptive phrase – "A Rule Play for Five Actors and a Posing Throne."

The conceptual base of *Svengali's* is as follows:

• The subject is that of sexual and artistic appropriation.
• The idea is that of reconstructed memory.
• The form is that of a series of acts in a cabaret setting.
• The text is that of scenes and selections from the novel *Trilby*, by George du Maurier.
• The other source material includes songs, dances, music cited in the novel; compositions by Rachmaninoff and Liszt; and a visual and performance vocabulary drawn from both nineteenth century theatrical forms (melodrama, Burlesque, Guignol) and from the apparatus of artistic endeavour (painting, posing, piano-playing, singing).

This project has been developed through a couple of workshops—just a few days in each case—and in 2002, Civilized Theatre (my little company) raised enough money to fund three full weeks of work. The complete artistic team occupied The Theatre Centre, Toronto, for this time. We rehearsed for a week and a bit. We opened the show to the public in the second week, for a series of eight developing "previews" (so to speak), at a graduated range of prices ($5-$10-$15-$20). And then, as a climactic conclusion of the three weeks, we presented the final evening's performance as a single gala event—with cocktails and oysters and cake and other sociable amenities—as a kind of first-night/last-night party ($30). Every element of the show (environment, set, lights, sound, costume, dressing, performance, the rules) was developed, progressively, from the first day of work to the last. The resulting presentation proved to be very entertaining; and I think it can be claimed, from the impact of the piece, that *Svengali's* was a successful Rule Play.

Svengali's is based on the nineteenth-century horror novel *Trilby* (1894), by George du Maurier. This work caused a sensation in its time; and it has maintained a life in popular culture (plays, films, versions), though its currency has now faded a bit. Among its hooks are its heroine, Trilby – a highly eroticized portrait of an artists' model who sleeps around but keeps her innocence; and its villain, Svengali – a highly demonized portrait of a musician who longs for sole possession of her and who attains it by means of hypnosis (he transforms her into a singer). The relationship between these two figures has become emblematic of a certain kind of obsessive love. And to this day, we use the word "Svengali," even if we do not know its source.

The novel retains provocative appeal because of the archetypal nature of its central relationship. Its definition of love as a form of hypnotic appropriation is powerfully transgressive. Also, the ethos of the novel—it is set in the bohemian world of striving visual artists—makes an eerie connection between hypnosis and the power of the artist's gaze. Not only the musician Svengali but also his three painter rivals are seen to be engaged in the attempt to "render" their object of desire. And all the characters are caught in a web of each other's gazing eyes. A play on the compulsions of looking and being looked at—in life, in art and in theatre—suggested itself: a piece based on the transformative hypnotics of performance.

Svengali himself supplies a rich centrepiece for such a drama – not just as a hypnotist and the villain of the story, but as the presiding genius (or demon) of the whole theatrical enterprise. The project is conceived as a framework for a fresh manifestation of this sinister spectre that continues to haunt our culture. But a sense of common fixation is also aimed at. The sexual dynamics and psychological compulsions of the story describe a dangerous and tempting power: the co-option of personality. The tale invokes our aptitude to make people over into something else; and it speaks to our readiness to be made over. The central idea of the show, therefore, is to provide a theatrical arena for an exploration of that species of transgressive, erotic and artistic appropriation which Svengali's character has come to represent: the transforming gaze.

The purpose of the show, at its simplest, is to tell the story of the novel—of Svengali and Trilby and of her other suitors—in concentrated terms. A cast of four men and one woman. A setting suggestive of an impoverished artists' studio – with a posing throne for Trilby to model on and a piano for Svengali to play. A continuous action, of about ninety minutes, encompassing all the main actions of the novel. The presentation aims to reconstruct the suspense of the original narrative and to explore its eerie erotic qualities and haunting themes.

The notion of a "hypnosis show" suggested period models and an environmental approach to the staging. The evening's events are mounted as a visit to a sinister and exotic nightclub—with tables and chairs, bar service, refreshments, music and a cabaret stage with a piano—all appointed in faux nineteenth-century style, like a miniature Grand Guignol. The nightclub—and the title of the piece—is *Svengali's*. The hypnotist himself presides over the establishment and the event, as proprietor and host. The theatrical premise is that Svengali is putting on a show (*Trilby's Foot*) that tells his story in the form of a series of vaudevillian enactments – a set of cabaret acts, in grotesque melodramatic style, which make macabre entertainment out of his obsessive and appropriative impulses.

The text for the presentation is entirely derived from the novel. I constructed a repertoire of some thirty dramatic scenes (none much longer than a couple of pages) that told the story. I gave them titles ("Trilby Sings," "The Bath," "The Fight Scene," "A Piece of Paper"). And I also constructed a repertoire of some twenty-five pages of descriptive passages (none much longer than a paragraph) that provided perspectives on the story. I organized them thematically; and I titled the categories ("Life in the Quarter," "The Look of Love," "Paralyzed Affections," "Posing," "Nudity"). This combined repertoire of dramatic scenes and descriptive passages constitutes the entire textual equipment for the performance of the piece.

In a Rule Play, the performers play a game with the dramatic material and vocabulary. And the story of this novel provides a foundation for a competitive game. Four men compete for possession of a single female, and the female seeks the most commanding male. It is a game of seduction. More broadly, all five characters compete to appropriate each other (in one sense or another), and all five characters compete to appropriate the story they are in. The whole show is fashioned as a contest of competing perspectives. It is a competition between characters, a competition between storytellers and a competition between players.

In the performance of the piece, a device is employed to justify this concerted, competitive effort of narration; and it is drawn from the novel itself. The "mystery" in the story derives from Trilby's double identity as humble model (her life with the artists) and glamorous diva (her life with Svengali). The dramatic crisis occurs when, in performance, Svengali dies of a heart attack, Trilby collapses and the artists recognize her as the woman they knew. At this point, Trilby remembers nothing. The artists return her to their studio and attempt to reconstruct her divided past, as a way of restoring her to health. But, as Trilby is made to recall her story, she again becomes possessed by the spirit (or ghost) of Svengali and is summoned by him into death.

In the play, this situation—the return to the studio and the attempt at recall—is the starting point for the series of enactments that tell the story (in the cabaret format). Trilby is introduced on stage as knowing nothing about her own history – she has been rescued and is in a susceptible state (perhaps, she has come from the street). The work of the players—her rescuers—is to reconstruct her past by means of enacted scenes and descriptions. And as this past is reconstructed, she relives it and again falls into the possession of Svengali.

So, in the performance of the piece, the rules require that the players insist on enacting the scenes in which they played a part. They vie with each other for what scenes they choose to represent, for the order in which they choose to represent them and for the emphasis they choose to place on them. At the behest of the proprietor, Svengali (and with his collusion and involvement), they mount the cabaret act "Trilby's Foot" in order to disclose the dynamics of their shared past. And, in acting it out, all the characters are compelled to re-experience it.

In *Svengali's*, the thirty pages of dramatic scenes and the twenty-five pages of descriptive passages provide much more material than can be included in a ninety-minute show. Seven of the scenes carry the main narrative line and are made obligatory. But, beyond these obligatory scenes, the demands of choice and selection are completely open, and they are imposed equally on all five players. Once the characters, settings and idioms of performance are established in the opening sequences, the players' theatrical mission is clear: They have to decide what scene to do next – and from a very wide range of options.

The procedure of choice-making is quite direct. Since the story is about her and since she is assumed to be ignorant of her history, the heroine, Trilby, is given the power of choice from the outset. The four male actors compete with each other to propose the titles of the scenes they favour ("Trilby's First Appearance," "Billee's Proposal," "The Death Scene," "Sandy's Problem," "Taffy's Discovery," "Trilby Disappears"); Trilby makes her choice and the scene is played.

But the directness of this procedure rapidly gathers complications. The heroine may delegate her decisions. The trio of artists may assert their respective—and differing—agendas (favouring their own characters, for instance, or disfavouring Svengali). Svengali, as proprietor, has special powers of arbitration and, as villain, can lay claim to certain rights of scenic appearance. Measures are provided to formalize disputes and conflicts as acted-out negotiations. The scenes themselves may be aborted, abandoned, repeated. And so on. The players are engaged in a collective endeavour to fashion a sequence of enactments that not only acquaint the heroine with her history but also demonstrate the competitive and erotic dynamics of which that history is composed.

Additionally, between each scene, all five players compete to deliver descriptive passages of their own choice from the repertoire of thematic categories. These passages provide personalized perspectives on the components of the narrative ("Feet" "Love," "Female Complications," "Svengali's Sensitivities"). They are delivered in direct address to the audience. By means of these "solos," each player lays claim to being a distinctive voice of narration, conducting the audience through the ongoing fabric of representations and urging a particular perspective and position within it. There is a formal limit of three such passages after each scene. And there are procedures for collisions – for the competition among players to claim both their preferred scenes and their own authority as presiding storyteller is, naturally, intense.

So, the story gets told, not only through the series of chosen scenes, but also through the glosses on those scenes—and on the whole situation—provided by the five participating storytellers, as the evening proceeds. No matter how partial or variously dispersed the scenes may be in performance, the central fable will emerge clearly from the constellation of enacted recollections in much the same way as a mystery story is reconstructed through an assemblage of clues, or a traumatic experience is reconstructed through an assemblage of retrieved memories. And no matter how different and various the choices of scenes and solos are, with each performance a distinctive pattern of experience will always emerge. The original story gets told, of course, and its shape can be inferred. But the shape we see is that of the telling. For we are watching a theatrical game: an encounter between five performers and some agreed material, within a given timeframe.

The dynamics of this encounter derive from a mixture—a collision—of intention and chance, of planning and spontaneity, like life itself. But the character of the fictional material—the artistic vocabulary, the roles, the rules, the use of time—is very precisely defined, as in a sport (what's going on with the ball). So the dynamic shape that emerges has the authority of the organic: it is a real response to a real situation. The story told each night will be a real story of a group endeavour played out for a crowd. And this means that the heart of the fictional material (the Svengali-Trilby relation and the species of appropriation it embodies) will be made to seem real in its turn – thanks to the transformative agreements of performance. In essence, the competitive dynamics of the game (the facts) are fashioned to fit the competitive dynamics of the archetype (the fiction). The fiction is rendered in terms of the facts. So the Trilby story is brought to life—and re-examined—each night, through the game.

The fascination of Rule Plays derives from the sense they communicate a set of interlocking, but various, criteria for performance, and from the mixture of skill, calculation and inspiration shown by the players in deploying them – especially in respect of the balance sought between competition and collaboration. The excitement of the work depends upon the fluidity with which these criteria for performance are manipulated. And their suspense, drive and energy derive from the concerted effort of the players to put the repertoire of available procedures—the given rules of the given game, however free, however fixed—at the service of a particular dramatic expression. The rules are not mere controls. They are instruments of investigation and enactment, within the arena of a specific, chosen subject. They are the means of a search for meaning. Each Rule Play, in other words, aims to create its own particular world, its own distinct ethos, its own total aesthetic. And that (for me) is the intention and the interest of the form.

A Short History of Rule Plays

The idea of Rule Plays originated in a company experience (at the National Arts Centre in 1969), which took a strange turn. After months of work on a collective creation, we found that we had a subject, themes, texts, set, lights, sound, props, costumes, characters, relationships, routines, scenes; but no play. We had failed to find a dramatic form to contain them.

At the last minute, an emergency procedure was devised. A set of "rules for the play" was imposed that guaranteed some kind of continuity of performance. The event was legislated from within, and its execution made to depend on decisions made by the actors, according to the agreed rules. The result was turbulent and unruly, and the show closed in disgrace.

I thought an interesting process and form had been discovered. The idea of rules suggested the expressive formalities of sports and games. The acting out of relationships between regulation and freedom, strictures and spontaneity, requirements and inspiration, codification and chance, inevitably generates powerful and transparent human dynamics – for both performers and onlookers. It seemed to me that, as a method for playmaking, the devising of rule systems might well provide a rich and varied vocabulary of dramatic expression, as capable of conveying theatrical meanings as a written, rehearsed and repeated script. And the "living" dimension of such performances—the choice-making, improvised aspect shared with sports—seemed likely to create an original theatrical excitement.

Since 1970 (when I came to Toronto), I have continued to explore and experiment with this formal idea of play creation. The first show I devised, based entirely on these principles, was called *Meat* (Villanova University, 1971). Its subject was murder; its idea was a training party for Hashashim; its form was that of the courses of a meal; its texts were *Titus Andronicus* and *Ten Little Indians*; its other material derived from superheroes and pop music.

As artistic director of the Theatre Second Floor, Toronto (1974–79), I devised three shows of this type: *The Robinson Crusoe Exhibit* – an island piece for a black and a white actor, from Defoe; *Jekyll Play Hyde* – a laboratory piece for "twin" male actors and a presiding doctor figure, from Stevenson and Wilde; and *Laura Walks* – a war game between an English, an American, a Canadian and a Native actor, from texts about the War of 1812.

I also devised two other Rule Plays for public performance – one in Vancouver for Simon Fraser University, from Shakespeare (*Getting the Shakes*, 1979); and one in Toronto for Necessary Angel, from ideas/texts about performance art (*Projekt Putz*, 1986). And I employed related procedures in classes I have given on the acting of Chekhov, Brecht and Shakespeare, which required some kind of presentation. I also used Rule Play methods to construct a formal, two-act drama, based on selections from the plays of Tennessee Williams: *The Strangest Kind of Romance* (for the Grand Theatre, Kingston, 1989). In this case, the text became "fixed" – though the effect of the piece depended on an impression of improvisation.

More recently, as artistic director of Civilized Theatre, Toronto (1995–present), I have devised and produced four Rule Plays: *The Freud Project* (1996); *A Club of Small Men* (1999) – a multi-disciplinary piece with a mixed-race cast, about the Canadian composer Colin McPhee and his transformative encounter, in the 1930s, with Balinese music and culture; *Confessions of an Opium Eater* (1999) – a small (twenty-five minute) piece designed for progressive repetitions over an evening, for a Caucasian male and an Asian female, based on De Quincey's essay; and *Svengali's* (2002) – a burlesque Guignol piece in cabaret format, based on du Maurier's horror novel *Trilby*.

(2004)

Enacting *This is for You, Anna*:
Re-enacting the Collective Process

by Shelley Scott

In the spring of 2004, I had the opportunity to direct a student production of the play *This Is for You, Anna* at the University of Lethbridge in Alberta. The play was done in our black box theatre with seating for about 200, as part of Theatrextra, a "second season" of plays intended to offer smaller or more "experimental" shows. In this article, I will consider how the play attempts to re-enact the circumstances and context of a real-life crime in a non-realistic, yet evocative, manner. I will also consider the fact that to perform *This Is for You, Anna* is, to an unusual degree, to re-enact the history of the play's creation through collective process. Finally, I will comment on the effectiveness of enactment as a tool of feminist pedagogy with student actors.

Students can have a hard time integrating theoretical knowledge into their own belief systems, which is why physically embodying an experience in the theatrical process may be of great benefit. In *Upstaging Big Daddy: Directing Theater As If Gender and Race Matter*, editors Ellen Donkin and Susan Clement write: "It may develop that theater itself, the moment of making dramatic action around 'someone else's problems,' will make possible certain revelations, providing the company an education through the body and heart" ("Editors' Introduction" 9). This is especially relevant when the "someone else" is a real person and the dramatic action revolves around an act of violence. *This Is for You, Anna*, like the event on which it is based, is a mass of causal factors, influences and societal forces that converge into one moment in time and then flare out again into the effects, the responses and the same set of regulating cultural determinants. The play is a shared interpretative occasion. Because it takes as its substance a culture's response to and complicity in a real event, it must enact that event in order to evoke its power.

In 1981, Marianne Bachmeier walked into a German courtroom and fired seven gunshots into the man who had killed her seven-year-old daughter. *This Is for You, Anna* is a Canadian work first envisioned by a group of women calling themselves The Anna Project. The play was their reaction to a newspaper article about Bachmeier's act of revenge. A unique performance piece, first staged by a collective of five women in 1983 for a Toronto women's festival, it has been recreated in different versions and has played throughout Ontario and toured to England. In 1986, the production was invited to the prestigious DuMaurier World Theatre Festival in Toronto. The version that we used in our production was published in 1985 and again in 1993 and was credited to four women: Ann-Marie MacDonald, Bañuta Rubess, Maureen White and Suzanne Odette Khuri. [1]

This Is for You, Anna is noteworthy for its feminist content and the opportunity it offers to explore provocative questions about motherhood, revenge and violence committed by and against women. But for me, the most intriguing aspect of the play is its fragmented, imagistic and non-linear structure. The main character, Marianne, is played by all the actors, sometimes simultaneously, designated as Marianne 1, 2, 3 and 4. Unlike in a traditional, realist play where one actor "becomes" one character, *This Is for You, Anna* is more typical of the collective creation model, which has been so integral to the development of Canadian and feminist drama, in that each actor plays multiple roles (see Scott). This technique can highlight notions of gender performance, since, in a Brechtian way, we see the actor don and discard the external signifiers of a "self" that is understood to be played, not somehow expressed.

As its subtitle, "A Spectacle of Revenge," suggests, *This Is for You, Anna* uses a highly visual, overtly symbolic and aggressively presentational style. The main story-line is intertwined with material from fairy tales and interviews with battered Canadian women and was developed collectively through improvisation, games and dream exercises. The play has eight scenes, each with a title, and even within the telling of Marianne's story, there is much shifting between time periods, echoing of lines and repeating of fragments of memory. In an early scene entitled "The Story of Marianne Bachmeier," the sad events of her life are catalogued by one narrator, and with each declarative line, a nail is placed in a circle on the floor. After this, all other facts and recollections are scrambled and fragmentary. It is not possible for Marianne to "make sense" of her life, to fix a coherent sense of self. She has never experienced herself in a position of agency, but rather as someone who is acted upon and reacts in order to survive. In describing the collaborative work of the feminist company Split Britches, Sabrina Hamilton has written:

> The text always makes emotional sense, though not necessarily logical sense. It is a product of an inclusive, horizontal process, open to the irra-tional, allowed to remain personal. The permission to include personal imagery that may feel somewhat obscure to the audience gives the piece a very particular aesthetic, unpolished by some dramatic standards but brimming with authenticity. (141)

Hamilton's words also serve to describe the way in which *This Is for You, Anna* evokes Marianne's experience and enacts her circumstances, without resorting to literalism.

The Anna Project was adamant that the performance not exploit Marianne's history of abuse, nor her revenge against Anna's killer. A note in the 1985 publication states, "The authors expressly forbid the graphic depiction of violence, weapons or blood in any production of this script" (128). Instead, the moment of the shooting is enacted in oblique ways. On two occasions, actors playing Marianne mime drawing and pointing a gun as they struggle to narrate the events of that day. The play suggests that Marianne's own experiences are barely real to her: her memories are confused;

they come to her in fragments as she disputes the accuracy of her own interpretations. In the Prologue, Marianne 1 says: "It was a sunny day. I walked up to the courtroom. I opened the door ... No. I must have dreamt it." Marianne 2 agrees: "Yes, it was a dream," but Marianne 1 then contradicts her(self) by saying "I'm glad I did it" (129). The narration is clearly about an event that has already occurred, but is made immediate by the visual gesture of a pointed gun. The other scene in which the shooting is enacted is similarly oblique. In "The Jury Scene," four women enter the courtroom at the trial of Klaus Grabowski, Anna's killer. The women comment on the crime and identify different people in the courtroom as lawyers, judges and the killer's fiancée. Then they see Marianne enter, and after the line "Here she comes. She's walking to her place," there is a handclap and the women fall to their knees, reacting to the fact that Marianne has begun shooting (160). In our production we added another visual symbol, as one of the women drops her purse on the floor, spilling its content of nails.

In reference to her own work as a director, Simone Benmussa has argued that, in order to succeed, theatre that rejects traditional narrative structure and is devoted to ideological disruption "... must exist and assert itself as political theatre, [for] it is radically opposed to the great edifying and reproducing machines that we see all around us at the moment" (qtd. in Sullivan 23). In addition to the obvious Brechtian influence, I drew upon the aesthetic of the Workers' Theatre Movement in the simple set, uniform costuming, highly regimented choreography and emphasis on songs, slogans, titles and repeated phrases that work as an incantation.[2] The strategy of presenting the cast of women as a kind of agitprop troupe allowed us to work against their traditional objectification as female bodies. As Liz Newberry points out in an article on gender performance, "The hegemonically feminine body takes up less space, averts her gaze, is gazed at, is less strong and muscular, is less assertive, and is valued primarily for her appearance" (21). By having the five actors mainly function as a team, dressed identically and speaking directly to the audience, often in a confrontational manner, we worked to strip them of the hegemonically feminine signifiers and "natural" victim status. We worked on making the transitions particularly sharp, as the actors paused for a moment to leave what had transpired to resonate, then abruptly shifted into their next positions for a new scene, marked by the title on an overhead transparency projection, as well as by music and lighting changes. There was a tightly choreographed and disciplined quality to all the movement, the precision suggesting a kind of clinical setup for each scene. Actors donned their costume pieces, picked up their props from a kitchen table, got into position and then launched into the next scene.

Thus, the scenes in which they appeared as victims of unequal social relations were that much more instructive. These incidents functioned as Brechtian lesson plays, as demonstrations of the constructed nature of these relations: not only as expressions of Marianne Bachmeier as an individual victim, but also Marianne as functioning within an ideological system. While the merits of "political" or "didactic" theatre are frequently debated, here I wanted to take the play's political nature as the given starting point and motivator for all other elements. I think that, if anything, rejecting traditional realism in as aggressive a way as possible was not only justified by the play's unusual structure, but also helped to make sense of it.

This Is for You, Anna holds an important place in the history and study of feminist Canadian theatre. It is an example of a "signal performance," an occasion that may initially have been seen by few people, but that has subsequently "activated a deeper set of relationships that accord it historical status" (Filewod 9). In the case of *This Is for You, Anna,* much of the play's significance is due to the way in which it is marked by its feminist collective process. The play went through radical revisions in a series of versions between 1983 and 1985, and continued to change even after publication. The published version continues to preserve traces of this refusal to be finalized, by indicating in the stage directions that what is reproduced on the page is only, in some cases, an approximation of what was done onstage and by offering alternatives, highlighting passages that were improvised each evening and even suggesting places where material might be changed. *This Is for You, Anna* has had no one home, cast or version. The insistence, even within the published text, that sections be improvised, positions it as an unfinalizable set of practices that must be activated by performers and observers. The play is marked with the social conditions of its initial creation: not only the feminism of the theatre workers, but also their relative poverty and theatrical homelessness, their collective work process and intention to tour to specific audiences.

In the version published in *Canadian Theatre Review,* the text is from the four-member 1985 production, but the accompanying photos are from the previous year when the company had five members. There is a disjunction between words and images that acted on me subconsciously when I was casting. I stopped after four, since there were four written parts. But when I decided to add one more, the balance of the production seemed better, even if the appearance of a fifth person, as in the production photos, further unsettled the stability of the text.[3] Our re-enactment of the play's original creative process was realized most explicitly when we all worked together to create a scene called "How to be a victim." The published version gives a sense of what this looked like in the original production, but also contains the greatest number of references to improvising. Bañuta Rubess, on behalf of The Anna Project, gave us permission to create our own version of the "How to Be a Victim" scene, and in fact suggested the scene would only work if we made it our own, thereby re-enacting the very process by which the production came to exist.

Female student actors are often eager to expose themselves as sexual beings onstage, but are conflicted about the limited ways that female sexuality is "read." I think that as young women they are wary of being trapped: whether in terms of an image they project, being judged in some way or making choices. As Rebecca Munford has written, the conscious performance of female gender "highlights the extent to which the politics of subjectivity requires an understanding of the agency within self-representation as well as the appropriation of that agency" (149). Not surprisingly for students in their particular age range, evocations of female power, whether through the use of sexuality or physical dominance, are highly charged. Interestingly too,

I found that the moments in the play when the actors were at their best were the incidents of resistance or anger, the potential occasions for revenge in lines such as, "I just wish I had got him in the face"; "And then she poked out his eyes"; "You're not so hot, baby"; "The next time he did it I threw a beer glass at his head. Now he thinks twice." Not surprisingly, they relished the moments of strength more than the position of victimhood.

This was the direct subject matter of our "How to Be a Victim" scene, which we created from a series of movement exercises and by working with images from magazines.[4] Just as the play uses a number of symbols, such as milk and nails, without defining them, so too did our scene evoke, in a non-specific and non-narrative way, the climate of sexualization that Marianne, and indeed the actors themselves, live in. As Jeffrey Weeks has written, "Identities are deeply personal but tell us about … multiple social belongings" (qtd. in Gallagher 172). The idea was not to express something about the character Marianne, which would limit the presentation to her particular and very unfortunate circumstances, nor to suggest that she is somehow an essentialist "everywoman," but rather to indicate the social context of power relations and a series of ambivalent sexual roles available to be played.

Without denying the specificity of Marianne Bachmeier's experience, and without judging or exalting her, the play is concerned with how she was portrayed in the German media, first as the avenging "good mother," and then as the sexually active "bad mother." In a 1995 article by Ann Wilson, *This Is for You, Anna* is discussed in the context of what Wilson calls a "culture of abuse" (160). Wilson writes that "Bachmeier's life, marked by her own sexual desire, was at odds with conventional notions of the mother as an asexual figure who selflessly devotes herself to her children" (165). Wilson further argues that Marianne Bachmeier had no real choice but to rely on her physical attractiveness and ability to please men for her economic welfare, but also for her sense of self-worth. Ultimately, Wilson concludes that the play presents a "suggestive portrait of the social production of femininity which predisposes women to be victims" (168). For me, I do not think it is as simple as calling Marianne an everywoman because that downplays the material conditions of her life and the enormity of her struggle. I think it is more accurate, and more useful for the student actors, to suggest that we exist in the same cultural immersion that she did.

Throughout the play, a character will ask, "Want a story?" The story told is always one of archetypal negative female experience—abandonment, rape, self-sacrifice, abuse—and concludes with the line "Now go to sleep." For the actors involved, this construction was freeing: They were able to both "drop into" the emotional truth of moments in the play, to empathize with a woman whose experience was different from their own, and yet to understand the social arrangements that they share. In her article "Teaching Against the Grain: Contradictions and Possibilities," Roxana Ng points out that critical, anti-racist and feminist pedagogy all share a concern with power and inequality (130). Ng quotes Barbara Thomas, who states, "It is unequal power that limits one's ability to earn a living, meet basic needs, make one's voice heard. It is unequal power that makes the struggle for self-respect … a formidable task" (qtd. in Ng 131). Although Thomas is here discussing anti-racist education, her description can apply as well to the gender- and class-based situation of Marianne Bachmeier and to the gender and age-related position of female students. Ng also quotes Dorothy Smith on the usefulness of treating individual experience for what it tells us about social organizations: "If you've located an individual experience in the social relations which determine it, then although that individual experience might be idiosyncratic, the social relations are not idiosyncratic. [All experiences] are generated out of, and are aspects of[,] the social relations of our time" (Smith, qtd. in Ng 134). So too, in Marianne Bachmeier's individual life, can we see not only her economic position, but also her experience as a product of gender oppression. The value of the play is that it enacts onstage not only the moment of her revenge, but the larger context in which it occurred.

For the student actors, because they all played Marianne, she did not physically belong to only one of them. Because of the fragmented structure and collective characteristics of the script and its creation process, they were inserted into the re-enactment of her story and the other women's stories in a way that allowed them an unusual amount of psychic space around potentially devastating issues. I think this allowed them to experience a range of theoretical issues and to work within a politicized pedagogical framework, while also being physically and imaginatively free.

(2005)

Notes

[1] References to the script are from the 1985 version published in *Canadian Theatre Review* 43 (1985). For more on the play's development process, see The Anna Project's "Fragments," in that issue. The play was also published in *The CTR Anthology*. See Filewod.

[2] The set designer was Trish Short; costumes were by Jordana Hawkins; the lighting designer was Meghan Johnson and the sound designer was Tara Johnston.

[3] The fifth actor operated the overheard projector and played characters other than Marianne, such as a friend who visits her twice (although in each visit the actor playing Marianne is different), the fiancée of the killer and a contemporary presence that disrupts the hysterical romanticism of a scene entitled "The story of Lucretia." I also mainly ignored the allotment of lines to M1, M2, M3 and M4, changing even which actor was assigned to which number from scene to scene.

[4] The actors and I developed the scene, with the invaluable contributions of Assistant Director, Mark Mason, and movement facilitators Lily Marquez Tamayo and Lisa Doolittle.

Works Cited

Anna Project, The. " Fragments: Afterthoughts." *Canadian Theatre Review* 43 (1985): 167–73.

——. "This is for You, Anna." *Canadian Theatre Review* 43 (1985): 127–66.

——. "This is for You, Anna." Filewod, *CTR Anthology* 249–81.

Donkin, Ellen, and Susan Clement. "Editors' Introduction." Donkin and Clement 1–9.

——, ed. *Upstaging Big Daddy: Directing Theater As if Gender and Race Matter.* Ann Arbor: U of Michigan P, 1993.

Filewod, Alan, ed. *The CTR Anthology: Fifteen Plays from* Canadian Theatre Review. Toronto: U of Toronto P, 1993.

——. *Performing Canada: The Nation Enacted in the Imagined Theatre.* Monograph. Critical Performance/s in Canada ser. *Textual Studies in Canada* 15 (2002).

Gallagher, Kathleen. "Dramatic Arenas for Ethical Stories." *Resources For Feminist Research* 29.3/4 (2002): 167–76.

Hamilton, Sabrina. "Split Britches and the Alcestis Lesson: 'What Is This Albatross?'" Donkin and Clement, *Upstaging.* 133–49.

Munford, Rebecca. "'Wake Up and Smell the Lipgloss': Gender, Generation and the (A)politics of Girl Power." *The Third Wave: A Critical Exploration.* Ed. Stacy Gillis, Gillian Howie and Rebecca Munford. Basingstoke, UK: Palgrave MacMillan, 2004. 142–53.

Newbery, Liz. "'Mirror, mirror on the wall, who's the fairest one of all?': Troubling Gendered Identities." *Resources for Feminist Research* 29.3/4 (2002): 19–38.

Ng, Roxana. "Teaching Against the Grain: Contradictions and Possibilities." *Anti-Racism, Feminism, and Critical Approaches to Education.* Ed. Roxana Ng, Pat Staton, and Joyce Seane. Westport, CT: Bergin and Garvey, 1995. 129–52.

Scott, Shelley. "Collective Creation and the Changing Mandate of Nightwood Theatre." *Theatre Research in Canada/Recherches théâtrales au Canada* 18.2 (1997): 191–207.

Sullivan, Esther Beth. "Women, Woman, and the Subject of Feminism: Feminist Directions." Donkin and Clement, *Upstaging.* 11–34.

Wilson, Ann. "The Culture of Abuse in *Under the Skin, This Is for You, Anna* and *Lion in the Streets.*" *Contemporary Issues in Canadian Drama.* Ed. Per Brask. Winnipeg: Blizzard, 1995. 160–70.

Mining "Turbulence": Authorship Through Direction in Physically-Based Devised Theatre [1]

by Bruce Barton

Motivated by a conventional practice that has assumed the weight of accepted wisdom, *authorship* is almost invariably associated with dramatic *texts*, while *directing* is understood as the realm of theatrical *realization*. But the clarity of such neat categorizations is itself, of course, the product of a desire for conceptual and practical efficiency rather than an accurate or productive demarcation of responsibilities or territories of activity. The relationship between, on the one hand, a writer's initial organization of ideas, images, and rhythmical patterning, and, on the other, a director's subsequent orchestration of substances, sounds, light and bodies, is a far more complicated, fluid, and negotiable field of interaction. Furthermore, not surprisingly, the complexity of this situation is multiplied exponentially when the role of "writer" is fragmented and dispersed among a collective body of creator/performers utilizing found, adapted, and invented text within a physically-based devised process of discovery. Issues of precedence and priority in terms of the relationship between text and movement emerge primarily in terms of the performer/creators' resistance to, and refutation of, conventional expectations (which thus remain a powerful and defining preoccupation). Within this context, the designation of authorial and directorial roles, rights, and functions becomes highly problematic.

Admittedly, "physically-based" and "devised theatre" are sufficiently broad references as to incorporate a wide range of very different objectives, techniques and styles. However, for the purposes of this argument, the terms identify an approach to theatrical creation and performance for which text is not accorded primary or originary status – indeed, in which text is often a secondary component, in both the qualitative and chronological senses of "secondary." Rather, the elements of visual and aural presentation, as well as the work's engagement with narrative, equally or more often emerge out of a set of processes that are based in movement, improvisation, physical discipline, and the set of creative instruments understood and experienced as *instinct* and *intuition*. [2] It is, in a sense, an *opportunistic* form of theatrical creation which, to an at times unnerving degree, relies upon an engagement with coincidence and the unpredictable through a heightened sensitivity to possibility and a rigorous ability to exploit its gifts. It is a form of theatre which, as Eugenio Barba contends, "must forge [its] own fortuitousness" (59).

Any attempt to gain a firmer understanding of the roles of direction and author-ship within physically-based devised theatre must first acknowledge that such designations are only negotiable subsequent to a preliminary consideration of the concepts of *writing* and *composition* within this complex and collaborative context. In particular, the role of *text* in a creative process that foregrounds what Eugenio Barba has called a "dramaturgy of changing states" (a concept to which I will return) is charged with anxiety and ambivalence, as inherently ambiguous physical move-ment—grounded in instinctive and intuitive performativity—wrestles with the conventional constraints of symbolic language, generating what Barba effectively calls "turbulence." Under these circumstances, I propose, composition within physically-based devised theatre can effectively be understood as a *montage*-based hybrid process of authorship *through* direction—an act of "mining turbulence"—in an effort to extract, manipulate and refine a distinctly visceral and substantial performance text.

The Case of Icaria

In the autumn of 1998 I witnessed a theatrical production that radically altered my understanding of performance. Staged in the dynamic (if economically desperate) confines of the Khyber Klub in downtown Halifax (Nova Scotia), the work was entitled *Icaria,*[3] and was the creation of Number Eleven Theatre. Led by director Ker Wells, a founding member of the now defunct but deeply influential Primus Theatre (of Winnipeg, Manitoba), the company included Primus co-member Sondra Haglund, as well as Varrick Grimes, Alex MacLean and Elizabeth Rucker – all alumni of Primus training programs. Having never seen a Primus production, and being only minimally familiar with the company's modes of training and performance, I was not prepared for the level of physical intensity, rigour and innovation that each member of Number Eleven Theatre brought to the execution of the demanding, wildly physical, yet intricate *Icaria*. Equally remarkable was the irresolvably elusive and eclectic use of diverse textual styles and sources that made up the symbolic mosaic of the play's narrative. For while a succinct synopsis of the play's "story" is conceivable, its recounting results in a misrepresentative diminishment of the performance to a degree far exceeding that in the case of traditional, text-based production. Swirling around a basic scenario depicting a young girl (Rucker) and her recollections of her distracted and disaffected mother (Haglund), her charismatic and abusive father (Grimes), and her idealistic and ultimately suicidal brother (McLean), *Icaria* unques-tionably created a deeply moving sense of context, character and resolution. Described by *Halifax Daily Mail* reviewer Ron Foley MacDonald as "part circus, part nightmare," the work tapped into instinctive and intuitive elements of anxiety and aspiration that, for this spectator, are seldom accessed in my regular visits to the theatre. Not since, perhaps, my equally startling discovery of Gilles Maheu and Carbon 14's[4] *Le Dotoir*, at the beginning of the 1990s, had I been so forcefully reminded of the potential of live performance.

Icaria is structured, both narratively and in terms of its physical design, to unfold as a dream or series of memories. The playing space is long and narrow, and the audience is seated on both sides (in only a single row in the first production, and usually no more than two). One end of the space features a huge, exaggerated proscenium arch, conspicuously constructed from cloth and papier-mâché, with an accordion-style set of curtains that repeatedly open to reveal successive scenes of fantasy or remembrance. Daphne—the woman who becomes a young girl as she recounts her family's story—seems to struggle to fix her memories in terms of participants, tone and significance. Her father appears as a man who combines ready humour and joyful enthusiasm with quick anger and brutality; her mother is at times loving and playful yet at others aloof, mysterious, and emotionally distant; and her brother, Thomas, exercises the entire spectrum from ecstasy through utter, resigned dejection. A dinner table argument erupts into a balletic battle with chairs between Thomas and his father. As if by sleight-of-hand, the tablecloth—complete with dishes and cutlery—is lifted, swirled and transformed into a picnic blanket, and the kinetic family feud becomes a pastoral gathering under an open sky. Thomas repeatedly fascinates and horrifies his sister with fantastic bedtime stories that conflate mythology, fairy-tale, and apocalyptic prophecy. Finally, locked in his room, Thomas does battle with a monstrous, stilt-walking manifestation of his father (whose steel-pointed gaff is swung powerfully through the air within inches of Thomas and within mere feet of regularly speechless audience members) before succumbing to the impulse to take his own life. The performance ends with his family apparently preparing his still erect and alert yet clearly "dead" body for burial (one of the few moments in the play when all the family members share a common focus and intention). As the lights dim, Daphne pulls a peaceful, haunting Thomas out through the curtains of her memory on a small wooden wagon that they have played with at numerous points in the play, the two characters having finally achieved a state of shared calm.

Proposing this narrative relationship between the events of the performance, however, requires a considerable feat of imposed interpretation. For at almost no point throughout these intensely choreographed sequences do the verbal texts being delivered directly address or elucidate the forward progression or comprehensive significance of this scenario. Rather the performer/characters employ a highly poetic rhetoric of allusion and metaphor, as if rejecting language's linear, expository function, and substituting instead the establishment of emotional environment and the governance of tempo and rhythm. Thus, while the storytelling of *Icaria* is powerfully and undeniably engaging, it is also a collaborative act of construction that is in large part determined by a spectator's horizon of expectations and experience. As Alistair Jarvis has suggested,

> The experience of watching these heterogeneous elements brought together seems akin to that of contemplating a quilt. One is amazed not only at the skill with which dozens of pieces of fabric have been stitched together to form a unified work, but also at the images and memories evoked by the individual pieces. Encountering a quilt, some may be impressed by the pattern or composition of the work as a whole, while others may be drawn to specific patches which for them contain

significance. Each scrap may contain imaginatively within its edges the full piece from which it once came, or perhaps another artefact [sic] made from the same fabric. What connects the viewing of a quilt to the experience of this theatre piece is that each individual viewer will have a highly personal experience of the work. *Icaria* is so dense (and wonderfully so) that ... it is impossible to take the whole piece in as it passes before our eyes – the spectator must choose between texts or segments that develop simultaneously, and highly physical actions that occur often at opposite ends of the playing area. It seems inevitable that, presented with such diversity, each spectator must construct his or her own experience out of this work by choosing what to observe. As a result, the potential for personal resonances elicited by these choices will differ from viewer to viewer. (94)

Yet, as Russ Hunt asserts, "in the end, we do make sense of it":

Because of the discipline and control of the production, we believe that every movement, every flick of an eyelash, is deliberate, planned, part of an artifice designed to move us. Every accident is planned. We feel everything is suffused with purpose and meaning, and are prepared to wait till it makes sense – at least emotional sense, if not discursive, rational sense.

How is it possible for such an elusively constructed narrative to nonetheless sustain such a high level of engagement and individual identification? What are the compositional strategies at work so effectively in such a performance text?

Changing States

Certainly, the most immediate influence on the art and craft of Ker Wells and Number Eleven is the legacy of Richard Fowler and Primus Theatre. Yet an understanding of this lineage comes most accessibly through an appreciation of the Odin Teatret, where Fowler had studied extensively, and of Eugenio Barba, with whom Fowler maintained an ongoing professional and developmental relationship. As Lisa Wolford has noted,

One might suggest that the Odin influence in Primus's work is most visually discernible in relation to the use of masks and stilt characters in certain productions, yet such an influence can also be traced in the group's rehearsal methods and process of developing performance text, the rejection of a naturalistic performance style in favour of overt theatricality, and a preference for what Ian Watson describes as a concatenate plot structure over a more conventional, linear narrative. Even more significantly, however, such an influence is reflected in Fowler's conception of a theatre ensemble as a living entity. (40)

As Fowler, himself, asserted, "The members of Primus Theatre are precisely that, members, the articulating limbs of a living organism; the theatre of which they are members is not a building ... but the social unit which is the manifestation of their collective relationship" (qtd. in Wolford 40).

Further, while Wells is respectfully uneasy about citing increasingly distant influences, the "idea" of Jerzy Grotowski is also a conscious presence in Number Eleven's practice and ethos. "Discipline," "integrity," and "honesty"—frequent and elusive, yet also deeply resonant terms and concepts throughout Grotowski's writings—enter into Wells' discussion of both the company's process and it objectives, along with a conscious insistence that every idea and every image be entirely "earned" in the moment (Interview). Clearly, this preoccupation with *merit* echoes Grotowski's rejection of fixed rules and stereotypes, and his insistence that all decisions be rooted intuitively in the body. As Grotowski asserts in *Towards a Poor Theatre*, "[t]he essential thing is that everything must come from and through the body. First and foremost, there must be a physical reaction to everything that affects us ... If you think ... [y]ou must think with the whole body, by means of actions" (204). Beyond this fundamental alignment of the intellectual and the intuitive, however, Well's expressed obligation to *earn* every moment is directly connected to Barba's emphasis on the *pre-expressive* in both training and performance.

There are, according to Barba, three different dramaturgies within theatrical creation and production, and while they occur simultaneously, they develop separately. The first is "an *organic or dynamic dramaturgy*, which is the composition of the rhythms and dynamisms affecting the spectators on a nervous, sensorial and sensual level." The second is a "*narrative dramaturgy*, which interweaves events and characters, informing the spectators on the meaning of what they are watching." The third, most elusive, and for the purposes of this discussion, most significant, is a "*dramaturgy of changing states*, when the entirety of what [is witnessed] manages to evoke something totally different, similar to when a song develops another sound line through the harmonics" (60). In an approach to performance that is often tightly choreographed and painstakingly rehearsed, the dramaturgy of changing states operates without "technical rules," "distill[ing] or captur[ing] hidden significances," and producing "leaps from one dimension to another ... from one state of consciousness to another with unforeseeable and extremely personal consequences, both sensorial and mental" (60). The instance in which the transforming table cloth of *Icaria* radically alters every aspect of the performance—plot, characterization, theme, tone, tempo, spatial and physical relationships—quickly comes to mind in terms of this reference. The result or, more accurately, *product*, Barba contends, is two-fold: on the one hand, "enlightenment," and on the other, what Barba calls "turbulence." Intriguingly, turbulence is proposed as the more significant of the two outcomes. Only *apparently* a "violation of order," turbulence is, in fact, "order in motion" (61), disrupting "continuity, rhythm, and narrative," forestalling unity and deferring meaning.

Ultimately, according to Barba, "[t]he dramaturgy of changing states concerns the performance as a physical and sensorial event, as an organism-in-life. It has nothing to do with the written text, with the dramaturgy of the words, in the way that the vibratory quality of the singing voice has nothing to do with the score" (62). The "coherence" of such a theatre, then, is located in the performers' bodies: "The actions of the actors should possess a coherence independent of their context and their 'meaning.' They should appear credible on a sensorial level and be *present* on a pre-expressive one" (62).

As defined by Helbo et al., *pre-expressivity* is an anthropological term that refers to a "level" which precedes and contextualizes the particular feelings, passions and concepts—that is, the "expression"—of a specific situation of performance (78). On this pre-expressive level, "the actor expresses nothing but his presence." Intentionally sidestepping the rich but problematic ambiguity inherent in the term "presence," the authors propose that

> The actor's presence strikes us every time we watch a form of theatre with conventions unfamiliar to us and whose meaning we find difficult to understand. On the other hand the actor's presence escapes us when it is *hidden* by conventions we all know and by meaning we can all understand. Our ability to comprehend overshadows, almost to its total disappearance, the seduction of presence. But the fact that this presence … escapes our attention does not mean that it does not exist, or that it is not an integral part of that same process of comprehension that is obscuring our view of it. (78)

For Barba, however, the relationship between the expressive and pre-expressive levels—understood, paradoxically, as a prerequisite and a defining consequence of a performer's preparatory training—is less absolute. And by extension, the relationship between intellect and intuition—between conscious expression and pre-expressive presence—is less predetermined and passive. In *A Dictionary of Theatre Anthropology*, Barba notes,

> … the long daily work on physical training, transformed over the years, has slowly become distilled into internal patterns of energy which can be applied to a way of conceiving or composing a dramatic action, a way of speaking in public, a way of writing. Thought has a physical aspect: its way of moving, changing direction, leaping – its "behaviour," in fact. This aspect also has a pre-expressive level which can be considered analogous to the performer's pre-expressive work, that which has to do with presence (energy) and which preceded—logically if not chronologically —real and actual artistic composition. (55)

As literal descriptions, the highly metaphorical quality of both Grotowski's and Barba's writings (despite clear differences in style and intention) produces a beguiling combination of explication and poeticization – one which generates both perpetual potential for interpretation and, for the non-initiate who has not experienced a *physical* understanding of the concepts through training, a frustrating degree of abstraction. Yet these quasi-philosophical (even, on occasion, "mystical") systems of intellectual and physical training undergo a critical transformation in the creative practice of Ker Wells and Number Eleven Theatre. Philip Auslander, in tracing the developing understanding of the body and physical presence from the modernist through the postmodernist sensibility (for instance, I propose, from Grotowski through Barba and Fowler to Wells), has proposed that

> the distinction between a modernist and a postmodernist artist is an epistemological, not a historical, difference ... Whereas the modernist artist believes that ideological and cultural codes may be transcended, or even annulled, through transgression, the post-modernist artist recognizes that she must work within the codes that define the cultural landscape. (93)

In ways both subtle and profound, the members of Number Eleven Theatre operate both within and through an understanding that the powerful influences of Grotowski, Barba and Fowler are, in fact, primary "codes" within their own cultural landscape. As a result, their engagement with metaphor is primarily aesthetic and narrative, rather than philosophical, in nature, and the productive turbulence of their creative process involves both an evocation and a continuous critique (at time conscious, at others not) of the traditions through which it has evolved.

From Composition to Authorship Through Direction

A direct consequence of this shift in focus and intention is a distinct redefinition of both *direction* and *authorship* within the company's compositional processes. Specifically, within Number Eleven's postmodernist reorientation, the largely unquestioned central authority bestowed by a systematic "disciple"-based philosophical body of teaching gives way to a more self-consciously subjective, collective concession to directorial agency. Granted, Wells's role as the pivot around which the hybrid act of "authorship through direction" revolves remains central – as with Grotowski and Barba (and, for that, matter, Fowler); yet Wells's authority is, in a sense, liberated through a heightened group awareness of its arbitrary status as a consensual function within a collaborative equation.

Drawing on methods acquired while in Primus and further developed through ongoing application, the individual performing members of Number Eleven (Grimes, MacLean, Rucker and Jane Wells [5]) begin the development of a project in isolation, as each conducts his or her own research and creates initial "actions" (patterns of movement and voice.) These may be inspired by any combination of personal reflection and memory, works of visual art and music, and found or created text (drama, fiction, poetry and songs). The troupe may begin with an agreed upon initial inspiration for a full-length work, but it is regularly multiple in nature, involving elements as general as "the Holocaust," as specific as select short stories by established or obscure authors, and as abstract and evocative as folks songs from a particular ethnic group.

Each performer is, at the outset, responsible for defining his or her own field of information collection and creation, and for shaping it into one or more short movement/voice sequences. These actions regularly incorporate both naturalistic and highly stylized, even acrobatic gestures, and most perform an intentionally inconclusive and unstable curiosity in numerous, only partially and/or tangentially related source materials. Then, under Wells' directorial eye and sensibility, and working from this already once digested raw material, the company begins the long collaborative process of establishing connections and interpenetrations of meaning. Specifically, Wells assumes the lead role in the troupe's search for points of resonance (through similarity, contrast and parallelism) among the individual preparatory sequences. At this stage, this resonance is primarily physical in nature (e.g., in terms of spatial dimensions, direction, size, tempo, rhythm, etc.). After carefully observing the performers individually, Wells begins to orchestrate multiple, simultaneous enactments of two or more sequences. Asking for bodily repositionings and modulations of scale, velocity, etc., the director initiates a process of sculpting in both space and time, seeking out the most evocative, striking and engaging points of physical correspondence (indeed, physical *conversation*). Such sculpting is seldom an end in and of itself, however, and the most significant points of resonance are those that the director interprets as *thematic*. His early responses therefore assume a dominant authorial influence, as he attempts to identify the initial conjunctions, or sites of relational meaning, in the embryonic narrative structure. The gradually emergent nature of this structure results in the operative paradox of the work's authorship *through* direction: on the one hand, Wells's remove from the individual, physical acts of creation purchases him a central authority over their manipulation as factors of signification; at the same time, however, his *authorship* is almost entirely dependent on the material generated by the performers, and is in large part a function of astute and innovative observation, suggestion and organization.

Thus, even in its earliest phases, the process draws upon two successive stages of composition that involve bringing together "fragments" of resistant—since decontextualized—material, both textual and physical. Contrary to traditional expectation and practice, this resistance remains a conspicuous and productive characteristic of both the formal and narrative structures of the resulting work. In effect, this resistance represents an implicit testament to the company's process and an explicit concession to the unavoidably composite quality of human experience and the means through which it is interpreted and understood. Further, this strategy effectively foregrounds the equally and inevitably composite quality of the source texts employed – all of which (including, arguably, those newly created by the performers in the preparation of their initial actions) are themselves the product of previous de- and recontextualization through the historical processes of recording, documentation and representation. Indeed, the product of this strategy is exponential as each new level of performativity is requested of the "original" source material (i.e., at each point it is recontextualized within a new proximal relationship with other action sequences).

Further, through their recontextualization—both in terms of their proximity to the other fragments brought into play and in terms of their utilization within a performance situation—these fragments can be seen to assume significance that is not only expressive (i.e., through importation into newly evolving physical and narrative situations), but in a sense *pre-expressive* (i.e., demonstrating the fundamentally abstract yet undeniable "presence" of decontextualized speech and gesture). Jarvis's reference to *Icaria* as a "quilt" is particularly interesting in this light. Certainly the individual fragments that construct an actual quilt have expressive significance—*meaning*—in terms of their recontextualized relation to the other fragments used. Yet the same act of juxtaposition also foregrounds each fragment's distinct, decontextualized materiality. Similarly, the "quilt" of *Icaria* is both integrated and compartmentalized, thematic and material: expressive and pre-expressive.

The initial text fragments may be transposed, modified, or discarded through the progress of this work, as the emerging meaning of the piece is developed largely through the evolution of a physical dialogue between the performers, the director, and the shared space through which they move. The motivations served by this process of compositional attrition are, as with any collaborative creation, multiple, as are the means by which they are achieved. Prioritizing spontaneity and the "fortuitousness" (following Barba) that is made possible by fluid responsiveness, Wells welcomes and, indeed, solicits the performers' input at virtually every step, attempting to remain sensitive to their unease, curiosity, criticism and creativity. Conversely, however, the director in this process must assume, with uncommon honesty and audacity, the weight of the work's central authorship, as the primary agent of selection, organization and modification. While these responsibilities attach themselves to virtually all theatre direction, Number Eleven's approach precludes a fixed (or even tentative) written text for the director to point to, consult for guidance, or hide behind. Thus, just as each of the performers has responded to the authors of their various source materials in their preliminary movement/voice compositions, so too Wells responds to the authors of those initial (and subsequent, evolving) actions—his performers— in the movement/voice composition of the work as a whole.

Intriguingly, Wells is insistent that at the base of this process is a commitment to "story." Indeed, the director has asserted that story is the only objective that can justify Number Eleven's creative process (Public Forum). Not entirely averse to the level of abstraction here attributed to the writings of Barba and Grotowski, Wells suggests that Number Eleven's compositional approach amounts ultimately to a search for the "best" story to be "discovered" within the specific conditions of a specific creative project (Interview). For Wells, however, the range of factors that culminate in a work's story are broad and variable – beginning with the source materials and extending through the physical space and place of creation, the length of available development and rehearsal opportunities, levels of physical and mental conditioning, clarity of individual and group focus, and the often random contributions and accretions of input that occur throughout the process, to name only the most conspicuous elements at play. As such, Wells contends, assertions of a single *correct* story are counter-productive.

Rather, what Wells terms the "best story" would seem more accurately to describe a composite understanding of narrative that overlays multiple, explicit, and conspicuously "spectacular" (and, thus, performative) modes of communication: dense, poetic and disjunctive passages of verbal text; tightly choreographed individual and group spatial negotiations; scale, rhythm and tempo of semi-autonomous physical movement; *a capella* aural variation, recitation and song. Wells insists that these elements must ultimately combine to produce an identifiable thematic focus and a progressive development of event and character. Clearly, however, these traditional narrative preoccupations are pursued through a highly unconventional and intensely physical struggle with material that is experienced viscerally as well as understood intellectually, and which is selected and generated in large part with an emphasis on its inherent resistance (physical as well as conceptual) to generally accepted strategies of dramatic storytelling.

Actors and Answers

Understandably, the experience of this creative process is as intimidating as it is liberating, and the company must be able to withstand prolonged periods of uncertainty and abstraction. These can only be sustained within a context where the performers' confidence in their director's ability to propose, foster, and distill from the group's explorations those elements that serve and enhance the (always) emerging narrative is absolute (while, ironically, always open to question). No one is more susceptible to anxiety in this situation than the director himself, who has on numerous occasions described the disappointment of performers (particularly student performers[6]) upon their realization that he does not, in fact, have a pre-established narrative structure to which he is adhering. Inevitably, this ready concession on the director's part results in a clear and possibly requisite juncture of challenged faith – which may only be momentary but which, in situations of limited personal familiarity and investment, can permanently define and curtail the possibilities inherent in Wells' approach.

Of particular interest here is the perceived degree to which conventionally trained actors (relying upon some variation of "method"-based psychological identification and motivation) can maintain high levels of personal focus and confidence, despite pronounced levels of experiment, when innovation is clearly contained within the traditional directorial parameters of "interpretation." Under this understanding, the "realization" of the pre-existing text, even when it involves conspicuous departure from prior materializations of that text, remains imaginatively contained within the relatively stable authority of the tolerant yet ultimately immutable script, earning for even the upstart and irreverent director highly elastic applications of poetic license. Conversely, however, when exposed to the far less common process of authorship *through* direction of devised theatre—that is, to the moment-to-moment creation of the work's aims and means of narration—such performers may quickly prove far fainter of heart. Further, when such performers are asked to directly bear a share of the responsibility of authorship (a level of centrality in the process that, ironically, so many of their informal personal strategies seem designed to purchase, whether or not consciously), the response is regularly expressions of protest and assertions that the director is either misinterpreting or outright abdicating her obligations. That the levels of indeterminacy which characterize these two different approaches (conventional direction vs. authorship through direction) are primarily distinguishable in terms of "type" rather than "degree" (i.e., in terms of the source of the indeterminacy rather than the odds that it can be resolved) attests to the power of familiarity and established categories of responsibility in the purchase of performer confidence and capability.

Unlike more traditional, text-based direction, then, which may also proceed through a process of inquiry and "asking questions," Wells's approach (as with much physically-based devised theatre) is not supported by preconceived solutions or goals towards which he is shepherding his actors. As the director is quick to assert, the answers, in large part, can only be provided by the performers through their individual explorations. Thus, again, Wells's authorship amounts to the precise articulation of the most relevant questions, the evocation of the most committed attempts on the parts of the actor/creators to respond, and the recognition of the most thoroughly *earned* answers. As the above discussion of story illustrates, however, despite the company's uncommon tolerance for/attraction towards multiple and inconclusive narrational strategies, the objective is not what, for instance, Erin Hurley has described as Carbon 14's self-consciously postmodern and mosaic-like "pastiche of unreconciled movement vocabularies" (29). Rather, Once again, Barba is an evocative filter through which to consider Number Eleven's process:

> Confusion, when it is sought after and practiced as an *end in itself*, is the art of deception. This does not necessarily mean that it is a negative state, one to be avoided. When used as a *means*, confusion constitutes one of the components of an organic creative process. It is the moment in which material, prospects, contiguous stories, and diverse intentions become con-fused, i.e., fuse together, mixing with one another, each becoming the other face of the other. (62)

It is, specifically, this final image that provides a potential avenue into the complex issue of composition as authorship through direction in physically-based devised theatre. However, Barba's mixing or "fusing" of elements would seem to propose a degree of unifying closure that is absent from the work of Number Eleven (and, for that matter, Barba's own Odin Teatret). Rather, I here propose a metaphor that I believe more accurately describes Number Eleven's wrestling with resistance – one that posits, on the one hand, a more rowdy and unstable site of meaning and, on the other, a more visceral and substantive understanding of performativity. The metaphor to which I refer is "collision" – the fundamental act and condition identified by Sergei Eisenstein in the creation of *montage*.

From Mosaic to Montage

Montage, Eisenstein asserts in his mid-twentieth century writings on the formal attributes of film, is *conflict* – it is "the collision of two given factors [from which] arises a concept" (37). While the "factors" are material, the "concept" is psychological and emotional. Of particular significance is Eisenstein's insistence that montage is not a linear or cumulative process – not, following his contemporary, Pudovkin, a "linkage of pieces" into a "chain" of signification. Rather, for Eisenstein, montage is a process of superimposition, effecting collision not merely *between* distinct elements but *through* multiple levels of interpretation.

Granted, Eisenstein was attempting to establish a "unified system for methods of cinematographic expressiveness that shall hold good for all its elements" (39), ascribing to filmic processes a degree of symbolic stability approaching that of the Japanese ideogram that provided both his inspiration and his overtly systematic model. But, as Patrice Pavis, amongst others, has argued, any attempt to restrain theatrical signification within a controllable and fully decipherable process of "communication" represents both an impoverishment and a fundamental misinterpretation of the performance context. [7] Indeed, Eisenstein's own application of the concept—both in his subsequent writings on the topic and, in particular, in his employment of it as a compositional strategy in his films—places increasing emphasis on montage's powerful effects of evocation, rather than direct communication (i.e., of connotation rather than denotation). Similarly, when relieved of the totalizing intentionality of symbolic stability, the concept of montage intersects with the conditions of physically-based theatrical creation—and, specifically, that of Number Eleven—at central points.

The proximity of montage to more arbitrarily symbolic systems of expression emphasizes the ways in which it both approximates and deviates from traditional forms of writing (specifically, in this context, theatrical "text-based" writing), much as Number Eleven's unconventional approach to narrative is complicated and articulated through their declared attachment to story. The model in which distinct material units are forced into a collision that produces psychological and emotional concepts accurately describes the physical process employed within Number Eleven's compositional strategies. Granted, in this latter context the model emerges in a manner that is far less contained and predictable than is anticipated in Eisenstein's early theoretical writings – yet one which is intriguingly similar to that utilized in films such as *The Battleship Potemkin* (1925) and *October 1917: Ten Days that Shook the World* (1928). The troupe's process of creating initially disconnected and unrelated sections of movement and text that are then, in a very real sense, brought into thematic, spatial, and rhythmical collision parallels—in terms of strategy and objective—Eisenstein's pursuit of psychological and emotional concepts. And both approaches to meaning effectively embody (and, perhaps, provide welcome concretization to) Barba's proposed "*dramaturgy of changing states*, when the entirety of what [is shown] manages to evoke something totally different."

Particularly intriguing and evocative in this context, however, is Eisenstein's assertion of *superimposition* as a fundamental characteristic of montage. As previously stated, the composite understanding of narrative that emerges out of Wells's work with Number Eleven involves a spectator's experience of numerous, self-consciously performative storytelling strategies. While the company employs spoken text, song, and a physical vocabulary that ranges from realistic gesture through acrobatics, the precise relationships between these modes of communication are constantly shifting and being renegotiated in a manner that denies them stable interaction. This, in turn, requires a spectator to, in a sense, look *across* the multiple, semi-autonomous planes of signification in the search for comprehension. Meaning, ultimately, emerges as a product of simultaneous and contingent—that is, *superimposed*—but never ultimately coalescing modes of articulation. Further, perhaps most evocatively (indeed, inevitably even when unintentionally) superimposed within physically-based narrative constructions are the expressive and pre-expressive levels of the performance. Yet rather than an exclusive, zero-sum gain relationship between expressivity and pre-expressivity (as suggested in the earlier quotation from Helbo, et al.), it is possible to imagine a conflictual, superimpositional, and productively "concept[ual]" (i.e. *meaningful*) montage of performative levels, a signifying turbulence composed in and through the collision of the raw material of the performer's bodies and voices.

Possibilities and Limitations

The implications of these observations for an understanding of Wells's work with Number Eleven are extensive, and can only be considered in a preliminary manner within the scope of this article. Ironically, popular film-based dramaturgical strategies (utilized primarily within the product of Hollywood and its many international counterparts), which emphasize linear progression with near (or literal) "template" predictability, are regularly cited as a domesticating influence on contemporary theatrical writing. But the cinematic models thus derided correspond much more closely with Pudovkin's understanding of montage as a form of "linkage" – as, in effect, a logic-driven, Aristotelian assertion of narrative inevitability. Eisenstein's interpretation of montage, in contrast, proposes an evocative, indeed transformative effect in which, through abrupt juxtaposition, evocations of emotion exert the *conceptual* impact of psychological connotation. In this context, the onus of storytelling is relocated from the pre-existing textual narration to an accumulative (rather than progressively linked) sequence of semi-autonomous action sequences. As a consequence, within Eisenstein's articulation of montage authorship is primarily a process of editorial orchestration, as the raw visual and aural material is selected, organized, and conceptually superimposed in an attempt to generate the most powerfully communicative collisions of thematically resonant yet materially diverse elements.

It is difficult to find a more immediately applicable access point into Ker Wells's work with Number Eleven. The initial research carried out by the entire company and the action sequences prepared by the individual performers yield preliminary visual and aural elements. Given the process through which this raw material is developed, its inevitably diverse and autonomous yet thematically resonant qualities require that Wells direct a developmental process of manipulation and juxtaposition—of orchestrated collision—the results of which must be interpreted across multiple, simultaneous elements of performance. And, as in the case of Eisensteinian montage, the product must meet the dual criteria of powerful evocation that is at once materially striking and thematically resonant.

There are, of course, clear (and instructive) limitations in this interpretive model, and these too demand a degree of further, detailed analysis that must extend beyond this document. Unlike the raw material of film, Number Eleven's preliminary sequences are highly mutable and generative, and thus open to an ongoing process of transformation. In a manner closer to the current flexibility afforded by computer generated imagery than traditional film editing, Wells can call for adjustments of considerable subtlety, and can quickly revise issues of scale, direction, and tempo in ways unimagined by the creators of early cinema. Indeed, the company's creative process is one in which the original individual sequences may exist in a final production entirely as thematic and gestural "echoes," having undergone utter reconfiguration through the extended stages of development.

Yet, as noted, the company establishes and maintains a definitive investment in an approach to composition that precludes the foundation of a pre-existing narrative structure. Rather, their creative process is, in effect, almost entirely responsive to the physical and conceptual explorations executed and earned in the generative moment of collaborative development. Thus, rather than facilitate a linkage of progressive sequences, within a montage-based dynamic of authorship through direction Wells is responsible for the facilitation (the incitement *and* containment) of a volatile *chain reaction* of material collisions that is sustained through the accumulation of productive turbulence generated within a *dramaturgy of changing states*. For this researcher, the inherent potential—in both the company's approach to theatrical composition/performance and in the critical framework here proposed—is a source of huge promise and inspiration.

(2006)

Notes

1 This article is one of two connected inquiries, first drafted in 2003, based on the creative processes of Toronto's Number Eleven Theatre. The focus of this article is a detailed and theoretically-based analysis of the relationship between direction and authorship—authorship *through* direction—in the compositional strategies of physically-based devised theatre and, specifically, Number Eleven Theatre and its founder-director, Ker Wells. The other article, entitled "Navigating 'Turbulence': The Dramaturg in Physical Theatre," explores the role and function of the dramaturg in Number Eleven's creative work and other, related approaches to devised theatre. The two articles emerge out of the same developmental experiences and share descriptive material; however, they proceed into distinct areas of study and present separate bodies of analysis and interpretation. The other article is published in *Theatre Topics*. See Barton.

2   For the purposes of this study, the following definitions of "instinct" and "intuition" are applied:

> • **instinct**: "[I]nherited behaviour patterns, or skills, with motivations for rewards and fears for avoiding danger, though it is not in consciousness. It might be described as *knowledge*, gradually discovered by natural selection and stored in the genetic code. Although individual learning is not transmitted for inheritance, instinctive knowledge is" (Penguin 727).

> • **intuition**: "quick and ready insight ... the power of attaining direct knowledge without evident rational thought or the drawing of conclusions from evidence available ... knowledge gained by this power" (Penguin 737).

Instinct is thus understood here as inherent, pre-rational, and common to a species at a particular stage of evolution. Intuition is understood here as acquired but post-rational – individual learning that has become *implicit* (see Kihlstrom, Mulvaney, Tobias and Tobis 30–35), and which can influence behaviour without entering consciousness.

3   The premiere of *Icaria* was staged in the Turret Room of the Khyber Klub on Barrington Street, Halifax, Nova Scotia, in November of 1998.

4   Celebrated physical theatre troupe from Quebec, lead by Gilles Maheau.

5   Following the first production of *Icaria*, Sondra Haglund left Number Eleven; Jane Wells—Ker Wells's sister and Primus-trained performer—joined the company at that time and has appeared, along with Grimes, MacLean and Rucker, in all subsequent company productions.

6   Wells is a regular instructor at Canada's National Theatre School in Montreal, Quebec and Humber College in Toronto, Ontario.

7   See Pavis (23–36).

Works Cited

Auslander, Philip. *From Acting to Performance: Essays in Modernism and Postmodernism.* London: Routledge, 1997.

Barba, Eugenio. "The Deep Order Called Turbulence: The Three Faces of Dramaturgy." *TDR* 44.4 (T168) (2000): 56–66.

———, and Savarese, Nicola. *A Dictionary of Theatre Anthropology: The Secret Art of the Performer.* London: Routledge, 1991.

Barton, Bruce. "Navigating 'Turbulence': The Dramaturg in Physical Theatre." *Theatre Topics* 15:1 (2005): 103–19.

Eisenstein, Sergei. *Film Form: Essays in Film Theory*. Trans. Jay Leyda. New York: Harcourt, Brace & World, Inc., 1949.

Grotowski, Jerzy. *Towards a Poor Theatre*. New York: Simon and Schuster, 1968.

Helbo, André, J. Dines Johansen, Patrice Pavis, and Annie Ubersfeld. *Approaching Theatre*. Bloomington: Indiana UP, 1991.

Hunt, Russ. Review of *Icaria* (Black Box Theatre, University of New Brunswick, November, 2001). http://www.stthomasu.ca/~hunt/reviews/icaria.htm.

Hurley, Erin. "Carbone 14's Intelligent and Responsive Body." *Canadian Theatre Review* 109 (2002): 26–31.

Jarvis, Alistair. "Review of Icaria." *Canadian Theatre Review* 99 (1999): 93–95.

Kihlstrom, John F., Shelagh Mulvaney, Betsy A. Tobias, and Irene P. Tobis. "The Emotional Unconscious." *Cognition and Emotion*. Ed. Eric Eich, John F. Kihlstrom, Gordon H. Bowere, Joseph P. Forgas, and Paula M. Niedenthal. Oxford: Oxford UP, 2000. 30–86.

MacDonald, Ron Foley. "Review of *Icaria*." *Halifax Daily News* 28 November 1998: 31.

Pavis, Patrice. *Languages of the Stage: Essays in the Semiology of the Theatre*. New York: PAJ Pub., 1982.

Wells, Ker. Personal Interview with the Author. 11 October 2003.

———. Public Forum, North American Cultural Laboratory's Festival of New Theatre, in the Catskill Mountains, New York. 15 August 2004.

Wolford, Lisa. "Seminal Teachings: The Grotowski Influence: A Reassessment." *Canadian Theatre Review* 88 (1996): 38–43.

Towards a Poetics of Popular Theatre: Directing and Authorship in Community-Based Work

by Edward Little

Community-based theatre in Canada is fundamentally concerned with issues of cultural diversity, access, the impact of public participation in the arts, audience/ performer relationships, empathy, activism and public discourse. As a consequence, this theatre offers complications and challenges, as well as an expanded repertoire of approaches to directing and authorship in Western drama. To evaluate these contributions, however, requires understanding their aesthetic terms of reference. But while considerable attention has been focused on the social implications of popular theatre —including its measurable impact on participants and communities—relatively little attention has been paid to community-based theatre as an art form. This paper proposes a provisional poetics of popular theatre that suggests ways in which the form might contribute its own aesthetic criteria for evaluating efficacy and "excellence" in art, as well an expanded, more socially and culturally inclusive vision of traditional Western aesthetics.

John Murrell has said that the role of all art is to ask difficult questions (1). I would add that this must apply not only to the questions that the work of art poses for its audience but to the questions that artists must continually ask themselves about their creative practice. In community-based theatre, the difficult questions remain obscured within a persistent either/or conceptualization of art and social action. This is a road well travelled, yet we continue to find ourselves bogged down in muddy debates in which aesthetic accomplishment and social efficacy are characterized as competing or mutually exclusive. Socio-cultural intervention is, in essence, the inspiring story or content of community-based theatre. To whatever degree the authorial or directorial roles are assigned to single individuals overseeing all aspects of staging or to a collaborating team working to the same ends, artists in popular theatre are inevitably working towards an integrated vision of art, life, popular education, and social action. Our difficult questions relate to the negotiated authorship and ownership of collaborative art, to the ethical practice of art that explicitly engages with local life, and especially to the ways in which our aesthetic expression integrates artistic and social goals. How then should artistic accomplishment in popular theatre be evaluated? And who defines "art" and social action?

To ask these questions requires that we examine our own complicity in the ideological agendas that are driving polarized and binary conceptions of art and social action. To consider publicly funded art as the exclusive realm of the professional, for example, can reinforce ideological, systemic, and formal impediments that continue to exclude voices and notions of authorship from beyond the current margins. To fail to question inherited notions of art, beauty, and utility risks reinforcing the kinds of already-decided cultural agendas that are stultifying the ability of our theatre to respond to the contemporary experience of multicultural life. This perpetuates the marginalization of artists—particularly those from socially and culturally diverse backgrounds—who wish to work outside Eurocentric frameworks or modernist traditions and who would explore a truly multicultural aesthetic.

Defining Art and Social Action

Augusto Boal, with his concept of "The Cops in the Head," adapted Theatre of the Oppressed to accommodate the complexity of socio-cultural contexts in which oppressor and oppressed do not fall so discretely into separate camps. This seminally altered our perceptions of theatre and intervention; yet, in spite of Boal, or perhaps *because* of Boal (I'm speaking of the widespread, often flawed application of his work) much of our thinking about community-based theatre remains rooted in unexamined notions of community, agency, authorship, and developing world conceptions of what constitutes social change. It is precisely this lack of ideological clarity that plays into the hands of those who would drive a wedge between art and social action.

Political theatre, participatory theatre, grassroots theatre, community plays, community theatre, community-based theatre, theatre for social change, theatre for development, *théâtre action, théâtre d'intervention* – all of these describe approaches to what artists in Canada commonly refer to as "popular theatre." Each shares a common commitment to include socially or culturally marginalized members of society in the creation of the work of art. Beyond this, the various names foreground localized practices as well as core (sometimes competing) ideological approaches to the work. Complicating matters, the discourse of popular theatre is by nature shifting and dynamic as it responds to exigencies within host communities and groups and in order to avoid colonization by the mainstream. Baz Kershaw contends that with the "promiscuity of the political in post-modernism," terms such as "political theatre" have outlived their usefulness. Kershaw draws popular forms together in what he terms "democratized performance," in which the "radical" impulse is characterized by "dialogic exchange, participatory engagement, performative absence, and aesthetic reflexivity" (*The Radical* 20).[1] Catherine Graham prefers the term "activist theatre." Graham was recently awarded SSHRC funding for a comparative analysis of activist theatre in five liberal democracies – Canada, the USA, the UK, France and Belgium. For Graham, activist theatre is defined by "the desire to broaden participation in the public life of specific local areas" (10).[2] Graham takes the premise that although "democratic decision-making is theoretically possible" in liberal democracies, "opportunities for participation in public life are declining" and "most forms of activist theatre are better understood as attempts to overcome the problems of liberal discursive regimes than as authentic representations of particular communities" (10,

15). All forms of popular theatre share a concern with countering globalization. They are often characterized by their use of theatre to help disenfranchised local groups bring concerns that are considered "too private" for public debate into the public eye and, in so doing, imagining collective options of redress.

For Graham, as for Kershaw and many others, any separation of artistic form and social utility is a false dichotomy because it is precisely the artistic choices and formal qualities of this theatre that generate reflection about the social life at the heart of the theatrical endeavour. This thinking is supported by recent liberal communitarian debates in which the use of the term community is not so much a reference to some pre-existing (perhaps even nostalgic) entity, but rather is indicative of a political strategy emphasizing collective responsibility for public life through actions designed to expose and affect power relationships at local levels.

Relationships of power, however, as Lib Spry reminds us, must be interrogated within both the structure *and* the formal choices of the popular theatre project (177). One of the many strengths of Jan Selman and Tim Prentki's recent book, *Popular Theatre in Political Culture*, is its forceful admonition to artists to recognize the need for intense self-examination and clear communication with regard to the ideologies informing particular projects and to the intentions and values inherent in the techniques and practices that collaborating artists choose to employ. Ideologies, intentions, and values, however, can be deeply naturalized. Our ideas of utility and beauty are often derived from inherited and unconscious categories and distinctions. Identifying and articulating these for discussion can be a difficult and time-consuming process – even amongst artists with considerable experience of working together. This process is invariably complicated when working across cultural and social differences.

Deeply held, and often unexamined, notions of community, for example, fundamentally inform the kind of public life a particular project seeks to enact or represent. Graham draws on the work of Seyla Benhabib to articulate tensions between integrationist and participatory views of community. The integrationist view of community posits that the problem of modernity arises from the loss of a coherent value scheme and system of belonging that would provide a solid foundation for public life. The participatory view holds that collective action can instead be based on sentiments of political agency and efficacy: in other words, on "the sense that what one does, makes a difference" and that "we have a say in the economic, political, and civic arrangements which define our lives together" (Benhabib, qtd. in Graham 77–81). Tensions between territorial and relational notions of community also have implications for popular theatre, especially as power in Western democratic societies is so often defined through land ownership, municipal and regional governments, or even locally based community and religious organizations. Yet while territorial approaches will be under pressure to identify and *include* diversity within a geographical area, relational approaches, by definition, tend to stress a commonality that may *exclude* such differences.

The communitarian ideal is the informing vision of what is known as the "collaborative community play" in Canada (the Colway community play in Britain). The communitarian ideal is, arguably, the most pervasively naturalized (and nostalgic) notion of community. It is predicated on traditional conceptions that, according to sociologist Derek Phillips, depend on four central characteristics: a common geographical territory or locale; a common history and shared values; widespread political participation (accomplished through collective activity); and a high degree of moral solidarity (10, 14).

Of course, as Benedict Anderson has pointed out, powerful illusions of continuity lending credence to any sense of common history and shared values is at root a narrative strategy that often depends upon the "remembering" of ostensibly "forgotten" histories. [3] Similarly, a "let's all work together on this" appeal to collective action can also serve to mask real inequities in political participation, and moral solidarity often wears the mask of reactive righteous indignation.

Other notions of how political agency and moral solidarity should and might be achieved pertain to distinctions between community education and community development – two ideological approaches that are often confused or conflated. Activists working on a project may push for more prescriptive approaches involving "education *of* the community." In such cases, the activist's view of the need to generate immediate preconditions for a healthy community may take precedence over a more developmental approach that requires the negotiation of a higher degree of consensus enabling community participants to more fully participate in the ideological framing and content of the project. [4]

There are polarized schools of thought within ideas of community development as well. Selman and Prentki draw attention to work informed by the "consensus or liberal view on the one hand, and the conflict or radical view on the other" (32). The consensus view sees society as an organism – its various parts contribute to the functioning of "the whole in much the same manner as the organs of the body work together to perform necessary functions." In this conception, society is made up of co-operating elements, and the emphasis is on common values and beliefs. Adherents of this view "approach social change in incremental and relatively optimistic terms," and community-based theatre practitioners often take comfort in "the positive on-the-spot experience which theatre can effect." This is seen as "a significant step in a long series of such steps" (Selman 32).

K. Rubenson contends that the consensus view tends to obscure the degree to which inequity arises from the vested interests of particular individuals or groups. This propagates assumptions that inequity is a natural consequence of the overarching needs of society taken as a whole and that because individual survival is "contingent upon the survival and well-being of society," inequity is inevitable, necessary, and even beneficial (qtd. in Selman 32). Rubenson stresses that "the system of classification in any society is essentially an expression of the value system of that society" and "the rewards accruing to certain positions are a function of the degree to which their quality, performance, and possessions measure up to the standards set by society" (qtd. in Selman 32).

In contrast, adherents of the conflict view believe that social inequity results from the fact that society consists of groups with fundamentally different, often incompatible interests, and those with privileged positions will seek to defend entrenched interests. As Mark Selman puts it, "for those who take this view, the belief that individuals succeed by equipping themselves better to fulfill roles important to society is seen as a myth, moreover as a myth which is useful for those in power as it tends to promote satisfaction with the status quo" (qtd. in Selman 32).

The implications of these various ideologies for authors and directors of popular theatre are, of course, tightly tied to the particular goals of specific projects and their various intentions to assist individuals or populations to variously cope with, and/or to intervene in, existing social structures. While these various ideologies may be able to work together towards the same goals within the same project, they are often, in fact, operating in unexamined contradiction even within individuals – principles of artistic meritocracy within notions of cultural democracy, for example, or struggles between activism and community development, or the inherent tensions between a prerequisite need to affirm common ground within a community in order to generate a platform for intervention. A key directorial function in popular theatre is to ensure that these ideological differences are recognized and accommodated – implicitly through aesthetic expression and explicitly through project planning. Any degree of failure in this regard results in both structural and aesthetic cross-purposes.

Towards an Aesthetics of Popular Theatre

Directors and authors of popular and community-based theatre are charged with the responsibility of discovering ways in which the ideologies, intentions, and values of projects can be expressed as an aesthetic weave and a social weft in the creation of an artistic fabric. The current polarized climate between art and social action, however, means that evaluations of *artistic accomplishment* in popular theatre are usually subject to a naturalized criteria of "artistic excellence" determined by, and for, mainstream theatre. To resist this (and taking a page or two from Brecht's Epic theatre and John McGrath's Working Class theatre), the following diagram suggests points of intersection within a comparative hierarchy of aesthetic values as a generalized starting point for a provisional "poetics" of popular theatre. [5]

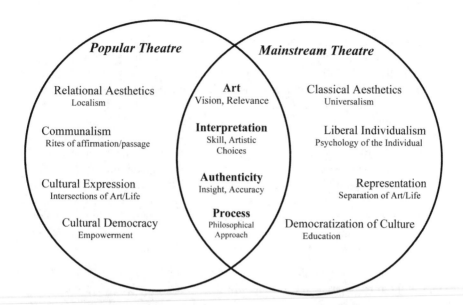

At the top of the hierarchy, both approaches aspire to vision, relevance and quality in the artistic product. Similarly, both value skill, originality and artistic choices in interpretation, and in accuracy and authenticity of insight. Mainstream theatre, however, traditionally favours a classical aesthetics that privileges liberal individualism through an emphasis on the skills and accomplishments of author, director, designer, and actor-in-role; seeks universality in representation; and advocates a clear aesthetic separation between practices involving "art" and the participatory life of the community. To achieve the widest possible dissemination of its artistic products, mainstream theatre subscribes philosophically to the democratization of culture.

Popular theatre, in comparison, values a relational aesthetics in which vision, relevance, interpretation and authenticity proceed from localized cultural expression that is rooted in a communal sense of utility, participation in art and public life, and a "grass-roots-up" inspired philosophy of cultural democracy.

A binary approach to this paradigm posits that these parallel sets of values *can* co-exist, but only as expressed in separate practices. This ignores the degree to which key aesthetic values are held in common. A *Ven*, or continuum approach, argues that they *must* co-exist – and suggests that they constitute central values informing the processes of "production" and the products of "consumption" respectively.[6] The continuum approach insists that cultural democracy and the democratization of culture be recognized as interdependent, complementary parts of a vigorous, inclusive, and expanded vision of theatre and cultural life. This offers a veritable Kama Sutra of aesthetic alternatives to the commonly prescribed missionary position in which categories such as "amateur/professional," "popular/mainstream," or "life/art" are seen as competing and/or mutually exclusive.

An Aesthetic of Cultural Democracy

Cultural democracy is predicated on direct public participation in the creation of a living, responsive culture. It defines the opposite end of the continuum from the democratization of *culture* – or what Roy Shaw, a past secretary of the British Arts Council during the Thatcher era, refers to as the "high arts." The democratization of culture is concerned with promoting wider public access to "high arts" through touring, regional funding, networking, and most importantly education. Shaw seminally championed the view that "high art" should, by definition, transcend such differences as class by appealing to our common humanity. The "sophistication" of "high art," however, means that in order to "inherit culture, you must make an effort, sometimes a considerable one," and therefore education must be the "prime factor in facilitating greater access to the arts." Advocates for community-based arts, such as Owen Kelly, counter that an exclusive practice of democratizing culture can also be seen as a system for the "popularization of an already decided cultural agenda" – one which values *consumption* of the arts over *participation* in the arts.[7]

Cultural democracy is a powerful mechanism of authorship in popular theatre. It generates the raw material comprising both the social weft and the artistic weave. It seeks to reconcile what Alison Beale calls "the antithetical relationship" between *culture* – defined "as a way or ways of life particular to peoples and nations" – and *art* – defined as "a set of activities chosen according to elite and traditional values for support and promotion of the state" (356). The aesthetic expression of cultural democracy is multiple: diverse voices foregrounding authenticity through direct community participation, artist/community partnerships, and interdisciplinary and multidisciplinary approaches to planning and artistic creation.

Cultural democracy represents and reflects the social and cultural diversity of streets, neighbourhoods and cities. To this end, authors and directors of community-based projects often integrate ritualistic elements not only into performances but into "gathering" (pre-production) and "dispersal" (post-production) phases of the theatrical event (Bennett 12, 96ff). These socially or culturally specific activities can range from conservative evocations of barn-raisings, dances, auctions, fairs, weddings, funerals, and the like to more radical practices involving gang initiations, street protocol, and the sex trade. Such elements of cultural expression serve to reflect or challenge local values or concerns while heightening the sense of authenticity and relevance of the project as an artistic expression of "a way or ways of life" (Beale 356). Audience participation in ritualistic elements adds a more visceral experience, and ritualistic gathering and dispersal activities break down amateur/professional and popular/mainstream binaries, blur the lines between beginnings and endings, and create an extended theatrical event in which art and daily life are not regarded as mutually exclusive. An aesthetic of cultural democracy is less about a specific performance event and more about an integrated vision of art and life that unfolds over a substantial amount of time. Local knowledge is essential to an appreciation of art created from the impulse of cultural democracy. Shaw called for considerable effort to comprehend high art – popular theatre also requires a commitment far beyond an hour and a half in order to render its particular social weft visible within its aesthetic fabric.

There are, of course, risks and pitfalls for authors and directors within an aesthetic of cultural democracy. Floyd Favel Star warns against simplistic and literal stagings of ritual onstage, advocating instead that art lies in finding the roots of the ritual and working with an embodied evocation of some aspect of this essence (84–85). Similarly, simply representing "life as it is lived" without editorial intervention—particularly when such representations involve instances of social injustice—can contribute to reductive and voyeuristic portrayals that may actually work against the initiating impulse to challenge marginalizing hegemonic structures. Furthermore, authors and directors working in an aesthetic of cultural democracy are often under considerable pressure to include too many contributions from the community—irrespective of their relevance to a project's artistic vision—and to represent consensus. This can result in a loosening of the kinds of condensation, timing, and immediacy that are common to modernist art, as well as in a dilution of ideas or dramatic conflict. [8] To counteract these liabilities, authors and directors must embrace an overarching narrative strategy that is capable of sustaining multiple points of view in dramatic suspension without evoking simplistic closure while remaining within a project's need for consensual participation. The artistic treatment of dissonant voices requires a directorial approach that renders such tensions a subject of creative theatrical exploration in a manner analogous to Boal's concept of "analogical induction": the simultaneous creation of multiple analytical perspectives (45).

Cultural Expression

Cultural Expression in popular theatre is the stuff of the social weft. As noted above, it embraces an ethos of direct and meaningful community participation in the creation of theatrical art. Subscribing to pedagogical principles of active learning, an aesthetic embracing cultural expression aspires—to varying degrees and in varying ways—to be a theatre *by*, *for* and *about* the members of its constituent communities. It resists the rigid separation of artist and audience common to professional models. Artists and community members work together to create varying types and degrees of authorship involving the aesthetic expression of both shared and individual experiences and concerns.

To ensure that participation is widespread and meaningful, any approach must recognize and accommodate divergent notions of community and social action. These are fundamentally drawn together under Raymond Williams' conception of community as "the necessary mediating element between the individual and the larger society" (95). This is often reflected in an aesthetic in which the community is positioned as protagonist with the internal and external struggles of individual members staged as elements of dramatic conflict. [9] An overarching intent common to community-based theatre is to create an iconic representation that celebrates negotiated values, privileges human creativity (as opposed to expensive and resource-consuming technological solutions), and affords a pragmatic appreciation of the potential utility of art as a resource-effective means of addressing community concerns. To this end, the directorial use of simple, yet creative transformations illustrates a central principle of a popular theatre – perceptions and reality are transformable through group action. This pragmatic sense of the potential social efficacy of popular theatre opens creative possibilities for a dynamic and dialogic experience that reaches out to new audiences and prepares the way for various additional kinds of communal input and dialogue extending into the dispersal phase of the project. Cultural expression values the local over the universal, and individual *emergence* within a community context over individual *accomplishment*. Boal characterizes this as a "rehearsal for change." In such ways, an aesthetic of cultural expression stages collective representation and activity as an emancipatory act, highlighting relationships between individual expression, growth and community development.

Communalism

Whereas liberal individualism in mainstream art tends to place great value on the skill of the actor-in-role, the aesthetics of cultural expression and communalism value the community *performer-as-role*. The local nature of the work means that community members will often know the everyday roles of any given performer, and this will be clearly in mind as they witness the performer onstage. The staging of personal testimony is often used as the most direct way of staging a *performer-as-role's* struggle against personal limitations, social conditioning, or cultural taboos. In community-based projects with multiple constituencies, a key directorial challenge is to make the principle of *performer-as-role* appropriately visible to audience members not from the particular performer's social or cultural background. The aesthetic expression of this can be analogous to the Brechtian narration of role, the use of allusion or dramatic irony in mainstream theatre, or even an in-joke.

The liabilities of an aesthetic of communalism often pertain to choices about localism, and about the treatment and positioning of *performer-as-role* within the aesthetic tapestry. Localism in content—local stories or legends, or even adapted universal myths or canonical texts—can fall victim to reductively self-congratulatory and sentimental representations. Authorial and directorial considerations for any particular text must also balance social efficacy and artistic merit: not in terms of a text's suitability as a vehicle for writers, directors, designers or professionally trained performers, but rather in terms of its ability to strike a creative balance between, on the one hand, staging community power relations and concerns and, on the other, the talents, skills, and personal realities of community participants. The sophistication (or lack thereof) of directorial choice and ideological clarity in these areas is a measure of artistic skill and interpretation.

Where cultural democracy and cultural expression largely constitute the social weft, communalism within a relational aesthetic makes up the aesthetic weave. This comprises the artistic treatment and realization of the negotiated intentions and values of communalism, cultural expression and cultural democracy. The directorial challenge is to stage community as a form of Brechtian Gestus – revealing such things as unexamined beliefs, social dynamics, relationships of power, and coercive tensions between socially and culturally specific notions of "public" and "private" spheres. Directorial choices that render the processes of creation visible in the performance event can be used to draw viewers' attention to the politics of production as a reflection of specific constructions of cultural expression and cultural democracy. Aesthetic accomplishment relates to the artistry with which such factors are rendered visible and constructed, and therefore are negotiable and subject to change. Theatre semioticians and anthropologists also challenge popular theatre directors to adopt an awareness of how theatre's formal qualities might be used to draw attention to unconscious distinctions and categories relating to inherited notions of beauty and utility. This might be done explicitly through the kinds of extended and participatory "gathering and dispersal phases" noted earlier, or more subtly through the creative positioning of rhetorical (form-related) and authenticating (locally-significant) conventions. Authorial and directorial choices establishing relationships between these conventions can provide a distancing effect or allow editorial commentary through the juxtaposition of local and universal significances. An aesthetic of communalism can be further evaluated by the sophistication of its engagement with resonant social and cultural roots within its host community. These can be expressed both in text and more formalistically through movement, gesture, music, linguistic rhythms, tones and idiosyncratic syntax that are arranged and deployed in ways that confirm authenticity while offering possibilities for analogical induction through de-familiarization. Casting *performer-as-role* against type can also serve this end.

A striking testimony to the power of communalism comes in the form of an anecdotal story that Jon Oram (a former artistic director of Britain's Colway Theatre Trust) tells about London-based critic Michael Billington's response to Colway's 1984 Dorchester community play (written by David Edgar and directed by Ann Jellicoe). An adapted version of the play was subsequently produced at the National Theatre under the direction of Sir Peter Hall, starring Dame Judi Dench and Tim Piggott Smith. Billington is reported by Oram to have compared the two productions by stating, "When I saw the community version, I was moved. When I saw the National's version, I was impressed!" [10]

As the Billington anecdote suggests, the effective staging of communalism and cultural expression is, to a very large degree, the source of power in community-based theatre. As in ritual, the community-based participant does not compete with the skill and conditioning of professional artists: rather, the community performer's greatest strength lies in its relational aspects – the authenticity, relevance and frame of reference of their performance for their host communities. In a post-modern context, to be either "moved" or "impressed" (or some combination of both) is a subjective experience that is largely contingent on environmental factors, which include an individual's sense of belonging within a matrix of geographic and relational communities and the degree and nature of an individual's participation in the theatrical event. A key directorial challenge within an aesthetic of communalism relates to striking a similarly dynamic balance along a continuum extending from *affirmation* (reification of a community as it is currently constituted and understood) to community *intervention* (cultural intervention, social change, or community advocacy in the face of a dominant or threatening other). [11] If the balance tips too far towards affirmation, the result can appear sentimental, nostalgic, self-indulgent or self-congratulatory, and lacking in either social or political analysis. Too far in the other direction, and the work risks the stridency of agitational propaganda and the alienation of community members. An artistic balance of the two presents the human condition of the community to itself in aesthetic ways that open space for new perspectives, dialogic engagement on both visceral and intellectual levels, and a demonstrated potential for social change. This is the measure of a project's relevance to its community.

Relational Aesthetics

To experience a popular theatre project's relevance to its constituent communities is to begin to recognize the aesthetic fabric in its entirety. Relevance with a relational aesthetic, however, must extend beyond simplistic portrayals of community and *performer-as-role* to evoke an examination of complicity. As noted, the qualitative measure of relevance is largely contingent on the creative and artistic balance struck between community affirmation and community intervention. If affirmation of identity becomes too tightly tied to a literal approach, there will be considerable pressure to "tell it like it is" and risk what Julie Salverson characterizes as the "lie of the literal": an approach that risks re-traumatizing participants, particularly in work involving personal testimony ("Art of Witness" 38). On the other hand, participants might express a desire to retreat from an unflattering portrait by invoking premature closure, or to project a sense of moral consensus or community solidarity where this is not yet in evidence. At the same time, what constitutes affirmation at a local level may well achieve intervention at broader regional, or even national, levels. In wrestling with the implications of Canadian policies on multiculturalism, for example, affirming participants' ability to cope at a local level with a status quo that Smaro Kamboureli characterizes as "a sedative politics" designed to "manage" ethnic diversity may well be an essential first step towards engendering future collective intervention that challenges essentialized conceptions of the immigrant experience as simply "an obstacle to be overcome" (82, 87). Finally, as Kershaw points out, elements of the "radical" may be found in nostalgic theatre, reminiscence theatre, or even museum theatre (*The Radical* 19). The responsibility for ensuring relevance through intervention, however, especially in terms of dramaturgy, narrative structure and collective authorship, falls heavily into the hands of the director(s), whose job is to ensure artistic integrity. Salverson cautions that reductive triads of victims, villains and helpers risk an "eros of injury" that prohibits explorations of complicity ("Questioning" 67). Rachel Van Fossen, in approaching writing for the large-scale collaborative community play, points out that the first time a community member says, "oh, the play can't be about that. You can't talk about that in the play," she almost invariably knows she has found a key social thread to be woven (Writing 10).

A relational aesthetic that would reconcile art and social action begins with a fundamental commitment to including community members "in both the creation and dissemination of theatrical work that opens space in public forums for people whose voices often go unheard" (Graham 11). The role of the director in this process is inevitably a form of creative mediation. The need for artistic self-examination and a corresponding re-examination of the primacy of art in this regard is receiving renewed theoretical attention in Canada from the likes of Graham, Selman, Salverson and Van Fossen. In a talk given at the Ontario Arts Council's 2003 Community Arts Conference, Salverson called for renewed attention to the "art" in community-based work and an end to the notion of artist as mere "facilitator" of the community's voice. Van Fossen, delivering the keynote address at a Regina symposium on community arts, called for artists to accept full responsibility for their role as co-creators in community-based work and for recognition that artists must also be (or function as) agents of change in themselves.

A Final Context

In late 1997, the Canadian Conference for the Arts released the Arts in Transition Report and Paper – one of several studies that informed the Canada Council's decision to implement the Artists in Community Collaboration Fund (ACCF). The report was undertaken with funding from the Samuel and Saidye Bronfman Family Foundation and the Department of Canadian Heritage, and was compiled after consultation with federal, provincial, territorial and municipal cultural departments and arts councils, and close to two hundred Canadian artists and arts professionals. The report concluded that audiences for the performing arts in Canada are either declining or not growing adequately and that there is an urgent need "to integrate the arts more deeply and widely in the broader community" (2, 3). The report warned that "unless the work of an arts organization is rooted in and meaningful to its community, its survival is precarious" (18). It stressed the need for meaningful *participation* in art (as distinct from spectatorship alone) and it suggested that arts groups and artists must do more to engage with the increasing cultural diversity of the country (30, emphasis added).

The report further noted that education, training and funding of artists in Canada continue to emphasise "modernist traditions" that place primary value on the artist as solitary creator – an approach overwhelmingly oriented to the development of artistic skills. As the report points out, this model "has produced and continues to produce many exceptional artists and works of art." At the same time, it found that many younger artists find (the modernist approach) confining, unable to accommodate their desire to work more closely with communities and incorporate social and ecological issues into their art (5, 6).

Conclusion

I believe we are charged with an urgent task to imagine and articulate criteria for artistic excellence that can inform directorial and authorial choices; engage with popular, community-based, and related theatrical expression on its own generic terms; and avoid using the criteria of oranges to assess the accomplishments of apples. Popular theatre shares with its mainstream counterparts the ability to evoke the communicative power of art: its resonant power of abstraction and its ability to engage contradictory ideological perspectives without imposing resolution or closure. Beyond this, popular theatre is making significant contributions to a vigorous, inclusive continuum of theatrical practice in Canada and abroad. Popular theatre promotes greater access and relevance in theatre arts, it encourages populist participation in art and social dialogue, and, through cultural democracy, it resists proselytizing the kinds of socially and culturally specific "missionary positions" which prescribe and limit the role of authors, directors, spectators, participants, or witnesses engaged in the theatrical act.

(2006)

Notes

[1]   Kershaw is talking both about the ways in which this kind of theatre can open space for the "Other" and about the kinds of multiple and excess meanings that this theatre can provide.

[2]   Dr. Graham has generously allowed me to cite from her unpublished document, "Theorizing Activist Theatre across Cultures."

[3]   Anderson's concern is primarily with the ways in which ideas of nationhood and nations have been "imagined" since the eighteenth century. I am suggesting that his work demonstrates the immense hegemonic capacity of these constructions at both the micro and macro level.

[4]   See, for example, Selman and Prentki's discussion of Brookfield's categories of community and adult education (35–37).

[5]   John McGrath's comparative schema of working class versus middle class aesthetics is explicitly concerned with qualities and values such as humour, variety, emotionalism, sentimentality, directness, immediacy, relevance, and overall effect.

[6]   The pictured diagram is commonly referred to as a Ven Diagram. It depicts points of ideological overlap between apparently competing ideas.

[7]   The debate between Kelly and Shaw is succinctly encapsulated in Kershaw (*Politics of Performance* 183–85).

[8] Consensus is of course an essential component of participatory community-based cultural democracy, and striving towards consensus can also be seen as a key indicator of power balance/sharing.

[9] This was also a common strategy in American historical pageantry: see Glassberg.

[10] I have heard Oram tell this story at many public talks he has given about Colway's work, and most recently at "The Gifts of Time Community Play Symposium" hosted by Everybody's Theatre Company (ETC) in conjunction with performances of ETC's Guelph Community Play Project, "The Gifts of Time." Eden Mills, Ontario, October 30–31st, 2004.

[11] Julian Hilton discusses community affirmation and community intervention within the anthropological context of "rites of intensification" and "rites of passage" respectively (60).

Works Cited

Anderson, Benedict. *Imagined Communities: Reflections on the Origin and Spread of Nationalism.* Rev. ed. London: Verso, 1991.

Beale, Allison. "The Dilettante's Dilemma: Speaking for the Arts in Canadian Cultural Policy." *Harold Innis in the New Century Reflections and Refractions.* Ed. Charles R. Acland and William J. Buxton. Montreal: McGill-Queens UP, 1999. 355–68.

Bennett, Susan. *Theatre Audiences: A Theory of Production and Reception.* New York: Routledge, 1990.

Boal, Augusto. *The Rainbow of Desire.* Trans. Adrian Jackson. New York: Routledge, 1995.

Canadian Conference for the Arts. "The Arts in Transition: Toward a Culture of Shared Resources: Building an Environment for the Long-Term Sustainability of the Arts in Canada." Ottawa, October 1997.

Favel Starr, Floyd. "The Artificial Tree: Native Performance Culture Research 1991–96." *Canadian Theatre Review* 90 (1987): 83–85.

Glassberg, David. *American Historical Pageantry: The Uses of Tradition in the Early Twentieth Century.* Chapel Hill: U North Carolina P, 1990.

Graham, Catherine. "Theorizing Activist Theatre across Cultures." Unpublished paper. 2003.

Hilton, Julian. "The Other Oxfordshire Theatre: The Nature of Community Art and Action." *Theatre Quarterly* 9.33 (1979): 53–61.

Kershaw, Baz. *The Politics of Performance: Radical Theatre as Cultural Intervention.* London: Routledge, 1992.

———. *The Radical in Performance.* London: Routledge, 1999.

Kamboureli, Smaro. "Sedative Politics: Media, Law, Philosophy." *Scandalous Bodies: Diasporic Literature in English Canada.* Don Mills, Ontario: Oxford UP, 2000. 81–130.

McGrath, John. *A Good Night Out – Popular Theatre: Audience, Class, and Form.* London, Methuen, 1981.

Murrell, John. The Graham Spry Lecture Series. ts. *Ideas.* CBC Radio, 1994.

Phillips, Derek L. *Looking Backward: A Critical Appraisal of Communitarian Thought.* Princeton UP, 1993.

Salverson, Julie. "Art and the Imagination in Community Art". *Kicking it up a Notch. The Community Arts Ontario Conference.* Toronto: Harbourfront Centre, May 2003.

———. "The Art of Witness in Popular Theatre." *Canadian Theatre Review* 90 (1997): 36–39.

———. "Questioning an Aesthetics of Injury: Notes from the Development of *Boom.*" *Canadian Theatre Review* 106 (2001): 66–69.

———. "Imagination and Art in Community Arts." *alt.theatre: cultural diversity and the stage* 3.2 (2004): 4–6.

Selman, Jan and Tim Prentki. *Popular Theatre in Political Culture.* Bristol: Intellect, 2000.

Spry, Lib. "Structures of Power: Toward a Theatre of Liberation." *Playing Boal: Theatre, Therapy, Activism.* Ed. Mady Schutzman and Jan Cohen-Cruz. New York: Routledge, 1994. 171–84.

Van Fossen, Rachel. "The Artist as Agent of Change in Herself." Address. Symposium: *The Artist as Agent of Social Change.* Common Weal Community Arts and CARFAC. Regina, October 2002.

———. "Writing for the Community Play Form." *Canadian Theatre Review* 90 (1997.) 10–14.

Williams, Raymond. *The Long Revolution.* Harmondsworth: Penguin, 1995.

Chocolate Woman
Dreams the Milky Way [1]

by Monique Mojica

I have been thinking for quite awhile about knowing and not knowing. What we know and *how* we know it. There's a saying in Spanish—"*saber sabiendo*"—literally "to know knowingly." But it also carries the connotation of knowing the unknown, the intuitively known or what we don't know that we know.

Most of the work that I have done over the past two decades reflects tapping this kind of knowing. I haven't always done it consciously and I haven't done it alone. Since 1991, I have collaborated with Floyd Favel and Muriel Miguel, among others, in performance research and laboratories searching out how to do consciously what we do *un*consciously. This work has resulted in studio investigations and produced performances that aim to identify and hone a methodology that Floyd has called Native Performance Culture. These two visionary directors have had an enormous influence on me and I will talk more about them later.

So, I have been doing this performance thing for a long time. It has been fifty years since I first started training (!), twenty-seven years since I first worked with an all-Native theatre company: *Indian Time Theater*, directed by Bruce King, out of the now defunct Native American Center for the Living Arts in Niagara Falls, N.Y. It has been twenty-four years since I moved to Toronto to be one of the early Artistic Directors of *Native Earth Performing Arts*. Those were the times just preceding the infamous "Native theatre explosion" in Toronto when our small circle included the Highway brothers, Tomson and René, Billy Merasty, Makka Kleist, Maariu Olsen, Gary Farmer, Shirley Cheechoo, Graham Greene and Doris Linklater. Over the years, I have accumulated quite a bit of material. Some there is no record of; some is in the form of drafts lost on floppy discs that my computer can no longer read. Some drafts hide in my not-so-organized filing cabinet, and still others are scraps of paper folded into notebooks: fragments of stories and notations of improvisations. As someone whose writing process includes doing laundry, making lists and sifting though papers, I excavated some two-decades old writings, dusted them off and had a look. What I found is that not only could I recognize recurring themes and imagery, but I could also trace a trajectory, a personal transformation as an artist and as an Aboriginal woman. This trajectory transforms amnesia through stories drawn from conscious memory, muscle memory, blood memory, then births organic texts, allowing me to emerge trusting the Indigenous knowledge encoded in my dreams, in my waking visions and in my DNA.

• • •

I have organized this chronologically so I am going to begin with some fragments from a writing exercise written during the development of *Princess Pocahontas and the Blue Spots* (1988), dramaturged by Djanet Sears. When I uncrinkled this and read it, it occurred to me that it contains many of the themes that I have worked with since and that it is something of a prophecy for my life's path.

> Once upon a time there was a little girl who lived in a stone cave, not entirely by herself – but almost. She lived that way, away from other people, because she was not entirely invisible – but almost (maybe about half). It made other people very uncomfortable that they couldn't see the other half of her even though she referred to it often and insisted that it actually was there and that it would bleed if she scraped it, and even scab over and get well.

> One day, the girl got tired of waiting in her stone cave for someone to believe her and she decided to leave. But she didn't know where she was going so she didn't know how to get there. So, she called to the spirit of heartbreak and sadness, the spirit of blood and rebellion, the spirit of back-breaking endurance and the spirit of transformation to help her make a map.

(The part of the story that follows has been lost but this is the next recovered fragment:)

> "Easy for you to say," said the girl, "but I only have one foot!"

> "Ah, ahhh," said the Grandmother spirits, "but just because other people cannot see your other foot doesn't mean it doesn't make an imprint when you walk. One foot in front of the other. Follow your own path, which is ours."

> So she did.

This is how elements from this exercise appeared in the final *Princess Pocahontas and the Blue Spots* script:

> **CONTEMPORARY WOMAN #1.**
> No map, no trail, no footprint, no way home
> only darkness, a cold wind whistling by my ears.
> The only light comes from the stars.
> Nowhere to set my feet
> No place to stand. *(rising)*
> No map, no trail, no footprint, no way home.
>
> *Sees basin of water; brings it to center.*

> He said, "It's time for the women to pick up their medicine in order for the people to continue." *(washes hands, arms)*

She asked him, "What is the women's medicine?" The only answer he found was, "The women are the medicine, so we must heal the women."

Washes from basin head, arms, legs, feet. Tiple theme begins.

Squatting over basin in a birthing position, she lifts a newborn from between her legs. Holding baby in front of her, she rises.

When I was born, the umbilical cord was wrapped around my neck
and my face was blue.
When I was born, my mother turned me over to check for the blue
spot at the base of the spine – the sign of Indian blood.
When my child was born, after counting the fingers and the toes,
I turned it over to check for the blue spot at the base of the spine.
Even among the half-breeds, it's one of the last things to go. (19-20)

"No map, no trail, no footprint, no way home," is a refrain echoed by the character, Lady Rebecca, as Pocahontas was renamed when she was converted to Christianity and then taken to England's Elizabethan court as an advertising gimmick. The theme of being lost in my motherland, finding no trail to follow because my grandmothers and great-grandmothers left no written records of themselves or their experiences, weaves through my early work. Narratives of wandering without a map, having forgotten my way, evolved to another recurring theme: memory/remembering/memorializing.

The following text fragment is from a writing exercise on 'amnesia' from *Un(tit)led* (1993), a piece co-written with Djanet Sears and Kate Lushington that explored the borders and boundaries of race and women's friendship. It was presented by Nightwood Theatre as a workshop production, facilitated by Clarissa Chandler, animated by Bañuta Rubess and directed by Muriel Miguel, with a set designed by Teresa Przybylski.

Amnesia fragments

Amnesia.
Long nightmare hallways,
lost, wandering.
Memory just slipped away.
All recognition of myself,
        who I was or am or might be
Where does the spirit of an amnesiac go to find refuge?
Does it hang around waiting to be recognized, brought home,
fed and warmed as the relatives on the other side do
when we forget to acknowledge them?
Plastic Halloween costumes,
        remnants of some vague need for ritual,
        walking in the night — not to wander

> nor to play but to be fed — Day of the Dead.
Sacred time to eat,
to celebrate,
to consecrate,
to pacify,
to subdue
Smoke filled hollows of spaces long neglected needing
> to be filled and fulfilled with the brimming nurturing
> sustenance of food
> of flavors on the tongues of we who are we who are we
> who make fire,
> who plant,
> who hands in the cornmeal bless the masa doug
> facing East.

I forgot.
I forgot the ant spray.
I forgot where I've been.
I forgot where I walked.
I forgot what it's like to walk on sand,
> to be in the ocean everyday,
> to sleep in a hammock,
> to wake at dawn and go with the other
> women in dugout canoes to the mainland
> to get water from the river in the forest.
I forgot what it's like to climb coconut trees and
> to know the jaguar watches over us
I forgot to remember.

The following is the piece that was actually scripted from this exercise and presented. It began as a monologue that I wrote and then we broke it up and Djanet and Kate added some character-specific images.

Forbidden Territory

> **MONIQUE.** In this forbidden territory, the landscape itself is
>   treacherous.
> **DJANET.** No Exit.
> **MONIQUE.** No entrance.
> **KATE.** No admittance.
> **ALL.** *(whisper)* Only, only us.
> **MONIQUE.** White lies in twisted words of "Discover America!"
>   *(singing)* "See the USA in your Chevrolet!"
> **KATE.** Poor Dinah.
> **MONIQUE.** Twisted words of nice hiding behind a Sunday school
>   smile.
> **DJANET.** Sssh, it's a secret.

KATE. *(singing)* *"Someone's in the kitchen with Dinah."*

MONIQUE. I always thought that meant Dinah Shore.

KATE. Poor Dinah.

MONIQUE. In this treacherous landscape where we by our natures are forbidden.

KATE. In secret we meet.

DJANET. It's a secret manoeuvre.

KATE. Sssh.

MONIQUE. Covert operation. Undercover. Under wraps. Under the stars, under the cover of night.

DJANET. Dinah never fooled me; I always knew she was Black.

KATE. In the shadows, in the margins…

DJANET. …our spines pressed flat against the wall, bellies pushed against our spines…

KATE. We gasp for breath to fortify us in our vigilance. Vigilance, unless I keep constant vigilance, I will forget everything

DJANET. …like a flower, a Black Cosmos, pushing up through the concrete.

KATE. I have forgotten who I am, I have forgotten who you are, I have forgotten why we are important to one another. The stars are going out inside my mind. I used to remember; how to dance, Pythagoras theorem, the capital of Australia.

ALL. We who are we who are we who are we… *(continues under)*

DJANET. …we who jump the borderline into this forbidden territory. Clandestine.

KATE. Clandestine.

MONIQUE. Clandestine mass graves – bones of my ancestors, bones of my ancestors, bones of my ancestors.

KATE. *(singing)* *"Dong dong bell, bodies in a well! Who put them in?"*

DJANET. Sssh, it's a secret.

MONIQUE. The souls of amnesiac Indians on the land roam like trick-or-treaters on a Halloween night in the suburbs.

DJANET. *(singing)* *"See the USA in your Chevrolet!"*

MONIQUE. White lies fall apart, shattered into millions of metallic mirrored pieces only to reproduce as mutant thoughts in the bodies of our unborn children.

KATE. Poor Dinah.

DJANET. Incognito we advance. Masked, veiled, disguised and hidden.

KATE. Subversive.

MONIQUE. We meet with a password:

ALL. Now!

The voice in the previous piece became a character I named Rebelda. Here is Rebelda's story:

There once was a woman named Rebelda. She has a plan. She has a memory. Rebelda knows they will come knock on your door, take you away and kill you. Rebelda knows they will burn your homes. Rebelda has no time to cry. Rebelda plans. Rebelda makes allies. Rebelda strategizes. Rebelda will not be wiped out.

She carries memorized in code: a recipe for cornbread, a song for birthing babies while under fire. Propaganda in her hand and propagation on her mind. A baby on each hip and a weapon in her hand. Rebelda has no time to cry. Rebelda plans. Rebelda makes allies. Rebelda strategizes. Rebelda will not be wiped out.

Like the coyotes, they haven't built a trap that will hold her. Like the raccoons, Rebelda spreads her brood. Rebelda steals. Rebelda eats garbage. Rebelda will not be wiped out.

• • •

Another one of the recurring images in my work is the bag of bones-carrying girl/woman. A character I will refer to as Bag of Bones/Rebecca first appeared in an early Native Earth production, *Double Take/A Second Look* (1983), written by Billy Merasty, Gloria Miguel, Maariu Olsen and myself and directed by Muriel Miguel. Rebelda is another aspect of the same character. In retrospect, they are both early versions of Esperanza, my massacre-collecting atrocity tour guide from Turtle Gals' *The Scrubbing Project* (2002 & 2005). My original inspiration for this character came from Gabriel García Márquez's *One Hundred Years of Solitude*, which I read for the first time at age sixteen. This is a passage from García Márquez's magical novel: "That Sunday, in fact, Rebecca arrived. She was only eleven years old ... Her entire baggage consisted of a small trunk, a little rocking chair with small hand-painted flowers, and a canvas sack which kept making a *cloc-cloc-cloc* sound, where she carried her parent's bones" (47). I carried this bag of bones around for a long time – these "bones of my ancestors," and with the bones, the history of Native women on this continent. The history of being the sexual commodities for the conquest, the stories from the female side of the colonization experience, were not being told in the course of the "Native theatre explosion." I wanted to work with other Native women who felt the void and who had the courage to tell their own stories.

Jani Lauzon, Michelle St. John and I first worked together in 1990 on the set of a CBC mini-series, "Conspiracy of Silence." At that time, during pre-dawn conversations on the way to the set in sub-zero temperatures, we discovered a common interest in a theme that had left its mark on us all. Each of us had, or knew someone who had, tried to scrub off or bleach out her colour. These conversations and recognitions were the first seeds of *The Scrubbing Project*. It was not until nearly ten years later that we gathered to create the work.

In 1999 Turtle Gals Performance Ensemble was formed. Its founding members included Jani Lauzon, Michelle St. John, Sandra Laronde and myself. For the first two workshop presentations in Nightwood Theatre's Groundswell and Native Earth's

Weesageechak Begins to Dance, *The Scrubbing Project* was performed by a four-woman ensemble. By our second Groundswell presentation in 2000, we had become a trio.

In *The Scrubbing Project*, the Bag of Bones/Rebecca/Rebelda character was fully developed and her story expanded to include the massacre imagery that I had been working with since The Centre for Indigenous Theatre's residency at the Banff Centre in the winter of 1995. This was a program that Floyd Favel and I co-directed that included Muriel Miguel, Pura Fé, Michelle St. John, Archer Pechawis, Maariu Olsen, Jennifer Podemski, Alex Thompson and others. There were several questions from this residency that carried over into the creation process of *The Scrubbing Project*. They were: 1) What are the consequences of creating art out of atrocity? 2) Is there such a thing as internalized genocide? (If so, what does it look like?) A question from a subsequent research project on memorials I did with Floyd Favel was: How do we create memorials to the holocaust in the Americas? To which Turtle Gals added: 1) Once Native women have put down the bundles of grief and multi-generational trauma that we collectively carry – then what? And 2) How do we get from victim to victory?

The Scrubbing Project is a study of the manifestations of internalized racism and genocide. Esperanza, my Earthplane character, is a persona formed from my deepest victimization. She carries with her at all times a bag of bones she recovered from a clandestine mass grave: bones which she scrubs, feeds and cares for. She also carries a bag filled with shoes she collected from massacre sites, which she treats as prayers and offerings, which the play's three characters transform into tobacco ties, to honour them – to memorialize.

Esperanza was further informed by this quotation from a document entitled *Guatemala: Memory of Silence: Conclusions and Recommendations* from the Report of the CEH (Commission for the Clarification of History) in 1999 (see Tomuschat). This is an excerpt of testimony made by a witness to the commission who arrived carrying human remains. I put these words in Esperanza's mouth:

> It is very painful to carry them ... it's like carrying death ... I'm not going to bury them yet ... Yes, I want them to rest, I want to rest too, but I can't yet ... They are the proof of my declaration ... I'm not going to bury them yet, I want a paper that tells me "they killed them" ... and they had committed no crime, they were innocent. Then we will rest.

In contrast, my Starworld character, Winged Victory, was created from my strongest vision of victory: the huge copper and bronze winged beings, round breasted and full in the thigh, who crown the tops of the triumphant neo-Greco/Roman statuary our colonizers have erected in order to commemorate *their* victories. She is also rooted to the knowledge that the Kuna Rebellion of 1925, led by Nele Kantule, and the Mayan uprising of 1994, led by the Zapatistas, are evidence that sometimes we get to win.

This is an excerpt from *The Scrubbing Project* where Esperanza crosses a threshold into a "Massacre Portal" and tells the story of the recovery of the bones. By the end of the story she cradles the bones in her arms and addresses them. When Turtle Gals performs this, there are pieces of text woven into the story and the character Ophelia's "Passion Portal" unfolds out of the "Massacre Portal" like a kaleidoscope before its conclusion. Here, I've put the sections back together in order to read it as a whole.

Massacre Portal

> **ESPERANZA**. Crack! /Thud! Crack! /Thud!
> *BRANDA tries to hang on to tradition. DOVE spirals down to*
> *Earthplane, back to OPHELIA.*
> **ESPERANZA**. It's that once you see you can't ever pretend you don't
>   see.
> And I see,
> I see the men lined up on one side, the women trembling on the other.
> I've never witnessed a massacre/I see them all the time.
>
>> I see the soldiers raise their rifles –
>>
>> I see
>> Skulls shatter
>> I see
>> Bodies fall:
>> Friends
>> Companions
>>   Husband
>
> Crack! Thud! (X2)
> I've never seen a body fall under the crack of
> Bullet splintering bone/I see them all the time
> And once you've seen, you can't ever pretend you don't see
> And I see…
> **ESP & OPH**. Little rivulets of blood…
> **ESPERANZA**. …soaked up by the thirsty earth.
> **ESP & OPH**. All the colours of the rainbow…
> **ESPERANZA**. …dried to a rusty brown crust.
> I've never seen my relatives' bodies piled on the
> blood soaked earth/I see them all the time.
> Spit on blood fades the stain.
>
> But once you've seen, you can't ever pretend you don't see
>   and I see.
>   (*as she gathers up bones*)
> I will carry you, I will care for you, I will feed you, and I
>   will sing you songs of comfort.
> I will wash away the dirt, and the ragged flecks of flesh and
>   skin
> And you will be warm

And you will be loved
And I will build memory.

I am very grateful to the process that Turtle Gals went through diving headlong into the dark places of our victimization. The willingness to go there has allowed me to use those depths as a springboard – a trampoline that offers me the possibility of grounding myself in another place: a place where I cease to identify with my own victimization and no longer recognize my reflection as "the victim."

• • •

I would now like to talk about two veteran theatre directors whom I consider to be light-bearers in our movement. They have consistently held up a beacon, shed light on the path and given me a direction through their incredible vision. They are Floyd Favel of Takwakin Performance Lab on the Poundmaker Reserve in Saskatchewan, and my aunt, Muriel Miguel of Spiderwoman Theatre in New York City.

I will start with this equation that Floyd created, and although it is somewhat "tongue in cheek" and pseudo-scientific, I think it works.

$$TrAd \text{ (social/ritual)} \times M = NpC$$

Or, Tradition, social or ritual x Methodology = Native Performance Culture.

Instead of trying to interpret what Floyd means, I will offer a quotation from an article he wrote called "The Shadowed Path":

> One of the ideas of Native Performance Culture is to search for accessible ritual and social structures that can act as a catalyst for creative action. I believe that there needs to be a bridge from a ritual and social action to the professional stage. Tradition needs to be filtered and transformed for the objective needs of the theatre. Without this bridge, theatre risks presenting "Artificial Trees" on stage. "Artificial Trees" is the superficial or clichéd presentation of ritual and social structures on the professional stage.

In another article entitled "Waskawewin," published in 2005 for *Topoi*, an international philosophy journal published in the Netherlands, Floyd defines the concept of "Artificial Trees" this way: "to take the traditional sacred dance as it is and transplant this to the modern stage. This process I feel turns the dance into folklore, or an "artificial tree." A tree cut off from its roots, a facsimile of culture and sacredness" (114).

He describes the methodology for Native Performance Culture he has been searching for in these words:

> One would have to isolate the technical principles of the dance and use these as starting points for contemporary performance. What is meant by technical principles is: the position of the body to the earth, the relationship of the feet to the ground, the head to the sky, the different

oppositions in the body, balance. It is the enigmatic relationship between these technical principles that create the dance. These enigmatic relationships are the shadow zone where ancestors and the unknown dwell, and this is where creativity is born, where the impulse is born.

In Japan, they call this the Ma, the pause between beats and notes. In my tradition, they say the ancestors dwell in the space between the dancers. (114)

One of the things that I love about Floyd is that he doesn't get stuck in his own dogma. He warns against his equation being applied as a formula, saying that each artist must work from his or her own equation. In a recent phone conversation he also said, "'Artificial trees' is its own valid form." And that is true. It is what my grandpa did performing Indian medicine shows – it is the "Lakota" commercial. Which provides the perfect segue to … Spiderwoman Theater.

I have known Muriel Miguel all my life; she is my mother's youngest sister. I grew up watching her, my mother, Gloria Miguel and their older sister, Lisa Mayo, perform long before Spiderwoman Theater was founded. They are my lineage and I am proud of the precious gifts that I have inherited from them.

As the director that I have worked with most consistently over the past two decades, Muriel has truly been the one to mold the raw material of my writing into performances. This is how she describes what she does. It is from the director's notes from *The Scrubbing Project* program.

As indigenous people, we see all disciplines as interconnected, with roots in traditional forms of storytelling. As the artistic director of Spiderwoman Theater, I have, over the past 30 years been using a methodology called *storyweaving* to entwine stories and fragments of stories with words, music, song, film, dance and movement, thereby creating a production that is multi-layered and complex; an emotional, cultural and political tapestry.

I have been thinking about the way Muriel works when she directs. She helps generate materials, she dramaturgs that material and weaves it together in a way that is very intuitive – not at all an intellectual process. In fact, it is a mistake to even try to justify something to her intellectually. She will wave it away with her wrist and say, "That sounds very intellectual" – as if to also say, "I can't do anything with *that*, Dearie – you're going to have to go deeper." Muriel does not allow an actor/creator to stay in her head. Muriel works from that place of what is unconsciously known, intuitively known – *saber sabiendo*: to know knowingly. Nor is she satisfied for a piece of theatre to be one or two-dimensional when it could be three, six, nine or even twelve dimensional. And dynamics! – do not play her the same note!

Then I had a brain flash. Maybe it was just menopause, but I could see, I thought, what Muriel does. She makes *molas* out of theatre. *Molas* are her palette and her dramaturgical tool. *Molas*: the art of Kuna women.

Molas are the traditional textiles of the Kuna nation from the autonomous territory of Kuna Yala, in what is known as Panama. Kuna women are renowned for their skills in creating their designs and combining colour. Originally the designs were painted and tattooed on our bodies. Kuna women wear two *mola* panels—front and back—sewn together to form blouses. Each *mola* tells a story. Each story is a layered narrative. When the women walk it is said, "We are walking stories." Kuna perception, Kuna cosmology, Kuna identity is encoded in the layers of our *molas*.

Molas are made by the combined techniques of reverse appliqué, appliqué and embroidery. They require several layers of fabric and the designs are cut out freehand to allow the colours from the layers underneath to show through. Stitching the edges of the designs with the tiniest of stitches is the most fastidious part because it is what connects the layers. The *mola* gets thicker and thicker. Sometimes a corner will be torn apart and another colour or pattern of cloth will be inserted. Some areas will be built up with appliqué and details embroidered on. There are no even edges and although symmetry and duality are central principles, even two panels of the same blouse will not be exactly the same. Ironically, sewing machines were introduced to make Kuna women's work faster, a more economically sound enterprise. They did make the work faster but these *molas* are thin with square edges to their designs and inferior overall. It is possible to trace the design of a *mola* and reproduce its outline but it would lack the multi-dimensional layers of meaning that make it Kuna. I have never made a *mola*, neither has my mother nor my aunts, but we all grew up living with them, touching them, tracing their texture and designs, smelling them, sleeping on them and wearing them. It is this thickness, this multi-dimensional knowing applied from the principles of Kuna women's art, that I believe is my inheritance from Spiderwoman's theatrical methodology. And I want that thickness in my work.

I still have a *mola* that was my mother's since before I was born. When I was very small I used to put in on to dance around our apartment. It was too long and fell almost to my knees; it would slip off my shoulders. I always wore it accompanied by a little red ballet tutu, and I would dance and create performances all by myself. I would spend hours dancing in my *mola* and red tutu to Tschaikovsky, Mendelssohn, Rimsky-Korsakov. I have not thought about that outfit in fifty years, but I can feel myself going back to where I began, only now with more experience and more information. *Saber sabiendo.*

In November 2007 I had the unique opportunity to try these ideas in a studio/ laboratory setting starting from a clear premise and intent. *Chocolate Woman Dreams the Milky Way* is a multidisciplinary collaboration among three senior artists; myself as writer/performer, Floyd Favel as director and Kuna visual artist Oswaldo (Achu) DeLeon Kantule as painter, design and cultural consultant. Our proposal was: 1) to collaboratively create a multidisciplinary live theatre piece that integrates traditional and contemporary art forms and incorporates visual imagery with text and performance, and 2) to build on a methodology of Native Performance Culture by applying principles and structures from traditional visual story narratives to script development. We also wanted to explore: a) how organically generated text and story narrative can support (not explain) the visual image and b) how a performer can embody the visual image such that it can be used as the framework for a narrative structure.

The first three days of the workshop process were spent looking at paintings from Achu's considerable body of work – stunning contemporary paintings rooted in the aesthetic of *mola* designs and pictographic writing. Then we poured through piles of *molas*, with Achu making us familiar with the principles in *mola* art from the most abstract (most traditional) to the most representational or figurative (most modern). We studied the *molas'* dissection of designs, their dualities, multiples of dualities and thematic abstractions. We then turned to the pictographic writings that notate the chants of the traditional Kuna healers and identified the literary structure of the chants: a repetition that builds through the accumulation of verbs – *dramatic action.*

From these principles, rooted in an indigenous cosmology, identity and aesthetic, we employed abstractions (a process Achu has been using in his paintings for some time) to create the beginnings of a form and a structure for *Chocolate Woman Dreams the Milky Way*. We also used the Kuna principles of presenting image and story metaphorically as if through the smoke screen of Chocolate Woman's smudge in order to protect its true meaning by encoding it.

We knew from the first improvisation "on my feet" that we were onto a process that worked; however, we were quite astonished when I was instructed by Floyd to notate that first improvisation using the process and my text emerged as pictographs written from right to left, then left to right. [2] We have now taken a first step towards developing a dramaturgy specific to an indigenous aesthetic and literary structure – in this case, one rooted in the principles of traditional Kuna visual art and literature. In Achu's words, "We are reclaiming cultural history." What is more, this same model could be adapted and applied by an Ojibwe artist investigating the bark scrolls, an Inuit artist examining the syllabic writing system, a Pueblo artist looking at rock paintings or a Mayan artist deciphering the glyphs.

This collaboration also gave space to a discussion about the evolution of Floyd's "formula" for Native Performance Culture. He has grown away from the term "methodology" as connoting something too fixed and product-oriented. He now prefers to call the transformative journey to the stage (and back to our origins) simply "process." So the "formula" now looks like this:

Tradition⇦⇨Process⇦⇨Performance

It is a fluid, multi-directional continuum where the three elements all relate to each other in an equal manner.

Tracing the themes in my work over the past two decades has allowed me to see up close my trajectory from victim to victory. Returning to the fragment from the development of *Princess Pocahontas* noted at the beginning of this piece, I can say that today I am no longer willing to call to the "spirits of heartbreak and sadness," "blood and rebellion," or "back-breaking endurance." I spent a long time digging around in massacre imagery and now I must call out to other spirits because transformation *is* a continuum and I must conjure myself into another place on my map. My writings and the theatre I create from them are my offerings, my prayers, my healing chants, my history, my identity – my *molas*. This is what the stories in *Chocolate Woman Dreams the Milky Way* are about.

Siagua, cacao beans, are what chocolate is made from. In the central part of the Americas (from Mexico south) they are very important. They are used as currency, they are burned as smudge to purify, pray and heal and they are an important part of the traditional diet. *Siagua*. Without it many Kuna have developed diabetes and high blood pressure. I have started eating these beans. In Kuna culture all the medicines are women, so *siagua* is referred to as Cacao Woman – *Puna Siagua*. Intrigued by the yummy image of a chocolate woman I began calling to Cacao Woman just as *Ixquic*, Blood Woman from the Mayan creation story, did when, bereft and alone, she cried out for help. This title piece of a new multidisciplinary collaboration evolved, in part, from a dream I had about ten years ago.

Chocolate Woman Dreams the Milky Way
an invocation

> In this time when my blood is held inside,
>> the cries of my dolphin children are carried farther out to sea
>>> into the arms of
>> *Muu Bili*, Grandmother Ocean.

> Now that my blood is held inside,
>> Purified by the smoke of Red Cacao Woman's beads – *siagua*
>> – here on *Abya Yala*
>> Land of Blood.

> *Puna Siagua, Siagua kinnit!*
> *Be an anwe be sagua waale waaletgin*
> *Wrap me in the arms of your purifying smoke*

>>> ~

> *Olowaili*, the morning star is the sister of the sun.
> My grandfather whose broad chest was tattooed with an eagle's
>> wingspan open full,
> saw *Olowaili* fall to earth over New York harbour and named me for
>> her.

> *Olowaili*, swirl and dance!
> Spiral and place your feet in mine!
> Fill my belly with starlight!
> *Olowaili guile birya birya!*

Be nak odoe an nakine
Be an saban enoge nizgana guallu gine

~

In heavy chocolate dreams I swim to shore
I am naked as the warm turquoise water breaks over my face.
I can see the shoreline. There are houses made from cane stalks lashed
    together
            their palm-thatched roofs hang low.
Swaying and rebounding in the sea breeze are the palms themselves
The beach burns brilliant
Sand blinding white. *Kuna Yala*!

I stand and walk out of the sea. Salt water slides off my naked skin.
Against the starkness of the sand there are *molas* neatly laid out.
A blanket of red layered and encoded with meaning.

To my left, a few steps away from the *molas*, stands a beautiful young
woman. She wears the clothes of *Kuna* women: a red *mola* blouse, sarong
skirt, a red and gold head-scarf, *winis* – beads wrapped tightly around
her wrists almost to the elbow, adorning her ankles almost to the knee,
a gold nose-ring and a gold necklace that falls over her entire chest like
a breast-plate. A delicate line of blue-black paint traces the centerline of
her nose. Her round cheeks are shiny with moisture and stained *achiote*
red. Her black hair cropped short frames her face. There is something on
her head like … a golden bowl whose sides undulate in constant motion.

She is smiling. Smiling at me. Her arms outstretched, fingers spread
wide. She shows me her *molas*, neatly arranged in rows on the sand. She
is proud of her work. She begins to spin and spin and spin. Faster and
faster.

Olowaili, guile birya birya!
Be nak odoe an nakine
Be an saban enoge nizgana guallu gine
Puna Siagua! Siagua kinnit!
Be an anwe be sagua waale waaletgine
Let my smile mirror the spinning girl on the beach!

~

Full moon hangs low over the Ocean.
It is December. The air is humid and night cocoons the narrow thread
of highway. Sugarcane fields whip past.
Shards of moonlight like fragments of broken disco ball bob in the
black water – laying a path of stars to the Milky Way – *negaduu.*

If I could place my feet upon those stars like stepping stones, I would follow them to visit my ancestors. And we would drink cacao – *siagua* mixed with ground, roasted corn from gourds. We would smack our lips; wipe our mouths on the backs of our hands and talk. Wouldn't we talk! *Tegi!*

I, too, am a granddaughter fallen from the stars
I call to Sky Woman: send me your courage!
The courage of the valiant Morning Star, *Olowaili,* when she rises each morning to greet her brother, *Ibeler,* the sun, at daybreak
And there, for some moments, we hang in the liquid pigment of
a watercolour sky.

(2006–08)

Notes

1 This essay is a revised version of two oral presentations, the first offered at the Distinguished Lecture Series, University of Toronto, in January 2006, and the second at the Honouring Spiderwoman Conference, Native American Women Playwrights Archive, Miami University, in February 2007. It was revised and updated in January 2008. An earlier version will appear in a forthcoming volume of essays on North American Native performance, edited by Steve Wilmer, to be published by Arizona University Press.

2 For much of the public reading of this work-in-progress presentation my text was read from pictographs.

Works Cited

Favel, Floyd. "The Shadowed Path." Unpublished.

———. "Waskawewin." *Topoi* 24.1 (2005): 113–15.

García Márquez, Gabriel. *One Hundred Years of Solitude.* New York: Avon, 1971.

Mojica, Monique. *Princess Pocahontas and the Blue Spots.* Toronto: Women's Press, 1991.

Tomuschat, Christian, Otilia Lux de Cotí and Alfredo Balsells Tojo. "Guatemala: Memory of Silence. Report of the Commission for Historical Clarification. Conclusions and Recommendations." February 1999. http://shr.aaas.org/guatemala/ceh/report/english/toc.html. Accessed 23 January 2008.

The Theatre of Urban:
Youth and Schooling
in Dangerous Times (excerpt)

by Kathleen Gallagher

New Introduction to Excerpt:

Following the practices of many renowned theatre-makers who devise theatre or find modes of collaboration to create theatre forms and stories, in my recently completed ethnographic study of youth experiences of schooling in two high schools in Toronto and two high schools in New York City, I engaged in such theatre "collaboration" with youth research participants, moving away from the traditional research "text" and structures so we could use forms of collaborative, devised and improvisational theatre to differently understand their experiences of life in urban high schools.

We used theatre to reframe the research context, which means positioning the researcher as "do-er" or improviser, rather than "observer." And as a "do-er"—in life and in art—you run the risk or gain the benefit of being in an area of not knowing how it is you know something. In this way, non-interpretation of a context, biding one's time, becomes as important as interpretation. The creative process of building a context together with research participants, as with art, takes considerable time and demands something we called "open readings." In an age of measured outcomes and time-bound curriculum events in schools, however, or of re-emergent scientism in the social sciences, or of market-driven cultural production, these choices are not always easily made by teachers or researchers or artists. Irish playwright Brian Friel charac-terizes well the arts and their uneasy fit in an age of "accounting" and measuring: "Flux is their only constant; the crossroads their only home, impermanence their only yardstick" (16).

So led by art, researchers, teacher and students moved differently, and here is what it looked like: we created an experiment in research that changed the terms of engagement, the levels of communication, and the modes of cultural production with a group of high school students. Convinced that working in improvised drama made available certain modes of communication, conduct and embodiment, we were drawn to this research approach for the quality of talk and interaction that we thought it would solicit and for the kind of new insight into young people's worlds we might uncover together with them. We aimed to create a dialogue with them, and they with each other, in which, just as in life, the point was to communicate, a project at once larger and more immediate than an overtly pedagogic one or a narrowly defined research-driven one. It is the quality of interaction in the improvised moment of creation between actors—a sociology of aesthetics—as I have come to understand it, which fosters a form of communication, and by extension, self-representation, not typical of the regimented social roles allocated to high school students.

This is theatre as methodology: theatre as a mode of devising a world in order to look at it, to collaboratively discover and artistically frame a problem or a context in order to peer inside it. Engaging youth in research theatrically provides a robust environment for questioning, as the work deals in metaphor, recreating "real life" situations in which collaborators are able to more freely experiment with alternate strategies and perspectives in testing the validity of their own theories and insights about the world.

K.G., November, 2007

Excerpt from *The Theatre of Urban*

In discussions and interviews with students, we were beginning to see emerge a theme from our data which I termed "Identity-Representation-Surveillance":

> First of all, I wouldn't have a jail. All I would ask the students [if I were the principal] is how they would like to see the school run. (Carter, grade twelve, Redmount School)

> I think the locked bathrooms, the I.D. swipes and the sweep rules are totally unfair. (Damien, grade eleven, Redmount School)

> It feels like we're a bunch of robots. (Adeline, grade twelve, Middleview Tech)

This would be the theme we would use to initiate a drama with the students. My research assistant Philip Lortie and I devised an extended improvisation activity that we hoped would allow students to imaginatively enter into a created world that would ask them to both improvise and reflect upon their understandings of, and responses to, this prevalent theme of their concerns about how they are represented and watched. Henry persuasively argues that "[t]he structures of qualitative research and of dramas take innovative forms in which means and ends, thought and action, intertwine in an unpremeditated, improvisational fashion. Both involve ways of knowing which people use in their everyday lives: existential knowledge" (51).

In short, on this particular day, in the second year of the study, we decided to move the research inside the art frame. Shifting into role as two uncaring bureaucrats conducting an employee review, we moved inside the questions; we went from asking "How does it make you feel when?" and "What would you do if?" to the matter itself. In doing so, the students were faced with choices not just about how to react, but who they were enacting. The fictional world was asking them to be attentive to the "aesthetics of self and questions of self-stylization" (Peters, qtd. in Besley 165) and the multiple and shifting dimensions and relations of power. In this meta-context, they were, in effect, "living out the drama of the post" as Best and Kellner describe it, an era [i.e., postmodern] which has produced "novel social conditions for today's youth who are engaging innovative and challenging cultural forms, and a dramatically worsening economic and political situation, and ever more complex and unpredictable life" (80).

It occurred to me, only in hindsight, that this methodological shift was resonant with what Smith sets up as an alternative to "established sociology." In this alternative, she does not treat experience as knowledge but as a place to begin inquiry, where the aim of the inquiry is not to explain people's behaviour but to explain to people the social—or society—as it enters into and shapes their lives and activities (96). Her alternative is built upon a social theory of knowledge, one which "begins in a world of activity, the doings of actual people" (98).

What we did with the students is artificial, to be sure. We created a "fictional" world/workplace of actual people in order to build theory together with youth, or as Foucault has suggested, to theorize in order to explain our experiences when we notice "something cracked, dully jarring, or disfunctioning in things." But is this theatre-making world any more "artificial" than a researcher's reconstruction of the "actual one" for the reader? *Theoria* (to "look at," "contemplate"), the form of knowledge that is called theory, comes from the same root as does the word theatre ("a place for viewing"). New theories, I would suggest, become imaginable in the moment of dramatic improvisation, the moment when our latent, embodied and experiential knowledge is called on, when our "actions" become the fodder for the creative responses of others, and when the quality of our communication depends on our ability to take others in. What had been emerging in our conversations with youth, we aimed to re-present through the verisimilitude of the created world. What it afforded us was a shared point of reference, across a range of very diverse lived experiences, to examine precisely how the social, the political and the ideological are entering and shaping our lives and activities.

"Interviewing" within a sustained improvisation, this analogous world, allows the researcher to consider carefully what "listening to" might mean. For youth, story and story-telling become an especially powerful means of communicating. If, as Lyotard has proposed, narrative knowledge is embodied in story-telling, the better question to ask, perhaps, is "How, as researchers, do we enter into young people's fictions and re-tellings?" We found one way to be through the remove of the fictional, the convention of creating an alternate world, that allowed us, ultimately, to co-construct knowledge with the youth.

There were about 25 students in the class on this day. The entire episode was recorded on video. We asked the group if they were prepared to go into role with us, to give us all another way to work through some of the themes and issues we had been discussing with them through the course of the research. They seemed quite keen to work with us in this different way. We reiterated that we would all be in role together, that Phil and I would be "employers," the bureaucrats, here for their six-month review. We also suggested that we would have time to "unpack" our fictional world together after the drama. Upon re-entering the room anew, we proceeded to call some "employees" up, while others were asked to wait in line. In role, I played the Processor, arbitrarily calling students up to be "fingerprinted" and verified in my laptop computer. I then sent them on to Phil, the Interviewer:

> INTERVIEWER (White, male, American-born). What department are
> you in?
> KAYLA (Black, female, Caribbean-born). [*straining to hear over the
> noise*] Excuse me?
> INTERVIEWER. What department are you in?
> KAYLA. I don't know ... I just started, nobody told me anything.
> INTERVIEWER. Hah! [*to PROCESSOR, loudly*] She doesn't know
> what department she's in! [*Laughs. The rest of class is momentarily
> quieted, then begins to react to INTERVIEWER's display of contempt.*]
> PROCESSOR (White, female, Canadian-born). [*to everyone waiting in
> line for interview*] We're assuming everyone knows what department
> they're in. [*to individual employee*] Do you know what department
> you're in?
> INTERVIEWER. You don't know what department you're in. Where
> do you go every day? [*pause*] This is a six-month review, you have
> been coming to work for six months and you don't know what
> department you're in?
> KAYLA. It's not my fault.
> INTERVIEWER. What do you mean it's not your fault?
> KAYLA. Because I am an employee, the employer is supposed to send
> me there.
> INTERVIEWER. Kayla Ford ... now I have to look through the
> alphabetical list. [*pause, looking for her name on list*] Okay you're in
> Gardening, just for future reference, you're in Gardening. You know
> all those flowers and stuff? That's what you do.
> [*looking over Manager's report*] Okay well this is fairly consistent ...
> You are giving your manager Monique quite a bit of resistance. She
> says that you also, several times after work, have been seen loitering
> around the building.
> KAYLA. [*very serious, surprised*] Loitering around? That's funny. Every
> time I'm here I am working. [*ten second pause*] If I am not shown
> respect, I will not give respect.
> INTERVIEWER. Okay, well that attitude is going to be problematic
> in a place like this. The customer comes first. If you expect the
> customers to hold your hand and bat their eyelashes at you....

Unsurprisingly, the heat of the moment swept us into ambiguous territory where our fabricated setting held real-world implications.

During the one hour of in-role work, students at the back of the room were engaging with each other while we fingerprinted and interviewed others at the front. The whole experience had the feeling of uncertainty both in terms of the improvisation and for us as researchers. It felt risky throughout, both dramatically and methodologically. While interviewing Alessandra, Phil barked out to the rest of the group:

> INTERVIEWER. If you don't have any identification, I don't know what you want us to do. I don't know you. You could be anyone. You need picture I.D. Could that be any clearer?
>
> SABICCA (Black, female, first-generation Canadian, Caribbean descent). [*calling from the sidelines where the PROCESSOR has seated her*] I have a question. So I don't have I.D. So what am I doing here? Can I leave?
>
> PROCESSOR. No you have to wait.
>
> SABICCA. I have to sit here?
>
> [*PROCESSOR does not reply but five minutes later calls SABICCA up to "fingerprint" her*]
>
> SABICCA. So what's all this for?
>
> [*PROCESSOR does not reply but directs her again to the side of the room to sit and wait*]
>
> [*three minutes later*]
>
> SABICCA. [*calling out*] Are we getting paid for this? Cause if not, I'm going back to work!
>
> PROCESSOR. Well you may not have work to go back to.

The final moment of our extended roleplay was signaled by Sabicca. Tired and frustrated at having waited in line the entire time without ever being processed or interviewed, she could no longer tolerate the injustice. She bellows out her objections, attracting the attention of everyone in the room, and is eventually backed by a semi-circle of employees as she leads the charge against the Processor and Interviewer.

> SABICCA. [*loud and angry*] It's not our fault that you do not know how to run your company, Sir! We have been standing here for two and a half hours!
>
> INTERVIEWER. If you don't have identification tomorrow, you won't be seen. We spent a lot of time today dealing with people who did not have proper I.D.
>
> MS. S. (White, female, Canadian-born). Will we get our identification back?
>
> INTERVIEWER. We do have some I.D. that we have reason to believe is false identification, so if you need that I.D. back, come back at 9:00 a.m. tomorrow.
>
> [*Huge outcry. The PROCESSOR and INTERVIEWER pack up to leave. They inform everyone that they are now going to take lunch, so the employees can either wait here, or leave and come back in 90 minutes. They exit the room, and the drama ends.*]

To the very last, our intent as Processor and Interviewer was to treat the employees with a disinterested discourtesy while forcing them to succumb to the privations of a badly-executed security and employment review. In doing so we anticipated that we could shape events in such a way that it would be nearly impossible for the students to participate, at whatever level, without making sense of a) why they were there in the first place, b) their reaction to what was happening, and c) the implications (both personal and social) of going through such an experience. It was obvious to the students, I believed, that our fictional world of the "employee review" was analogous to their depictions of the practices of bureaucracy and surveillance in their schools. They also understood that we were asking them to think critically about the many complaints they had previously made to us in interviews and in general classroom discussions about the dehumanizing processes of schooling. In retrospect, our dramatic goals neatly corresponded with our goals as researchers inquiring into the knowledge students produce in drama classrooms in urban schools, an equivalence which, in our view, strengthened the argument for moving our research inside the art experience itself.

Our encounter with the fictional gave our subsequent interviews with students a quality and depth I imagine would be difficult to reproduce without having experienced, together, such a shared context – without having, however briefly, transformed our space. As bell hooks beautifully captures the idea, "Spaces can be real or imagined. Spaces can tell stories and unfold histories. Spaces can be interrupted, appropriated and transformed through artistic and literary practices" (153).

The students' bodily reactions, even from those who did not speak throughout the entire role-playing event, conveyed sophisticated understanding of the terms of our engagement. The following debriefing exchange stands out for us as an example of how fluid the boundaries are between the social performance in the classroom and the performance within the drama. In the following passage we ask the students what was going on in the various corners of the room while our interviewing process was happening at the front. There were, after all, 25 people in the room, in role for close to one hour, and Philip and I could only deal with one, or at most two, at a time:

> SABICCA. I wanted to know what happened to him [*Andre, who was being interviewed by us*]. I wanted to know what did he say to you.
>
> PHILIP. Yeah, you were the one who was like, "Now wait, there were three people, three people have been let through." Like you were keeping track of everything that was happening.
>
> SABICCA. That's exactly what I do, I always keep track.
>
> PHILIP. Your whole thing was you were looking for justice.
>
> SABICCA. Yes I was. There wasn't any though.
>
> PHILIP. You were saying this is unfair.
>
> SABICCA. It *was* unfair. It was completely unfair. Because one guy didn't have I.D., and he got in before people with I.D. got in, and he got accepted for a job. And I was like, "What the Hell?!" And I was like, I have been sitting here for how long? And then Charlie went before me, I was the only one without I.D. that didn't go. And then that came at the end, and then you guys gave me a hassle. You said I have to go to Human Resources. I was like, "Oh what the Hell,

> Human Resources, where? I've been here for so long, they'll put me
> on hold again? No, I want the answer right now!"
> [*noisy reaction from several students*]
> **ANDRE.** [*smiling mischievously; to SABICCA*] Coming unprepared,
> and always wanting to get in front, like, shut up.
> **SABICCA.** Get in front?! See that's the attitude I'm talking about.
> [*general laughter*] I didn't say I couldn't wait. I would wait! But the
> fact that people were going before me and I came before them and
> they didn't have I.D. either ... that was unfair. So shut the hell up!
> [*everyone laughs*]

A fascinating shift occurs during Sabicca's recounting: she becomes upset all over again at the memory of being relegated to the back of the line and seems to enter back into that context (as suggested by a shift from past to present tense). Andre responds in kind by chastising her character for coming unprepared and expecting equitable treatment. This banter is reminiscent of their "characters'" talk during the drama. Despite the obvious levity, this is a picture of students taking their learning seriously. They are exploring the basis for claims of privilege, justice, the influence of perception on reality, and the meaning-making of individuals and the collective. And although this dialogue involves one-upmanship of a certain familiar adolescent kind, it is on its most basic level a collaboration, a dance between two selves and their performances. As Susan Sontag strikingly portrays the relationship, "Art is seduction, not rape. A work of art proposes a type of experience designed to manifest the quality of imperiousness. But art cannot seduce without the complicity of the experiencing subject" (22).

(2007)

Works Cited

Besley, A. C. "Hybridized and Globalized: Youth Cultures in the Postmodern Era." *Review of Education, Pedagogy, and Cultural Studies* 25.2 (2003): 153–77.

Best, Steven, and Douglas Kellner. "Contemporary Youth and the Postmodern Adventure." *Review of Education, Pedagogy, and Cultural Studies* 25.2 (2003): 75–93.

Friel, Brian. *Brian Friel: Essays, Diaries, Interviews: 1964–1999.* Ed. Christopher Murray. London: Faber & Faber, 1999.

Henry, Mallika. "Drama's Ways of Learning." *Research in Drama Education* 5.1 (2000): 45–62.

hooks, bell. *Black Looks: Race and Representation.* Boston: South End, 1992.

Lyman, Stanford M., and Marvin B. Scott. *The Drama of Social Reality.* New York: Oxford UP, 1975.

Lyotard, Jean-François. *Phenomenology.* Albany, New York: SUNY P, 1984.

Smith, Dorothy E. *Writing the Social: Critique, Theory, and Investigations.* Toronto: U of Toronto P, 1999.

Sontag, Susan. *Against Interpretation.* London: Vintage, (1966) 2001.

The Social Impresario: capitalizing on the desire to be remembered for as long as it takes wood to rot

by Darren O'Donnell

Like so many of us in the culture industries, I am pulled by two seemingly conflicted concerns: I want my work to be politically engaged, ameliorating aspects of this horrible world and making it a better place, but, on the other hand, I want to be rich and famous, an A-Lister with tons of power, glory and influence. Initially, my method was to oscillate neurotically between these two poles, trying to nurture one while obliterating the other. Then there was the more successful attempt at synthesizing them to produce art *in response* to the problems in the world, in a have-cake-eat-too strategy. This was pretty good; it worked for a while and it won me points in the local entertainment weeklies. There was a big temptation to stop at that point, resting on the belief that working with political content is the same as political engagement, perhaps some of the insights of contemporary physics having convinced me that witnessing is doing. And maybe in some cases it is but, for the most part, it's not.

So rather than trying to overlap these two concerns by creating *responses*, I've decided to conflate the two to create *interactions*. My own understanding of my identity within this undergoes a shift. By accepting my dueling desires, I don two masks at once: the social worker and the opera impresario, leading to a new figure: the Social Impresario, an individual who shamelessly, flamboyantly and aggressively promotes socially ameliorative acts for the expressed purpose of making *MY* world a better place. But, if done ethically, the selfishness of this actually leads to more honest and effective results.

Case Study: *The Floating Curator*

In my own practice this has yielded a series of events that I term social acupuncture, small interventions that attempt to disrupt or redirect social flows. With much of my work in this realm, it's important to note that small, intimate projects possessing aspects of my intentions serve as the basis for larger-scale events that bring the ideas more fully into fruition and, in turn, feedback into further experimentation. Components are tested in isolation, with full appreciation of the incompleteness of the event. While this might sound like I'm apologizing for the shortcomings—and I am a bit—it's important to understand the event as part of a group of events and always as research for *other* events. You don't design a car and a stereo at the same time but when they're combined you've got a nice set of wheels. I also want to point out that I create this work with the confidence that not only does artistic meaning occur during the actual event but that, because of the conceptual simplicity, the event easily continues in conversation and in my documentation and analysis. In other words, I consider this article, too, as part of the performance and, without it, the work loses a crucial dimension. This would be the concern of the press-obsessed impresario.

The Floating Curator brings together the social worker and the impresario by creating a highly charged event where social fortification is combined with conceptual aggression and flamboyance in one of the smallest, intimate and most socially charged dynamics: communication and friendship between a stranger and a child.

The Floating Curator was undertaken for curator Christine Shaw's *Public Acts* project, which assigned the themes of the 29 issues of the cultural theory quarterly *Public Access* to artists across Canada. In the summer of 2006, Shaw traveled the Trans-Canada Highway to document these 29 public acts (http://www.publicacts.ca/). I was assigned Public Act 21 (http://www.publicacts.ca/act21/), "Childhood," and in an act of childish mischief, I designed a project that placed the onus squarely on Christine, using her as the subject of a social experiment.

The concept was simple: I drafted an airtight contract that required Christine to spend an hour-and-a-half per day for five days in August floating in the shallow end of the Alexandra Park outdoor pool, approaching children and becoming their friends. Marks were assigned for—among other things—participation, convincing the kids to take her photo, time spent with the children outside the confines of the pool area and connecting with kids of different races. If Christine did not achieve a mark of 50% or more, she had to remove all traces of the project from her website and accompanying material and, when referencing the 21st Public Act, she had to declare: "Children do not exist."

The Contract

The Floating Curator is an artistic contract between Christine Shaw (hereafter referred to as The Curator) and Darren O'Donnell (hereafter referred to as The Artist).

1) Over the course of August 3, 2006 – August 7, 2006, The Curator shall spend 1.5 hours per day (5 days) floating in the shallow end of the Alexandra Park outdoor pool located at Bathurst and Dundas, Toronto, ON.

2) The Curator shall not be accompanied by any friends or associates and will only bring a towel and sunscreen onto the pool deck. All reading material is forbidden.

3) The Curator shall spend as much time in the shallow end of the pool as is comfortable.

4) Wrinkling fingers shall not constitute discomfort but shivering shall.

5) The Curator shall a) initiate extended conversations with the children playing in the pool, b) convince them to take her photo, c) spend some time outside the pool with at least one child first met at the pool and who is of a different race than The Curator and c) attempt to be photographed with said child. Each of these activities is assigned a percentage value. (See 14.)

6) An extended conversation shall be defined as an exchange lasting more than one minute and in which the child asks The Curator at least one question.

7) The Curator shall keep track of her daily and accumulative totals and submit a daily email or phone report to The Artist.

8) In the daily report The Curator shall inform The Artist as to when on the following day she shall be at the pool.

9) The Artist shall make occasional and unannounced checks to confirm that The Curator is at the pool during the stated times. In the event the Curator is absent the contract is void. (See 11.)

10) The Curator shall score at least 50% or more.

11) In the event The Curator scores less than 50% the contract shall be considered void and The Curator shall be forbidden to speak, document or refer to the contract/project/Artist with respect to the contract/project in any way and must erase all traces of the contract/project/Artist from any previously written material concerning the contract/project including any blog, proposals, suggestions or any other material pertaining to The Curator's Public Acts project.

12) In the event The Curator scores less than 50% The Curator shall write "Public 21. Childhood. Children do not exist" in any and all instances where the details of The Curator's Public Acts project is mentioned when those details necessitate the inclusion of the 21st Public Act.

13) In the event The Curator is successful The Curator shall have the right to document the contract/project in a manner that is acceptable to The Artist. The Artist shall not unreasonably withhold consent.

14) The Curator shall give copies of all documentation to The Artist.

15) Whatever The Curator scores, The Artist reserves all rights to the contract/project and may document and/or reference it in any way, in any media throughout the universe and in perpetuity.

16) The activities and their value:

Activity	Value	
	Daily %	Total%
1.5 hours of floating per day for 5 days.	5%	25%
An extended conversation with a child a day for 5 days	5%	25%
A daily email or phone call to The Artist for 5 days	1%	5%
A photo of The Curator at the pool taken by a child.		10%
Out-of-pool social time with a child first met at the pool		15%
Photo of The Curator with the child outside the pool		10%
The child is a different race than The Curator		10%
TOTAL		**100%**

Needless to say, Christine was angry and nervous about being perceived as a pervert. I sympathized but felt that, at worst, they would think she was a batty lady and, in the event they did vilify her … well, what can I say, art is risky and there's nothing romantic about taking a risk.

> If you could have peered into my apartment the weekend you emailed me The Contract you would have seen me pass through a whole range of affective tonalities: anger, fear, sadness, tenacity, resilience, joy, will, determination. I think I might even [have] been heard muttering "Bring it on, Darren." Needless to say, you and this contract got under my skin. I was immediately aware of the potential risks and receptions involved as soon as I received the contract that night back in June: perversion, repulsion, anxiety, alienation, social fatigue, insecurity, vulnerability…. (Shaw, "You think this is easy?")[1]

I was impressed with Christine's strategy – she simply went up to the staff at the pool and explained the whole project. Even when approaching the kids she, again, thoroughly outlined the premise. I thought this was the best and certainly most respectful approach, assuming a sophisticated understanding on the part of the kids. On the second day she met Elise, an 11-year-old who lived near the pool and spent nearly every day there. They hit it off and I joined them, the three of us spending portions of the rest of the week as an ad hoc family, chilling together outside the pool, going for dinner, playing in the park and spending time with her parents.

The only consistent contact kids have with the world outside the institutions of family and school are almost exclusively with the consumerist world of corporate visual culture: films, the internet, television, pop music. *The Floating Curator* invokes the notion of the uselessness of art, of art as completely devoid of any instrumentalism and, in so doing, was able to sneak past one of the most rigid social prohibitions: children talking to strangers. Like a magic cloak of invisibility, the diaphanous shroud of art can be cunningly instrumentalized, turned against the culture's dominant economic imperative. By contemporary social codes, the situation we created is atypical, yet when the shroud of "art" is draped over the activity, it becomes the easiest thing in the world. What is art, then, that it can so easily yet so radically change the terms of social engagement?

The first thing the social impresario needs to examine is where the project sits along the continuum stretching between the two prevailing imperatives that culture is currently being subjected to. First, there's the move by the state to put culture in service of the community, thereby forcing artists to fix social problems by engaging youth and other under-serviced communities. (In Ontario, funding to arts programs in education has been cut at the same time as arts organizations are required to include a youth component in their work. A crafty move—artists are cheaper than teachers—we're accustomed to working without benefits, for next to nothing.) Second, artists are being asked to provide content and activities to keep the information-age rolling in large-scale spectacular art events like Toronto's Nuit Blanche and the whole Live with Culture campaign. So we see the artist being deployed as cheap glue for the social fabric and cheap grease for wheels of the economy. The need to conflate these two is what the social impresario attempts, looking to bring the community into the realm of the spectacular and vice versa.

Public Acts was a national event, involving over 30 artists from Victoria to Halifax, and included public works that were intended for wide participation and more intimate events. With *The Floating Curator*, intimacy was pushed to the limits, the social aspect of the agenda taking precedence over the impresorial except with the conception itself, which was relatively obnoxious and flamboyant. This is where I locate the showmanship of the work: in the very idea of pinning someone down and demanding that—in order to retain the project—little kids would have to be approached in the pool. But once we get over the irrational stranger-danger, all we've got left is an earnest attempt to make the social sphere a more generous place.

The social impresario is concerned with diversity for the same reason that everyone is concerned with diversity: fairness. However, that's just the social side of the equation; the impresario also understands that it makes good business sense to involve and attract a diversity of participants. But cold hard capital is only one consideration; the impresario also appreciates the social, cultural and emotional capital that is generated in creating diverse networks, the possibilities that are created by encounters with difference. This, the impresario undertakes strictly to make himself a better person, in a proudly self-serving gesture. Including diversity in the contract with Christine was intended to make the world a better place, Christine a better person, but also to enrich my social circles – the impermissibility (for obvious reasons) of me playing with the kids at my favourite outdoor pool a yearly source of summertime frustration and sadness.

The impresario, then, relies on atypicalness, of generating unusual and flamboyantly charged encounters that produce new and meaningful contexts, questioning current social flows and throwing things into as much turmoil as possible. This, in contrast to the social worker who tries to introduce stability and normalcy and, rather than disrupting social flows, helps others to swim along more comfortably with the prevailing current. Not always, of course, but even when working with clients for whom conforming would mean death, there's still a disavowal of antagonism. The impresario, on the other hand, knows that antagonism sells, but not just any antagonisms, *fruitful* ones where friction and tension are triggered and the ensuing dynamic examined in a performative arena and under the gossamer shroud of Art, where all is easily forgiven. The impresario, being the ever-alert opportunist, looks for ways to maximize antagonism, turning to accepted hierarchies as a way in. In this, the two figures find agreement, with the social worker, too, struggling against the effects of hierarchies. In *The Floating Curator* we have the fruitful antagonism of the nice curator approaching children in the pool combined with the nervousness and weakness she feels, where, ultimately, the kids have the power to blow the whistle on this aberrant behavior.

> 2:22 p.m. – The Curator sees that the boy has finally settled into the pool and is having fun with his father. She approaches them to introduce herself. The boy's name is Ryan. The Curator tells the father about the Floating Curator Contract. He is at first guarded because he thought The Curator meant she wanted to take pictures of his little boy. She clarifies, "No, I want him to take pictures of me!" He likes the idea but defers to his wife, "You need to ask her. She is very sensitive about this sort of thing."
>
> 2:29 p.m. – The Curator … shows the father how to use her camera thinking he might want to explain it to Ryan. Ryan grabs the camera from The Curator with his tiny hand and immediately shoves it in the Curator's face, toggling the zoom and clicking the shutter. The Curator is stunned: "He knows how to use it!" She laughs, in amazement. His tiny hands clasp the camera as it dangles over the water. The Curator is a bit nervous and controls her impulse to suggest that Ryan move away from the water. The camera is about 6 inches away from her face. The father, The Curator and Ryan hover at the pool edge while Ryan shoots many, many pictures of the Curator. (Shaw, "Daily Report #3")

Social assumptions were materially addressed in the doing of this project. The pool staff who were approached by Christine, the parents who fielded her requests to play with their children and the children themselves had to face common (and in my mind incorrect and damaging) assumptions about the safety of the social sphere. A realistic assessment of the risk to kids reveals not so surprising facts:

> Five hundred thousand kids every year are classified as "throwaways" (children whose parents or guardians will not let them live at home, as distinguished from "runaways"). As many as 800,000 are beaten horribly. Even more are subject to emotional abuse and neglect. How much attention do they get? Instead, we focus our attention, almost all of it, on stranger-danger: things like abductions, of which there are between 100 and 200 annually. Our carefully controlled outrage is generated for our own purposes, certainly not to protect the children. (Kincaid)

The Social Impressario provokes a performance in which social assumptions are turned on their head so that everybody is confronted by the visceral and undeniable fact that the assumptions are baseless. Christine and I became friends with Elise, and spent time with her parents and family friends outside the pool, creating a new social dynamic that had much in common with the notion of the past as a place when things were simpler, kids were free to roam and perverts didn't exist. Well, they did exist but no more than they do now, the fetish for safety more a disguise for social control than any mechanism to protect the children.

The social impresario uses the social sphere as the venue for activity, trying to bring the spectacular out of the realm of privatized entertainment and into the public, but always—as dictated by the social side of the duality—with ameliorative effects in mind, contaminating the grease with the glue. Situating the activity in public proves a challenge to the impresario, who knows that caché is developed by increasing demand by decreasing access—to a point—and that public transactions are harder to metre than those occurring in private. The Social Worker, however, wins this round, trumping the impresario with the fact that—in the long run—the public realm is the place where all the power is located. This is an act of faith; not the impresario's strong suit. On the other hand the public field does provide the opportunity to engage and entice additional participants, providing an opportunity for wider involvement in the project. In the case of *The Floating Curator*, the children who were approached got involved, contributing insights.

> 3:20 p.m. – The 2 people swim towards The Curator.
> The Curator asks, "Are you kids? Do you think of yourselves as kids?"
> They laugh.
> The female replies, "I'm not a kid."
> The male replies, "I'm a kid. I don't have to pay rent yet!"
>
> 3:25 p.m. – Together they begin to talk about the concept of "youth," what constitutes being a kid and how it is an abstract concept. Donna (16 yrs of age) refuses to be thought of as a kid and reiterates once again that she is not a kid, without explanation. Tyson (15 yrs of age) tosses out a range of different examples that trouble the concept of childhood and youth. They all laugh together. (Shaw, "Daily Report #1")

The social impresario, then, is keen on generating beauty and amazement, wanting to dazzle, but seeking the civic sphere as the challenging arena for these encounters, anxious to make the world a better place while still providing the requisite thrills, spills and chills. I adopt this identity as an experiment, developing and testing criteria, wanting, ultimately, my neighborhood to be a better place, even as I yearn for a statue to be erected in my honour. But it will be a wooden statue, only around long enough to inspire a generation or two before it's absorbed back into the same ground that will devour me.

Criteria to determine Beautiful Civic Engagement

1) Gluing the Grease and Greasing the Glue: conflating the imperative to grease the wheels of commerce with the imperative to glue the social fabric; in other words, hauling the community into the commercial and the commercial into the community to spread, or equalize, power.

2) Diversity: age, race, sexual orientation, religion, occupation, etc.

3) Atypical Encounter: people doing things they wouldn't ordinarily do, or would ordinarily do but in an unordinary context with people they wouldn't ordinarily do it with.

4) Inversion of Hierarchies: those who normally have the power give it up, or participate in service to other less powerful participants.

5) Offering Agency: creating a context that provides agency to those who would not ordinarily have it.

6) Questioning Social Assumptions, Imperatives: creating a context where taboos are challenged by actions that reveal the taboo to be based in social control.

7) Atypical Use of Public and Public/Private Space: playing where we're supposed to work and working where we're supposed to play.

8) Fruitful Antagonisms: triggering friction, tension, and examining the ensuing dynamic in a performative arena where all is easily forgiven.

9) Volunteer Ownership: providing opportunities for volunteers to participate to foster a wider sense of ownership. Examples.

10) Blurring of Roles: passersby become observers; observers become participants; participants become collaborators; and volunteers become creators.

11) Generating Buzz: where the media is on par with other aspects of the project; the media as collaborators—slippery collaborators—but collaborators, nonetheless.

(2007)

Notes

[1]   A full account of *The Floating Curator* can be found on Christine Shaw's blog, "ACT 21. CHILDHOOD": http://www.publicacts.ca/act21/.

Works Cited

Kincaid, James R. "Little Miss Sunshine: America's Obsession with Jon Benet Ramsey." Slate.com. 21 August 2006 http://www.slate.com/id/2148089/. Accessed 2 January 2008.

Shaw, Christine. "Daily Report #1." *The Floating Curator* http://www.publicacts.ca/act21/.

———. "Daily Report #3." *The Floating Curator* http://www.publicacts.ca/act21/. Accessed 2 January 2008.

———. "You think this is easy?" http://www.publicacts.ca/act21/. Accessed 2 January 2008.

Making *Radium City*:
Annotations (excerpts) [1]

by Alex McLean and Robert Plowman

DIRECTOR'S NOTE

Alex McLean: I view the theatre as a meeting place where a highly sophisticated and invigorating exchange takes place between people. It is a meeting on high ground, to which all parties must travel a distance. When we get there, there is cause for celebration; we play together. This play generates electricity, a wild and unpredictable light that illuminates the sky.

"SEEK ELECTRICITY" is written on a piece of bristol board that we post on the wall during Zuppa Circus rehearsals. We carefully structure each creative process to allow for the unpredictable. As director, I have learned to seek this through the play of autonomous elements: contrary to traditional scene work, in which the directed actor interprets a text with vocal and physical action, I attempt a scene work in which neither the text nor the action is subordinate to the other, but rather a tension is cultivated between all the components of the performance. As a younger artist I witnessed electricity generated in this manner and it became one of the central features of all my subsequent work.

My approach to directing is strongly informed by North American practitioners in the tradition of Jerzy Grotowski and Eugenio Barba. My first solid acting training came from the late Primus Theatre of Winnipeg, led by Richard Fowler, an alumnus of Barba's Odin Teatret. I was then directed and mentored by Ker Wells (a former member of Primus) while I worked as an actor with Number Eleven Theatre in Toronto. Over the eight years I worked closely with Ker, I realized that underlying his suspicion of mainstream theatrical devices and conventional ways of constructing meaning was a deeply felt love of life and a compassion for human predicaments. Often he was able to bring actors to touch on something very truthful and beautiful by forging an indirect but carefully constructed relationship between their action and text. In this work, an actor's physical and vocal actions could be read in multiple ways at once, all separate from the words being spoken: as subtext, as manifestations of emotional throughlines, as representations of daily behaviour, as shards of memories, as echoes of other moments in the show, et cetera. Witnessing this work, my imagination was able to dance and experience something very personal.

When I began directing for Zuppa Circus, I knew the type of experience I wanted to create for audiences and for my colleagues. Yet I hesitated to fully apply

Ker's working methods; I knew that I was not my teacher and I didn't want Zuppa Circus to be an imitation of Number Eleven. Zuppa was its own thing.

This being said, I frequently worked with the Zuppa actors as Ker had worked with me. When I felt we needed to surprise audiences or crack open a scene that was otherwise becoming predictable, I would ask actors to make what we in Number Eleven had called Actions – an Action being a repeatable physical score, usually two or three minutes in length, and usually created and performed by a solitary actor. In Number Eleven rehearsals, these individual Actions then met with Actions created by other actors, along with text and/or music. Almost always, though, the initial stage was one of solitary work.

Zuppa Circus was founded on the principle of *complicité*, as interpreted by Parisian clown and *bouffon* master Philippe Gaulier, the mentor of the company's actors. When I first worked with the company in 1999, their scene work always involved two or more people. As their process was infused with the idea of play and marked by cofounder Ben Stone's highly social and gregarious spirit, it was clear to me that independent work could not serve as large a role in a Zuppa Circus rehearsal as it did with Number Eleven. We did create Actions, but also spent a lot of time with actors improvising as a group, trying things, failing, and trying again. Where improvisations often seemed chaotic and sloppy, our early work with Actions frequently felt static, formal and lifeless.

The emphasis of the Zuppa actors on playfulness provided a new element to my work as director. I began to apply the rules of a game to an actor's performance of an Action. For example, the foundation for a new scene might come from two actors performing their Actions while playing a game of Capture the Flag and speaking text at the same time. The fun of the game helped prevent frustration; failure was part of the work. Overt traces of the game would be gradually removed as the scene developed, but the spirit of it would remain, keeping the impulses of the actors alive.

A major breakthrough in our practice came with *Uncle Oscar's Experiment* (2003), a show that grew out of an earlier work titled *Between Wonder & Amusement, Uncle Oscar Was Silent* (2002). The earlier piece was structured as three interrelated one-act plays, each borrowing from a different theatrical genre. The first story was a Greek tragedy, the second a medieval mystery play, and the third a melodrama. When we subsequently decided to redevelop *Between Wonder & Amusement*, concentrating on our favorite story of the three, the melodrama, there were performance elements from the other two segments that we wanted to preserve. We took music that had been used in the earlier show and made minor adjustments (including to lyrics, in vocal pieces). We kept the rhythm and vocal delivery of some dialogue, but altered the words. Most significantly for me, we took the action of whole scenes, stripped of text, and began inserting this action into the melodrama. We were constructing the shape of the performance without a predetermined meaning.

This proved to be an exciting and successful experiment. The actors had a previous relationship to the transplanted action. They knew it well and were easily able to play with it. Many of my favorite scenes in *Uncle Oscar's Experiment* were the result of taking text written by Peter McBain (the project's writer) and colliding it with pre-existing ensemble physical scores. This was transplanted Group Action, whole scenes divorced from previous context. The lengthy process of determining how to adapt and reinterpret this action involved much trial and error, but it was worth it. We created undercurrents, images and surprises in scenes that we would never have invented had we simply interpreted the text in a conventional manner. We were finding our own way of dancing.

As we approached our next show, *Radium City*, I saw it as an opportunity to explore more intentionally what had been dictated by necessity in *Uncle Oscar's Experiment*. It was also marked by the challenge of pursuing a new model of collaboration. We had never worked with a writer in the way we were planning to work with Robert Plowman. He was the author. *Radium City* was very much his play and we would have no say in the overall storyline. It was understood, though, that we would cut and possibly rearrange his text. It was also understood that, with the writing happening concurrent to the rehearsal period, we would often be creating action for scenes before text existed. From the script to the ensemble work to the music, the entire process was structured to allow for the play of autonomous elements.

In the course of the show's 10-week rehearsal period, we tested our latest understanding of our work in the light of all the difficult compromises and happy accidents of the collaboration.

Of course, since *Radium City* in 2004, our practice has continued to evolve, informed by the challenges of that ambitious project. Given the epic spirit of the play, we knew at the time that we were working on the first stage of the show's development. It is a piece we are still anxious to revisit, a body of work we look forward to playing with again, with new strategies for sparking electricity.

THE STORY

Robert Plowman: At the start of our collaboration, I called it a mad scientist play. I said it was a trickster story. It was about shamanic initiation. It was the story of becoming a god.

For the longest time, it had no story. When at last I wrote the story, it came fast. It came after months of being buried in books, studying how the visionary experience was put down in words. I studied accounts of saints and mystics, separated by continents, by centuries, by circumstances, and by cultures. I read over 100 years of drug memoirs (from Thomas DeQuincey's *Confessions of an English Opium-Eater* to William Burroughs' *Junky*), with a particular focus on clinical researchers who'd self-experimented with psychotropic drugs (like Arthur Heffter with mescaline in the 1890s and Albert Hofmann with LSD in the 1940s). And then I turned to scientists who were visionaries in either the metaphorical sense (James Watson was descending a spiral staircase at Oxford one day when he suddenly realized that, contrary to all available data, the structure of DNA must be a double-helix) or in very real terms (electrical pioneer Nikola Tesla had a series of mystical experiences throughout his life, which he credited with revealing to him the mechanism of alternating current). I read about tricksters, about schizophrenia, about how cities are made, about the evolution of language… trying to complete a circuit of ideas and images, to illuminate the landscape of *Radium City*.

At the start of 2004, after the months of reading and daydreaming and brainstorming with my collaborators, I wrote a sketch of the first act of the play, its first sixteen scenes. The sketch was meant to do more than tell the story; I wanted it to map out *how* the story might be told, its language and its theatrical challenges. It was an invitation for Zuppa Circus to the heart of the play I imagined, its world of ideas, its flavour, its underneath.

Zuppa Circus responded with a staged reading of this sketch, giving us a glimpse of the meeting points, as well as the push and pull, between my writing and the company's aesthetic. And as our work on the project continued, the sketch of the story remained the central document of the collaboration. This common source allowed writer and ensemble to work independently, pursuing separate processes, without losing sight of each other.

SCENES 10 & 12: THE LAND OF VISIONS

RP: As a playwright, I am more and more interested in finding a theatrical language that cuts past the surface of things, that flaunts the rules of how people talk and behave in order to tease out deeper truths. And so, I came to this collaboration with Zuppa Circus imagining my writing would be a good fit for the ensemble. When I'd seen their plays I came away excited not just for the stories they told or the joy with which they told them or even their technical virtuosity and daring, but for their poetry of thought, their ability to find theatrical expression for the ineffable. Action and music and words come together in their work in a way that bypasses the everyday and speaks straight to the imagination.

Though the rules of how we would work together were clear from the start, precisely what in our work would work best together was something we had to discover as we went. And staging the Land of Visions was the occasion for many of those discoveries.

. . .

AM: I knew that staging the Land of Visions would be a major challenge. We had to enter a different world with different rules. In the end, we likely devoted more time to creating this material than to any other part of the show. To tell the story of Tom Violence's journey to a place of pure imagination that lies between life and death, we distilled actions from four primary sources: the Potato Scene, the Dances, the Cooking Show, and the Grand Guignol.

"The Potato Scene"

Earlier in the year, I had taken a three-day directing workshop with the accomplished actor and director Henry Woolf. In the context of that workshop I had invented a scene with which I was very happy. Based on reading I had done regarding the cruel agricultural practices of some major food companies, the scene that I now taught to the Zuppa actors went as follows:

A corpse is lying under a blanket on a table. Two undertakers stand peeling potatoes over the body. A fourth person enters and pulls the blanket back, revealing the face of the corpse to the two undertakers. Then, one of the undertakers initiates a game of keep-away with the blanket, and the three living characters run through the space, playing with the blanket. Suddenly, the corpse sits up and begins frantically reciting a text in a foreign language, trying to get the attention of the three involved in the game. As a last resort, the corpse picks up a sack of potatoes and dumps them all over the floor. This gets the attention of the others, who race back to the table and pull the empty sack over the corpse's head, restoring the body to its lifeless state.

"The Dances"

I asked the actors to choreograph dance routines to pop songs, which they would sing while dancing. There were three different themes I proposed for The Dances—"the sorcerer's apprentice," "the village idiot," and "Rene Duplessis"—which each performer could interpret however they wished in the song of their choice. At the time, I thought this might be a useful way to construct vocal scores: I was interested in how the fun and exertion of the dance would affect each actor's voice. Ben made a dance based on a medley of Milli Vanilli hits, Kiersten [Tough] on Bruce Springsteen's "Born to Run," Sue [Leblanc-Crawford] on Sloan's "I Can Feel It," and Sandy [Gribbin] on "People Are You Ready?" by Lyrics Born. As each actor taught their dance to the ensemble, I began to see more potential in the choreography than in the vocal work for which The Dances had been created.

"The Cooking Show"

At one point, early in the rehearsal period, I thought that the feast of the Land of Visions would provide the foundation for the production's *mise-en-scene.* I imagined a scenario in which food was prepared throughout the first act of the show, served to Tom Violence in the Land of Visions, and then spewed all over the stage and shared with the audience during the carnival, at the start of the second act. With this in mind, I asked Sue and Kiersten to develop a clown cooking show, in which a bossy clown ordered her clown co-host around the kitchen. After comically mangling a number of delicacies, their scene culminated with the grinding of potatoes in an old-fashioned meat grinder. (While food did not, ultimately, play as large a role in the production as I'd envisioned—and found more of a place in our next show, *The Open Theatre Kitchen*—traces of this abandoned *mise-en-scene* survived in the form of the folding banquet tables used as the principal set pieces.)

"The Grand Guignol"

When I first began to meet with Robert to discuss *Radium City*, two touchstones he used when speaking of the mood of the play were silent films and Grand Guignol. Zuppa had played with elements of Grand Guignol previously, in *Uncle Oscar's Experiment*. To explore how that style of performance might fit the present show, I assigned the actors the task of staging an actual Grand Guignol play.

• • •

RP: Grand Guignol is delightfully perverse. In late-nineteenth-century Paris, Grand Guignol distilled melodrama into a sublime pornography of bloody stage magic. For the half century it remained in vogue, this genre brought relentless inventiveness to enacting all manners of torture and death with shocking realism. Seductive and repellent at once, Grand Guignol thrives in the place where the question of what we desire and what we don't becomes murky. From the time I began writing the story of *Radium City*, something of this flavour made sense for the show.

Alex asked the performers to stage a play called *A Murder In the Madhouse* (1925), written by André de Lorde, the Shakespeare of Grand Guignol, in collaboration with Alfred Binet. We did not have access to the script, but rather used a brief plot synopsis, along with three production photographs, and an engraving from the original poster. Working outwards from these images, the ensemble created a 10-minute version of the play.

The story went as follows: Louise (Sue) is a young woman about to be released from an asylum. She assails her grotesque fellow inmates—One-Eye (Ben), the Hunchback (Kiersten), and the Normandy Woman (Sandy)—with stories of the happiness that awaits her and talks incessantly of how her fiancé adores her beautiful eyes. Finally, tormented beyond endurance by Louise's impending freedom, the inmates unite against her. In the violence that ensues, One-Eye blinds Louise with a pair of knitting needles; and, out of her thwarted desire for Louise, the Hunchback retaliates by throwing a pot of boiling soup in One-Eye's face. From the deliberate pacing of the scene's opening moments, punctuated by the tok-tok of the knitting needles and the stirring of the soup, the horrific outcome was never in doubt; the pleasure was in watching it unfold.

• • •

AM: Work on these four pieces—the Potato Scene, the Dances, the Cooking Show and the Grand Guignol—was prompted by very different courses of investigation. The work on each of these began before there was any text for the Land of Visions. It began without any predetermined sense of how each piece might be used in the play. For several weeks, we continued to rehearse and refine these pieces as independent islands of material, while other actions began to find homes in distinct scenes. After Robert produced his first draft of the text for the Land of Visions, these four pieces began to migrate towards that section of the play, finding a like sensibility in the language of the Monsters.

• • •

RP: The company had a language all its own. And as I began to work with Zuppa Circus, I enjoyed not knowing the ensemble's creative shorthand—with the pleasure of a traveller for whom words have become dull tools—enjoyed hearing their shared history come out in esoteric and obscene non-sequiturs, clearly conveying multiple meanings I had no access to. And then sometimes the members of the ensemble really spoke their own language: in fact, it's called the Ooo Language. To speak it one simply substitutes all vowel sounds with the sound "oo," as in the words "snoop" and "hoop."

I suggested that the Ooo Language be made the language of the Land of Visions. Approaching the writing of the scene, I knew that the Monsters needed to have a very specific way of speaking and had toyed with using elaborate storybook rhymes or giving them a vocabulary and grammar of my own invention. But the Ooo Language had the advantage of, when spoken by an expert, being totally opaque and absolutely clear at the same time.

It was a way of feeding the process back into the work, of using the pleasure the company brings to rehearsal as content. "It's true!" became "Oot's troo!" "Eat, eat!" became "Oot, oot!"

• • •

AM: The first run-through of all *Radium City* material to-date happened five weeks into the rehearsal period. At this time, an adapted version of the Grand Guignol was performed in place of the first Land of Visions scene (followed by the song "Downtown," which later shifted to scene 14). Ben and Sue had swapped Grand Guignol actions, to line up "Tom Violence beset by the Monsters" with "Louise beset by the other inmates." As the Monsters, Kiersten and Sue wore clown noses and Sandy an oversized mask. (Originally built for a character called the Honka Beast, the giant, full-head mask was an artifact of one of Zuppa's earliest shows, *Nicholas Knock,* an adaptation of the Dennis Lee poem.) The second Land of Visions scene began with the Potato Scene, leading into a series of tableaus that had been selected from the Cooking Show. In their new context, the nineteen tableaus (with names like "stretching the skin," "intestinal discomfort," "spaghetti," and "honeydew melon") now told the story of the monsters opening up Tom Violence's body and removing his internal organs.

This attempt at roughly slotting action into the narrative framework for the Land of Visions made sense to me. I decided these were the right pieces, and our work began to focus on taking apart and reassembling the available elements to craft the scene. None of Robert's text was, as yet, paired with scenes 10 and 12.

• • •

RP: I watched the ensemble slowly reshape the actions to suit the new context of the Land of Visions. They stripped the text of the Grand Guignol scene and ran it as a piece of choreography. Then Alex began to layer in my words, feeding the performers a line here, a line there. There might be a flurry of exchanges and then a long silence, then an answer to an unasked question, then one half of a dialogue. He was trying to uncover a new structure in the intersection of the action and the words. When the baseline action went slack, Alex might rearrange the sequence of events within a source scene, or import a segment of, say, the Cooking Show into the midst of the Grand Guignol.

. . .

AM: Robert wrote a few different drafts for the Land of Visions, in response to the work we were doing in rehearsal. We made cuts and rearranged his initial two scenes into a single scene and he responded with proposals for new text and better edits.

We finally arrived at a densely layered baseline action for the scene:

Wandering through a strange, unreal landscape Tom Violence finds that he is observed by a pair of Monsters (now wearing *commedia*-style half-masks in place of the red noses). Kiersten and Sue's clown interplay from the Cooking Show became the groundwork for their action, as the two Monsters introduce themselves, speaking the Ooo Language in unison. As the third Monster, Sandy hovers in the background, just as he did in *A Murder In the Madhouse*, popping in and out of the scene, startling Tom Violence each time he appears. Inviting him to a feast, the pair of Monsters aggressively peel potatoes at Tom Violence, forcing him back onto the table, while the Honka Beast, laughing, drops potatoes on the floor from a large sack. Once Tom Violence bolts away from the table in an effort to escape the increasingly perilous situation, the Grand Guignol action again dominates: the three Monsters huddle around a large pot of mashed potatoes, and when Tom Violence's stomach gets the better of him ("These are horrifying dishes! I shall have to sample them all!") they pounce on him – the action identical to the inmates' assault on Louise. Here the blinding is replaced by force-feeding. As the Honka Beast straddles Tom Violence, one of the other Monsters ladles spoonful after spoonful of mashed potatoes into his mouth, finally plunging the wooden spoon into the mound of overflowing food. (The feeding was accompanied by the *a capella* chant "Oonvoosoobool," written by David Christensen.) In celebration, the pair of Monsters break out in dance, as the Honka Beast leads Tom Violence away.

The Dances were the last element of physical action to arrive in the Land of Visions. The four actors had learned each other's dances and assimilated the best elements from each into a single routine, which Sue and Kiersten now performed (to the manic, calliope-like music of "The Monster's Ball," composed by Jason MacIsaac). Tom Violence returns to the stage and joins in the dance. His transformation into a Monster—signalled by his new mastery of the Ooo Language and the fanged and horned Indonesian mask he wears—brings the scene to an end.

. . .

RP: The success of the staging of the Land of Visions was that the flavours of its component elements were still alive in the scene: the silliness of the Cooking Show and the gleeful horror of the Grand Guignol, the joy of the Dances and the beguiling dream logic of the Potato Scene were fused together in the transformation of Tom Violence. The scene conveyed much more than I had written, while using perhaps a third of my text.

In the course of the collaboration, I learned that the strengths I saw in my writing were not the same strengths Zuppa Circus found there. When I first wrote scenes 10 and 12, I'd worried the material was too simple (the Ooo Language too easy, all of it skewing too far towards comedy), when, in fact, what the writing needed was to be made much simpler. The simpler it became, the better it supported the baroque action and staging of the Land of Visions.

Something that only began to be apparent to me once we were running the show was that, in certain other scenes, my writing and the ensemble's staging were occasionally too close together. All the elements—action and words and music—had been created separately from one another, to be sure, with no one part designed to literally illustrate another. Being too literal wasn't the problem. It was the abstraction in my writing coming up against the abstraction in Zuppa's staging. Text and action that were strong on their own terms, that felt vital when paired together, sometimes faltered in the context of the full play: texture layered on top of texture resulted in something curiously flat. In these cases, the affinity between my work and the company's, which drew us together, became an obstacle.

We were testing the combinations: there were times when the words deferred to the action, or the action to the words, and times when physical scores and dialogue would collide and work together with an eerie serendipity. Some of the combinations we tried in the 2004 workshop were instructive by their failure. And the parts of the collaboration that felt richest were also the most labour intensive. The sifting and resifting of material that went into creating the Land of Visions scene gave us a model for how we might take our work further in the next incarnation of *Radium City*.

(2008)

Notes

[1] A staged reading of *A Sketch for "Radium City"* was presented at the *Shifting Tides: Atlantic Canadian Theatre, Yesterday, Today, and Tomorrow* conference, hosted by the University of Toronto Graduate Centre for Study of Drama, in Toronto, Ontario, on March 27, 2004; and, again, as part of the North American Cultural Laboratory's Catskill Festival of New Theatre, in Highland Lake, New York, on August 15, 2004. The reading was performed by Ben Stone and Kiersten Tough, with a live musical score by David Christensen, under the direction of Alex McLean.

The workshop production of *Radium City* was performed by Zuppa Circus at the North Street Church in Halifax, Nova Scotia, November 23 – December 5, 2004.

Mr Whisper, *the tycoon*	Sandy Gribbin
Dr Vox, *the scientist*	Kiersten Tough
Flora, *his daughter*	Susan Leblanc-Crawford
Tom Violence, *the thief*	Ben Stone
The Count, *the foreigner*	Susan Leblanc-Crawford
Ms November, *the architect*	Kiersten Tough
Writer	Robert Plowman
Director	Alex McLean
Composers	David Christensen & Jason MacIsaac
Stage manager	Lea Ambros
Technical assistant	Christine Oakey

Work With Your Hands

by Ker Wells

> Our fine arts were developed, their types and uses were established, in times very different from the present, by men whose power of action upon things was insignificant in comparison with ours. But the amazing growth of our techniques, the adaptability and precision they have attained, the ideas and habits they are creating, make it a certainty that profound changes are impending in the ancient craft of the beautiful.
>
> (Paul Valéry, *Pièces sur l'Art*, qtd. in Benjamin 571)

> Beyond talent lie all the usual words: discipline, love, luck, but, most of all, endurance.
>
> (James Baldwin 77)

August 17, 2007

I recently had photos taken for my new solo performance *Living Tall*. In the photos I am wearing my costume, a business suit. I emailed the photos to my mother, who lives in Prince Edward Island, on the farm where I grew up, because I knew she would enjoy seeing me so respectably attired. Her response was that she did not recognize me in the photos, which I took as an indication that the costume worked in the way that one hopes a costume will, as a disguise of sorts. Then she added, "… until I saw your hands in one of the photos. Your hands in that one photo are your father's hands."

My father, who died in 1998, was a journalist, a foreign correspondent, who, at about the age I am as I write this (forty-three), became a farmer. In 1974 my father, my mother, my two sisters and I moved from Europe to a farm on PEI adjacent to the one on which my father's grandparents had worked and lived.

I look at my hands in the photo my mother had mentioned, and I can indeed see my father's hands: smallish, like mine, his fingers slightly curled as they hovered over the keys of his manual typewriter. In the photo in question I appear to be looking at my hands in a sort of stunned contemplation, and it brought to mind a comment my father made to me a few years before he died. We were talking about the life I had chosen and the work that I was doing. At the time, I was a member of a theatre troupe called Primus. Our work together, which included a rigorous daily physical training, was predicated on a strong—some would say fanatical—work ethic, and on a determined autonomy in, and control over, the circumstances in which we created and presented our work. In practice this meant doing almost all of the work, including the performing, the administrating, the building of sets, props and costumes, and the heavy moving of touring, ourselves.

"Your trouble," my father said, "is the same as mine; deep down, you think that real work is something you do with your hands." My father attributed this buried conviction to our lineage of subsistence farmers and particularly (in his case) to the influence of his grandfather, whom my father knew as "Pop." As a boy my father had spent most of his summers in PEI, working for and alongside Pop. Like many farmers of his and earlier generations, Pop was by necessity also a blacksmith, a veterinarian, a mechanic, an agronomist, and so on, as the daily demands of mixed subsistence farming required. He died at the age of 82, the year before I was born, struck by a car as he was leaping from the back of a horse-drawn sleigh. It was a few years after this conversation with my father that I first heard the term "Devised Theatre," and I liked the term immediately because it seemed to suggest a mixture of improvisatory skill and adaptability similar to that possessed by Pop (a few years ago I was both amused and flattered when a student in a class I was teaching at The National Theatre School referred to me as a "theatrical MacGyver.")

At the time I am writing this I am in the midst of a ten-day visit to the farm in PEI. Our farm is no longer active—we have sold much of the land that we worked when my father was alive—but my sister Emily and my mother still live in the farm-house and one of the two barns is still standing. Until this spring there was also, bordering the northwestern edge of the farmyard, a low out-building about 80 feet long. In the years when we still kept sheep, this building and the adjoining paddock it created were where our 80 or so sheep were wintered, and where, during the spring lambing season, they would give birth. The shed was built when I was eleven, the summer after we arrived in PEI. I remember shingling the roof with my father and my grandfather, Pop's son Jimmy, who had only one arm, and who amazed me with his ability to drive roofing nails one-handed into the asphalt shingles. That was over thirty years ago, and great swaths of the shingles had blown off and the shed had begun to sag and collapse. Emily had hired someone (a local fellow with the nickname "Killer") to tear it down. He had done a thorough job, and had salvaged much of the lumber: weathered spruce boards and cedar posts that were now piled at the edge of the wildflower garden that Emily had planted where the shed used to be. Her concern now was that with the sheep shed gone there was nothing to block the north wind and the snow it would carry into the yard in the winter. We decided that I would build a fence using the salvaged lumber from the shed, and so it is that I have spent much of my time here digging post holes, pulling rusty nails and spikes, and erecting a hun-dred-foot-long fence, about five feet high, along the edge of the yard. The physically hardest part of the work has been digging the holes, for which I used an admirable old hand tool called a posthole auger, and a heavy iron pry bar to break through layers of shale and rock in the sandy red soil. The posthole auger is the same one I recall using to dig postholes with my father, and the pry bar I borrowed from our neighbour Dave, a retired housepainter. My hands are blistered, my arms and back feel well-used from the digging, and I love the work.

Why do I love it, and why is it an easier love than my chosen vocation as a theatre artist? As I dig, my father's words about work with the hands come back to me, and I consider how this work of digging holes in the earth compares to the work I do when I make theatre. The two are fundamentally different, of course, with regards to their practical purpose, and I do not presume to add anything new to the age-old debate about the utility of art. But I can say that like many artists (and especially those who grew up on farms, I suspect) I have chronic doubts and questions about the "use" of what I do, of making theatre in a time and a society in which theatre seems, much of the time, to hover in a limbo between irrelevance and extinction. But as is often the case when I am consumed by a consuming work, revealing parallels and contrasts between what I am doing and all other aspects of life seem to emerge as I dig. I think about Dave, who lent me the pry bar and consulted with me on the most effective design for the fence. Dave spends most of his free hours carving birds from wood salvaged from old telephone poles, so I imagine him to be a secret fellow-traveller in a place where no one calls himself an "artist," but I suspect even he thinks I am a little fanatic, or crazy, for digging all the holes by hand, when I could hire someone to dig them all in an hour with a tractor-mounted auger. Why do I dig them by hand? My conscious reasoning is a mix of the ideological (why enlarge my carbon footprint?), the practical/economical (it is cheaper if I dig them by hand), and the hedonistic/sensorial (I actually enjoy the work and the particular quality of reflection it seems to afford me). But beyond that, this situation, this choice, is deeply familiar to me. I consider how often I think, when I am directing or acting, of "earning" a moment, or an image, or a prop, or a set piece. I reflect on this chronic wariness of mechanical assistance – whether in the form of a tractor-mounted posthole auger or in the form of recorded and amplified music in theatre (because the latter allows one to command attention and dominance of the space without "earning" it). I consider the possibility that this preoccupation with working with my hands, with earning, is simply a sublimated Scots Presbyterian instinct towards self-deprivation/flagellation. Although I was not raised with any religious affiliation or observation, that genetic strain is present on both sides of my family, the fierce, even punitive Scots preoccupation with humility and hard work and our modest place in creation. I think about the terms "work" and "creation."

Earlier this year I attended a talk by Peter Brook during which he said that he preferred not to call himself "a creator," that the term seemed too grand or presumptuous (and overused) to describe the process he engages in with his colleagues when they make theatre together. The humility of his statement appealed to me. It also corresponded to my experience, even in the making of a new work, which is often, at least initially, not so much an act of conjuring something new magically into existence, but rather of turning and adapting, combining pre-existing ideas, images and other elements to reveal something new. Bruce Barton, a friend of mine (who says he is paraphrasing the Russian film director Sergei Eisenstein), has described this kind of creative process as one of "collision"; the collision of pre-existing elements that, when juxtaposed, evoke something entirely new and different and, often, unexpected.

The sometimes wondrous alchemical change of this collision can eclipse the often slow, attentive, persistent work that precedes and allows it.

August 18, 2007

This morning as I came out to work on the fence, I ran across the yard to where the posthole auger lay in the grass, covered with a coating of dew. I ran because I was excited to get back into action, back to work on the fence, even though at the end of the day yesterday I realized that I needed to pull up some of the posts and re-do many of the holes.

I start digging and my thoughts turn to presence and action. I use these terms a great deal when I am teaching and directing, and they were constant themes, and goals, of the physical training I did in my years with Primus. In the context of actor-training, and of creating performance material, they are the *sine qua non*; without presence, an actor is at best invisible and ineffectual, and without the impetus, necessity, and effect that true action (intention-driven movement, as distinct from empty representation or indication) contains and imparts, an actor's movement, the progress of a scene, the story of a play, all amount to nothing. In that context both presence and action are at once critical and elusive, and much time is spent trying to define and find them. But here, as I dig (and re-dig) my postholes, presence and action seem simple, essential and inextricably part of what I am doing, part of the effort and effect of my work. I am unquestionably present and engaged in action, and of course I am unplagued by questions of utility, relevance and authenticity – the work is what it is, and that seems to be, unassailably, enough. And so I run to it.

August 19, 2007

I am trying to think of the opposite of what I am doing, of this completely practical work. I try to think of "art work" that would seem to be completely *im*practical, and set myself the task of defending that work with the same rational/emotional/sensorial/moral values that come into play for fence building. I think of artists who do work that is provocative, inflammatory, minimalist, conceptual. I think of Marcel Duchamp and his *readymade* urinal, which he did not make. And I think of Gerhard Richter, a contemporary German painter whose work I admire. A significant portion of Richter's later and best-known work consists of paintings based on photos, many of them portraits, in which the painted copies are blurred, as if the image was being viewed through frosted glass. I read about Richter's work before I saw it, and was primed to like it, but found it difficult when I first encountered it in reality. It was frustrating, and I felt a petulant impatience with the blurring, this apparent deliberate impairment of my perception of the image. But then something happened. I saw his paintings of the death of the German terrorist Andreas Baader (part of his 1977 cycle of Baader Meinhof paintings) and I glimpsed something of Richter's work, his real work in the creation of this image, of the way it raised questions for me about truth. And I was flooded with admiration for his courage and his diligence. I have a book of Richter's writings about his work over the past 50 years. His words are inspiring, challenging and clarifying – truly useful when I need to be inspired, challenged and clarified. He is rigorous and lighthearted, deeply committed, and resistant to ideologies and dogmas, but is not afraid to make categorical statements ("There is no way to paint except the way I do it" [34].) His book is called *The Daily Practice of Painting*. The simplicity of the title suggests the daily dedication, the simple stubbornness necessary to continue, but conceals from view the contradictions and debates and playfulness that emerge in the writing and the thoughts, and in any artistic work.

August 20, 2007

Today I was thinking about an old man in Italy named Aniello.

Sixteen years ago, early in my years with Primus, we spent a summer living and working in a mountain village in Southern Italy. The village, called Nocelle, is home to a hundred or so people, and sits on a mountainside on the Amalfi Coast over-looking the Mediterranean. At the time we were there Nocelle was accessible only on foot, a half-hour walk from the nearest paved road along a winding path of steps carved into the mountain. The town itself, like many in the region, was built of terraces and steps and narrow streets just wide enough for a man and a mule to pass. Our agreement with the people of Nocelle was a barter, an exchange in which we were given space to work in the little town schoolhouse and in the adjoining village square or piazza, and in return we would create a performance which we would present to the village at the end of the summer. The villagers were somewhat wary of outsiders, and the agreement was only possible because our director, Richard Fowler, had been living in the village for some years.

Each morning we would begin work at 7 a.m., allowing us to finish before the worst of the afternoon heat descended. We would start with physical and vocal training, followed by work on a new stilt performance. Quite reliably each day, as we were parading the length of the piazza on our stilts, with our drums, bells, and various outlandish props and bits of costume, Aniello would arrive. He was one of the elders of the village, about 65 or 70, and he would appear, descending the steps that led into the piazza from the higher reaches of the village, and above that from the steep and rocky mountainside covered with olive trees, wild thyme and rosemary, myrtle bushes, and Prickly Pear cacti. I say Aniello would "appear," although in fact he himself was invisible, bent double under a load of branches which he had cut on his land up on the mountain, and which he was now carrying down through the piazza to give as feed to his cows, kept in the same compound where he and his family lived. He would have gone up the mountain at dawn or before, his short machete hanging from his belt, and spent the morning cutting and piling the branches in a bundle which now sat like an enormous turtle shell on his back. His descent into the piazza was remarkably slow and steady. He came at a pace I came to recognize and appreciate as I watched the villagers carrying their various loads and packages along the long winding path into town. Whether they were carrying groceries, or firewood, or (as I saw on one occasion) a refrigerator, they all seemed to move at this same unhurried but inexorable rate along the streets and up and down the hundreds of stairs.

Aniello would descend the steps, and rolling his great bundle from his back to the low wall that surrounded the piazza, he would sit on the wall and rest and watch us as we worked. The first time Aniello appeared, Richard walked over and greeted him, and we continued to work as they exchanged words. We, the actors, complete newcomers to this beautiful, isolated and (to us) exotic place, were still very curious about the villagers and their opinion of us, and we were, at least at this early stage, somewhat self-conscious about our artistic work in this village of hard-working, deeply practical people. That day at lunch we quizzed Richard about what Aniello had said after watching us work. "Nothing," Richard said. "We talked about the weather, and our gardens." And so it continued for several weeks. Most mornings, a few hours into our work, Aniello would appear with his branches, he would stop and sit, and he and Richard would exchange greetings and discuss the progress of their tomatoes and peppers, and we would continue working. Aniello watched us openly for the minutes he was there—I remember his very large, clear blue eyes following us, a slight smile on his lips—and then he would take up his branches, cross the edge of the piazza, and sink from view, descending the steps down past the town cemetery, towards his home and his cows. For the final steps only his bundle was visible, sinking gracefully from view: step, pause, step, pause, step. His appearance, presence and departure came to feel like a part of our work.

Then, a month or so later, Richard announced at lunch one day that Aniello had broken the pattern. That morning, he said, they had exchanged their usual greeting, and then, sitting together on the wall, they had watched us for a few minutes. Then Aniello had spoken. "This is a good work you're doing," he said, pointing his chin at us doing our parading and kicking, drumming and sweating in the hot morning sun. "I see you here every day," he continued. "You work hard. I see progress." It was not intended as a blessing—Aniello was too modest a man, I think—but I know that I received it as something like that. Why did it matter to me what this stranger thought of my work? In part, because my father was right, because I share his respect for those who work hard with their hands, but also because I saw in Aniello's approach to his work, in his slow steady walk, a quality that I know is critical, and sometimes hard to find, in my own work when I am making something new, when I am creating.

September 22, 2007

I am now back in Toronto, where I live, and I have just opened a three-week run of *Living Tall* in the theatre. Opening night was great; an audience full of friends and colleagues and I felt on top of my game as I performed, while also feeling that new things were revealing themselves to me as I moved through the show and the audience responded. The work I have done over months of rehearsal was clearly there, but I could feel that I was taking leaps, generating inspired moments of change. Afterwards I felt fulfilled and exhilarated – I felt that my work was succeeding. The second night of the performance, in contrast, is a classic second night; I am to some degree trying to repeat the experience of the night before, but the audience is far less vocal in response. I feel as if I am simply stubbornly repeating what I have developed in rehearsal. Rather than feeling like I have taken leaps, I feel that I have simply endured something. The audience is appreciative, but I feel that I have somehow failed. When I was digging postholes, the trajectory seemed much simpler: with each hole, as I recalled how to use the auger effectively, my technique reliably improved.

September 24, 2007

The first week of the show is over. The audiences following the opening night surge have been small, but the performances are satisfying – I feel the work continuing to develop. I am thinking again of Aniello's work and of my work on the fence, in comparison to this work of creating and performing. In these days it is clear to me again the ways in which these kinds of work are different, and the difference is not simply one of the utility of what I am making. It is a fundamental difference in approach, intention and result. Aniello knows his task and his path every day; the spot where he finds his branches may differ, but every day his feet will follow more or less the same route down the mountain and back to his home. If he gets lost and does not return in time to feed his cows, he has failed at his task. But when I am making something new, *if* I am to make something truly new, I *must* get lost, truly lost, in order to find something I have not made before. That is Richter's blurring of the image, the push away from certainty, from knowing what the image is, but in a way that cannot be calculated – if the leap is a leap into the known, then it is not a leap. This is true both in the act of creating and rehearsing the piece, but also in the nightly act of performing it. I must go out there not knowing, and ready. That is the nature of the leap, of the "risk" that is so often spoken of as a critical element of artistic creation, and particularly in live performance.

This is what I want, whom I want to emulate, Richter-plus-Aniello, every day going up the mountain determined to work, but also determined to get truly, diligently lost, and sometimes to return with something worth carrying.

(2008)

Works Cited

Richter, Gerhard. *The Daily Practice of Painting: Writings and Interviews, 1962–1993.* Trans. David Britt. London: Anthony d'Offay Gallery, 1995.

Baldwin, James. "The Art of Fiction LXXVIII." Interview with Jordan Elgrably. *The Paris Review* 91 (1984): 48–82.

Benjamin, Walter. "The Work of Art in the Age of Mechanical Reproduction." *The Critical Tradition: Classic Texts and Contemporary Trends.* Ed. David H. Richter. New York: St. Martin's, 1989. 571–88.

Cultural Meeting in Collaborative Intercultural Theatre: Collision and Convergence in the Prague-Toronto-Manitoulin Theatre Project[1]

by Barry A. Freeman

The Prague-Toronto-Manitoulin Theatre Project (PTMTP) attracts significant public attention. In 2004, the PTMTP was featured on the front page of a Prague daily and became a news item on three television stations. The May 9, 2004 Prague opening of the show was attended by Pavel Dostál, the then Czech Minister of Culture. Shortly thereafter, in Canada, the project was featured in a recurring segment on Bravo! Television and was celebrated in June 2004 at a gala event at the Czech Consulate in Montreal. The University of Toronto at Scarborough acknowledged the project's contribution to the campus's profile by partially funding its fourth incarnation in 2006. Among the individual supporters of the project have been theatre producer David Mirvish and prominent Czech author Josef Škvorecký.

It is not surprising that the PTMTP has been so publicly endorsed, premised as it is on fostering relationships and learning among artists from different parts of the world. In the program for the 2004 project, director Jan Schmid writes that the purpose of the project is "to perceive and realize the individuality and distinctiveness of each person ... [To] be able to distinguish them, but at the same time discover common denominators between people, minorities, nations, etc., all of whom jointly create the richness of the world." The myths of different cultures, he continues, are "most certainly rooted in our ancient past, and I would be happy if they could help us to orient ourselves in today's world and help us find our place in it" ("Program"). The story of the project as Schmid tells it is one for which many are hungry in our turbulent world: that despite our different histories, traditions and languages, we can cooperate and learn from one another. It is also *trans*cultural in that it purports to be able to *trans*cend specific cultural codes in order to access "universals of the human condition," perhaps even *pre*cultural in its suggestion that we can tap into a shared repertory of stories or understandings that *pre*cedes culture.

The force of such *trans*- or *pre*-cultural narratives is strong, and variations on them have to-date served as the first and last word about the PTMTP's nature and value in the absence of a more scholarly treatment. Theatre work of this kind often goes unanalyzed, as Peter Eckersall observes: "Exchange in the majority of cases is unproblematized and a sense of ambiguity or a continued unwillingness to consider intercultural politics is evident" ("Trendiness" 52). However, I have been uniquely positioned to undertake a more extensive academic study of the PTMTP on account of my participation in it over the course of seven years, and after having done some qualitative research on each of its three contexts. This essay begins with what is for me an important early observation about the work: that there is a disconnect between, on the one hand, the official narratives of the project and the image of transcultural harmony projected by its public performances and, on the other, the experience of its participants, for whom the cultural and artistic dynamics of the work are often difficult and unresolvable. The ordered cultural harmony drowns out a discordant chorus of voices, all roughly following the conductor but each seeking the tune. It is my belief that this strange music is profoundly meaningful. What are its qualities, and how can it best be heard? In seeking answers to these questions, my aim is not to devalue the PTMTP or to challenge the actions or intentions of its facilitators. On the contrary, my goal is to add to its impact and value by extending the intercultural conversation it initiated. In the words of one of the project's Canadian participants, expressed to me in an interview, "It's never a learning experience if you don't analyze it. It's just an experience" (Interview 3, June 2 2006). This essay, then, draws on intercultural theatre theory and my experience with the PTMTP to extend the conversation about the work and to argue that an approach to intercultural analysis is needed which looks beyond the theatrical product into other important sites of meaning-making.

The PTMTP is an example of what I call collaborative intercultural theatre: theatre that sees groups from different parts of the world come together to create performances combining the skills, stories and languages of the participants. My use of the term *inter*cultural concurs with Jacqueline Lo and Helen Gilbert's definition of the intercultural as "a hybrid derived from an intentional encounter between cultures and performing traditions" (36). The PTMTP is not a single production, but a theatrical project that operated between 1999 and 2006. It produced four separate public performances with four different ensembles. I was absent from only the second of these four projects, participating in the first as a performer, the third as Assistant Director and performer, and the fourth as Assistant Director.

The project began as a collaboration between its founders and principal facilitators, Michal Schonberg and Jan Schmid. Schonberg, the project's dramaturg, is a professor in the Drama program at the University of Toronto at Scarborough, where he directs performances in the campus's Leigha Lee Browne Theatre. Schmid, the PTMTP's director, is a professor in Prague at DAMU, a theatre school under the auspices of Charles University. Schmid is also known in Prague as the Artistic Director of the professional and popular Divadlo ypsilonka (Ypsilon Theatre), which he has led since its founding in 1963. Schmid and Schonberg began to discuss the possibility of collaborating in 1998 while the latter was guest-directing at Ypsilon. Their idea was to have students under their tutelage work together on a performance to be created and staged in each of their respective theatres. Their devising would begin with only a general theme, which for the first project in 1999 was to be *Muž a žena,* or *Man and Woman.* The success of *Man and Woman* led the two to collaborate again in 2002 with a new group of students who started with the theme *Já a ostatní,* or *I and They.* For the third project in 2004, themed *Myty Které nás spojují* or *The Myths that Unite Us,* the facilitators invited a third company into the collaboration, the De-ba-jeh-mu-jig Theatre Group (Debaj). With this inclusion came two more collaborators: then Artistic Director of Debaj Ron Bertie (now Artistic Producer) and Delaware poet-playwright Daniel David Moses. The same collaborators worked together again in 2006, completing a fourth project themed *Umění Žít*, or *The Art of Living*. By 2006, then, the project had become quite large and complex, comprising 32 performers and 10 facilitators and administrators, and seeing performances in Prague, Toronto, and in Wikwemikong on Manitoulin Island.

The facilitators cited a number of reasons for welcoming Debaj into the project. In the first place, Schonberg was impressed by Debaj's work after seeing a performance of theirs in Toronto. He imagined that the students of the PTMTP would benefit from being exposed to their culture and ways of working. It was also felt that Debaj would have much to contribute to a project taking myths as its subject, as Schonberg expresses in the program for the performance that resulted from the collaboration: "The participation of the First Nations theatre professionals provides us with an important guide in the search for myths that unite us" ("Program").

The devising process of the four projects differed slightly, but a general description is possible. Each time, the groups began by each working separately on the theme in its own way according to its own preferences and talents. This phase of the work was exploratory, doubling both as a way for the performers to get to know one another (if they did not already) and also as generative of potential material for the performance. Schmid then traveled to Canada to co-facilitate a two-week workshop. At this point, Schmid was accompanied only by Jan Jiráň, a composer at Ypsilon who acted as composer and musical director of the PTMTP. Building on what had been generated prior to their arrival, the facilitators led the Debaj and UTSC ensembles through more structured creative work. In the case of each project, for instance, participants had been asked to produce written responses to a set of questions on the theme, from which Schmid and Schonberg chose items to dramatize. (Debaj, less inclined to work from text, elected to devise only physically for the fourth project.) Meanwhile, Jiráň taught the participants music of his own composition, with lyrics provided either by participants or, later, by Daniel David Moses. These elements—personal reactions and musical interludes—were then combined with tightly choreographed sequences of movement, gesture and sound of Schmid's own composition. The end result was presented as a "workshop performance" for an invited audience only. Schmid and Jiráň then returned to Prague and soon after directed the Czech students through a similar process. Some months later, the UTSC and Debaj groups travelled to the Czech Republic for a three-week stay. The groups spent the first and second days in Prague getting acquainted and performing their work to one another, leaving only seven days to merge the material together into a public performance on the main stage at Schmid's Ypsilon Theatre. The performances thus emerged as a sequence of connected—and mostly comedic—variations on a theme punctuated by vocal and instrumental music. None boasted a central narrative aside from the connections that arose organically out of segues or a general thematic movement, say, from birth to death. After the Prague opening, the ensemble travelled to the north Bohemian town of Liberec, where they performed at Naivní divadlo (Naive Theatre).

Two weeks after the UTSC/Debaj ensemble returned to Canada, it hosted the traveling Czech group. Though the ensemble had already performed for an audience, the performance was still adjusted and refined at this point (there was never a sense within the group that the work was "finished"; Schmid typically came backstage during intermissions with directions). In Toronto, the show was performed at the University of Toronto at Scarborough and the Graduate Centre for the Study of Drama in Toronto. The entire ensemble then travelled to Manitoulin Island, where performances were held at Pontiac Public School in Wikwemikong and at Manitoulin Secondary School in West Bay.

While some of the facilitators remained the same over the years (such as myself), each of the four projects was created with an almost entirely new ensemble. A brief word about each of the participating groups serves as an introduction to the different theatrical and cultural contexts involved:

University of Toronto at Scarborough (UTSC): The group from UTSC comprises students of the Drama Program offered there by the Department of Humanities. Participants from this group have usually been first- or second-generation Canadians of a multitude of cultural backgrounds, such as Italian, East Indian, West Indian, Chinese and Irish. Being between the ages of 20 and 24, and being in a non-conservatory program, these students have always had some experience in community and university theatre, but have rarely had experience in professional theatre. While they are likely to have had an opportunity to create original theatre collectively during their studies, most of their training and experience would have involved character development from canonical scripts. Some students of the UTSC Drama Program go on to be drama educators, administrators, or scholars and some go into professional theatre, but many graduates have pursued careers in other fields.

De-ba-jeh-mu-jig Theatre Group (Debaj): Debaj is a professional theatre company based in Wikwemikong, Ontario on Manitoulin Island. Most of the artists who have worked at Debaj throughout its 23-year history have been of Native ancestry. PTMTP participants from Debaj have been a mix of its more experienced artists (who are deemed Arts Animators within the company's parlance) and younger interns training with the company under its National Aboriginal Arts Animator Program. The company sometimes works from scripts but has in recent years been mainly devising original work collectively. Debaj shares with the UTSC group an emphasis on training and development. Its members, too, are from numerous cultural backgrounds: Debaj participants in the PTMTP have been of Cree, Ojibwe and Potawatami backgrounds (Debaj properly regards its own work in remote northern communities as "intercultural").

Divadelní fakulta Academie múzických umění v Praze (DAMU): The Czech participants are students of Jan Schmid at DAMU (English translation: the Theatre Faculty of the Academy of the Performing Arts in Prague). They are all training with Schmid and others within an "alternative" curriculum stream (which is complemented at DAMU by another more "classical" program). DAMU is regarded as a prestigious school in the Czech Republic, one of only two university-based conservatory theatre training programs in the country (the other is JAMU, in Brno). Hundreds show up for DAMU's annual auditions, from which a cohort of about a dozen students is chosen. Accordingly, their training is rigorous and practical and they are resourceful performers. All, for example, are expected to be able to play multiple instruments, sing, and do acrobatics and puppetry. Students of the "alternative" stream exclusively create new work collectively; when they do work from a known text they adapt it significantly. Their work is performed in repertory at their small student theatre, the DISK theatre in the centre of Staroměstká, Prague's Old Town, but Schmid also employs some of the students to create performances for the smaller stage at his own Ypsilon theatre.

Even these cursory descriptions of the process and the constituent groups suggest the more complex dynamics of the collaboration. In the first place, the groups are differentiated not only by geography and culture, but also by professional orientation. The focus of the program at UTSC is dramatic literature and history. DAMU students, on the other hand, are being trained to be professional performers. Members of Debaj are already working in a professional context, though one that is uniquely situated both culturally and geographically. Also, while the pretense of the project presents the three groups as representatives of Canadian, Native and Czech culture respectively, their cultural composition is in fact variegated, presenting only the first problem with speaking in terms of a Canadian or Czech "perspective." Finally, the project must be seen as a collaboration on a number of levels beyond that of its core facilitators. Schmid, Schonberg, and everyone else work within constellations of institutional and professional organization that offer the significant practical and financial support that makes such an undertaking possible. Consider that while the 2006 project cost each participant group tens of thousands of dollars, all public performances of the project were free. While this required extensive fundraising on the part of the organizers and participants, the project also depended on the patronage of the participant institutions in terms of personnel, space and funding.

During my work on the PTMTP, I began to develop a methodological and theoretical approach to analyzing the PTMTP that could critically engage with the many overlapping contexts and conditions I was watching in operation. I have wanted my analysis to honour the spirit of the project by contributing to the meaning-making and therefore the value of intercultural work. Conscious of the way in which writing about the experience *post facto* further contains and closes meaning and sometimes excludes those interpretations that do not fit, I have sought ways to write about intercultural theatre work that resist the fixing of meaning. This has meant building a framework that opens up and explores the complex working contexts and conditions, yet, like the work, remains moveable and open to revision.

I soon learned that such an approach would have to depart from much of the existing scholarship. Rooted in semiotics, the academic discussion of intercultural theatre has focused on the practice in the Western theatre of borrowing stories and techniques from non-Western cultures. Two influential models have both conceived of the intercultural event in terms of the interactions of groups and their attendant systems of signification. In his 1992 book *Theatre at the Crossroads of Culture*, Patrice Pavis articulated a widely cited "hourglass" model. The model describes how culture —a system that can be read semiotically—is in the theatre removed from its original context and refashioned to suit a new context. In this model the upper and lower chambers of the hourglass represent the source and target cultures respectively, while the neck contains a series of filters. The hourglass metaphor suggests a closed system, a straightforward unidirectional flow of culture, and cohesive, homogenous source and target cultures. In 2002 Jacqueline Lo and Helen Gilbert proposed a remodelling of intercultural theatre praxis to better align it with contemporary practice and with post-colonial theory. Cultures in their model are still subject to the same filters identified by Pavis, but both participating cultures are considered cultural sources along a continuum with the target culture positioned between them. More accurately it is a *moving target* culture in that the representation of the groups changes in different contexts. This model is better suited to an emergent type of intercultural collaboration characterized by the active maintenance of equitable relations between partners, a focus on the processes and politics of exchange rather than on product, and a desire "to explore the fullness of cultural exchange in all its contradictions and convergences for all parties" (39). Lo and Gilbert's model improves on that of Pavis by calling attention to the ways groups' self-representation changes as they travel through different performance spaces. They have made the assimilated culture of Pavis' model a partner in the collaboration – but an unequal partner that must guard against being appropriated even while sharing the space of the other. The unequal partner must monitor "ideologically laden sign systems" (46) like language, space, and the body to ensure that they do not insidiously amplify the voice of one group while silencing another. This model allows for a dialogical interaction between groups and turns critical attention toward the ethics of representation and the wider politics of production.

Yet, while Lo and Gilbert's model addresses the politics of representation in dynamic contexts, it for the most part still thinks of intercultural work in terms of the interaction of group cultures, monolithic and describable as such, as though participant groups in collaborative intercultural theatre can be said to unproblematically represent the source cultures of their origin. The model is built on a structuralist premise: that by reading the ideologically-laden signs of the theatre, we may arrive at a picture of a culture and, subsequently, a picture of cultures interacting. The framework I am pursuing, however, begins with a post-structuralist premise: that individuals are agents—subjects and not objects—influenced but not fully determined by the norms of their source cultures. The structuralist perspective sees culture as *being* – a set of fixed practices and values, a set of rules that are obeyed and passed on through tradition. The post-structuralist perspective refuses to see culture as an ontological category of existence outside of human experience. This makes it at least *possible* that human beings may create, maintain, and change culture.

The view of culture as *being*, as something fixed to which we are all obedient, is powerful and persistent. Collaborative intercultural theatre generates an expectation, on the part of an audience if not also on the part of the participants, that somehow participants from each group "represent" their group in some sense, an expectation not normally placed upon them in each of their own working contexts. That cultural ideas can be resisted and deconstructed does not make them less persistent, and they must be constantly negotiated. Cultural meaning is always threatening to close, to make itself available as a commodity to be exchanged. Cultural commodities are present in the rehearsal rooms of collaborative intercultural theatre, and can be traded with ease among individuals without much knowledge of one another. Sometimes, however, people struggle with how (or whether) to perform images of themselves that they do not accept, or, for that matter, even clearly comprehend. Many reactions are possible: while working on the PTMTP I observed instances where participants variously rejected, accepted, revised and embellished cultural stereotypes, at times consciously and parodically, at times (seemingly) not.

It is my view, then, that enlarging the cultural and political potential of collaborative intercultural theatre requires an approach that takes the individual as its basic unit of observation and understanding. The individual has a relationship to the group, certainly, but the individual remains a subject with unique ideas. Of course, at the level of individual, culture is decidedly more slippery. Individual perspectives reveal themselves in conversations, are intersubjective, and are open to revision. But this shifty territory is worth traversing, since the individual gives us access to the intercultural. If interculturalism is the space between cultures, a performative space opened up by collaborative intercultural theatre, it is individuals that occupy this space, and whose opinions, personal struggles and actions create the possibility of change.

All this informs another critical paradigm of my own making. It sees collaborative intercultural theatre not as a process of group evolution or equalization, but rather as a series of cultural collisions and convergences that must be understood individually and in context. A collision is an experiential moment of cultural misunderstanding or perceived difference, whereas a convergence is one of cultural understanding or perceived commonality. I group these together as two possible outcomes of *cultural meeting*. Clive Barker, from whom I have stolen the term, describes cultural meeting as follows: "I encounter the otherness of people and in so doing I change. My personality develops and becomes richer by moving beyond the cultural definitions of my nationality" (255–56). The quotation comes from Barker's concluding essay in Pavis' *Intercultural Performance Reader*, in which Barker suggests some of the ways intercultural work might avoid being "an imposition of one set of cultural patterns on an alien people" or an "appropriation of cultural devices for exoticism or spurious novelty" (256). The multiple possibilities of cultural meeting, for Barker, are alternatives to these common pitfalls.

In the case of the PTMTP, identifying illuminating instances of both forms of cultural meeting—that is, of collision *and* convergence—involves looking beyond the order of the public performances produced by the projects. The patchwork and unlinear style of the PTMTP performances notwithstanding, even *as performances* they possess a semiotic and ontological unity that organizes an otherwise unstructured and unresolved experience. Moreover, these performances of the four projects—all of the same style—have had a disarming charm, seeming like a spontaneous intercultural cabaret of song, movement and personal reflection. Whatever image these shows presented of intercultural interaction from moment to moment, it was always uncomplicated and positive. Yet from my perspective as a practitioner and academic, interactions behind the curtain seemed only to become more fraught and unresolvable over the years, such that the public performance grew to less and less accurately reflect the conflicted feelings about the work circulating among the ensemble. This confusion was not merely the uncertainty one might normally expect in collective theatre work. Confusion is sometimes consciously employed and tolerated in devised theatre as a means of disrupting entrenched understandings or habits. Peter Eckersall, for example, highlights confusion in his analysis of the Australia-Japan collaboration *Journey to Con-Fusion*. That project, according to Eckersall, used confusion as a means to "imbricate a healthy sensibility of discomfort and destabilization into a genre that too often privileges one aesthetic discourse over another" ("Theatrical" 209). Bruce Barton also points to the importance of collision in physically-based devised theatre, suggesting that collision is the act and condition of *montage*, a dramaturgical strategy by which "distinct material units are forced into a collision [producing] psychological and emotional concepts" (109). In the case of PTMTP, the confusion was largely unacknowledged, resulting from participants not having sufficient knowledge of the contexts, traditions and decisions at play in rehearsal.

It was in search of other sites of cultural meeting that I conducted interviews with PTMTP participants throughout 2006 and 2007. My goal was to investigate participants' experience by asking them how they understood the work they were doing, who they were doing it with, and the contexts in which they worked. The participants understood that their opinions would contribute to an academic study. I guaranteed them anonymity because I wanted them to feel free to say whatever they wished about the work, though I openly acknowledged that such conversations are always conditioned by interpersonal relationships – including my own friendship with them. Like them, I was also implicated in the work, sometimes being perceived as a fellow participant and sometimes as a facilitator. I embraced my own implication in the work by sharing my own experience and opinions with them and dispelling the perception that I was a detached researcher. One of the many themes that emerged in my conversations was confusion, manifested in the following examples as ambivalence about the performances of the project:

> *A Debaj participant:* I love being in rehearsal. I love it. I love working with the artists. I love seeing what people are doing and coming up with. I love seeing that process … And the product to me is not – Like I don't have a huge attachment to it. So it isn't necessarily mine, really. There are parts of it that I think are fun. (laughter) (Interview 1, 2 June 2006)

A Czech participant: Because actually the show doesn't bring me any success … That would make me like … Like I did a good job. I don't feel this, actually … I don't mind. I really had a relaxing time with Canadians. But me as a like, for an actress, I would expect more. (Interview 2, 10 June 2006)

A UTSC participant: It's like you're entertaining the audience …. [We] don't have the facility to actually interact with the audience and find out like, how … Did you like it? … How did you respond to it? Did you recognize that certain parts were … You know, like are the mistakes – do you really recognize that these are mistakes being represented, or are you just laughing at a funny sketch? Do you know what I mean? Are you actually thinking about it? And I have no idea. (Interview 3, 2 June 2006)

Given that it is common for participants in collective theatre work to feel a special sense of ownership, it might be surprising that the first two participants quoted express their detachment from it, choosing instead to highlight their interest in the process and the wider intercultural experience. Conversely, the third participant did not find it so easy to detach, expressing an anxiety about what messages the performance was sending to its audiences. This related to this participant's wider frustration with not always understanding the cultural meanings circulating and motivating certain decisions; a potential problem in any theatrical work, perhaps, but a special problem in intercultural work in which artistic choices made can from the standpoint of one cultural or theatrical tradition make a lot of sense, while from another can range from bizarre to offensive. Unfortunately, with such a large ensemble and so little time to do the work it was not always possible in rehearsal to explain the choices being made, which often left participants to seek out their own meanings in conversations outside of the theatre. As these comments (and many others I could cite) indicate, this led to a sense that the most meaningful intercultural exchange was taking place in the extra-theatrical contexts of the project.

Some contemporary collaborative intercultural projects, such as the aforementioned *Journey to Con-Fusion*, have built into their processes opportunities to discuss the exchange itself and how the groups were understanding one another and the work. In the case of the *PTMTP*, such discussion was always extra-theatrical and informal. There may have been some practical reasons for this, but in this case the dramaturgy was shaped by the interests of its facilitators. While the project has clearly always been about learning from the intercultural experience, it was never focused on opening up dialogue within the ensemble about cultural politics. Director Jan Schmid, in particular, was instead interested in the project's theatrical elements, attempting to find some aesthetic synthesis between groups of different attitudes and styles that would prove interesting and entertaining to its audiences. The intercultural learning was meant to arise, it seems, from the exposure to different traditions and from performing to one another and to foreign audiences. Certainly that did happen, though it seems to me that those experiences only became meaningful as the participants discussed it later and connected their experience in the theatre to that outside.

For this reason, I add to my evaluation of the work those meanings that circulate extra-theatrically. It is necessary to do so, I believe, because this extra-theatrical experience—travelling to different communities, absorbing the energy of new spaces, seeing theatre performances elsewhere, seeing how people live elsewhere, discussing all of this over drinks—is another site of meaningful intercultural exchange that has deep and lasting significance for the participants. Such experience was so powerful for some participants that the performance they were creating almost became merely a pretense for the experience of traveling and experiencing a different culture:

> *A UTSC participant:* I know the rehearsal process is like slow for a lot of people, and they were expecting a little bit more, but ... you can't really dwell just on that one aspect when there's so much more going on while we're doing this whole thing, you know? (Interview 4, 7 June 2006)

> *Another UTSC participant:* [T]here were sort of cultural connections, and education about cultural experiences and attitudes, despite, perhaps, instead of, because of, like, *the project per se*, like I think that were made on a personal level. And that carries over into the process. (Interview 3, 2 June 2006)

> *A Czech participant:* [The] performance is just 10% of the whole project. The whole project for me is having fun, meeting people, seeing new places, being all together ... what I really appreciate is like all the people. (Interview 2, 10 June 2006)

Comments such as these lead me to consider how the extra-theatrical experience of intercultural work may be uniquely significant. In thinking about this, I find it useful to borrow from Ian Watson's writing about Eugenio Barba's "barters" his concept of the "event-narrative." The term "barter" was first used by Barba himself in 1974 to describe a performance situation in which two groups meet to perform for each other. In a barter, different forms of performance are exchanged, such as folk songs, dance, poems and stories. Barters were all unique, ranging from spontaneous performance exchanges to more orchestrated events of several hours, in which audiences were ushered around multiple performance sites. Even the more orchestrated events, though, were typically followed by a period of unstructured dialogue between groups. This was very important because, in Barba's opinion, the performance and the techniques, the products, were less significant in barter than the act of communicating across cultures itself. Writes Barba: "A man cannot meet another man if not through *some thing*, from this comes the paradox of the utility of apparently useless things ... The theatre as barter is connected to the utility of waste, of *potlatch*, of the dissipation of energies not used to produce things, but to produce relations" (103). For Barba, such "useless" things as techniques and stories were only a pretence for the sharing of a temporary community. Barters were to cultural dialogue what phatic conversation is to everyday dialogue: they existed to establish or maintain social relationships rather than impart information. Event narrative, then, is the term Ian Watson uses in application to Barba's barters in order to draw attention to the wider experience of the barter, its arc of development from beginning to end. Writes Watson:

"Barter is an orchestrated performance in which the entire event is a socio-theatrical metaphor of its intentions, which are to induce contact and an exchange between cultures" (100). Event narrative is the story of the whole performance event. In Barba's barters, the event narrative was often changing on the fly and didn't always have a clear start or end point.

Thinking of barters as prototypical collaborative intercultural theatre projects, the event narrative opens up as a possible broader, more inclusive site of cultural meeting beyond the process and product. This takes the entire experience of the participants, inside and outside of theatrical space, to be significant. Normally, when we create contemporary theatre, we are part of a creative process for a few hours, after which we go home and go about our daily lives, to return to rehearsal again perhaps on the next day. Collaborative intercultural theatre projects, however, usually remove people from their daily lives and normal social contexts. That removal defines the start and endpoints of the event narrative. Where the PTMTP differs from Barba's barters is in the event narrative's duration and richness. A barter typically lasted only four or five hours, whereas the PTMTP lasts four to five weeks.

This raises one potential further area of exploration: the temporalities of inter-culturalism. Owing to the influence of semiotics on intercultural discourse, I would argue, the predilection of intercultural theorists has been to think of intercultural negotiation in visual or spatial terms. But what of the temporal? Just as a meeting between unacquainted individuals can range from a simple handshake to extensive conversation, so too the results of cultural meeting varies. The brevity of Barba's barters led Ian Watson to observe that while barter is a site of "cultural meeting," it is not necessarily a site of "cultural engagement" (106). Watson feels that Barba's barters only ever achieved epidermal contact. Considering how much of human experience and understanding we identify as one's culture—the social, the civic, the political, the religious, the linguistic, the psycho-behavioral, the artistic—how much of this could possibly be accessed within the context of barters only several hours long? However, relating this back to the PTMTP, how much can be accessed in weeks? And then, how much in years, for those participants (like myself) who continue to be involved in the project? As Jane Turner has pointed out "[It] does not necessarily follow ... that all contemporary performance that plays with cultural signs and performance practices ... challenges cultural understandings" (15).

I asked most participants I interviewed what they would have changed about the design of the project, and in every case the response included the suggestion that more time was needed for the individuals and groups to get to know one another. Yet while that may have helped individuals understand one another and the process, it would be mistaken to assume that more lengthy collaboration necessarily means more mean-ingful collaboration. The PTMTP operated with a very compressed schedule, but the extent to which more time would have allowed for different dynamics is uncertain. What seems evident to me, at least, is that a compressed time schedule can eliminate time for reflection and shape a creative process that admits little confusion. The management of time, always within given circumstances of production, ultimately makes some meanings possible and others not. This has significant implications. Who, and in what circumstances, has the opportunity to ask questions about the work? Who is able to question or challenge cultural representations as they material- ize in the rehearsal room? Admitting such interventions into the process and sorting through moments of collision takes time, and the exigencies of time and production are such that critical reflection can be glossed over in favour of priorities less compli- cated – such as, for instance, the story of pre- or transcultural harmony mentioned at the outset of this essay. Lo and Gilbert, who would call such a story a "universalist vision," propose that it may be disrupted within intercultural "sites of intervention" such as language, space, the body and costume (46). Time, while less readable as semiotic text, can be understood as an additional site of intervention.

The comments of the PTMTP participants and Barba and Watson's comments about barters both point, I think, to process and event narrative as particularly impor- tant sites of meaning-making in the intercultural context. Some participants expressed a detachment from the theatrical product – because they didn't understand it, they didn't feel ownership over it. Yet however much rehearsals of the PTMTP might have actually looked like Barba's barters, the project is more than potlatch, undoubtedly providing for its participants valuable exposure to different ways of working and theatrical traditions. Difficult and unresolved experience is still experi- ence—perhaps of the most valuable kind—and I hope that my ongoing conversation with participants helps them, and me, find further meaning in it.

These preliminary practical and theoretical considerations are intended to only suggest a direction for further analysis. The paradigm of cultural meeting, for instance, like that of Pavis and Lo and Gilbert's models, is of course reductive: there are a range of possible outcomes of cultural meeting that go beyond the collision/ convergence binary. Also, collision and convergence are not necessarily mutually exclusive. A single exercise or scene from rehearsal or performance can be—indeed was often—interpreted as both during my interviews. In the absence of more thor- ough knowledge of the contexts and traditions at play, participants would sometimes patch together an understanding that was either quite different from or a complete reduction of that of others. What this might mean requires further theoretical exploration that would benefit from consulting those who approach interculturalism from a psychological perspective. James Herbeck, for example, has analyzed how the self experiences the other in the context of intercultural theatre and he argues that "through the Other's symbols, one can become more fully one's self" (13). Considering such a conclusion along with its Jungian premises might be a way to approach the experience of "understanding" in theoretical terms, though it would have to stop short of the unadvisable end of constructing a restrictive typology of experiences of intercultural interaction.

The public accolades and support for the PTMTP cited at the outset of this essay have given the impression that the work was a success, but this discussion has aimed to begin to make it successful in a different way: by offering individuals a chance to reflect on the value of the experience, and by using this data in a case study that considers meaning-making in the context of intercultural theatre. Doing so has required looking beyond the readily available story of transcultural harmony to explore how the work is understood by its participants. I have not offered a model to replace those discussed earlier, arguing instead for a post-structural paradigm that is most interested in the individual's theatrical and extra-theatrical experience. In a form of theatre premised on reconciling multiple cultural perspectives, it will be important to be aware of the particular way-of-seeing that this framework for analysis privileges, such that the theoretical tools it provides help to interpret sites of meaningful intercultural interaction without producing restricting arch-narratives of its own.

(2008)

Note

[1] An earlier version of this essay was presented at the 2006 annual conference of the *Association for Canadian Theatre Research*, where it was awarded the Robert Lawrence Prize for outstanding paper by an emerging scholar.

Works Cited

Barba, Eugenio. *Beyond the Floating Islands*. New York: PAJ Pub., 1986.

Barker, Clive. "The Possibilities and Politics of Intercultural Penetration and Exchange." *The Intercultural Performance Reader*. Ed. Patrice Pavis. London: Routledge, 1996: 247–56.

Barton, Bruce. "Navigating Turbulence: The Dramaturg in Physical Theatre." *Theatre Topics*. 15.1 (2005): 103–19.

Eckersall, Peter. "Theatrical Collaboration in the Age of Globalization: The Gekidan Kaitaisha-NYID Intercultural Collaboration Project." *Diasporas and Interculturalism in Asian Performing Arts*. Ed. Hae-kyung Um. London: Routledge-Curzon, 2005: 204–20.

———. "Trendiness and Appropriation? On Australia-Japan Contemporary Theatre Exchange." *Alternatives: Debating Theatre Culture in the Age of Con-Fusion*. Brussels: Peter Lang, 2004: 23–55.

Interview 1. Interview with De-Ba-Jeh-Mu-Jig participant in *The Art of Living*. 2 June 2006.

Interview 2. Interview with Czech participant in *The Art of Living*. 10 June 2006.

Interview 3. Interview with UTSC participant in *The Art of Living*. 2 June 2006.

Interview 4. Interview with UTSC participant in *The Art of Living*. 7 June 2006.

Lo, Jacqueline and Helen Gilbert. "Toward a Topography of Cross-Cultural Theatre Praxis." *TDR* 46.3 (2002): 31–53.

Pavis, Patrice. *Theatre at the Crossroads of Culture*. Trans. Loren Kruger. London: Routledge, 1992.

——. "Towards a Theory of Interculturalism in Theatre?" *The Intercultural Performance Reader*. Ed. Patrice Pavis. London: Routledge, 1996: 1–21.

Program for the *Prague-Toronto-Manitoulin Theatre Project 4: The Art of Living*. Trans. Michal Schonberg. Prague: Ypsilon Theatre, 2004.

Turner, Jane. "The 'Third' Spectator." in *Crossing Borders: Intercultural Drama and Theatre at the Turn of the Millennium*. Ed. Bernhard Reitz and Alyce von Rothkirch. Frankfurt: Wissenchaftlichter Verlag Trier, 2001. 11–16.

Watson, Ian. "The Dynamics of Barter." *Negotiating Cultures: Eugenio Barba and the Intercultural Debate*. Manchester: Manchester UP, 2002. 94–111.

Cosmopolitan Time and
Intercultural Collaborative Creation

by Modupe Olaogun

In Toronto in 2005, a Toronto-based theatre company, AfriCan Theatre Ensemble, created and publicly staged a theatrical piece of entertainment called *Market of Tales*. The creation began as stories, which members of the group transformed into theatre. The Ensemble members who participated in the project met in Toronto, a cosmopolitan centre that reflects the face of modern Canada as an immigrant and multicultural society. This location influenced the composition of the Ensemble members, who were all Canadian residents, and whose national or cultural backgrounds were as follows: an Eritrean, an Ethiopian, a Kenyan, a Sudanese, two Canadian-born Anglo-Caucasians, a Greek, a Zimbabwean and two Nigerians from different ethnic and linguistic backgrounds.[1] The stage, imaged as a "Market of Tales," became a metaphorical projection and a metonymic extension of the world. *Market of Tales* was a hybrid at many levels: the linguistic medium; the source material; the temporal reference of its various segments; the constituent genres; and the emotive evocation and association of the component stories. The aim of this analysis is to examine the cosmopolitan contact zone that shaped *Market of Tales* and how this contact zone hybridizes the temporalities of the stories that it absorbs into its public memory.

Migration is a key factor in the formation of the location where the composition of *Market of Tales* took place. Implicated in migration are the ideas of movement, relocation, space, place, citizenship, memory, temporality and displacement. In the shaping of *Market of Tales*, time played a critical role, as the stories that constituted the source material indicated different temporalities. As categorized by the dramaturge, the stories as reconceptualized in *Market of Tales* were creation myths, tales about origin of society, folktales with life lessons, historical accounts and contemporary events. This analysis asks: what are the assumptions about time and temporality in *Market of Tales* as an intercultural aesthetic, as a theatrical practice, and as an instance of a hybrid creation and performance? What are the kinds of anteriority that *Market of Tales* performs and from which it departs? What drives the departures? What kinds of new temporal and cultural spaces does *Market of Tales* create?

The idea of framing the new creation as a "Market of Tales" was the starting point. Once the idea took hold, the next question was: where are we getting the tales from? The dramaturge, Ronald Weihs, was attracted to creation myths, origin stories and folktales, and had assembled many of these from existing cross-cultural anthologies. Early in the exploration meetings, the ensemble members took turns to read these stories. As they read the stories, the dramaturge elicited more stories from the ensemble members, who contributed their own, some of which were additional creation and origin stories and folktales and, quite importantly, historical and biographical accounts and contemporary events, as well. There were a great number of stories, but the collaborative selection criteria of the ensemble began to mediate the choices. These criteria took the form of the entertainment value ascribed by the ensemble members to particular stories and the preferences they expressed in respect of the thematic and aesthetic possibilities of the stories in light of the dramatic adaptation in view.

The categories into which the ensemble placed the source materials contributed to shaping the creation of *Market of Tales* by helping the ensemble to determine connections between the source materials and to see possible ways in which the new creation could be made coherent. Arriving at possible categories took place alongside the imagining of a market as a place where drama and stories happen. The ensemble members considered a physical market as a place of selling and buying, of rendezvous of various kinds, a place where acquaintances and strangers meet, where people drive bargains and some make money while others lose, where people make friends and enemies, and so on. They talked about the kinds of dramas and stories that these various activities are capable of generating. In conceiving of the market as a place which draws an assortment of people and characters from all kinds of places, it was not difficult for the ensemble members to imagine a mingling in the market of beings from this and alternative worlds. Many ensemble members recalled the tales they heard in their childhood featuring ghosts and other supernatural beings and animals in fables who plied markets, taking advantage of the crowdedness of the markets and the free interactions to mingle and pursue relationships with humans. Other dramas and stories the ensemble members imagined in a market included love, disputes, magic and spectacle. These various dramas and stories suggested proto-categories correlated with the subject-matter.

The categorization evolved further in the gathering of the stories both from the written and the oral sources. Through the reading aloud of the published sources during the early exploration workshops, the ensemble performed a re-oralization of the initial origin myths and folktales. This process of re-oralization could only be a partial one, as the recording medium, print medium and the translation and the editing choices of the printed texts had mediated the transmission of the stories in certain ways. Let us look at two examples of the transformations that began with finding the stories and visualizing them in the ensemble's chosen categories.

One of the source stories is "How the World was created from a drop of milk" from an anthology compiled and edited by Ulli Beier called *The Origin of Life and Death: African Creation Myths*. The attribution appended to the story by the editor is simply "a Fulani story (Mali)"; this attribution suggests a communal cultural narrative. Ulli Beier, a German with Jewish background, was born in Glowitz, Germany in 1922. After studying linguistics at the University of London, he came to Nigeria in October 1950. He taught at the University College, Ibadan (which became the

University of Ibadan), and immersed himself in the local culture and language, Yoruba, in which he became quite fluent.[2] There is no statement in Beier's book about how he came upon the story and the seventeen other stories in his anthology, which altogether represent seventeen different languages and ten countries from Africa. Beier is not known to speak all these languages; however, he is interested in collective identities and universal motifs, as his statements in the introduction to the book suggest:

> But more important than "influences" or borrowings is, I think, the fact that similar ideas will occur to human beings in different places and at different times independently of each other. The story of the flood exists also among the Eskimos, where direct Oriental influence seems out of the question. The Aztecs of Mexico built the pyramids, even though they could not have had contact with Egypt. From a literary point of view, however, the origin of a particular motif is of little interest. Rather it is the particular version, the slant given to it, the style of the telling, that is of interest. (viii–ix)

The difficulty with each of the stories in Beier's collection, however, is that it is difficult to know the "slant" for which the collector and editor is responsible and the slant for which other people might have been responsible. The story, "How the World was created from a drop of milk," illustrates Beier's incitement of speculation, for it is the only narrative in the whole anthology that is presented in a remarkably poetic format. All the other stories are in prose form. What might have been responsible for the uniqueness of this story in terms of form in this anthology? Did the Fulani of Mali recite this story in a beautiful lyrical form that we glimpse through the English translation? How did Beier obtain this particular version? What was lost in the translation and the scripting? What was gained? Therefore, contrary to the suggestion by Beier, slant in this context, which is intercultural, is not a transparent, lineal category. It is at best fractured, mongrel-like, intermittent, cumulative and partially transparent. This interculturality is characteristic also of the cosmopolitan context of *Market of Tales*.

Remarkably, in the ensemble's adaptation the source words remain intact. It is the syntactic re-organization of these words in the ensemble's version, which will be picked up in a perceptive reading, which makes the decisive difference. As performance, the differences are further sharpened:

Beier version
At the beginning there was a huge drop of milk.
Then Doondari came and he created the stone.
Then the stone created iron;
And iron created fire;
And fire created water;
And water created air.
Then Doondari descended the second time. And he took the five elements
And he shaped them into man.

But man was proud.
Then Doondari created blindness and blindness defeated man.
But when blindness became too proud,
Doondari created sleep, and sleep defeated blindness.
But when sleep became too proud,
Doondari created worry, and worry defeated sleep;
But when worry became too proud,
Doondari created death, and death defeated worry.
But when death became too proud,
Doondari descended for the third time,
And he came as Gueno, the eternal one,
And Gueno defeated death. (Beier, 1–2)

For the ensemble's use of this story in *Market of Tales*, the company's dramaturge broke it into two separate semantic units titled "A drop of milk" and "Origins of the Elements" and restructured the text syntactically:

AfriCan Theatre Ensemble's adaptation in *Market of Tales*

At the beginning there was a huge drop of milk
Then Doondari came and he created the stone.
Then the stone created iron;
And iron created fire;
And fire created water;
And water created air.
Then Doondari descended the second time. And he took the five
    elements
And he shaped them into man.

But man was proud.
Then Doondari created blindness
And *blindness* defeated man.
But when blindness became too proud, *Doondari* created sleep.
And *sleep* defeated blindness;
But when sleep became too proud, *Doondari* created worry.
And *worry* defeated sleep;
But when worry became too proud, *Doondari* created death
And *death* defeated worry.
But when death became too proud, *Doondari* descended for the third
    time.
And he came as Gueno, the eternal one
And Gueno defeated death.
(Italics added to syntactic changes)

It may be noted that milk is a staple diet among the Fulani of sub-Saharan Africa, which includes Mali, so linking milk in their lore to the origins of life and the subsequent unleashing of creativity and diversity of human activities and states is a brilliant observation on the part of the Fulani whose myth we encounter here.

The ensemble's version foregrounds a nuance in mythological time. It makes it possible to see time as a whole as comprising a combination of continuums and stages and phases – discrete moments knitted together by ongoing organic activities that occupy time. By breaking the narrative into two distinct segments, the ensemble's version draws attention to moments in the event narrated and even makes it possible to think of what is happening in the story as multiple events rather than one single event. The dramatic break between the first and the second segments takes a cue from the first coordinating conjunction "but" in the source text: "But man…." The ensemble's adaptation makes productive use of this signifier of contrariness by intensifying the dramatic tension around it. It achieves this tension through the repositioning of the clauses, "and blindness defeated man" / "and sleep defeated blindness" / "and worry defeated sleep" / "and death defeated worry." The clauses are transferred from middle positions (in Beier's version) to beginning positions, where they initiate sentences. In so doing, the noun components of the clauses—"blindness" / "sleep" / "worry" / "death"—become foregrounded as protagonists with agency, and in this new position cause the syntactical position of "Doondari" to change (see the italicized sections of the ensemble's version above).

The coordinating conjunction "and" in the new position proposes the equality of the syntactical and structural importance of "blindness," "sleep," "worry" and "death" as agents, and of "Doondari," who occupies an originating position syntactically throughout Beier's version. In the ensemble's version, the position of "Doondari" shifts and becomes more varied. Consequently, Doondari, as creator in the myth, becomes humanized in the dramatic adaptation of *Market of Tales*. The foregrounded agency and volition of the various creations of Doondari in the ensemble's version present a more democratized vista of society, the metonymic extension of the created world, than in Beier's version.

The second example is a story titled "The Explanation of the Origin of Murder" from Volume 2 of Edwin Smith and Andrew Dale's *The Ila-Speaking Peoples of Northern Rhodesia* (present-day Zambia). Smith and Dale classify this story under "etiological and explanatory tales." There is a lexical change in AfriCan Theatre Ensemble's dramatic adaptation, which re-classifies it into a category titled "origin of society." In the ensemble's adaptation, this story becomes a segment called "The Eagle and the Child." The ensemble's lexical change in the new title creates greater semantic suggestiveness for the story and broadens its frames of reference.

After adaptation the source stories became "A Drop of Milk"; "Origins of the Elements"; "The Eagle and the Child"; "Luanda Magere," a legend about a cultural hero of the Luo of Kenya – contributed by ensemble member Muoi Nene; "The Two Sons," a Urhobo folktale – contributed by ensemble member Tony Adah; "All the Fierce Animals," an adaptation of "Rabbit and the Carnivores," a Gbaya/Cameroonian folktale by Daniel Ndaga, recorded by Philip Noss; "Lobengula," about the nineteenth century King of the Ndebele (present-day Zimbabwe); "Mbuya Nehanda," about the spirit medium, warrior and key leader of the Shona (present-day Zimbabwe) against British colonization in late nineteenth century; "Madiba (Nelson Mandela)," about the South African anti-apartheid fighter and first president of South Africa following a multi-"racial" election; and "Graça," about Graça Machel, a notable member of the Mozambican liberation struggle, social activist and first lady of Mozambique who became widowed and subsequently married Nelson Mandela. Ideas for the two historical accounts and the contemporary events were synthesized by the ensemble's dramaturge, Ronald Weihs, from a number of published sources.

One of the things the ensemble noted about the stories it was zeroing in upon for its composition of *Market of Tales* was their different temporal frameworks and the different occasions and motives for their prior narration. From the frequently unnamed narrators of the oral tales, who were the oral performers or native informers for the mostly Western or Western-trained ethnographers who collected the tales of origin and the folktales, to the ethnographers who participated in the tales' translations, editing and publication, to the ensemble members who are contemporary theatre practitioners and who became their cultures' interpreters as *Market of Tales* was composed, we have quite an assemblage of "voices" embedded in this creation. At a fundamental level, therefore, the product being forged was polyglot. Would there have been this degree of polyglot in a much less radically cosmopolitan location than Toronto? This is not likely. How these embedded voices intersect, interrogate, counter or supplement one another becomes an issue in forging a play from such constituent elements. For the play becomes an entity with a new life and a certain framework of coherence.

A second observation that can be made is the poly-temporality of the constituent stories. It is a poly-temporality inherent also in cosmopolitan space. The city of Toronto, as in many cosmopolitan spaces, is a palimpsest and hybrid of cultures. Newer settlements with distinct concentrations of cultural and linguistic groups in specific areas constantly redraw the cultural map of the city. Thus we have ethnically-named "towns," "neighbourhoods" and even nations within the city: "Chinatown," "Little Italy," "Black neighbourhoods," and so on. But these ethnic enclaves are ambivalent spaces that perpetuate the signs and features of the Old World and the New World simultaneously. Many first generation immigrants who seek Toronto to make it their new home talk about their desire for new opportunities for themselves and their progeny, while at the same time they attempt to maintain a distinctive cultural identity which may be articulated through their strictly observed religious and cultural rituals that they have brought from "home" – in this instance, their originating countries.

A common jocular affirmation of the Old World in the New World is reflected in such popular culinary "inside" knowledge as "you'll find more authentic and better Italian pasta in Toronto's Latino neighbourhoods than anywhere in Italy."[3] The point of separation from the Old World becomes solidified and reified as an unchanging and authentic image of the Old World. This willful suppression of the element of change in respect of the Old World is an anchoring device for the immigrants dealing with the uncertainties of the New World society for which they are only partially exchanging the Old World. In such a situation the time reference is polycentric and hybrid, integrating past/present/future simultaneously.

The impact of the categories mapped for *Market of Tales* on this dramatic creation can be gauged further through their structuring of this play. The categories indicated a time grid in which the presumed events take place. The creation myths suggest an abstract, imprecise time; the origin of society stories suggest a not-so-remote but still somewhat inexact time; the historical accounts suggest a closer time than the legends, which are often stories about a cultural hero or heroine from a presumably historical time that is distant; the contemporary events suggest a here-and-now temporality; and the folktales with life lessons suggest an imaginary time, one that can be any time.

The category chart constructed in *Market of Tales* bears a remarkable similarity to Isidore Okpewho's qualitative approach to oral narratives. In "Rethinking Myth," Okpewho observes both clock-wise and counter-clockwise movements between the axes of historical time and mythical time, and suggests a qualitative weighting of the relative fact and fiction based upon the various permutations available in these movements. The continuums might help, for instance, make a distinction between a legend which has a greater tendency toward fact versus a legend which has a greater tendency toward flights of fancy. But, quite importantly, Okpewho maintains, the creative temperament of the narrator or composer greatly mediates the degree to which a factual account is fanciful. Though folktales and fables generally defy the constraints of time, they can exercise a liberty to be set within a historical time and they will do this by converting into mythic legend. Unimaginable events can be set sometimes in the time of a historical figure. The dual movements in Okpewho's continuums make considerable time leaps conceivable within a single narrative (5–23, especially 14–19). In this regard, the time leaps within *Market of Tales* will be seen to be "logical." As a form and as a play, then, *Market of Tales* performs its unifying action through its process of subjecting its constituent stories to the "mythic" form. "Myth" here is understood as in the definition supplied by Okpewho – that is, not really a particular type of tale but "that quality of fancy which informs the creative or configurative power of the human mind in varying degrees of intensity" (19).

But while the ensemble played with the source stories by exploring them, devising dialogues, mimes and other treatments, and creating market scenes, not much happened at first in terms of the successful generation of a play with an organic coherence. The day the dramaturge asked the ensemble what *Market of Tales* should begin with, the formulation of what can be considered as a cohesive play began to emerge. The question enabled the ensemble to focus upon the kinds of stories it wanted to use and their temporal references. The ensemble members determined the sequence of the episodes by imagining a human life cycle. They decided that *Market of Tales* should start with a market scene where people interact. As these characters interacted, and the ensemble incorporated the stories they had worked upon, it soon became clear that the figures so created needed to be capable of morphing across different timeframes. So conceptualized, *Market of Tales* becomes both a process and a product. The ensemble members decided that the particular performance of *Market of Tales* they were working on should end with episodes involving contemporary events capable of suggesting both an ending and a beginning simultaneously. In this instance, it was Madiba's and Graça's love story. In between this opening and ending, "something happens," they said. What? A dramatic frame needed to be created to justify the radical temporal shifts between the segments of *Market of Tales* to make the movements between the segments logical and the overall dramatic tension unified.

The response to the ensemble's question at this stage was provided through the following reasoning: something is happening now; something happened before; something will happen next. The ensemble members also proceeded to determine the stories that "resonated" with one another. The ensemble was keenly aware of not just the different temporal frameworks of its source stories but also the different occasions and motives for their prior narration. The stories morphed through acting them and as a result of the environment in which they were being turned into a play. We can illustrate the foregoing observations through the segment, "The Two Brothers" or "The Upside Down Old Woman" in *Market of Tales*.

This story is about a family in which there are two wives who each have a son. One day one of the women becomes angry with her son, so she sends him to the forest. The boy encounters an old woman standing upside down with her teeth on the ground. When the old woman asks the boy for help to get her to stand the right way on her feet, he obliges cheerfully. To show her gratitude the old woman invites the boy into her home, where she lodges him. Before the boy goes to bed, the old woman informs him about some rats that may come into the house to eat up her food. She asks him to let the rats do as they please. When the rats come, the boy does not allow them to do as they please; he chases them away. The following day the old woman invites the boy to her farm, where she informs him about some crows that may come to eat up her crops. Again she asks the boy to let the crows do as they please. The boy does not allow the crows to do as they please; he chases them away. After the episode at the farm, the old woman decides it is time for the boy to return to his house, but before he departs, she asks him to choose a gift from a set of pots – one big, one small. He is to break the pot when he gets back home. The boy chooses the smaller pot. When he arrives at his house, his mother's temper has cooled down. The boy recounts his experiences and breaks the pot as he has been instructed by the old woman. The pot contains gold, other treasures and money. Another woman of the household, seeing what has happened, feigns anger with her son and sends him to the forest, as well. The other son also encounters the upside-down old woman, who gives him similar instructions as she had given to the first boy. However, when the rats come to the old woman's house, the other son allows them to do as they please. The following day at the old woman's farm he allows the crows to eat the crops. The boy follows the old woman's instructions faithfully. He too is presented a set of pots—one big and one small—from which he is to choose one. He chooses the bigger pot. Back in his house, when he and his mother open it, poisonous snakes, rather than treasures, issue from the pot.

The ensemble member who contributed the story understood its lesson to be that each brother got what he deserved. That was how the story had been interpreted where (and when) he grew up and heard it told. But many of the other ensemble members were puzzled by the fate of the second brother. What is the social value or personal quality for which one brother is being rewarded and the other punished? What is the ecological framework of the societ(ies) being encountered in this tale? They were thinking also about the values typically privileged in similar folktales, such as helpfulness and obedience to parental and older and wiser figures. The brother who received the snakes in the pot was, after all, helpful, obedient and respectful to the old woman, they believed. The ensemble member who contributed the story cared that the "authentic" African sources of the stories being adapted be carried forward. However, this authenticity is already problematized, interrogated by the new location, which is the cosmopolitan environment in which the stories are being retold, and by the experiences of the co-collaborators. In the negotiations that took place among the ensemble members over this story, bridges needed to be created to make the story meaningful. If frugality rather than improvidence, and initiative rather than blind obedience, are being emphasized, the ensemble members decided that the improvidence of one of the brothers would have to be exaggerated, rather than subtly presented, and the old woman's instructions about the rats and the crows would need a hint of irony.

Some of the conclusions to be drawn from this account and analysis of *Market of Tales* include the following. In the adaptation, a process of re-oralization of the material taken from published sources took place. As the members of AfriCan Theatre Ensemble members read aloud or told the stories, the stories came alive and so did their dramatic potential. New uses of the past and the present took place. *Market of Tales* is a departure from an African form it probably most closely resembles, the "concert party theatre" of West Africa, which is a variety show in dramatic form. *Market of Tales* forges its organic unity through its enactment of a story with a beginning, a middle and an end that is potentially a new beginning. This story is a cycle of human life featuring birth/creation, life on earth, death and rebirth. Consequently, it features tragedies, comedies and emotional states. It is akin to the drama suggested by Johannes Fabian that "never really ends." Fabian contrasts this drama with the tragic plot structure which delineates a series of events which end in doom (180).

Market of Tales is poly-temporal, polyglot and poly-generic. It is primarily a drama that enfolds into its form storytelling, mime, songs and dance. In the performances of oral narratives in the African societies described by Ruth Finnegan, there is a single narrator who may impersonate the characters in his or her narrative, not multiple actors (501). In *Market of Tales* there are multiple actors and the performance begins with these multiple actors in a linguistic exchange that morphs into a choral performance and changes into a short narration that reverts to dramatic form.[4] Morphing is an organizing principle in *Market of Tales*, seen not only in the interchange between the genres but also in the porosity of the different time periods implied by the stories. These stories that are embedded in *Market of Tales* are fragments of time. Fittingly, this strategy and quality of morphing were manifest in the costumes created for the performance at Artword Theatre in Toronto.[5] These costumes consisted of layering, peeling off and transformative uses of fabric and clothing items on stage in full audience view. The product which emerged from this collaborative creation was a staged performance and a scripted text that continued to change—to morph—until the last day of the performance.

(2008)

Notes

[1] The participants in the creation of *Market of Tales* in 2005 were Seifu Belachew (cast member), Alexandra Drossos (cast member), Teddy Masuku (cast member), Muoi Nene (cast member), Aktina Stathaki (cast member), Waleed Muoi (music director), Judith Sandiford (set and costume designer), Ronald Weihs (director and dramaturge) and Modupe Olaogun (artistic director and part costume designer). *Market of Tales* was first explored in 2004, leading to a pilot performance of two of the stories, "The Eagle and the Child" and "Luanda Magere" at ATE's AfriCan Soirée on November 20th, 2004. The ensemble participants in the short pilot were Tony Adah, Selina Chiarelli, Shannon Kitchings, Teddy Masuku, Muoi Nene and Kurt Spenrath.

[2] Gbemisola Adeoti calls Ulli Beier a "German-born Yoruba." See Adeoti. See also Ogundele.

[3] A Chilean gentleman living in Toronto said this to me sometime in 2007.

[4] For elaborate descriptions of the concert party, see Okpewho, *African Oral Literature*, and Cole.

[5] *Market of Tales* premiered at Artword Theatre, Toronto, 75 Portland Street, from November 9 to December 3, 2005. This production was directed by Ronald Weihs and designed by Judith Sandiford, with costume design by Modupe Olaogun and Judith Sandiford. A subsequent touring version, modified and directed by Tony Adah, was performed at a number primary and high schools in the Greater Toronto Area between February 7 and March 7, 2006.

Works Cited

Adeoti, Gbemisola. "Cultural Biography of the German-born Yoruba." http://www.africanreviewofbooks.com/Review.asp?offset=45&book_id=98. Accessed 23 January 2008.

Anonymous. "How the World was created from a drop of milk." Beier 1–2.

Anonymous. "The Explanation of the Origin of Murder." *The Ila-Speaking Peoples of Northern Rhodesia*. Ed. Edwin Smith and Andrew Dale. New Hyde Park, NY: University Books, 1968 (1920). 350–51.

Beier, Ulli, ed. *The Origin of Life and Death: African Creation Myths*. London: Heinemann, 1966.

Cole, Catherine. *Ghana's Concert Party*. Bloomington: Indiana UP, 2001.

Fabian, Johannes. "Theater and anthropology, theatricality and culture". *The Performance Studies Reader*. Ed. Henry Bial. London: Routledge, 2004. 175–82.

Finnegan, Ruth. *Oral Literature in Africa*. Nairobi: Oxford UP, 1976 (1970).

AfriCan Theatre Ensemble. *Market of Tales*. Performed by AfriCan Theatre Ensemble, Artword Theatre, Toronto. 9 November – 3 December 2005.

Ndanga, Daniel. "Rabbit and the Carnivores." *African Folklore*. Ed. Richard Dorson. Bloomington: Indiana UP, 1972. 485–94.

Ogundele, Wole. *Omoluabi: Ulli Beier, Yoruba Society and Culture*. Bayreuth African Studies 66. Bayreuth: Eckhard Breitinger, 2003.

Okpewho, Isidore. "Rethinking Myth." *African Literature Today* 11 (1980): 5–23.

———. *African Oral Literature: Backgrounds, Character, and Continuity*. Bloomington: Indiana UP, 1992.

The View Beyond the Stage:
Collective, Collaborative and
Site-Specific Performance in Vancouver

by Jerry Wasserman

Vancouver has long been known for its extraordinary natural beauty, but only recently has it begun to develop a lively theatrical culture that complements and utilizes the unique environments of city and region in imaginative, adventurous ways. The names of a couple of its most established companies, Theatre Under the Stars and Bard on the Beach, suggest how they have operated in harmony with the outdoors. A Vancouver institution since 1940, Theatre Under the Stars offered some of the city's first homegrown professional work. Semi-professional today, TUTS presents open-air musicals in Stanley Park's Malkin Bowl, surrounded by magnificent trees where the songs of shows like *Grease* and *Oklahoma* compete with the sounds of eagles and herons returning to their nests for the night. The Bard on the Beach Shakespeare Festival sold out its entire eighteenth summer season of four plays in 2007. Bard stages its shows in tents on the south shore of False Creek. The backs of the tents open to views of the water and the north shore mountains, so the backdrop to *Romeo and Juliet*'s balcony scene might be a sailboat coming in to harbour in the twilight of a Vancouver summer sunset. As Reid Gilbert points out, "no spectator can ever ignore the view beyond the stage" (119).

Viewing the most exciting work on and beyond Vancouver's stages these days means watching companies without their own buildings or even their own tents, companies that create new material themselves rather than recycling Shakespeare or American musicals. Many of them began as collectives and some still function that way. Their dramaturgical strategies frequently focus on developing site-specific work outside traditional theatre spaces; and in many cases the thematics of their work reflect the diversity of the company's own make-up, and in turn the make-up of the community. This diversity may be ethnic, a reflection of Vancouver's rich multicultural fabric. But it may also mean extending a show's economic and social range to include performers and audiences from outside theatre's typically middle-class demographic, or integrating physically or mentally challenged actors into an otherwise normative cast.

Electric Company Theatre, The Only Animal, Boca del Lupo, Theatre Replacement, neworldtheatre and Radix Theatre are at the centre of a new cultural ecology that has been transforming theatrical performance in Vancouver since the mid-1990s. Most of these companies were birthed from local post-secondary programs at the University of British Columbia, the actor-training program at Vancouver City College's Studio 58, and especially Simon Fraser University. They have made their mark on west coast theatre by virtue of original, self-created work and unique performance protocols, reinvigorating the local and, increasingly, the national scene. Like other collective and site-specific performance companies in contemporary Canada (see Shaver), their creative configurations resemble and yet differ from those of the alternative companies, working collaboratively, that revitalized Canadian theatre in the 1970s: Tamahnous, Theatre Passe Muraille, Codco and the *Paper Wheat* collective among others. Tamahnous was a Vancouver phenomenon; the latter three swept through the city in the 1970s at a time when it was still really just a big frontier town—Terminal City, the end of the line—a place where locally rooted professional theatre, especially the kind not cloning shows from Broadway or the West End, was struggling to gain a foothold.

In the late 1960s and early 70s collective creation became a popular element of the new Canadian alternate theatre for many reasons, most having to do with the countercultural and nationalist impulses of the era. Canadians looking for new theatrical paradigms found them in international alternatives to the commercial mainstream, like New York's Performance Group, Joan Littlewood's work in London and Peter Cheeseman's in Stoke-on-Trent, which offered collective, improvisational models (see Filewod, Johnston). According to Diane Bessai, "collective creation became the solution to the lack of written Canadian material" – given that there were so few experienced Canadian playwrights in a professional theatre that was just getting off the ground, actors getting together and improvising their own work provided a source of indigenous material. Bessai also cites "an aversion to the tyranny of the text – a trend initiated by the counterculture with its dedication to the creativity of the actor," as well as "the challenge of the informal, often improvised performance space – with its altered relation between performer and audience…" (27). The Tamahnous collective, whose members lived together communally, spoke for many of these emerging companies in the early 1970s when they described their concern "with the breaking down of the roles that exist in production—i.e., writer, director, actor—and with developing a working situation in which everyone is concerned with the central concept of the project" (qtd. in Usmiani 68). An additional motive, I would add, was the lack of opportunity for the baby boomers just coming out of theatre schools to get work in the mainstream regionals and Stratford.

Above all these particular elements was the overriding ideal of creating work not just generally Canadian but rooted specifically in the regional or local, the kind of work pioneered by Theatre Passe Muraille's Paul Thompson, who argued at the time that "in this country it's a political act to discover things about yourself" (qtd. in Wallace 62). Prototypical Passe Muraille shows of the 1970s, such as *The Farm Show* and *1837: The Farmers' Revolt*—of which Vancouverites saw both touring versions and multiple local productions, especially at the colleges and universities—influenced other young Canadians to organize their own companies collectively; to create their own shows about local material, collaboratively, improvisationally, and with a nationalist flavour; and to utilize non-traditional venues beyond not just the fourth wall but all four walls of the theatre. Passe Muraille shows also featured a stripped-down style of intense theatricalism that showcased the talents and imaginations of the actors while reflecting an attitude of what I call *Can-do Canadianism* back to its audiences, a style that other alternate companies of the 1970s would pick up, and that, along with many of the other characteristics of Passe Muraille dramaturgy, would be revived in Vancouver a quarter-century later.

Jump that quarter-century to the 1990s and you find British Columbia in recession and Vancouver theatre in a rut. But at the same time the city's demographics were radically changing with the influx of large populations of immigrants from Asia. And a new generation of theatre graduates, impatient with the status quo, were starting up their own companies, looking at a return to the collective, collaborative model, adding an embrace of the environment (Vancouver was the original home of Greenpeace), and emulating elements of the *Québecois* theatricality that gained high profile in the 1990s through the emergence into international prominence of Robert Lepage and Cirque du Soleil. Another influence was Caravan Farm Theatre, a working horse farm located 400 km northeast of Vancouver in rural Armstrong, BC, which stages its original shows and adaptations outdoors, utilizing the horses and other aspects of the rural environment. Many of the pioneers of new "alt" Vancouver theatre spent time at the Caravan.

Although the companies that emerged in Vancouver in the mid-1990s emulated strategies of the 1970s alternates, only some of the same rationales that motivated the earlier companies pertained to the new ones. International influences remained important. Radix co-founder Stephen O'Connell came to Simon Fraser in the 1980s with a BFA in Dance from Rutgers. The Only Animal's Kendra Fanconi, American-born and educated, trained and worked in the UK, Poland and France before arriving in Vancouver in 1997. The Asian heritage of neworld's Camyar Chai, Marcus Youssef and Adrienne Wong, Boca del Lupo's Sherry J. Yoon, and Theatre Replacement's Maiko Bae Yamamoto has manifested itself in much of their work. James Fagan Tait, an increasingly important figure tying together many of these companies, studied with Lecoq in Paris and directed in London before taking residence with Caravan on his way to Vancouver. Grotowski-based New Yorker Linda Putnam taught many of the future Boca del Lupos at Simon Fraser. Yet the influences cited by these artists are as likely to be indigenous as international: Caravan Theatre, Quebec's Carbone 14, Toronto's Mime Unlimited and Darren O'Donnell, and Vancouver's own HIVE collaborations in which these companies have co-created alongside each other.

Canadian nationalism per se is largely absent from their work. In the rare cases where it appears, as in neworld's *The Adventures of Ali and Ali and the aXes of Evil*, it gets critically examined and parodied. In many ways these companies take their Canadianism for granted. In their Canada, compared to Paul Thompson's, self-discovery through the theatrical investigation of one's environment involves a different kind of politics. Regionalism and localism are more likely to be implicit in the site-specificity of production than explicit in the subject matter or theme of the work, which has become increasingly internationalist, intercultural, and even interdimensional: the Middle Eastern concerns of neworld's shows, Electric Company's fascination with American technological pioneers, Theatre Replacement's *Sexual Practices of the Japanese*, the multiple, alternative worlds of The Only Animal's *Other Freds*. Boca del Lupo, typically, maintains that one of its "core values ... is to embody an international perspective as we operate locally, find partners nationally, and search for collaborators in other parts of the world" ("International").

Unlike the earlier Canadian collectives, these companies would have no shortage of good Canadian scripts or skilled, experienced Canadian playwrights to provide material for them if they were interested in simply producing pre-created work or working within the traditional hierarchy of writer–director–actors. With their formal theatre school training and a more extensive, varied theatrical marketplace in which to ply their trade, these artists also have much greater opportunity to simply plug themselves into the Canadian professional theatre than their predecessors had. But they have chosen a similar collaborative path.

In many ways the most successful of these companies is Electric Company Theatre, whose work has toured widely and been published. On their website they explain, "We create and produce original works with an emphasis on collective creation. Our projects are the result of collaborative writing with our scripts being authored by the core members of the company" ("Mission"). The core members are Kim Collier, David Hudgins, Kevin Kerr and Jonathon Young, the same four who started the company when they were students at Studio 58 in 1996. Collier had spent a year in Toronto studying with Mime Unlimited and had seen the work of Lepage, Carbone 14, and various dance companies that piqued her interest in a kind of physical theatre she was neither seeing in Vancouver nor learning at Studio 58. That institution taught primarily text-based, traditional acting technique, although all the "Electrics" took classes there with Wendy Gorling, whose physically-oriented mask work would result in her collaborations with Morris Panych on *The Overcoat* and other movement-based shows. Hudgins had worked on outdoor Shakespeare in Montreal, and all had had some alternative theatrical experience – on what Young calls "the borders of the production, where the fakery ends and real life begins" (qtd. in Ditor 93). The Electrics also cite the important influence of playwriting instructor John Lazarus, who taught a class in writing the one-person show. "You were given the tools of how to make things for yourself," Collier explains. [1]

Kerr had stumbled on the story of Nikola Tesla, the Hungarian inventor who immigrated to New York in the 1880s and competed, unsuccessfully, with Thomas Edison to popularize electric light and power. The four decided to create a play out of Tesla's story for the Vancouver Fringe Festival and took the company's name from its subject. Much like Passe Muraille under Paul Thompson, they divided up their areas of research and collectively improvised around the material they brought back to the rehearsal room. They even used the same term Thompson used to describe Passe Muraille's collective developmental dynamic: "jamming." Out of this process came *Brilliant! The Blinding Enlightenment of Nikola Tesla* (1996), authorship and direction ascribed to Electric Company Theatre, although in subsequent remounts direction is credited to "Electric Company with" an individual outside director (Electric 2–3).

In its subject matter, *Brilliant!* would be a paradigm for much of the Electrics' subsequent work, which Young describes as "our relation to new technology and the creative mind," seen again in *The Score* (2000), a play about genetics which the company has also done as a film for CBC television, and *Studies in Motion: The Hauntings of Eadweard Muybridge* (2006), about the nineteenth century American experimental photographer whose sequential photographs of bodies in motion prefigured cinematic technology. The process of creating *Brilliant!* made the Electrics aware of their individual strengths within the collective. Though all four would continue to perform and share writing, directing and design duties, Kerr became the *de facto* "head writer," Collier the primary director, Hudgins the key designer, and Young variously involved in all those roles with an emphasis on performance.

For their second show, *The Wake* (1999), again collectively researched and "jammed," the three men got co-writing credits and Collier and Kerr co-directed. *The Wake* chronicles three generations of a fictitious family living on Granville Island in Vancouver as it evolves from a Native fishing camp into the industrial centre of the city and, ultimately, to its post-industrial status as farmers' market, tourist site and performance centre, with the city's densest concentration of theatres. *The Wake* added one more element to what would become the Electric Company signature – its site-specific orientation – staged outdoors on Granville Island itself and in False Creek. The Electrics' attraction to site-specific work derived in large part from Collier, Young and Kerr's experience attending shows at nearby Caravan Farm Theatre while growing up in Kamloops. They learned to love what Young calls the "explosive theatricality" of work presented *in situ*, as well as the surprise and excitement audiences exhibited in a non-traditional theatrical environment. Their site-specific experimentation continued with *The Fall* (2003), a play about labour relations, a love triangle, and murder in a factory, brilliantly staged in a large abandoned warehouse.

Though all these works were collaboratively created, the company soon decided that they "had to break their model and do something different. We wanted to find ways to create but not always be in the room together," Collier explains. Young has since done a lot of freelance acting. Kerr went off and wrote *Unity (1918)* for Touchstone Theatre, which won the Governor General's Award, and has temporarily left the company to be playwright-in-residence at the University of Alberta. *The Fall* and *Studies in Motion* were co-produced with the University of British Columbia's Theatre Department. All these shows had large casts, which meant having to share the core members' creative vision and defer to somewhat more traditional playmaking methods. But even as the Electric Company continues to evolve, and its work becomes more polished and in many ways more astonishing, it does so with its core collective values intact, as it showed in its collaboration with The Only Animal and that company's artistic visionary, Kendra Fanconi.

Fanconi had co-created and performed in three productions with the Radix Theatre collective before starting her own company, originally called The Only

Fanconi. She also collaborated in 2002 with Boca del Lupo on *The Last Stand*, their first site-specific show high in the trees of Stanley Park. That same year she brought to the Electrics *The One That Got Away*, a remarkable play about a girl whose wicked, dying grandfather steals her heart and turns it into a fish. As he runs off with it, she follows him into the afterworld, staged in two adjacent swimming pools (originally in Vancouver's Jewish Community Centre), where the grandfather meets a singing, dancing chorus of his ex-wives and restages for his granddaughter the disastrous events of his early life in Russia. The play is credited to "Kendra Fanconi, created with Electric Company Theatre." Collier directed and Young was one of the performers.

Fanconi's The Only Animal extravaganza *Other Freds* (2005) has been perhaps Vancouver's most spectacular instance of site-specific theatre to date. Exploring the possibility that each of us exists simultaneously in multiple dimensions, seven identically dressed actors (including Theatre Replacement's James Long) played Fred simultaneously in a gigantic production staged on Granville Island and on boats or literally in the waters of False Creek, utilizing over 100 performers (mostly community volunteers), some of whom performed a bicycle ballet on the far shore of False Creek that the audience could see only via binoculars provided with the program. The performers, says Fanconi, "dealt with full immersion in the ocean, bird shit, rats, harassment from boaters, kayaking in active waterways and acting at the same time … Site-specific theatre is not for the faint of heart, diva or wuss" (qtd. in Strilchuk 102).

Boca del Lupo has a history similar to that of Electric Company. Boca began as a six-person collective at Simon Fraser in 1997. The role of Boca's *de facto* dramaturg/director was assumed by Sherry J. Yoon when the group got together in the rehearsal room to do their "woodshedding"—their word for what Passe Muraille and Electric Company call "jamming"—each member improvisationally riffing on assigned research material. For five years Boca operated as a pure collective, every member bearing the label "co-artistic director." Then, like the Electrics, they decided that the model was no longer functional. None of them had worked with anyone else but the collective and they felt that their process was getting stale, so they restructured, with Yoon taking on the role of artistic director and Jay Dodge artistic producer. They also took on as artistic associates graphic artist Jay White, musician/composer Joelysa Pankanea and writer/director James Fagan Tait, the latter two a potent project team that has immensely influenced Vancouver's new theatrical styles. All together, they have refined Boca's multidisciplinary storytelling techniques and its mission to create "new performance works using unique processes of collaboration and extra-ordinary interactions between performer and audience" ("Artistic Mission").

The "extra-ordinary interactions" have been accomplished primarily through their free, all-ages, site-specific outdoor summer shows in Stanley Park. Adapted from folk tales, they are staged in and among the trees in the park, with the audience following the action through the forest. Tait joined the collective as head writer to script *The Last Stand* (2002), *Lagoon of the Lost Tales* (2003), *Vasily the Luckless* (2005), starring the Electrics' Jonathon Young and *The Shoes That Were Danced to Pieces* (2006), as well as *Quasimodo, or The Bell Ringer of Our Lady of Paree* (2007), his adaptation of Victor Hugo's *Notre Dame de Paris*, staged beneath Vancouver's Burrard Street Bridge. Even more than their scripts, musical and design concerns—especially Jay Dodge's interest in climbing and rigging—dictate the narrative structure of these highly physical spectacles. Dodge says of the Boca del Lupo philosophy, "I don't think people of this generation see the difference between disciplines. In our company you're a story-maker in whatever discipline you work in. Our approach is, 'How can we work together to tell a story?'" In 2008 they premiered *My Dad, My Dog*, co-created by Yoon, Dodge and White, with Tait in the cast, the story of a North Korean woman convinced that her dead father has returned to life as a dog.

Two of Boca's original members, James Long and Maiko Bae Yamamoto, left in 2003 to form their own collective, Theatre Replacement. According to its website, key elements of the company's mandate include the intention "to continu[e] the evolution of collaborative theatre making," to "further our artistic practice through creative collaborations between artists of different disciplines and approaches," and to seek "diverse audiences." These impulses are not limited to Vancouver-based companies. Ric Knowles has written about Kitchener's MT Space, "a company based on difference *within* the collective … [and] the conscious bringing together of actors from different cultures to forge new, explicitly 'multicultural' or 'intercultural' dramaturgical forms" (8). Theatre Replacement's two best shows have accomplished these goals with great success. *Sexual Practices of the Japanese* (2006), collectively created by Long, Yamamoto, Manami Hara and Hiro Kanagawa, offers a brave Canadian take on some widely held notions about Japan and its sexual and cultural habits. For *BIOBOXES: Artifacting Human Experience* (2007), Yamamoto and Long directed six actors, each of whom performed for one audience member at a time on a "stage" which is a box that fits over the actor's head. Each playlet, written by the individual actors, derived from interviews they did with first-generation Canadians of the same national background as themselves – French, Italian, Serbian, German, Japanese, Chinese. Each playlet was performed bilingually. The effect, as I wrote when I saw the play at the 2007 PuSh International Performing Arts Festival in Vancouver, is "theatre that really does push your playgoing brain into another dimension" (*"BIOBOXES"*).[2]

Interculturalism and diversity—along with strong political positions—also define the neworldtheatre collective. Currently comprised of Camyar Chai, Marcus Youssef and Adrienne Wong, neworld was started by Chai in the 1990s after he graduated from UBC. Originally from Iran, he began by staging Persian folk plays. But after seeing a Caravan Farm Theatre show, he decided to go the collective route to bring other people's ideas and experiences into the mix. Among them were Lois Anderson, Stephen Hill, and the omnipresent James Fagan Tait. With Chai they collectively created *Devil Box Cabaret* (1998), a Brechtian political cabaret staged in a Commercial Drive storefront. Each member of the collective took a scene and led a day's work on it, with Chai functioning as what he calls "the distiller." After the substantial success of *Devil Box*, neworld instituted an annual rotating *de facto* artistic directorship. Hill took the first turn and came up with a concept he named Leaky Heaven Circus, a zany, irreverent, family-oriented free-for-all collaboration that incorporated the skills of acrobatic performers like Colin Heath and Manon

Beaudoin, who had worked with Cirque du Soleil, and that took care of the problem of childcare by putting their kids into the show, along with a developmentally challenged young man and a dog, all of whom became Leaky Heaven regulars. This was a paradigm for the politics of neworld: what Chai calls "changing the model" to create "theatre that wants to be involved in social health." Leaky Heaven Circus proved so popular that it became an annual event, eventually becoming an independent company under Hill.

Then, says Chai, "I started to get dissatisfied with that kind of collective creation. The chaos was wonderful but it didn't have room for finesse and subtlety. That's when Marcus and I started to discuss *hybridizing*, how to maintain that chaos and energy and add what a script gives you, which is structure and control." The first such hybrid show was *Opiate Karim*, a Persian tale scripted by Chai with significant input from the cast. *Opiate Karim* eventually developed into *Asylum of the Universe* (2004), starring Tait and incorporating a variety of physical theatre styles. Tait followed with his own epic adaptation of Dostoevsky's *Crime and Punishment*, which swept Vancouver's 2005 Jessie Awards. That show employed a large, ethnically diverse cast that included physically disabled and economically disadvantaged performers from Vancouver's Downtown Eastside neighbourhood.

neworld's most significant success has come with *The Adventures of Ali & Ali and the aXes of Evil* (2004), the company's challenge to the post-9/11 world order and Canada's role in it (see Wasserman, "Bombing"). The play was collectively created with Guillermo Verdecchia from political skits Chai and Youssef were doing for CBC radio. Chai explains, "We'd improvise, then all three of us would write different things, pass the scenes off to one another, improvise again, then write again." The neworld process and *Ali and Ali*'s metatheatrical aesthetic also allowed the actor playing the Scottish stage manager—originally Tom Butler, then John Murphy—to incorporate his own audition reel into the show, and led to neworld's producing Murphy's own extraordinary solo piece, *The Heretic* (2006), a scathing diatribe against Catholicism. Chai explains that it fit neworld's diversity mandate perfectly: "a Scottish-Catholic upbringing is as completely 'diverse' as a Persian-Muslim upbringing." neworld's *Adrift on the Nile* (2006) was adapted by Youssef from Naguib Mahfouz's Egyptian novel with the collaboration of the ethnically diverse cast, which included actors Maiko Bae Yamamoto and Adrienne Wong playing Egyptians. Chai, who directed, says "[W]e want all our shows to look like what you'd see walking down the street in Vancouver."

The last company I want to mention actually appeared first. Radix Theatre, another group of Simon Fraser alumni, lists over twenty productions since 1988. On its website Radix describes itself as a collective whose "productions are staged outside of traditional venues in an attempt to highlight the theatricality of unusual sites, and to look at ordinary spaces with a heightened perception." Andrew Laurenson and Paul Ternes have operated as co-artistic directors since 1998, the latter having performed with both Tamahnous and Boca del Lupo. Radix has developed an increased profile in the past decade with site-specific, collectively created shows like *The Swedish Play*

(2002), staged inside an IKEA store, *Half a Tank* (2004), performed in a parking lot with audience members sitting in their own cars, and *Final Viewing* (2005), a murder mystery of sorts that took the audience from a downtown pub to an office building where they viewed events unfolding live on the street below. For Radix, says Andrew Templeton, "locations are not simple settings or thematic tools but are integral to decoding experience" (49).

The collaborative synergies developed by Radix in conjunction with the five other companies I have discussed found an apt metaphor in HIVE, a 2007 collaboration of those six plus five additional local theatre operations. These eleven companies staged three evenings of individual short pieces for small audiences in the cloakroom of an old Vancouver funeral home (make of that specific site what you will). The plays, or theatrical installations, were presented simultaneously in a single room around a central bar where audiences and the companies themselves had the opportunity to cross-pollinate. HIVE 2 will be produced at the Magnetic North Theatre Festival in Vancouver in 2008.

All these views beyond the traditional stage reveal Vancouver's collective, collaborative, site-specific theatre to be a vital part of twenty-first century west coast culture. Vancouver is a very different city today than it was in the 1970s: bigger, more sophisticated, more diverse, more expensive, and in many ways more alienating. While echoing the ideology of the 1970s collectives, its current theatrical activity reflects a revised sense of place and cultural identity, a desire both to explore the here and now and to recapture some of what has been lost. Its site-specific work investigates classic urban spaces—streetscapes, bridges, warehouses—as well as the (urbanized) remnants of the natural world within the city: False Creek, Stanley Park. The pervasive influence of Caravan Farm Theatre's rural idyll and the nostalgic folktale quality of so many of these shows are not coincidental.

In a city with both the highest housing costs in the country and the poorest neighbourhood, collective creation and collaborative work among individual theatre artists and companies reaffirm communal values across economic and ethnic divides. Theatrical collaboration in Vancouver today replaces the self-conscious Canadian nationalist politics of earlier eras with an outward-looking sense of a larger stage, a polyphony of voices, and an international audience. Its mantra could be one of the paradigmatic slogans of the 1970s: think globally, act locally.

(2008)

Notes

[1] All unattributed quotations and much of the information about the artists and companies in this chapter derive from interviews, conversations and email exchanges I had with Kim Collier, Jonathon Young, Jay Dodge, Camyar Chai and Kendra Fanconi in 2006 and 2007. Dates in parentheses indicate year of first production.

[2] Norman Armour, another Simon Fraser theatre graduate, has steered the PuSh Festival since its inception in 2005. By giving Theatre Replacement, The Only Animal, Boca del Lupo, Radix and Electric Company opportunities to showcase their work alongside other cutting-edge companies from around the world, he has been instrumental in helping to raise their profile and effect international collaborations. The participation of the new alt Vancouver companies in recent editions of the Magnetic North Theatre Festival has also been important in giving their work national exposure. My quoted comment on *BIOBOXES* comes from my review of the show posted on my website www.vancouverplays.com. The *BIOBOXES* review can be found in the archives along with my reviews of various shows from every company discussed in this chapter.

Works Cited

Bessai, Diane. *Playwrights of Collective Creation.* Toronto: Simon & Pierre, 1992.

Boca del Lupo. "Artistic Mission." Company website. http://www.bocadellupo.com/mission.htm#mission. Accessed 23 January 2008.

———. "International." Company website. http://www.bocadellupo.com/mission.htm. Accessed 23 January 2008.

Ditor, Rachel. "On Site with the Electric Company: What Lures Artists out of the Theatre and into the Woods?" Houston and Nanni 92–97.

Electric Company. *Brilliant! The Blinding Enlightenment of Nikola Tesla.* Victoria: Brindle & Glass, 2004.

———. "Mission." Company website. http://www.electriccompanytheatre.com/mission/. Accessed 23 January 2008.

Filewod, Alan. *Collective Encounters: Documentary Theatre in English Canada.* Toronto: U of Toronto P, 1987.

Gilbert, Reid. "Vasily, Hamlet and Fred: Site-Specific Work in Vancouver, 2005." Houston and Nanni 119–21.

Houston, Andrew and Laura Nanni, ed. *Canadian Theatre Review* 126 (2006): *Site-Specific Performance.*

Johnston, Denis. *Up the Mainstream: The Rise of Toronto's Alternative Theatres, 1968–1975.* Toronto: U of Toronto P, 1991.

Knowles, Ric. "Collective Differences in MT Space." *alt.theatre: cultural diversity and the stage* 4 (2006): 8–11.

Shaver, Andrew. "Thoughts for the New Alternative: Histories, Boundaries and the Space Apart." Houston and Nanni 130–33.

Strilchuk, Amy Lynn. "Documenting the Creative Process of Kendra Fanconi: The Force behind *Freds.*" Houston and Nanni 98–102.

Templeton, Andrew. "Sex, Cars and Shopping: Meditations on Social Disabilities." *Canadian Theatre Review* 122 (2005): 45–49.

Usmiani, Renate. *Second Stage: The Alternative Theatre Movement in Canada.* Vancouver: U of British Columbia P, 1983.

Wallace, Bob. "Paul Thompson at Theatre Passe Muraille: Bits and Pieces." *Open Letter* 2nd ser. 7 (1974): 49–71.

Wasserman, Jerry. "*BIOBOXES: Artifacting Human Experience.*" Review. Theatre Replacement production, January 25 – February 4, 2006. Vancouverplays.com. http://www.vancouverplays.com/theatre/reviews_theatre/review_bioboxes.shtml. Accessed 23 January 2008.

———. "Bombing (on) the Border: *Ali & Ali and the aXes of Evil* as Transnational Agitprop." *Modern Drama* 51.1 (2008): forthcoming.

Youssef, Marcus, Guillermo Verdecchia and Camyar Chai. *The Adventures of Ali & Ali and the aXes of Evil.* Vancouver: Talonbooks, 2005.

The Very Act

by Yvette Nolan

These are the ingredients we needed to create *Death of a Chief*, Native Earth Performing Arts' all-Aboriginal adaptation of William Shakespeare's *Julius Caesar*.

> • *The original text, by Will.*

My first Shakespeare, one I watched on television as a toddler, with my mother, an autodidact, who quizzed me afterwards.
Mom: And what happened to Caesar?
Me: They stabbed him.
Mom: And what did Caesar say when they stabbed him?
Me: *Tee hee, Brutus.*

> • *A company of curious artists.*

The project began when an actor brought me a notice of funding for professional development: "Why don't you apply for money to offer a Shakespeare intensive for Aboriginal women?" We applied for and received funding, and I contacted Kennedy C. (Cathy) MacKinnon to teach the workshop. A former Stratford coach, she is, like me, in love with the Bard, believes, like me, that everything is in Shakespeare. She works with a diversity of players, from Stratford to the Centre for Indigenous Theatre, from Mozambique to Humber College. Seven women took the workshop and developed an appetite for Shakespeare. Cathy suggested we produce a Shakespeare. I confessed my desire to do an all-Aboriginal *Caesar* because of its resonance in the Native community.

The artists brought themselves to the work. One of the things we struggle with, and against, as Aboriginal artists is the idea of pan-Indianism. In spite of some shared values, some shared history, we are not all the same. We are different nations, with different practices, different traditions. Some come from nations that practice the sweat lodge; others don't. Some nations frown on their women drumming; others don't. Ceremonies differ from nation to nation. This became one of the primary things we explored as we worked on the text. How do we agree to a new set of rules for an intertribal group like the company of *Death of a Chief*? And by extension, how do we as contemporary Aboriginal people negotiate a new set of rules that we will use to govern ourselves in the very near future?

The artists brought their bodies to the work, and in their bodies, their histories, their languages, their voices. In the first workshop, we distilled the story of *Julius Caesar* to a seven-minute physical piece, incorporating voice and drum. This prologue remains in the production version of *Death of a Chief*, a prologue that tells the whole story in a physical way, before we attack the text. The only text in the prologue is "abuse of greatness is, when it disjoynes / Remorse from power" (II.i.18), a line that became symbolic for all the issues the company struggled with in talking about how the play resonates for us. As we struggle to reclaim our traditions, as we take first steps towards self-government, we try to choose a leader who will serve our communities, who will not turn out to be so ambitious that he "disjoynes / remorse from power." This is what the company explored throughout the development process: how "th'abuse of greatness" in our communities threatens the health of the whole. The very act of working together to adapt *Caesar* to *Death* is the subject of our Story; the community working together to find a way to coexist, to produce together, to move forward together.

•*Time.*

The time, and the breathing space to develop a project, is treated as a luxury, and yet it is critical to the development of almost all new work, but especially collectively created or devised work. That initial text workshop was in the spring of 2004. In the spring of 2005, we did the first week of workshop on *Julius Caesar*, and another in August. In September 2005, we did yet another, and presented what we had created so far at Native Earth's festival of new work, Weesageechak Begins to Dance. That showing lead to an invitation to present at University of Toronto Graduate Centre for Study of Drama's Festival of Original Theatre (FOOT) in February of 2006, which afforded us another week of workshop. A showing at the Macdonald Stewart Art Centre in Guelph in cooperation with the Canadian Adaptation of Shakespeare Project (CASP) bought us another two days of workshop in October of 2006. And then, miraculously, the National Arts Centre in Ottawa came on board as a producing partner and that bought us an additional two weeks of workshop in June of 2007, enough time to finish the adaptation. Six weeks and two days over two years and nine months to develop a piece that is ready to go into rehearsal. Fallow time between workshops. Time for the work to sit inside the artists. Time for the piece to reveal itself, like Michaelangelo's statue inside the marble. Time for Cathy and me to respond to the revelation, to digest, to talk, to evaluate, to plot out a direction, the next step.

• *Resources.*

Just as it takes a village to raise a child, so does it take an entire community to develop a piece of theatre. Each workshop of course moved the project forward, but the biggest leaps came in the last two. The two days in Guelph were critical to the company. On the second day, the day we showed the work to students and the community, one of the actors said, "It feels like an *ensemble* for the first time." Some of the players had been with the project since the beginning, others had come and gone, but for the first time we felt like we were an ensemble. The investment of the National Arts Centre allowed us to finish the text; until June 2007, the adaptation only went as far as the end of the third act. The two weeks that the NAC bought us, without the pressure of a showing, gave us the opportunity to find our way through to the end of Will's text.

• *Perspective.*

Early in the development of *Death of a Chief*, the project garnered a lot of attention. Perhaps it is the eternal appeal of Shakespeare, perhaps the seeming novelty of Indians doing Shakespeare. Regardless, the critics, the academics, the teachers began to pay attention, to document, to interview, to analyze. Instead of being distracting, this attention became a tool in the development of the piece. Most significant was the Guelph workshop in October 2006 that resulted in the video "What Means This Shouting?" by Marion Gruner and Sorouja Moll. The filmmakers were frustrated by not having workshop video to include in their documentary, so they raised the funding through University of Guelph's CASP for a two-day workshop at the Macdonald Stewart Art Centre. This, as mentioned before, was a critical workshop, where the company gelled into an ensemble.

• *Production.*

The beauty of production is the wonder of a deadline. Once the National Arts Centre committed to the project, Native Earth was able to confirm production dates. Nothing moves a project along like the threat of an audience, and while I believe that first production is a part of the development of a piece of theatre, and not the end of it, production does deliver an incontrovertible urgency to the process. At this writing, we are mere weeks away from rehearsal, the next and perhaps most telling stage of the process, a process that so far has resulted in the development of both a piece of theatre and a community of artists.

(2008)

Suggested Further Reading

Canadian Authors

Anderson, Peter. "Breaking All Four Walls: Open-Air Theatre at the Caravan Farm." *Canadian Theatre Review* 76 (1993): 8–12.

Arnott, Brian. "The Passe Muraille Alternative." *The Human Elements*. Ed. David Helwig. Ottawa: Oberon, 1978. 97–111.

Barton, Bruce. "Dancing with Spirits: Zuppa Circus's *Open Theatre Kitchen*." *Canadian Theatre Review* 128 (2006): 20–25.

———. "Making Change: The Composing Body in Devised Theatre." *Space and Composition: A Nordic Symposium on Physical/Visual Stage Dramaturgy* (Symposium Proceedings). Ed. Miriam Frandsen and Jesper Schou-Knudsen. Copenhagen: NordScen, 2005. 110–22.

———. "Navigating 'Turbulence': The Dramaturg in Physical Theatre." *Theatre Topics* 15:1 (2005): 103–19.

———. "The Razor's Edge between Performativity and Theatricality in Bluemouth Inc.'s *American Standard*." *Canadian Theatre Review* 126 (2006): 23–26.

———. "*Still Ringing*: Sounds Collaborative." *Canadian Theatre Review* 129 (2007): 25–29.

———. "Through a *Lenz* Darkly: Bluemouth Inc.'s S(t)imulated Schizophrenia." *Canadian Theatre Review* 127 (2006): 54–59.

Bessai, Diane. "Documentary Theatre in Canada: An Investigation into Questions and Backgrounds." *Canadian Drama/L'Art dramatique canadien* 6.1 (1980): 9–21.

Brask, Per, ed. *Contemporary Issues in Canadian Drama*. Winnipeg, MA; Blizzard, 1995.

de Guevara, Lina. "Sisters/Strangers: A Community Play about Immigrant Women." *Canadian Theatre Review* 90 (1997): 28–31.

Ditor, Rachel. "Questioning the Text." *Theatre Topics* 13.1 (2003): 35–43.

Filewod, Allan. *Collective Encounters: Documentary Theatre in English Canada*. Toronto: U of Toronto P, 1987.

———. "The Interactive Documentary in Canada: Catalyst Theatre's *It's About Time*." *Theatre History in Canada* 6.2 (1985): 133–47.

————. *Performing Canada: The Nation Enacted in the Imagined Theatre.* Kamloops, BC: Textual Studies in Canada, 2002.

————. "Theatrical Nationhood in Radical Mobility: *The Farm Show* Futures and the Banner / Ground Zero Collaborations." *Canadian Theatre Review* 125 (2006): 9–15.

Fitzsimmons Frey, Heather. "Dramaturgy and a Collective Theatre." *Canadian Theatre Review* 123 (2005): 73–78.

Fowler, Richard. "Epilogue: Why Did We Do It?" *Canadian Theatre Review* 88 (1996): 54–55.

————. "Grotowski and Barba: A Canadian Perspective." *Canadian Theatre Review* 32 (1981): 44–51.

Gilbert, Sky. "Dramaturgy for Radical Theatre." *Canadian Theatre Review* 87 (1996): 25–27.

Graham, Catherine. "Performing Community in English Canada and Québec." *Theatre Topics* 10.2 (2000): 101–11.

Harvie, Jen. "DV8's *Can We Afford This*: The Cost of Devising on Site for Global Markets." *Theatre Research International* 27.1 (2002): 68–77.

Hengen, Shannon. "The De-ba-jeh-mu-jig Method: Making Stories: The 'Four Directions' Creative Process Moves Script Development Beyond the European Model." *Canadian Theatre Review* 115 (2003): 35–38.

Ives, Patricia L. "The Very Best Bad Girls Create…" *Canadian Theatre Review* 55 (1998): 30–33.

Jarvis, Alistair. Review of *Icaria. Canadian Theatre Review* 99 (1999): 93–95.

Johnston, Denis W. *Up the Mainstream: The Rise of Toronto's Alternative Theatres.* Toronto: U of Toronto P, 1991.

Knowles, Richard Paul. "The Mulgrave Road Co-op theatre and the Community in Guysborough County, N.S." *Canadian Drama/L'Art dramatique canadien* 12.1 (1986): 18–32.

————. "Stories of Interest: Some Partial Histories of Mulgrave Road Groping Towards a Method." *Theatre Research in Canada/Recherches théâtrales au Canada* 13.1/2 (1992): 107–19.

Nunn, Robert. "Performing Fact: Canadian Documentary Theatre." *Canadian Literature* 103 (1984): 51–62.

O'Donnell, Darren. *Social Acupuncture: A Guide to Suicide, Performance and Utopia.* Toronto: Coach House, 2006.

Ondaatje, Michael, dir. "The Clinton Special: A Film about *The Farm Show.*" Mongrel Media, 1974.

Quirt, Brian and DD Kugler, eds. *Canadian Theatre Review* 119 (2004): *Creative Research and New Play Development.*

———. "Pure Research." *Canadian Theatre Review.* 119 (2004): 40–43.

Ross, Nadia. "Natural Emptiness: Thoughts About Theatre and the Body." *C Magazine,* 92 (2006): 31–35.

Salverson, Julie. "The Art of Witness in Popular Theatre." *Canadian Theatre Review* 90 (1997): 36–39.

———. "Imagination and Art in Community Arts." *alt.theatre: cultural diversity and the stage* 3.2 (2004): 4–6.

———. "Questioning an Aesthetics of Injury: Notes from the Development of *Boom.*" *Canadian Theatre Review* 106 (2001): 66–69.

Scott, Shelley. "Collective Creation and the Changing Mandate of Nightwood Theatre." *Theatre Research in Canada/Recherches théâtrales au Canada* 18.2 (1997): 191–207.

Taylor, Heidi. "Deep Dramaturgy: Excavating the Architecture of the Site-Specific Performance." *Canadian Theatre Review* 119 (2004): 16–19.

Theatre Passe Muraille. *The Farm Show.* Toronto: Coach House, 1976.

Van Fossen, Rachel. "Writing for the Community Play Form." *Canadian Theatre Review* 90 (1997): 10–14.

Vogt, Gordon. "The Politics of Entertainment: George Luscombe at TWP." *The Human Elements.* 2nd Series. Ed. David Helwig. Ottawa: Oberon, 1981. 132–60.

Wagner, Anton, ed. *Contemporary Canadian Theatre: New World Visions.* Toronto: Simon & Pierre, 1985.

Wallace, Robert. "Paul Thompson at Theatre Passe Muraille: Bits and Pieces." *Open Letter.* 2nd ser. 7 (1974): 49–71.

———. *Producing Marginality: Theatre and Criticism in Canada: Essays by Robert Wallace.* Saskatoon: Fifth House, 1990.

Weiss, Peter Eliot. "The Collective from a Playwright's Perspective." *Canadian Theatre Review* 49 (Winter 1987): 59–66.

Webb, Brian, ed. *The Responsive Body: A Language of Contemporary Dance.* Banff, AB: Banff Centre P, 2002.

Zimmer, Jacob. "All Statements Are Insecure Questions: Eight Words toward a Theatre." *Canadian Theatre Review* 119 (2004): 9–12.

International Authors

Auslander, Philip. *From Acting to Performance: Essays in Modernism and Postmodernism*. London: Routledge, 1997.

Babbage, Frances. *Augusto Boal*. Abingdon, Oxon: Routledge, 2004.

Banes, Sally and André Lepecki. *The Senses in Performance*. London: Routledge, 2007.

Barba, Eugenio. "The Deep Order Called Turbulence: The Three Faces of Dramaturgy." *TDR* 44.4 (T168) (2000): 56–66.

———. *Beyond the Floating Islands*. New York: PAJ Pub., 1986.

———, and Savarese, Nicola. *A Dictionary of Theatre Anthropology: The Secret Art of the Performer*. London: Routledge, 1991.

Bicât, Tina and Chris Baldwin. *Devised and Collaborative Theatre: A Practical Guide*. Ramsbury, Marlborough, Wiltshire: Crowood, 2002.

Bigwood, Carol. "Renaturalizing the Body (with the Help of Merleau-Ponty)." *Hypatia*. 6:3 (1991): 54–73. Rpt. in *Body and Flesh: A Philosophical Reader*. Ed. Donn Welton. Malden, MA: Blackwell, 1998. 99–114.

Boal, Augusto. *Games for Actors and Non-Actors*. 2nd ed. Trans. Adrian Jackson. London: Routledge, 1992.

———. *Theatre of the Opressed*. Trans. Charles A. and Maria-Odilia Leal McBride. New York: Theatre Communications Group, 1985 (1979).

Bobgan, Raymond. "Defining Collaboration." *Canadian Theatre Review* 88 (1996): 35–37.

Brian, Crystal. "Devising Community." *Theatre Topics* 15.1 (2005): 1–14.

Broadhurst, Susan and Josephine Machon, eds. *Performance and Technology: Practices of Virtual Embodiment and Interactivity*. Houndsmill, Basingstoke: Palgrave MacMillan, 2006.

Brown, Rich. "Moisés Kaufman: The Copulation of Form and Content." *Theatre Topics* 15.1 (2005): 51–67.

Burleigh, Louise. *The Community Theatre in Theory and Practice*. Boston: Little, Brown, 1917.

Carter, Alexandra, ed. *The Routledge Dance Studies Reader*. London: Routledge, 1998.

Conquergood, Dwight. "Performing as a Moral Act: Ethical Dimensions of the Ethnography of Performance." *The Community Performance Reader*. Ed. Petra Kuppers and Gwen Robertson. Abingdon, Oxon: Routledge, 2007. 57–70.

de Certeau, Michel. *The Practice of Everyday Life*. Trans. Stephen Rendall. London: U of California P, (1984) 2002.

Douglas, Mary. "The Two Bodies." *Natural Symbols: Explorations in Cosmology*. London: Routledge, 1996 (1970). Rpt. in *The Body: A Reader*. Ed. Marian Fraser and Monica Greco. London: Routledge, 2005. 73–77.

Eckersall, Peter. "Theatrical Collaboration in the Age of Globalization: The Gekidan Kaitaisha-NYID Intercultural Collaboration Project." *Diasporas and Interculturalism in Asian Performing Arts*. Ed. Hae-kyung Um. London: Routledge-Curzon. 2005. 204–20.

Farrell, Michael P. *Collaborative Circles: Friendship Dynamics & Creative Work*. Chicago: U of Chicago P, 2001.

Fraser, Miriam, and Monica Greco, eds. *The Body: A Reader*. London: Routledge, 2005.

Gordon, Robert. *The Purpose of Playing: Modern Acting Theories in Perspective*. Ann Arbor: U of Michigan P, 2006.

Kelleher, Joe and Nicholas Ridout, eds. *Contemporary Theatres in Europe: A Critical Companion*. London: Routledge, 2006.

Kershaw, Baz. *The Politics of Performance: Radical Theatre as Cultural Intervention*. London: Routledge, 1992.

———. *The Radical in Performance*. London: Routledge, 1999.

Kihlstrom, John F., Shelagh Mulvaney, Betsy A. Tobias, and Irene P. Tobis. "The Emotional Unconscious." *Cognition and Emotion*. Ed. Eric Eich, John F. Kihlstrom, Gordon H. Bowere, Joseph P. Forgas, and Paula M. Niedenthal. Oxford: Oxford UP, 2000. 30–86.

Krasner, David, ed. *Method Acting Reconsidered: Theory, Practice, Future*. New York: St. Martin's, 2000.

Kuppers, Petra and Gwen Robertson *The Community Performance Reader*. Abingdon, Oxon: Routledge, 2007

Kumiega, Jennifer. *The Theatre of Grotowski*. London and New York: Methuen, 1985.

Lepecki, André, ed. *Of the Presence of the Body: Essays on Dance and Performance Theory*. Middletown, CT: Wesleyan UP, 2004.

Malina, Judith and Julian Beck. *Paradise Now: Collective Creation of The Living Theatre*. New York: Random House, 1971.

McCullough, Christopher. *Theatre Praxis: Teaching Drama Through Practice*. London: MacMillan, 1998.

Merleau-Ponty, Maurice. *Phenomenology of Perception*. Trans. C. Smith. London: Routledge, 2004 (1945).

Mertz, Annelise, ed. *The Body Can Speak: Essays on Creative Movement Education with Emphasis on Dance and Drama*. Carbondale and Edwardsville: Southern Illinois UP, 2002.

Mitter, Shomit. *Systems of Rehearsal: Stanislavsky, Brecht, Grotowski and Brook.* London: Routledge, 1992.

Mock, Roberta, ed. *Performing Processes: Creating Live Performance.* Briston, UK: Intellect, 2000.

Parviainen, Jaana. *Bodies Moving and Moved: A Phenomenological Analysis of the Dancing Subject and the Cognitive and Ethical Values of Dance Art.* Tampere: Tampere UP, 1998.

Pavis, Patrice, ed. *The Intercultural Performance Reader.* London: Routledge, 1996.

———. *Theatre at the Crossroads of Culture.* Trans. Loren Kruger. London: Routledge, 1992.

Phelan, Peggy. *Unmarked: The Politics of Performance.* New York: Routledge, 1993.

——— and Jill Lane, eds. *The Ends of Performance.* New York: New York UP, 1998.

Rayner, Alice. *To Act, To Do, To Perform: Drama and the Phenomenology of Action.* Ann Arbor, MI: U of Michigan P, 1994.

Ritchie, Rob, ed. *The Joint Stock Book: The Making of a Theatre Collective.* London: Methuen, 1987.

Sawyer, Keith R. "Introduction." *Creativity in Performance.* Ed. Keith R. Sawyer. Greenwich, Connecticut: Ablex, 1997.

Schechner, Richard. "From Ritual to Theatre and Back." *Ritual, Play, and Performance.* Ed. Richard Schechner and Mady Schuman. New York: Seabury, 1976. 196–222.

———. *Performance Theory.* New York and London: Routledge, 1977.

——— and Lisa Wolford, eds. *The Grotowski Sourcebook.* London: Routledge, 1997.

Slowiak, James and Jairo Cuesta. *Jerzy Grotowski.* London: Routledge, 2004.

Stanislavski, Constantin. *An Actor Prepares.* Trans. Elizabeth Reynolds Hapgood. New York: Theatre Arts, 1964.

Tait, Peta. *Circus Bodies: Cultural Identity in Aerial Performance.* London: Routledge, 2005.

Theatre Topics. 12:1 (2002): *Praxis.*

———. 15.1 (2005): *Devising.*

Thomson, Lynn M. "Teaching and Rehearsing Collaboration." *Theatre Topics* 13.1 (2003): 117–29.

Tufnell, Miranda and Chris Crickmay. *Body Space Image: Notes Towards Improvisation and Performance.* London: Dance Books, 1990.

Wolford, Lisa. *Grotowski's Objective Drama Research.* Jackson, MI: UP of Mississippi, 1996.

Wangh, Stephen. *An Acrobat of the Heart: A Physical Approach to Acting Inspired by the Work of Jerzy Grotowski.* New York: Vintage, 2000.

Way, Ruth. "Collaborative Practice and the Phenomenal Dancer: Yolande Snaith's Theatredance." *Performing Processes: Creating Live Performance.* Ed. Roberta Mock. Bristol, UK: Intellect, 2000. 51–60.

Wood, John. *The Virtual Embodied: Presence/Practice/Technology.* London: Routledge, 1998.

Notes on Contributors

Bruce Barton is an Associate Professor at the University of Toronto, where he teaches playwriting and dramaturgy. He has published in numerous scholarly and practical periodicals and essay collections, and his book publications include *Imagination in Transition: David Mamet Moves to Film* (2005), *Marigraph* (2004), an anthology of Canadian Maritimes playwriting and *Canadian Devised Theatre* (2008), an anthology of devised performance texts (co-editor). Current research includes a SSHRC-funded study on the material conditions and practices of new play development in Canada and projects focused on the dramaturgies of the body in physically-based devised theatre and intermedia performance. Current creative practice includes writing and dramaturgy for multiple devised theatre projects and the creation of aerial-based interdisciplinary performance. Bruce is also an award-winning playwright.

Paul Bettis worked for more than thirty years in Canadian theatre, as director, actor, teacher, writer and creator of original projects. As one of the early workers for Factory Theatre and as Artistic Director of the Theatre Second Floor, he gave Toronto the first productions of George Walker, Michael Hollingsworth, Des McAnuff, Jim Garrard et al., along with other innovative presentations. He worked subsequently for most Toronto venues and was Artistic Director of Civilized Theatre.

Per K. Brask teaches Theatre at the University of Winnipeg. He has published essays, poetry, short stories, translations and interviews in a variety of journals. His books include *Aboriginal Voices: Amerindian, Inuit and Sami Theatre* (co-editor), *Contemporary Issues in Canadian Theatre and Drama* (editor), *Essays on Kushner's Angels* (editor), *Seven Canons* (co-editor), *A Sudden Sky: Selected poems by Ulrikka S. Gernes* (co-editor, co-translator) and *We Are Here: poems by Niels Hav* (co-translator). He has also written plays and libretti.

Diane Bessai is Professor Emeritus of English at the University of Alberta. As well as author of *Playwrights of Collective Creation* (1992), she has published numerous essays, articles and reviews of modern Canadian theatre and drama in books and journals. She is the general editor of the *Prairie Play Series* for NeWest Press and from 1976–1988 she served as theatre editor for *NeWest Review*. In the 1990s she initiated the collecting of Edmonton professional theatre records in the University of Alberta Archives.

Chris Brookes was a theatre director before he became a radio journalist. During the 1980s he reported out of war zones in Central America and was a documentary producer for Canadian network radio. More recently as an independent radio producer his documentaries have won awards, including the Peabody and the Prix

Italia, and have been broadcast in a dozen countries. He is also a published author and playwright and has produced TV documentaries, and his television writing has been nominated for the Gemini award. Brookes currently directs the production company *Battery Radio* with studios at the bottom of the cliff where Marconi received the first trans-Atlantic wireless message in St. John's, Newfoundland.

Barry A. Freeman is a doctoral candidate at the Graduate Centre for Study of Drama at the University of Toronto where he is completing a dissertation about collaborative intercultural theatre. Barry is an Editorial Assistant at *Theatre Research in Canada/Recherches théâtrales au Canada* and has publications forthcoming in that journal and in *Canadian Theatre Review*. Barry's varied research interests include interculturalism, drama-in-education, folk music and culture, Native theatre, Newfoundland theatre and Czech theatre. Barry recently returned from an exchange to Masaryk University in Brno, Czech Republic, where he studied Czech theatre and language.

Alan Filewod is Professor of Drama in the School of Literatures and Performance Studies in English at the University of Guelph. His books include *Performing Canada: The Nation Enacted in the Imagined Theatre* (Textual Studies in Canada, 2002); *Workers Playtime: Theatre and The Labour Movement Since 1970* (with David Watt; Currency P, 2001); and *Collective Encounters: Documentary Theatre in English Canada* (U of Toronto P, 1987).

Kathleen Gallagher is Associate Professor, Canada Research Chair in Urban School Research in Pedagogy and Policy, and the Academic Director of the Centre for Urban Schooling at the University of Toronto. Dr. Gallagher's books include *The Theatre of Urban: Youth and Schooling in Dangerous Times* (U of Toronto P, 2007); *Drama Education in the Lives of Girls: Imagining Possibilities* (U of Toronto P, 2000). Her edited collections include: *How Theatre Educates: Convergences and Counterpoints with Artists, Scholars, and Advocates* (U of Toronto P, 2003); *The Methodological Dilemma: Creative, Critical, and Collaborative Approaches to Qualitative Research* (Routledge, 2008). Her research continues to focus on questions of inclusion, engagement, and artistic practice as well as the methodological and pedagogical possibilities of the arts.

Erin Hurley is an Assistant Professor of English at McGill University. Work in her specialty areas of Quebecois performance and national performatives has been published in *Theatre Journal, Theatre Research in Canada/Recherches théâtrales au Canada, Canadian Theatre Review*, and in edited volumes. Forthcoming publications include a special issue on the performing arts in Quebec for *GLOBE: Revue internationale d'études québécoises*, which she edited and to which she contributed an article on Cirque du Soleil, as well as articles on Céline Dion in Las Vegas (for *L'Annuaire théâtral*) and Nancy Huston.

Ric Knowles is Professor of Theatre Studies at the University of Guelph, editor of *Canadian Theatre Review*, and general editor of Critical Perspectives on Canadian Theatre in English. Among his books are *The Theatre of Form and the Production of Meaning* (1999), *Shakespeare and Canada* (2004) and *Reading the Material Theatre* (2004).

Edward Little is Professor and Chair of the Department of Theatre at Concordia University. He is also editor-in-chief of *alt.theatre: cultural diversity and the stage* and associate artistic director of Montreal's Teesri Duniya Theatre.

Alex McLean was born in Montreal and raised in Dartmouth, Nova Scotia. He is the director of Halifax's Zuppa Circus Theatre, with whom he has created and directed nine original shows, most recently *Penny Dreadful*. He was a founding member of Number Eleven Theatre, with whom he created and performed *The Prague Visitor* and *Icaria* (1998–2006). Alex was a student at University of King's College, Double Edge Theatre, Primus Theatre and Philippe Gaulier. He has worked on projects with the Dalhousie Theatre Department, Rising Tide Theatre in Newfoundland and the International Theatre Institute's 2006 *Moving Stage Lab* in Copenhagen. He won the 2005 Robert Merritt Award (Nova Scotia) for Emerging Artist.

Monique Mojica is an actor and playwright from the Kuna and Rappahannock nations. Her play *Princess Pocahontas and the Blue Spots* was produced by Nightwood Theatre and Theatre Passe Muraille in 1990, broadcast on radio by CBC and published by Women's Press in 1991. She is the co-editor, with Ric Knowles, of *Staging Coyote's Dream: An Anthology of First Nations Drama in English*, vols. I & II. She is a former Artistic Director of Native Earth Performing Arts, a long-time collaborator with Floyd Favel in Native Performance Culture and a co-founder of Turtle Gals Performance Ensemble. Monique played the title role in *Death of A Chief*, Native Earth Performing Arts' adaptation of Shakespeare's *Julius Caesar*, at the National Arts Centre in 2008 and can be seen in the role of Martha on the new series *Rabbit Fall* for APTN. Upcoming projects include *Chocolate Woman Dreams the Milky Way*, a new multidisciplinary collaboration with Floyd Favel and Oswaldo DeLeon Kantule.

Yvette Nolan is a playwright, dramaturg and director. Her plays include *Annie Mae's Movement, BLADE, Job's Wife, Video*, the libretto *Hilda Blake* and the radio play *Owen*. Directing credits include *The Only Good Indian…, The Triple Truth, Tales of an Urban Indian, The Unnatural and Accidental Women* and *Annie Mae's Movement*. As a dramaturg, she works across Canada, most recently as the Festival Dramaturg for Saskatchewan Playwrights Centre Spring Festival. She is currently the Artistic Director of Native Earth Performing Arts in Toronto. She is also one of the National Arts Centre's Playwrights-In-Residence for the 2007–2008 season.

Robert Nunn taught dramatic literature and theatre history and theory at Brock University until his retirement in 2000. He has published numerous essays on Canadian plays and playwrights, including Hrant Alianak, David Fennario, David French, Sharon Pollock, Judith Thompson and Drew Hayden Taylor. Two of his essays were awarded the Richard Plant Essay Prize. He was co-editor of *Theatre Research in Canada/Recherches théâtrales au Canada* from 1993 to 1996, and is on the editorial board of that journal as well as *Essays in Theatre/Études théâtrales.*

Darren O'Donnell is a novelist, essayist, playwright, director, designer, performer and artistic director of Mammalian Diving Reflex. *The Chicago Reader* has called his first novel, *Your Secrets Sleep with Me,* "a bible for the dispossessed, a prophecy so full of hope it's crushing." His latest book, *Social Acupuncture: A Guide to Suicide Performance and Utopia,* was published in spring 2006 and prompted *The Globe and Mail* to declare, "O'Donnell writes like a sugar-addled genius at 300k/h." His performances include *Haircuts by Children, Slow Dance with Teacher, Ballroom Dancing, A Suicide-Site Guide to the City, Diplomatic Immunities, pppeeeaaaccceee, [boxhead], White Mice, Over, Who Shot Jacques Lacan?, Radio Rooster Says That's Bad* and *Mercy!*

Modupe Olaogun is an Associate Professor of English at York University, Toronto, where she teaches African and postcolonial literatures. She has published articles and presented papers on different genres of African literature. Her current research focuses on the aesthetics of African literature and theatre and on African literature which explores the subject of migration and dispersals from Africa within the last century. She provides a venue for the dissemination of African drama as the artistic director of AfriCan Theatre Ensemble (Toronto), which she founded in 1998.

Robert Plowman is a Halifax-based playwright and journalist. His passion for ensemble-based creation has lead him to collaborate, as a writer and as a dramaturge, with a number of collectives, most recently Zuppa Circus Theatre. He is currently at work on a new draft of *Radium City* for the company, slated for production in fall 2008.

Julie Salverson has worked in community related theatre since 1981, when she founded Second Look Community Arts. Plays and librettos include *Thumbelina, Over the Japanese Sea, Boom* (with Patricia Fraser) and *The Haunting of Sophie Scholl.* Her essays have been published in book anthologies and journals including *A Boal Reader, Between hope and despair: pedagogy and the remembrance of historical trauma; Theatre; Theatre Research in Canada/Recherches théâtrales au Canada; Theatre Topics* and *Canadian Theatre Review.* Current projects include: a libretto for a clown opera about the atomic bomb (composer Juliet Palmer); a book entitled *The Highway of the Atom: Memory, the Witness and the Archive* (with Peter van Wyck); and a book entitled *Witnessing A Tragic World: theatre, testimony and the courage to be happy.* She is Associate Professor of Drama at Queens University, Kingston.

Shelley Scott is an Associate Professor in the Department of Theatre and Dramatic Arts at the University of Lethbridge where she teaches Theatre History, Canadian Theatre, and special topics courses in Dramatic Literature and Theory, and where she occasionally directs department productions. Most recently she directed *Cloud Nine* in October 2007. Shelley's major area of research interest is Canadian women playwrights. Her PhD thesis was a study of Nightwood, a feminist theatre company in Toronto. Shelley is an active member in the Canadian Association for Theatre

Research and has published in *Modern Drama, Canadian Theatre Review, Theatre Research in Canada/Recherches théâtrales au Canada, Resources for Feminist Research* and the *British Journal of Canadian Studies*. In February of 2007 her book *The Violent Woman as a New Theatrical Character Type: Cases from Canadian Drama* was published by The Edwin Mellen Press.

Renate Usmiani, Prof. Emeritus at Mount St. Vincent University (Halifax), was born in Vienna, Austria, and obtained her graduate degree from Harvard University. She has taught Comparative Literature as well as World, Modern and Canadian Drama, and published widely in these areas. She has directed numerous amateur and student productions, including the world premiere in English of Michel Tremblay's *Damnee Manon, Sacree Sandra*. Books on Canadian drama include *Gratien Gélinas, Michel Tremblay, The Alternative Theatre Movement* and *The Theatre of Frustration*, a comparative study of Michel Tremblay and Franz Xavier Kroetz. She is also the editor of *Kelusultiek*, a collection of writings by First Nations women of Atlantic Canada.

Robert Wallace is Professor Emeritus of English and Drama Studies at Glendon College, York University, in Toronto. He is author of *Staging a Nation: Evolutions in Contemporary Canadian Theatre* (2003), *Theatre and Transformation in Contemporary Canada* (1999) and *Producing Marginality: Theatre and Criticism in Canada* (1990); co-author of *The Work: Conversations with English-Canadian Playwrights* (1981); editor of *Quebec Voices* (1986) and *Making, Out: Plays by Gay Men* (1992). In addition to writing and lecturing widely about theatre and cultural policy, he has produced 10 radio documentaries and edited more than 20 volumes of Canadian plays.

Jerry Wasserman, Professor of English and Theatre at the University of British Columbia, has published widely on Canadian theatre. His books include *Modern Canadian Plays*, now in its 4th edition, *Theatre and AutoBiography: Writing and Performing Lives in Theory and Practice*, co-edited with Sherrill Grace, and *Spectacle of Empire: Marc Lescarbot's Theatre of Neptune in New France*. Jerry is also an actor with more than 200 professional credits for stage and screen, and theatre critic for *The Province* newspaper in Vancouver.

Ker Wells was a founding member of Winnipeg-based Primus Theatre from 1989 to 1997. In 1998 he co-founded Number Eleven Theatre, with whom he created *Icaria* (1998 and 2000), *The Prague Visitor* (2003) and *The Curious History of Peter Schlemihl* (2004). Other recent work includes *The Confessions of Punch and Judy* (2004) and the solo performance *Living Tall* (2007). As an actor, director and teacher, Wells has toured across Canada, and to the U.S. and Europe. Wells lives in Toronto and is a returning guest faculty member at the National Theatre School of Canada and the Humber College School of Performing Arts.